THE BEST
OF THE
REVIEW — 2

PATHS OF RENEWAL
FOR RELIGIOUS

Edited by
David L. Fleming, S.J.

Imprimi Potest: Robert T. Costello, S.J.
Provincial
Missouri Province

Imprimatur: Most. Rev. Edward J. O'Donnell, D.D.
Auxiliary Bishop of St. Louis
June 20, 1986

Foreword

Vatican II's image of the "Pilgrim Church" *(Lumen Gentium,* Ch. 7) has been a major catalyst in the Church's renewal efforts. Being a pilgrim Church puts us all on a journey. We have a direction, we know our destination, but the journey takes in many daylight hours and dark nights, many choices of roads, paths, and byways, and the necessity of always moving on into the new territory of our pilgrimage.

Religious life recognized as a special gift of God for the life and holiness of this pilgrim Church has had to follow its own paths of renewal since the call of Vatican II. The journey over the past twenty years has not been an easy one. From being a clearly defined "state of life according to the evangelical counsels" with its own call to perfection, religious life seemed to flounder in the universal call to holiness that Vatican II emphasized for all Christians and which appeared to take away the "specialness" of being a religious. Works, too, previously identified as the activity of religious, were increasingly being done by the lay Christian and even by some secular arm of the civil society.

For religious, another path toward holiness was being pointed out—one less involved with prayer structures and formulas, yet more demanding of a specifically contemplative quality of a person's life and of a community's activity. A depth of understanding the vows as our way of following Christ, viewed not so much as individual areas of obligation but as aspects of the same one reality—the total gift of self to God—had to be made one's own as a new source of empowerment. The sheer gratuitousness of the gift offered—the special charism of invitation to follow Jesus more intimately—called forth anew the realization of the joy of response which only a free person could profess and live out publicly in community and in the Church.

Religious chastity had clearly to be an expression of personal celibate love lived out in relationships between individuals, within community and through ministry. The religious meaning of poverty had to be tied to work and more concretely to the material poverty which was more evidently dehumanizing an ever-growing number of the world's peoples. Religious obedience called for an adult relationship of responsible dialogue and ready service, necessary for bringing a certain order to a life and a work motivated by love of Christ and his Church.

Religious living in community felt the strain of these many new ideas and approaches and new ways of acting. Different ways of living community sprang up, often in conjunction with new apostolates or new groupings of individual apostolates. Unity in the midst of different approaches became a major concern both for a life together and for a sense of corporate ministry.

REVIEW FOR RELIGIOUS has been privileged to record the kinds of struggles and the attempts to respond that have been a part of religious life on this recent part of the Vatican II journey. The articles collected in this volume represent a glimpse into various aspects of the understandings and practices of religious renewal. Each article contributes significantly to another step forward, another path taken, another vision of what is ahead.

After an original introductory article in which I try to present an overview of religious life in its principal elements as it emerges from Vatican II, I have grouped the articles under four major headings: 1) religious charism and consecration; 2) religious vows; 3) religious community; and 4) religious apostolate. Rather than choose a logical progression within each section, I have deliberately chosen to keep a chronological order of the articles since each author presents a way of thinking more consonant with a certain time period and points the way to later development. The postscript includes those articles selected for their challenge to the future.

I intend that this collection will be helpful for religious men and women to discover some sense of the way we have come on our pilgrimage. These articles talk about our lives in realistic and hopeful ways. Although they are about the recent past, they point the way to our continued journeying. I also hope that those younger in religious life will be able to hear a bit of the story of our latest journey, and that they can enter into its appreciation through these readings. More generally, anyone who wants to understand a little better the renewal process in the lives of religious will, I believe, find insight through this collection.

I am grateful to each one of the authors who have cooperated with me in the editing of this book. I am especially indebted to the staff of the REVIEW, who both encouraged me in this project and then had to assume much of the correspondence and the work because of my sabbatical absence during that stage of its preparation.

God's gift of religious life is very precious for the vitality of Church life. May we religious, keepers and transmitters of such a charism, continue to seek the grace to understand more clearly the Lord's call in our time and to respond more eagerly to his lead on our journey together—for the good of our Church and our world, and for our own good.

David L. Fleming, S.J.

Table of Contents

Introduction

Religious Life: Act of Hope, Challenge to Human Weakness

by David L. Fleming, S.J.

In his book *Discipleship: Towards an Understanding of Religious Life,* Father John Lozano, C.M.F., observes that every Christian commitment is "an act of theological hope and a challenge to human weakness" since every Christian commitment has its origin in grace and is similarly an answer to it (p. 274). My own reflections about contemporary religious life are framed within this graced prism: it is seen as an act of hope, a challenge to human weakness.

When religious life is treated in the documents of Vatican II, there seems little intention of presenting radically new or revolutionary ways of thinking about this particular form of Church life. The newness of approach we find in the Constitution on the Church (*Lumen Gentium*) is rather in the wholeness of vision in which all the vocations within Church life are seen in the context of the universal call to holiness. The tradition of the vowed life of chastity, poverty and obedience is given new realization by its integration into the life of the one People of God, a pilgrim people all on the one journey in following the footsteps of their Lord.

Similarly in the decree on the up-to-date renewal of religious life (*Perfectae Caritatis*), there were no startling new insights into understandings about religious life. The newness of approach is found in the comprehensive way that the historical development and the traditional practices of this special form of Church life, designated as "religious," have been amalgamated. The Council took evident pains to interweave all the rich threads of development so that none of God's gifts of understanding this life identified with certain evangelical counsels and choices taken in living it out should become obscured or lost. Instead of fixing on a single scholastic or later tradition, Vatican II brought our attention to the whole storeroom of religious life history out of which we can bring forth goods that are both old and new—all centered on the following of Jesus.

All more recent official ecclesiastical developments—the writings of Pope Paul VI and Pope John Paul II and the documents of the Congregation for Religious and for Secular Institutes—have continued to be reflections upon the integrated approach first proposed in the treatment of religious life by Vatican II. It is my conviction that we, the Church, will continue to grow in our own understanding of religious life as we examine its wholeness, as we look at its various elements in the light of their integration into the one phenomenon we call "religious life." Moreover, we religious need to bring the various elements of our lived experience, our grace, our questions and difficulties into the forum of Scripture and Church tradition, as outlined in the documents of Vatican II and subsequent documents. It is in our trying to fit it all together that the Lord continues to grace us with insight and with courage for living this type of life. We religious must know our story if we are to continue to live it.

I intend to review five principal elements that come together for our story. The first element overrides all the others since it takes in the total reality—from God's initiating action to our graced response. It is the element of 1) choice and consecration. The lived reality of such a consecration is spelled out in the next three elements: 2) religious chastity for the sake of the kingdom: 3) renunciation and religious poverty; and 4) charity and religious obedience. Our dedication to the person of Jesus and to the service of his Church is enfleshed in the final elements, 5) community and ministry.

Choice and Consecration

The first *element* which all followers of Christ must consider is the reality of the call. There is an invitation which comes from Jesus to follow. The New Testament is the story of Jesus' call and our response. The call has always been understood as one of choice—Jesus' choice. And so the call is a grace, a gift freely extended to a person out of love, and open to refusal. Jesus does not condemn those who refuse; he rather acknowledges how hard it is to be a disciple.

Many Catholics do not remember much about the first call to be a follower of Christ because their parents and families provided the context of their own response in the sacrament of baptism as an infant. But sometime within the more adult decisions about our life values and direction, we come to make the Catholic following of Jesus our own personal choice as a way of life. It may happen at the time of marriage or on the occasion of educating children or at some personal crisis, or it may come about less dramatically and more a choice of hands and feet than noticeably one of head and heart. Regardless of how we come to it, the choice to follow Jesus must be lived by a Catholic faith which embodies our free and personal response.

Baptism is the Church's way of signing and sealing our choice/response to Christ's choice of us. Our baptismal identifying with Jesus draws us through the evident physical and personal life which is given at birth to an entering into a whole new way of living enjoyed completely now by the risen Lord. Traditionally we speak of our plunging into the waters of baptism as going down into death with

Jesus so that we might rise from the tomb of water into the new life of his resurrection. The sacrament of baptism proclaims the reality of the newness of life—a totally different dimension of life-with-God's-life.

We call God's action in us, entering us into this new dimension of God's life, a *consecration*. By baptism, people are marked as freely responding to the Lord in love as the Lord of their lives, and so they are dedicated to his service in all that they do. Consecration is entering into God's world. When we speak of people being consecrated, we talk of the power of God in them that affects their values and their direction in life. Consecration, then, signifies our relationship with God and with everything of our life seen in relationship to God. In Christ, the reality of our being brothers and sisters to one another is incarnated for all times and places, and so we proudly bear the responsibility of being called *Christian*. We as baptized persons are meant to grow in living out consciously and deliberately this gift of consecration which is ours in baptism. This consecration remains the empowering source of grace for our following of Christ throughout our lives. Other sacraments provide a power source for specific areas of need or strength, as in reconciliation or anointing or in matrimony or holy orders. But the consecration in baptism—our being identified with the risen Jesus in our response to his call—remains the seed and source of all our Christian growth and development.

Jesus does not call just once into our lives. Jesus continues to call to us at various moments in our journey, especially at the times of choices and decisions which affect our living out of our relationship to him. We identify as very special those times of life decisions or choices—whether Christ's call for us is to marry or to remain single, whether to marry this or that person, whether Christ's call to us is a renewed invitation to be identified with him by means of a dedication of an exclusive love-relationship. In the experience of this last type of call, it is as though the doors of our baptismal consecration have opened into a more central chamber of living as Christ lives. The invitation of Jesus to be identified with him in death and resurrection remains the same call, but, to use a musical image, pitched now in a different key. This new invitation calls forth from us a way of responding that makes all our previous responses seem like no response at all. We find ourselves caught up in that mysterious human experience in which we so love someone that it makes us feel that we never knew what love meant until this moment. Or this new call to us by Jesus is like having a certain breakthrough in praying to God that makes all our previous prayer seem like only a pale image of praying, not really worthy of the name *prayer* at all.

This invitation from Jesus which calls forth a new response of an exclusive choice of Jesus as the center of our life and the dedication of all our powers to his service remains an intensification of the one same consecration of baptism. Moved by the grace of God, we want to do more. Yet how can we do more, when everything of holiness is already demanded from us in living as Christians—to love God with our whole heart, with all our mind, and with our total strength, and to love our neighbor as ourselves? We know that we esteem martyrs for doing the more; the holiness of total love remains the same, it is true, but the martyrs *embody* the gift of their loving totally by the witness of their violent death. Like martyrs, we want to respond to this new call of Christ—a special movement of grace within us—to give ourselves in a total and exclusive love of Jesus, and to spend our lives in the service of his Church. To the call of Jesus at this moment in our lives we desire to respond in love with such a total and exclusive dedication of self to him that our original consecration is borne out anew in a type of life (in Church documents, the expression used is *genus vitae*) known as "religious life."

Religious life, then, is founded on the total dedication of a person through the consecration of baptism; only now the dedication is so exclusively focused on the following of Christ—the choice of us by Christ's love being met by our own love—choice of him—that it results in a new type of life *embodying* the values and directions of Jesus' life. For the past seven hundred years, such a renewed consecration was signed and sealed by the public profession of the vows of chastity, poverty, and obedience in the Church.

Vatican II has identified religious life primarily as a consecration: baptized Catholics enter into a wholly new and total dedication of self to Christ in love, and, in imitation of him, offer their lives to the service of the kingdom. Consistent with the sacramental nature of the Church's life, the offering of self is made at once to Jesus (God) and to his Body, the Church. More concretely, the Church is most often seen represented as a particular religious community which provides the ambit for both the life and the ministry of this dedication.

The Church in Vatican II, by laying stress on the reality of consecration founded in baptism, has drawn our attention to the free-choice initiative of both God and God's people in the theology of vocation. The Council has emphasized again that just as the initiative always begins with the Lord, so too God is the one who consecrates, who graces, who draws us into a wholly other dimension of divine life and meaning and value. For our human part, we spell out the dedication of self essential to consecration in various ways, usually by our own action of committing ourselves by vows or by some sacred bonds. But whatever form our dedication takes, the essential gift of total life and service for the Lord is captured in its graced nature by the Church's word, *consecration*.

Because of consecration, religious life has sometimes been described as a "setting apart" from the ordinary Church life. Vatican II has made clear that the reality is just the opposite; religious life calls us more to the center of the Church community, because the consecration represented in religious life can have no other source than a deeper entry into the one source that identifies all Christians with Christ—the consecration of baptism. For this reason, the council declares an esteem for the gift and call of the Lord to those in religious life since by their very dedication they are meant to reflect the life and holiness of the whole Church by the way they *embody* a following of Christ. Let us examine more closely this chosen way of *embodying* a following of Jesus.

Religious Chastity for the Sake of the Kingdom

Chastity for the sake of the kingdom of heaven is said by Vatican II to "tower above" all the grace-gifts that the Lord has given to his followers. Vowed celibacy stands preeminent among the traditional three vows associated with religious life. And yet, during the first centuries of Church life, religious chastity is ordinarily not mentioned as a significant step in a special following of Christ. It is true that consecrated virginity among Christians was given recognition and esteem early on, with perhaps an overly Hellenistic or Roman religious emphasis on the physical integrity of the female body. Consecrated virginity could sometimes emphasize far more the sacredness of the physical body, akin to the vessels and other "things" for altar sacrifice, rather than the rightful emphasis on the heart and the will involved in the personal dedication of one's life out of love. A residue of this more pagan-influenced understanding of virginity remained in the Church through the centuries.

Perhaps the personal love aspect of dedicating one's life to the Lord was so much a presumption in both the early religious-life forms of the anchorite and the cenobite (just as it tended to be de-emphasized in the vocation of the consecrated virgins) that it was considered unnecessary as a special step, in the sense of a bond or promise, in a following of Christ.

We might reconstruct the thinking of these early religious in the following way. If the call is from the Lord to us and it is a call of his love-choice, then what would move us to respond? Surely not a love to be single or a love to be a part of a particular community-group or even a love for a kind of work. One love and one love alone can base our dedication—a return love of the Lord and our choice of God as the total and exclusive love of our life, so much so that no other exclusive love relationship has a place. And so we live a celibate type of life, a life that is not just single, but a life dedicated in love to the Lord and consequently a life spent in his service.

By the qualifying adjectives and phrases which the Council uses when speaking of religious chastity, we realize that consecrated celibacy has little to do with a chastity based on ascetical motives or on some esteem for a physical or sexual purity in itself. Christianity, with its foundations in a fleshly incarnation, a suffering crucifixion, and a bodily resurrection which results in a consistently sacramental religious expression, has no fixation on some ritual or ascetical purity. The Christian virtue of chastity cannot be self-centering, which a self-perfecting ascesis tends to emphasize, but rather chastity in its conjugal or dedicated forms is always seen in a relational or self-surrendering way.

Celibacy in itself was not esteemed in the Jewish society of Jesus' time. It is likely that Jesus had to face the prejudice of the people of his day, similar to the way our contemporary society treats various of its members who are considered "different" in their lifestyle. Just as "queer" is an offensive put-down kind of word in our times, so "eunuch" was an offensive and put-down kind of word in the time of Jesus—and perhaps still is. Jesus takes this very word *eunuch*— possibly after having it hurled at himself—and says "There are eunuchs who have made themselves that way for the sake of the kingdom of heaven. Let anyone accept this who can" (Mt 19:12). In the context of that whole chapter in the

Gospel of St. Matthew, we see Jesus' agreeing that for us humans it would be impossible, but *with God* all things are possible, and the freedom to respond to such a gift as celibacy is ours.

Jesus sees himself as a eunuch because of his own free choice—to respond in love to his God and to spend his life in God's service. In the history of religious life, the gift that Jesus continues to offer certain men and women is the same kind of love-choice of himself as the central and exclusive love of their lives; and so they too make themselves "eunuchs for the kingdom of heaven."

The documents of Vatican II also draw our attention to the example and teaching of St. Paul in order to understand the scriptural foundations of consecrated chastity. Paul, in writing to the Church members in Corinth (1 Co 7), acknowledges the gift of his own celibate life. In his exuberance for the love of Christ which this gift represents in his life, he says that he would want that everyone could have such a gift. But he grants that the Lord gives many gifts towards our life decisions, and that marriage too is such a gift of the Lord. As Paul reminds us, the Lord has not expressed a preference, identifying one way of life as better than another. All we know from the evidence of Christian life is that the Lord distributes his gifts to the members of the Church, that the gifts differ, and that they all are signs of his love. Of course, this still does not dampen Paul's own enthusiasm for the celibate gift which is his.

Paul's particular emphasis is to try to draw the comparison between the personal loves of husband and wife and the necessary concerns that must be taken on in such a love, and the personal loves of a celibate and our Lord and the parallel necessary concerns of spending one's life in the service of God. The clarity which Paul provides is that Christian celibacy necessarily is guided not only by the subjective response of love of the Lord but also by the consequent spending of one's life about the affairs of the Lord. So Christian celibacy always includes the apostolic, just as Jesus' celibacy did—for the sake of the kingdom.

Because a celibacy for the sake of the kingdom can be grounded in the Gospels as truly an *evangelical* counsel proposed by Jesus, and then further elucidated in the witness and writings of St. Paul, some theologians suggest an understanding of celibacy or consecrated chastity that would place it as the basis or foundation of the whole consecrated life. Our very dedication in religious life is expressed primarily in the love of the Lord to whom we give ourselves completely, and for whom we desire to spend our lives. I believe that we can understand now the early Church's apparent indifference to a special vow or bond of religious chastity since the very life of dedication found in the religious vocation seems necessarily to involve the exclusive love commitment of a celibate type of life. It is also apparent how Vatican II can speak of consecrated chastity as preeminent, and why it is now commonly listed first among the traditional three vows of a religious life dedication.

And yet traditionally poverty was more consciously identified with the special dedication of a religious life. Poverty was usually spoken of first in the triad of the evangelical counsels. How did this come about?

Renunciation and Religious Poverty

The most striking aspect of the call of Jesus to his first followers portrayed in Scripture lies in the immediacy with which they leave all things to follow him. The emphasis which Jesus placed on himself or on the Gospel as primary in the hearts and lives of his followers always demanded a renouncing of any other personal ties or values that might stand in conflict. No matter that after leaving boats and nets and fathers and homes, the apostles are still found later in the Scripture accounts to have boats and nets, homes and wives. The point has been made that for all followers of Jesus, the Christ must be the center of their lives, their one principle and foundation. We recall that this remains the basic meaning of our Catholic baptism—a wholly new life now rooted and centered in Jesus.

Historically in Church life, the people who responded to the call of Jesus to a special type of life dedicated to him placed a heavy emphasis on the primacy of renunciation. Perhaps these men and women, following so closely upon the age of martyrs, needed to stress the cost and difficulty of renunciation for themselves and their contemporaries. The danger that such a stress was then (and is still in our day) remains that of focusing on a means so much that it becomes purposeful, and so an end in itself. From Jesus' own example and the best of the Church tradition, we know that the grace of the call is "to follow Jesus," and only in view of our following do we detach ourselves from whatever loves (of things or of persons) that would get in the way and be an obstacle. Christianity has never had a theological position that doing the hard thing (like renunciation) is "better" just because it is hard. The spirituality of Christianity remains firmly based on the dynamic of love just as Jesus expressed it, and not on penance, abnegation, or renunciation—all of which remain only means and, if misunderstood or misused, contain the seed of vitiating the creation which God called good, the redemption in which Christ is making all things new, and by which the human body becomes a temple of the Spirit.

In a particular instance of this renunciation, the early monks read the Scripture passage of the call to the rich young man as particularly applicable to the invitation which they experienced from Christ, to "sell what you own and give the money to the poor" (Mt 19:21), and so follow Jesus. A true material poverty, stemming from their distribution of personal possessions among the poor, forced these early monks to work for their own sustenance, often by tending a small tilled garden for their own foods. The renunciation of things (our riches) and their distribution to the poor were the important prerequisites for a following of the Lord. These early religious continued to live their chosen poverty state in following Jesus by laboring for their daily sustenance in the service of the Lord.

As the monastic communities began to form, the emphasis on a material poverty shifted toward a sharing of goods and works for the common life of all the members. The scriptural inspiration came from the earliest Christian communities described in the Acts of the Apostles (Ac 2:44-45), in which everything was held in common. Individually everyone remained poor in the sense of having no personal possessions. But inevitably there came a certain loss in real material poverty when the community group itself could become a possessor of buildings, lands, and products that resulted from common labor and gift.

The rise of the mendicant orders in the thirteenth century brought a return to material poverty even for community life and holdings in common. The choice of poverty now took its primary inspiration from the scriptural passages dealing with Jesus' sending his disciples out to preach (Mt 10, Lk 10). The one who preaches the "good news" should make no provision for clothing or sustenance, but should live on what is provided by those who receive the ministry.

Apostolic orders founded especially from the sixteenth century to our present day have tended to weave a way of observing poverty from both the ideals of the mendicant and the monastic traditions. Although individual members lived a life free of possessions, the community sense of poverty differed according to the apostolic purposes and ministries characteristic of the group. So the apostolate or the mission work of each apostolic order influenced the resources possessed and used by the members. For example, there were apostolic groups specially devoted to education and to hospital works, where land, buildings and equipment gave little semblance of material poverty, but were meant to be at the service of the mission and not for the members, either individually or as a community.

Vatican II took all these threads of living religious poverty, along with their scriptural inspiration, and pointed out directions leading toward a balance in this type of chosen value. The Church emphasized the notion of religious being identified as poor because they must work for their livelihood; the Council also stressed that communities, too, must observe a poverty of solidarity by their sharing of their resources with those less fortunate. In all of this, the Council acknowledged the call to a kind of material poverty which is particularly appropriate to and expected of religious men and women vowed to poverty in our times.

In this context, Vatican II draws attention to another traditionally cited Scripture text from St. Paul: "[Christ] became poor for your sake, to make you rich out of his poverty" (2 Co 8:9). In a theological understanding of poverty as it comes through both Old and New Testaments, we need always to remind ourselves that the word *poverty* understood in a religious sense does not start with the meaning of material poverty. And yet, as we use it commonly in the English language, *poverty* centers all its meaning around material lack. Saint Paul recalls that Jesus' poverty is first and foremost the poverty of being human like us. In another text, the Son of God is described by Paul as "emptying himself" to become incarnate (Ph 2:5-7). In this sense, poverty is possessed by all humankind, for we are all fundamentally needy. As a religious choice, then, material poverty can be lived in a sacramental way—signifying externally how truly poor we are before God.

God's preferential love of the poor inspires our religious choice of vowed poverty: our desire to be identified by a life stance of human neediness before God (which only God can fill) and our desire to hold to a freedom of detachment from everything that is not God. All Christians are required by their baptismal calling to live this kind of basic poverty in their following of Christ. Poverty, then, is not a gospel counsel peculiar to only certain followers of Christ. To follow Christ is to know "how hard it is for a rich person to enter the kingdom of heaven" (Mt 19:24). Jesus acknowledged that this kind of poverty, which draws us to the common depths of our human neediness and which makes possible our freedom from various enslavements, can only become ours through the grace of God. Religious, by their vow of poverty, profess with God's grace to enter more deeply into this Christian sense of poverty, and thus to live a life touching into actual material poverty by their lack of possessions and non-accumulation of goods both individual and as community groups.

Although poverty is not strictly speaking a gospel counsel distinguishing a type of life for following Christ the way celibacy is, still poverty can be appreciated as a natural corollary of a celibate life for the kingdom. In fact, paradoxically, poverty can be claimed as central and foundational, a "first" in the human acknowledgment of neediness which can flower into the exclusive love relationship with Jesus realized in celibacy. This approach to poverty gives rise to the long-standing practice of listing poverty as the first of the evangelical counsels.

Charity and Religious Obedience

If the meaning of the lived practice of religious poverty remains obscure without examining its historical development in the Church, religious obedience makes an even greater demand on us to return to its beginnings and to observe its development in order for us to accept its integral place in the vowed lives of religious. It is fact that the religious vow of obedience only slowly developed as a distinctive part of this type of life called a life of the evangelical counsels. Other than general remarks in Scripture from Jesus or from the writers of the epistles to the early churches about obedience to those in authority, there is no Gospel evidence of a counsel of obedience distinguishing a follower of Jesus.

Rather early on in the religious life tradition, there was a master/disciple relationship which laid a stress on the docility-obedience necessary for being directed in the spiritual life. But this docility-obedience was not understood as a special promise or vow, and it usually did not last beyond the time of a "noviti-ate period."

Following the emphasis on renunciation which was so closely tied into the understanding of poverty, the early anchorites and cenobites began to praise highly a submission/obedience because giving up or renouncing one's will was harder and worth more than all the fasting and corporal austerities of subduing one's body and renouncing material things. Instances are related in the history of this tradition which glorified this submission-obedience in itself, going beyond all common sense and human reasonableness. Although there will always be a truth in the renunciation effort required by a vow of obedience, the free giving over of oneself to the direction of another human being is not to be valued just as an ascetical act. Again the desire to seek and find God's will must always be the context and end of religious obedience. The free submission to the will and direction of another is only chosen as a means aiding the doing of God's will.

As monastic life became community centered, a form of charity-obedience became prevalent, both for good relationships within the community and for the coordination and good order of community life and work. Franciscan obedience follows more along the line of this tradition, with a further nuance of stressing the obedience necessary for mission. This aspect continues to receive greater emphasis within the apostolic orders founded over the last four hundred years.

Underlying all understandings of obedience is the inspiration and example of Jesus in relation to the God he calls Father. Vatican II calls our attention to the emptying of the Son to become man so that he might live out an obedience—"obedient, even to accepting death, death on a cross" (Ph 2:8). A similar quotation from the Letter to the Hebrews, referring to how Jesus "learned obedience through what he suffered" (Heb 10:8), has traditionally been suggested as providing an insight into aspects of the religious obedience inspired by the example of Jesus.

Obedience, then, is even less identifiable than poverty as a gospel counsel related to a type of life peculiar to the following of Jesus. There is no doubt that the biblical inspiration for obedience comes more generally from the theme of obedience as the necessary stance of the human person before God—the call for a "listening faith." This listening faith is lived out to its fullest by Jesus in his obedience to God and in his labors for the coming of the kingdom. But the development of obedience as a vow has been more practically than theologically oriented. From the direction given by Vatican II, there is a renewed emphasis on the attitudes of docility-obedience and charity-obedience, both of which are founded on an adult-to-adult relationship, with proper dialogue, and in the context of a true exercise and acceptance of legitimate authority.

The renunciation of self-will and self-direction embodied in the vow of religious obedience gives foundation to an understanding of the core value and central place of this vow. Since obedience touches into our most precious and unique gift of freedom, obedience is sometimes seen as key to the total life of dedication represented by the life according to the evangelical counsels. So obedience, like poverty and like consecrated chastity, can truly be said to capture in a most central way—each vow in its own unique way—the total gift of dedication. Each vow could arguably represent a total gift of self to the Lord and to the service of the kingdom. Perhaps in such a personalistic time as this Vatican II age, we might expect religious obedience to be viewed as the most difficult for people to freely take on and as the most critical of the vows.

In the light of the Council, obedience as a vow remains key to the existence and vitality of religious life, especially as the development of obedience is so much tied in with the elements of community and ministry in its story.

Community and Ministry

When the Church reemphasized the rooting of the religious vowed life in baptismal consecration, the natural flow of this life into community form and into ministry was also indicated.

It is a fact that the special call of following Jesus in a unique type of life patterned on his own originally led the people who responded to an anchorite life. But quickly enough for practical purposes of sharing experience, of formation, and also for peer support, a kind of community life developed. Then the monastic community took hold, and maintained its prominence as the religious-life form until the rise of the mendicant orders. Whereas community had come to be the total ambience of the monks—a faith world in which they spent their lives, community for the mendicants served as the formative and support group out of which they moved to minister and to which they returned. And so even with a great deal of movement among many peoples, the mendicants still retained the community as the central place of their faith world. As the apostolic orders developed, the apostolate or ministry became primary to the coming together of the group. The community is no longer held as the primary center of their faith world. Community retains its importance for formation and support purposes, but the apostolate is central to the ambience in which they find God, they pray and they work.

Just as in baptism, we are not put only as individuals into a relationship with Christ, but we become part of the Body of Christ, so to enter more deeply into this mystery of identification with Christ through the vowed life, we necessarily find ourselves called into relationship with others. Although Vatican II makes special mention of the validity of the hermit vocation for the Church, this kind of solitary life must also remain founded on the double commandment of love of God and love of neighbor for holiness and salvation. The more usual outcome of the special call to the consecrated life of the vows flows rather, as we have seen borne out historically, into some kind of closer community association. This phenomenon keeps religious life in practice true to its baptismal roots.

The other element common to religious life—apostolate or ministry—is similarly a natural outflow from the roots of baptismal consecration. As members of Christ's Body, we can never divorce ourselves from relationships with others. Our central act of worship as Catholics—the Eucharist—continuously calls us to lay down our lives with Jesus for others as Jesus laid down his life for us. Since we are called in religious life to a type of life embodying certain values of Jesus' life, we find ourselves necessarily responding to ways of serving as he served. In history, religious groups have responded to human needs in a great variety of ways. By apostolate or ministry, religious have tried to make present the touch, the care, the attitude, the faith and love of Jesus to a total way of living a Christian life (as life in an enclosed monastic community) or to a particular area of human living (as in the more apostolic groups serving in orphanages, hospitals, schools, publishing houses, and so on).

In the light of Vatican II, we would not be tempted to try to define or give value to religious life solely in terms of works or ministries. The apostolate or ministry flows naturally from consecration, as we see from the baptismal consecration of all Catholics. But the deeper identifying with Jesus in the type of life chosen by vow retains its precedence over work itself and gives the personal Christlike value to the ministry whatever form it takes. The Council made no attempt to focus the ministry of religious men and women in one particular direction. For choice of ministries, we are guided only by the traditional categories of service within the Body of Christ:

1) a primary importance is given to prayer as ministry, and so the contemplative orders will always be considered especially precious;
2) the ministry of good works is divided into two major efforts:
   a) works of evangelization, in which whatever form the work takes, the effort of spreading and deepening the faith is intended;
   b) works of charity, in which the relief of human want and suffering remains the purpose, thereby witnessing to Christ's loving care and making no direct attempt to evangelize.

So much always needs to be done in the areas of prayer, Gospel truth and the love ministries that religious men and women have consistently been called and graced by Christ to do in the freedom of their choice and their special charismatic identity as they respond to the perennial wants of our Church and our world.

In addition, Vatican II has removed the sharp distinction that was often made between the contemplative and apostolic contributions of differing religious orders. Consistently the Church has re-expressed the necessity for all religious to be both contemplative and apostolic. Because of the differences in founding charisms, religious groups will always vary in the emphasis given to the two parts of the contemplative-apostolic equation which forms religious life. Jesus as the one model of the contemplative and apostolic life draws religious today into the struggle of this integration so essential to a consecrated life of the vows.

An Act of Hope

From the renewal begun through the documents of Vatican II, religious life has come to represent even more clearly an act of hope, even in the midst of the more evident human weakness of those who try to respond to this call of Christ. It is difficult enough to live a Catholic life today and to claim to be following a call of the Lord in our adult decision to do so. But it is a stepping forward truly in hope to respond to another call of Jesus which is addressed to those who choose to identify with him in a type of life embodying the very life values and orientations with which he lived.

I call it an act of hope—to profess to hear a call to make Jesus so much the center of our love life that an exclusive love relationship is so formed that this dedicated love assumes a celibate lifestyle. To live the Catholic values of the virtue of chastity is difficult and much under attack today, with even good people doubting its possibility or perhaps its value. I call it a challenge to human weakness—to make ourselves eunuchs for love of Jesus, knowing the human impossibility and relying totally on the grace of God for making this type of life possible.

I call it an act of hope—to try to live a life divested of anything that might be claimed as our "riches." Everyone has something which becomes a prized possession, perhaps in some way inhibiting freedom and in some way vying with God as an idol. We hope to be totally free and not grasping—to be free like Jesus. I call it a challenge to human weakness to realize that our poverty starts with our very selves and to be dignified and free about it so that God can make us rich. Paradoxically, sharing in the richness of identity with Jesus roots the challenge to remain materially poor before the Lord.

I call it an act of hope—to trust in the direction of God for our growth and service coming through human authority, and to freely submit to it. To use freedom to be submissive for the sake of our following Jesus demands a trust in God's providence—his ordinary way of working with and through human persons in dialogue with one another. I call it a challenge to human weakness so deeply desirous of doing things "my way." Or at the opposite extreme, I call it a challenge to human weakness that tries to evade all responsibility in the false name of obedience. I call it a challenge to human weakness to dialogue and to enter into a discernment, and then to obey the decision of authority.

Vatican II and the subsequent Church documentation has brought the two-thousand-year old history of religious life into a holistic picture. All the elements of religious life can continue to receive a better integration as we understand our story. We religious are fortunate to have the renewal struggle of our age to give new life and depth to this integration. For our Church and for our world, as well as for ourselves, we give witness today to an act of hope, a challenge to human weakness, in our following of Christ.

I. Religious Charism and Consecration

Christianizing Religious Life

Sister Agnes Cunningham, S.S.C.M.

Volume 32, 1973, pp. 336-346.

What does it mean to speak about "Christianizing religious life"? Does it not seem impertinent—irreverent even—to suggest that religious life is less—or other—than Christian? Any attempt to offer answers to these questions may, or may not, be convincing. But given the evidences of history, both past and present, the subject must be taken seriously.

The discussion of religious life in these terms, however, seems to overlook the fact that religious themselves are aware that it is increasingly difficult to distinguish their lifestyle from any other mode of Christian living. The documents of Vatican II, the "new" ecclesiology, the witness and leadership of Christian men and women in every area of concern for human life: these are all so many factors provoking from religious the sometimes painful question: "What makes religious life *different*?" The question becomes increasingly problematic as external, identifying "signs" of religious life gradually disappear and as the number of those who choose to withdraw from religious life "in order to become more Christian" increases.

There is another question abroad in the Church today, which challenges the suggestion that religious life must be "Christianized." This is the question that grows out of a conviction that religious life is, actually, no "different" from what is called the "ordinary" Christian life, since all of Christian living exists as a response to the Person of Jesus Christ revealed in the gospel. Is religious life, then, still necessary in the Church?

Indeed, the need for religious life in the Church and the understanding of religious life as a differentiated mode of Christian living are both contingent upon the effort to Christianize religious life. This is an effort which is asked of all Christians today, lay as well as religious.

Religious life, of itself, is not necessarily Christian. The phenomenon of what at least one author has called, "a lay reforming movement,"[1] can be found as early as the sixth century before Christ. Discovery of the Dead Sea Scrolls brought to light, some twenty-five years ago, signs of religious communities in pre-Christian Judaism. In recent years, Buddhist monks have attracted attention through self-immolation in the cause of peace and concern for a people. These few examples are in no way exhaustive. They do point to the fact that religious life is not an "original" Christian contribution to the history of man.

The existence, then, of pre-Christian monastic types cannot be contested. Nevertheless, while the roots of Christian monasticism can be traced to both Jewish and Egyptian ante-types, the clear sign of the gospel call marks the beginnings of the "religious" way of life in Christianity. From the earliest ages of the Christian era, there could be found within the believing community the "exceptional witness" given by those, who, in the words of Paul VI[2] manifest "a steady firmness in seeking for God . . . an exclusive and undivided love for Christ, and an absolute dedication to the growth of his kingdom." Religious life, as we know it today, follows in the strong tradition of this witness, as it was variously expressed in the lives of martyrs, virgins, hermits, cenobites, and as it gradually developed toward monasticism.

Non-Christian Elements in Religious Life

In spite of the evangelical dimension which underlies the very existence of religious life, the historical development of monasticism is linked to the assimilation within Christianity of non-Christian elements. Religious have not been exempt from the dialogue between Athens and Rome. They have not been ignorant of the encounter between Christianity and humanism. They have not escaped the confrontation of Church and world. On the contrary, monastic contributions to the *contemptus mundi* debate[3] have, more frequently than not, influenced the climate in which all Christians seek to determine their status in "the city of this world."

It ought not be surprising, then, to discern in religious life today remnants of an extra-evangelical character that have never been demythologized and that, consequently, tend to militate against the gospel spirit to the extent that they are mistakenly identified as "Christian." These non-Christian elements, certainly, are not the exclusive property of religious. The nature and role attributed to religious life in the Church throughout the centuries, however, have tended to intensify and make more explicit qualities and traits which exist in more diffuse manner in the whole Church. Furthermore, to the extent to which religious forget or abandon their raison d'etre within the Christian community, to that extent do they fail to be a movement of reform—that is, of renewal and adaptation—in the Church. To that extent, also, do they maintain cultural accretions which are discarded with greater or lesser difficulty, as recent experiences in liturgical renewal have taught us.

Acculturation, therefore, to some extent explains, though it does not excuse, the continuity in religious life of ascetical practices adopted by the early Christians from Egyptian hermits, but not sufficiently transformed in the subsequent development of Christian spirituality as the Greek and Syrian traditions developed. Acculturation also accounts for the static self-perpetuating concepts of "religious" ethical behavior envisioned as an assured means to "perfection," or, for that matter, the notion of "perfection," itself, especially as this has been modified by Jansenistic or Puritanical overtones. Still another element which threatens the true Christian spirit is a kind of spirituality which develops as a tradition in its own right, fostering not only that necessary degree of withdrawal which any life of commitment demands, to some extent or other, but also giving rise to a separation from the life of the Church itself on the presumption that religious are to live a life in the Spirit that is not "simply" Christian.

Evangelica Testificatio

There is a suspicion among many religious today that the greatest effort toward renewal of religious life must be effected in the realm of interpersonal relations and reverence for human values. In a sense, this is a way of admitting that the central teaching of the gospel regarding Christian love has, to some measure, failed to touch religious life. This single fact alone would be reason enough to call for the Christianization of religious life as a necessary endeavor in the Church today. The task, rather, lies in the areas of application and implementation, for the call to *make* religious life *Christian* was launched as a challenge by the Second Council of the Vatican. At the present time, programs of renewal and adaptation in religious life, though of unequal value and achievement, have been in existence long enough to merit evaluation. The norms and criteria for such an evaluation come from the gospel message. They have most recently been re-articulated in the apostolic exhortation *Evangelica testificatio,* issued in June, 1971 by Paul VI. At one level, the exhortation can be understood as a concerned question addressed to religious by the Holy Father: *What are you doing to make religious life Christian?* At another level, it is an attempt to answer that question through a discussion of the evangelical, ecclesial, and historical dimensions of religious life as a mode of response and witness to the gospel.

The need for a document such as the apostolic exhortation has been felt among religious almost since the close of Vatican II. It would be unrealistic to suppose that the fathers of this Council were any more aware than their predecessors in conciliar history of the implications of the work of the Spirit in their midst. It would be naive to pretend that they, more than earlier Council fathers, could foresee the consequences of response throughout the Catholic world to the message contained in the documents of Vatican II. The intuition of the Council fathers to speak to the problems and aspiration of religious in the contemporary world was sure. Religious were encouraged to "renew" in inner reality of their commitment to a chosen mode of Christian living. They were asked to "adapt" the external forms and structures through which this commitment was made explicit. The message was, at best, ambiguous in its initial form. Even today, after volumes of competent study and reflection, *Perfectae caritatis* invites conflicting interpretations in some areas. Religious quickly learned to trace the guideline of their efforts toward renewal through documents other than the one addressed particularly to them. What seems not to have emerged with any great clarity was that the point of the entire renewal project was: *To Become Christian.*

Becoming Christian

The contemporary Christian in a world of multiple human values must learn to live in terms of the demands placed on him by the gospel, the Church, and the situation of his relationship to the Christian God revealed in Jesus Christ. These realities constitute the core of renewal understood as a process of Christianization in religious life. In the apostolic exhortation, Paul VI clarifies the message and challenge of Vatican II and provides guidelines for the future of religious life as a mode of gospel living in the Church.

Evangelica testificatio, as a discussion of renewal in religious life, necessarily took into consideration the fundamental elements of renewal as one historical aspect of any reform movement. The first of these elements concerns essential values: their discernment, reevaluation, reaffirmation. The second deals, rather, with the external forms and structures which transmit, perhaps translate, the values which assure continuity of the reality to be renewed. Pope Paul treats both values and structures in this document. The accent, however, is clearly on the inner values as constitutive of and constituting religious life. In other words, the internal reality of religious life is found in those values which make it possible for religious life to exist. *The gospel constitutes religious life.* These same evangelical values determine the manner in which religious life is to be lived historically, with attention not only to the preservation of those "signs" which assure its presence in the Church *as* religious life, but also with accommodation for those changes and adaptations necessary from one age or culture to another to assure its continuity as the *Christian* life.

The message of the exhortation can be summed up quite simply in the affirmation that religious are called to be men and women of the gospel, of the Church, and of prayer. In the persevering effort to become so, they maintain and foster the process by which religious life becomes increasingly *Christian.*

Men and Women of the Gospel

Religious are called to be men and women of the gospel because Christianity is an existential response to the gospel. Thus, religious life is meant to be a life of evangelical witness. The opening words of the exhortation speak of the "gospel witness" which clearly manifests to mankind the primacy of the love of God. There is, then, a sense in which religious life, of itself, gives witness to the reality of the love of God. There is another sense in which this witness is given only to the degree that religious, as individual persons and as communal groups, incorporate into their lives and lifestyles the authentic elements of the gospel, in order that the witness may be verified, meaningful, and effective. The evangelical witness given by religious must be *sincere,* in the most basic sense of the word: there must be no *wax*-filling in the cracks of the "sign" we present as gospel people.

The "cracks" will be there, nonetheless, in the burden of the humanity we bear. But it is because of this that religious life has built into its objectives the possibility of growth toward what Paul calls the "fullness of Christ": the aim, the goal of religious life, as indicated in the exhortation, is the *pursuit* of perfect charity, in surrender to the Spirit who calls us to the freedom of the children of God. We are not to fear, then, that some arbitrary mode of "perfection" is to be put on, like a piece of clothing, by those whom the Church recognizes as religious. In some way, the identification of religious men and women is caught up in the "sign" of this *pursuit* of perfect love, which the Holy Father sees in the light of the "dynamic process" of renewal desired by Vatican II.

Religious life, then, is bound to the gospel. It is, in fact, because of the gospel that religious life can exist at all. The exhortation reminds us that religious life is "born of the gospel": through the profession of the evangelical counsels, this mode of living the Christian life *comes to be.* As value and as institution, the state of life known as "religious" exists because of the gospel.

Seeking the Lord of the Gospel

Another way of expressing this, and one with which religious themselves are more comfortable, is to say that religious life exists because of the Lord of the gospel—because of Christ. Here is the first motive for the choice of religious life as a mode of living the gospel, of "pursuing perfect charity," of professing the evangelical counsels. The ancient Christian tradition of the *imitatio Christi,* the "following of Christ," the seeking and going after Jesus, that characterized his first followers, remains today the supreme reason for which Christians choose freely to live in a manner which calls for a given, explicit statement of the witness which all those who profess Jesus as Lord and God are called to proclaim in their lives.

This response to the person of Jesus Christ is rooted in the mystery of baptism through which Christians are initiated into the believing, worshiping community of the *ekklesia theou.* It is through an understanding of this mystery of baptism, then, that religious come to realize their incorporation into Christ through sacramental life as the reality to be expressed and developed in religious "consecration." Religious consecration, understood as rooted in and expressing more fully the prior, Christian consecration of baptism, is a reinsertion into the paschal mystery, lived in the whole Church. Because of the death/resurrection mystery of the Lord, religious are called to live in such a way that the cross becomes a reality of their lives. This is not merely a pious statement. Paul VI sees suffering as a necessary portion of the experience of religious. The death dimension of the paschal mystery marks religious life at many levels. There is the reality of humanity, from which religious are never exempt. There is the ascesis that comes from an effort to "pursue" perfect charity in a fraternal community of celibate love shared for the sake of the kingdom. There is the peculiar suffering that derives from fidelity to the counsels and from the labors of apostolic service to the Church. The paschal mystery, then, stands at the heart of the religious life, as of every mode of the Christian life. Neither the death nor the resurrection can be denied or set aside by those who have given the Lord of the Gospel priority in their lives.

Men and Women of the Church

Religious cannot be men and women of the gospel, however, unless they also respond to the call to be men and women of the Church. This is so because Christianity is an historical religion. The reality of the gospel, in historical time, is incarnated in those structures which provide for the limits and extensions of human activity.

Historically, the phenomenon of a lifestyle that foreshadowed what we know as religious life today has been present within the Christian community from the beginning. Furthermore, the effort to live the Christian life in a manner which expresses evangelical witness in specific terms has resulted—in the past as in the present—in communities or groupings which can be recognized as *ecclesiolae,* symbols of the whole Church in miniature.

The basis for such a claim rests on the need within the Christian community for implementation of a principle enunciated in the early ages of Christianity: Unity of faith does not require nor call for uniformity of expression. The principle, itself, initially referred to the manner and moment in which early Christians celebrated the memorial of the Lord's resurrection. Faith and worship, belief and *praxis,* value and structure were at stake in the early Easter controversy. The debate was resolved in an affirmation of *diversity in unity.* So, too, on a broader level, the gospel as response to the Person of Jesus calls for a multiplicity of witnesses, and for witness to the evangelical values which assure the universality and catholicity of the Church of Jesus Christ.

In religious life, therefore, forms must exist which complement one another and which together contribute to a fuller expression in every age of the mystery of Christ, Center of time and space. So it is that modes of the contemplative and the apostolic life exist in the Church. So it is that a variety of religious families continue to exist, throughout the ages, as the charism of each founder or foundress gives expression to still another manner of hearing and responding to the call of the gospel. The Church, in order to be Church, needs religious life. Every mode of Christian witness stresses and gives expression to essential evangelical values. In the renunciation of some terrestrial, temporal goods, in the celebration of others, both creation and redemption are constantly affirmed in the *ekklesia.* For this reason, each form of religious life must give priority to some fundamental gospel principle. For this reason, too, each form of religious life must affirm those gospel values which do not hold priority in one or another Christian lifestyle. For instance, some dimension of apostolic witness—of resonance within the Church—must mark the contemplative life; so too, in the lives of those who engage primarily in apostolic activity, there must be some dimension of contemplation. In this way, that essential ecclesial mission, *to proclaim the word of God,* will be shared by all religious and will shape the proper character of their witness.

It would be impossible to speak of evangelical witness in religious life, if the subject of the counsels were not addressed. In the language of the exhortation, these are "essential commitments" emerging from the historical experience of those who have endeavored to live the gospel throughout the Christian past. There is no question, here, of trying to find a fully elaborated "theology of the vows." This lies beyond the intention or scope of the document. Nor should we expect a discussion of chastity, obedience, and poverty that is novel or strikingly "different" from what has been taught in the past. The doctrine in the exhortation does not differ greatly from what the Church has taught consistently regarding the evangelical counsels. What is new in this case is a recognition that the challenge of the twentieth century calls for a new perspective through which religious can seek to find dimensions of witness that speak to the anguish, the confusion, and the achievement of our century.

Religious Chastity

In speaking of evangelical chastity, therefore, Paul VI stresses the fact that consecrated celibacy is a charism, a gift given by the Spirit to the Church. This charism directs and liberates the human capacity to love so that the lives of those who profess it in faithfulness can bear fruit for the whole body. The new perspectives introduced into the discussion of evangelical chastity include an emphasis on community as a newly perceived human and Christian value which provides for the expression and support of celibate love. Both this relation of chastity to community and that of chastity to contemplation, understood as the prayer to which all Christians are called, are yet to be explored more fully in their theological and spiritual dimensions. The most radical insight expressed in the discussion on consecrated chastity (#13) is that which calls for a witness to the integrity and fidelity of human love in an age when misplaced and deformed expressions of sexuality and interpersonal relationships so widely prevail. There is a message here for religious to explore in a special way the domain of friendship as a human experience open to evangelical witness on the part of those who profess celibacy for the sake of the kingdom.

Religious Obedience

Evangelical obedience, again, does not emerge in the document in a way that differs markedly from our past understanding of it, with one exception. The heart of evangelical obedience is, in a peculiar way, the paschal mystery, the mystery through which we participate in the death and resurrection of Jesus. It is in faith that we embrace this counsel, the document insists. To be obedient, then, is to "hear," to "listen to" the word of faith, the word of the Lord. As the Spirit of God acts and speaks to the community of the whole people of God, religious obedience, insofar as it is evangelical, will be open to those modes of dialogue which enable religious to listen to, to hear one another for the building up of their service to the Church. Without denying the role of that person whose first service in the community is to show forth an exercise of authority, the document does not disregard the role of those whose obedience is expressed in a service of response to authority through responsible sharing in the burden of discerning through consultation and discussion the will of God for each community. Pope Paul considers the relation that must exist between authority and the individual conscience, authority and the reality of individual freedom, authority and the communal response to it. Here, he recalls the experience of the paschal mystery, of the cross, that often marks this domain of religious life. He reminds us that a share in the death of the Lord is not separated from a participation in his risen life.

Religious Poverty

The discussion on consecrated poverty is, perhaps, the most noteworthy section on the counsels to be found in this document. Essentially, it is simplicity of life—with all that implies in terms of lifestyle, activities, dress, use of terrestrial goods, affirmation of human values, and fraternal sharing—which is stressed as the basic evangelical value. Beyond this, there is a call to religious to reexamine their witness to consecrated poverty in the light of their awareness and attention to the "cry of the poor and the needy." Questions of social justice, of indirect participation in or compromise with social injustices are highlighted. Religious are challenged to re-evaluate their acceptance of the universal mandate to work and their actual sharing in the lot of those whom they serve in apostolic activity. Communities, as well as individuals, are challenged to examine in truthful discernment their actual witness to evangelical poverty, and to seek to renew this according to the needs of the "world" in which they live.

Religious, then, are called to be men and women of the gospel and of the Church. This twofold call is dependent on a further challenge: the call to be men and women of prayer.

Men and Women of Prayer

One of the most important sections in *Evangelica testificatio* is that found in numbers forty-two through fifty. Authentic renewal depends on a twofold principle central to the Christian life: The man of prayer is a man who is made strong in God. The courage to be a disciple, as Bonhoeffer would express it, is the courage to accept that necessary discipline of life which assures the freedom of the children of God. Gospel freedom, in the last analysis, consists in the liberty to impose on oneself those limits which are necessary and appropriate to assure growth in Christ, the pursuit of perfect charity, the capacity to give evangelical witness. This implies, as well, an understanding of the need in the Christian life for an integration of the gospel values of contemplation and apostolic service. Authentic renewal thus calls for an attention to prayer that reaches into the domain of the ecclesial as well as of the personal. Worship is to be liturgical, individual, and communal. In this matter, the exhortation speaks to the phenomenon of the charism that is manifest today, both within the Christian community and among those who profess another religious or human tradition, in the quest for wisdom and love. It encourages religious to be open to receive this same gift.

After the exhortation has affirmed that religious life is, essentially, a life in which renewal becomes a process of Christianization, along the lines of evangelical, ecclesial and contemplative/apostolic realities, what does it say to religious men and women about their historical situation? Does the Church "need" religious life? Will religious life continue to exist in the Church? What are religious to do, practically speaking, to assure the continuity and effectiveness of their mode of life? Does the exhortation speak to these concerns? And, if it does, to what degree is this document to be taken seriously? At what level of consciousness does it speak to religious men and women?

The Church's Need for Religious Life

The concern shown for religious in the documents of Vatican II, as Paul VI recalls in *Evangelica testificatio,* is one sign of the need in the Church for Christians who choose to live that lifestyle which we call "religious life." There is recognition in the document that the modes and structures of religious life are in evolution today, that the present age calls for adaptations which may bring about important changes in the structures of the life itself. There can be no doubt, however, of the need within the Christian community for the type of witness that has been found at every age within the Church in one form or another from the beginning. This is a witness that has come to be identified with what has traditionally been called the "spirit of monasticism." It is safe to assert, without reservation, that "religious life," in this sense, will always be a reality within the historical Church. Furthermore, as a community that is both mystery and institution, the Church calls for lifestyles that witness to both the incarnational and eschatological dimensions of ecclesial reality. In what it has to say to the renewal of these internal, evangelical values, the exhortation does, indeed, address the question of the survival of religious life, historically. The affirmative character of the reflections is encouraging.

Beyond this, the exhortation provides principles, guidelines, reaffirmation of essential values as norms for that kind of renewal which will assure continuity of the evangelical witness proper to religious life in the Church. There is, surely, a tone of inspiration and idealism in the document. But the note of realism is not missing. Without presuming to deprive religious of their personal and communal responsibility for implementation of the principles of renewal in programs of adaptation, Paul VI has felt free to suggest the areas in which this adaptation might appropriately take place.

For religious themselves, the realms are those of lifestyle and commitment, in fidelity to the challenge and norm of evangelical living. For others, the exhortation takes into account those characteristics of our age which modify the climate within which apostolic activity and service are to be enacted. One of the most striking examples of this kind of concern is found in what the Pope himself calls a "burning question": *How can the message of the gospel penetrate the world? What can be done at those levels in which a new culture is unfolding, where a new type of man is emerging, a man who no longer believes he needs redemption?* (#52). There is no attempt to solve the problem for religious. There is expectation that they will know how to do that for themselves.

Conclusion

The need for a document of this kind has been longstanding among religious. Unfortunately, its advent has been strikingly unheralded in most quarters. Because it is not an encyclical—or a papal bull—some religious have concluded that it is of little, if any, importance. Because it is a papal document, others have concluded, in advance, that it has little, if anything important to say. As a document that stands low on the ladder of authoritative ecclesiastical documents, the apostolic exhortation is above all a word from a Christian who is, himself, an apostle. It is a word from a father to his children. It is a message from one concerned Christian to another. The fact that the apostle, the father, the Christian, is also the Vicar of Christ, first among bishops, adds solemnity to the message. The fact remains that the intention, here, is to encourage, to motivate, to "exhort," those who are addressed in the typical language of ecclesiastical documents as "beloved sons and daughters," to live as "lights which announce the kingdom of God with a liberty which knows no obstacles and is daily lived by thousands of sons and daughters of the Church" (#3).

The exhortation, then, is to be taken seriously. It is a sign of hope for religious today as they try to discern the specific character of their mode of living the Christian life. It is a mark of the concern of the whole Church for the "anxiety, uncertainty, and instability" that beset many religious men and women in this time of transition and change in the Church and in human society. It is a vote of confidence in religious themselves as persons of sufficient intelligence and integrity to undertake the project of renewal and adaptation in fidelity to the gospel and in attentiveness to mankind. It is an encouragement to religious, engaged in authentic renewal and appropriate adaptation, to "proceed with greater sureness and with more joyful confidence along the way" they have chosen. It is a blueprint which provides guidelines for renewal as a process through which, in fidelity to evangelical witness, religious may continue to make their life more deeply and more unequivocally *Christian.*

NOTES

[1] James A. Mohler, S.J., *The Heresy of Monasticism* (Staten Island: Alba. 1971).

[2] Paul VI, *Evangelica testificatio,* #3.

[3] An abundance of contemporary literature can be found on the *mepris du mone* theme, including much of the material surrounding the "secular city" debate in recent years.

Signs of Hope in Religious Life Today

Stephen Tutas, S.M.

Volume 42, 1983, pp. 3-8.

One of the most important contributions religious women and men can make to the Church in any era is to be signs of hope, encouraging others in their own response to God's call by a witness of joyful dedication. This call to religious to be signs of hope is as urgent today as in any other time in the history of the Church. The preparatory document for the 1983 Synod of Bishops states that "the dominant characteristic of our era seems to have become that of tensions and divisions . . . situations of incomprehension, of estrangement, of conflict, of schism, of reciprocal condemnation. . . ." In response to this, I believe it is absolutely necessary that we religious today strive to be outstanding men and women of hope. We must really believe—and show our belief—that the Holy Spirit is active in the Church today, and that this active presence of the Spirit is the basis for our hope.

Points of Convergence

For some time now, I have been especially sensitive to the signs of hope found in religious life. I was privileged to see some of these signs of hope as I met with other superiors general of both men and women religious congregations. The various formal and informal meetings in Rome and elsewhere were for me inspiring moments when we were able to share with each other what we experienced in our visits to communities. It was very heartening for me to see how many points of convergence there were as we discussed the main themes of religious life and were able to refer to so many encouraging examples of what was actually being realized on a day-by-day basis in religious communities throughout the world. My personal experience included contact with communities of the Society of Mary (Marianists) in thirty one countries on all the continents. As I found in my exchange of views with others, my experience reflected well the general thrusts in religious life as I came to identify these through visits and reports.

Obviously, not all that I experience is positive and encouraging. I am painfully aware of the inadequacies in my own life and in the lives of others. It is always true that the Church "is at the same time holy and always in need of being purified."[1] But while recognizing our failures as religious, I believe it is much more life-giving to look at the signs of hope so evident in the lives of many religious women and men and build on these so that together with other members of the Church we can move forward to the third millennium in a spirit of hope. I often pray in the words of Pope Paul VI that "the world of our time, which is searching, sometimes with anguish, sometimes with hope, be enabled to receive the Good News not from evangelizers who are dejected, discouraged, impatient or anxious, but from ministers of the gospel whose lives glow with fervor, who have first received the joy of Christ, and who are willing to risk their lives so that the kingdom may be proclaimed and the church established in the midst of the world."[2]

After completing my terms of service as Superior General, I was privileged to have several months to devote to prayer and reflection before taking up my new assignment as Director of the Marianist Formation Center in Cupertino, California. Most of this time of prayer and reflection was spent in the Motherhouse of the Dallas Province of the School Sisters of Notre Dame in Irving, Texas, where I served as chaplain under ideal conditions that made it easy for me to look back with gratitude and to look forward with hope, while sharing my experience of gratitude and hope with the community as I tried to live fully in the present.

Now that I have taken up my new life and work in California, with the specific responsibility to promote continuing formation in the Marianist Province of the Pacific, I would like to share with the readers of REVIEW FOR RELIGIOUS a summary of the signs of hope that I see in religious life today.

Ten Signs of Hope

I have selected ten signs of hope that I find particularly striking. It is evident that these signs do not exist everywhere. And where they do exist, the signs vary in clarity and intensity. But these signs *do* exist, and my daily prayer is that they become ever stronger and more general throughout the Church, I hope the readers of this article will find in the list a confirmation of their own experience, and a further encouragement to continue working to make these signs ever more clear and ever more general.

1. *A strong commitment to ongoing renewal,* emphasizing:
   - personal and communitarian prayer, making union with God clearly the

basis for religious life;
- the building of community, recognizing this bonding in view of a shared ideal as the sign of being a true follower of Christ;
- the concern for a greater simplicity of life;
- the positive understanding of celibacy as a way of loving rather than as a simple renunciation of marriage and of family.

These four points constitute a truly radical change in religious life which is often unnoticed as we ourselves go through it. It is not that the value of prayer, community, simplicity and celibacy were lacking in the past, but that we have been able to give new expression to these values in a changing world.

I have selected these four characteristics of renewal as being the most life-giving. First and foremost, of course, must be the contemplative dimension of religious life. I find it significant that the "Conclusive Document" just issued by the Vatican as a follow-up to the 1981 International Congress of Bishops and Others Responsible for Ecclesiastical Vocations declares, in speaking of religious states, that "the contemplative dimension is the true secret of spiritual renewal and apostolic fruitfulness in religious life."[3] All renewal programs begin with this contemplative dimension.

Efforts are also being made to emphasize community as a sharing of faith; faith is given expression in a concern for simplicity of life; the community of faith is always being urged to look beyond itself. These are outstanding features of various renewal programs.

Perhaps never before in the history of religious life has so much attention been given to providing assistance for continuing formation. This itself is certainly a great sign of hope.

2. *A rediscovery of the relevance of the founding charism,* along with a renewed interest in the person of the founder or foundress, and also a renewed understanding that the founding charism is just as important for the Church of our time as it was at the time of the actual foundation of the community.

The document, "Mutual Relations between Bishops and Religious," is an important encouragement for us religious to renew the offering of our charisms to the local church, and this with a renewed awareness that we are needed and wanted for the specific gifts God has entrusted to the various religious families in the Church.

General chapters, especially in writing constitutions in response to the Second Vatican Council, have expressed very forcefully how the founding charism is able to meet the urgent needs of the Church in our time.

3. *New directions in evangelization,* in continued response to that great document of Pope Paul VI, *Evangelization in the Modern World,* which followed the 1974 Synod of Bishops on Evangelization.

I found it very rewarding to read Archbishop Robert Sanchez' address to his fellow bishops at Collegeville last summer in which he gave heavy emphasis to the dynamic orientations implicit in Pope Paul's statement, saying that "it would be difficult to exaggerate the importance that this document will have in revitalizing and preparing the Church for the future. . . ."[4]

For us religious, this Apostolic Exhortation has sparked and encouraged a gratifying transition from concern about ourselves—even about our survival—to a greater sense of mission and outreach.

4. *The greater insertion of religious communities in the local church* and a more ecclesial thrust in solidarity with other religious and in collaboration with all others in the local church. As we look back over the past twenty-five years we can appreciate what dramatic changes have taken place in terms of greater collaboration among religious themselves, but also in terms of the active involvement of religious in the life and structures of the local church. The Unions of Superiors General and the national conferences of superiors have provided excellent leadership in this regard. At the same time, more and more bishops are recognizing the unique contribution religious communities can make to the life of the local church.

Here, as with the other signs of hope, much needs to be done, but the first step in making this sign clearer and more general is to acknowledge the great strides that have already been realized.

5. *The increasing concern for the promotion of justice and peace.* I am tempted to write more extensively about this sign than any other because, as President of the USG Commission Justice and Peace during most of my years as Superior General, I was able to witness first hand the response religious have made to the call of the 1971 Synod's document on Justice in the World. Perhaps the simplest statement is best: if the movement to promote justice and peace has developed so strongly in our time, it is in great part due to the courageous initiatives on the part of so many religious throughout the world.

6. *The promotion of the laity.* It may be surprising to some that I have chosen to underline the promotion of the laity as a sign of hope for religious. But I believe the attention that has been given to the vocation of the laity since Vatican II has served to clarify even more the specific vocation of religious men and women in the Church. Among the significant consequences of this clarification has been greater attention by religious to the witness they give by the quality of their religious life. There is a definite priority given today to being. Religious life, then, will not be evaluated simply in terms of doing. As important and vital as our work may be, the first and most important contribution we religious can make to the Church is in terms of our life. This emphasis religious give to being is a wonderful response to the call of the Church in our time, as this was stated so clearly by Pope John Paul II shortly after his election: "What counts most is not what the religious do, but what they are, as persons consecrated to the Lord."[5]

I also find it encouraging that more and more religious are emphasizing a greater collaboration with the laity, recognizing the unique values that each can offer the other. One of my hopes, as a consequence of the last Synod of Bishops on the Christian Family, has been for a more effective collaboration between the community of religious and the Christian family in the local church.

7. *Collaboration in the promotion of vocations.* Ever since the Second Vatican Council, the Church has been calling upon all Christians to work together in promoting all Christian vocations. The Conclusive Document referred to earlier is an excellent guide to help toward the realization of this objective put forward by the council. What I find as a heartening sign of hope is that so many religious communities are making well-organized efforts to collaborate with each other in the promotion of vocations rather than seeking unilaterally to promote their own vocations.

Religious who see clearly their responsibility to promote a sense of vocation in the lives of all, and who offer their own charism to those whom God may call are themselves great signs of hope for the Church in our time.

8. *Trends in formation and government that assure the best conditions for human development,* such as:
   - concern for affective maturity;
   - emphasis on freedom and personal responsibility;
   - endorsement of animation as a way of exercising authority;
   - general application of the principle of subsidiarity;
   - appreciation of collegiality on all levels.

Each of these points is itself a sign of hope. Taken together, these trends offer great promise for the future of religious life.

9. *A reassessement of the role of religious life in the churches of Africa, Latin America and Asia,* featuring both a new thrust (from missionary to collaborator) and new foundations to implant various expressions of religious life for greater and longer-lasting service to the local church. The kind of thinking sparked by Buhlman's "The Coming of the Third Church" has been both challenging and stimulating for many religious communities.

The transition from missionary to collaborator is not easy, but it is being done, and done very well, in so many places.

The new foundations, despite the overall decline in numbers and the steadily advancing age of communities, are remarkable signs of confidence in God's Providence, that a generous response to the evident needs of God's people is the only way to live.

10. *The spirit of hope that is evident in so many leaders of religious today.* I am strongly convinced of what I like to call "the apostolate of administration." There is nothing more life-giving than a religious leader who is a man or woman of hope and is able to share that hope with others. We religious are blessed in having many women and men of hope among us at this time in the history of religious life.

As I look at these ten signs of hope, I sense in religious life today a real desire for a way of life that, in the words of Cardinal Pironio, is committed, serious, profound, fraternal, ecclesial.

Something really tremendous is happening in the Church today, and this amid the tensions and struggles of life. And so it is very life-giving for us religious to look beyond the day-to-day struggles, the evident failures and shortcomings, to see how God is at work in our lives and to share this experience with each other. Not all that is happening in religious life can be attributed to the Spirit. There is need for continual discernment. But the good that is evident in religious life is a sign of the Spirit at work among us and deserves to be recognized and proclaimed.

We are in an age of transition as we experience the death of much of what was familiar and as we experience the birth of a new era in the history of religious life. May our constant prayer be for the grace to believe in the potentiality of our religious communities, recognizing that religious life does have a great mission in the Church today, and that each religious community is called to serve the Church in a special way, offering its particular charism to be incarnated, adapted and enriched in so many different people.

NOTES

[1] *Lumen Gentium*, n. 8.
[2] *Evangelii Nuntiandi*, n. 80.
[3] *The Conclusive Document*, p. 53.
[4] *Origins*, Sept. 2, 1982, p. 181.
[5] October 1, 1979, quoted in *The Conclusive Document*, p. 53.

Discipleship: Root Model of the Life Called "Religious"

Elizabeth A. Johnson, C.S.J.

Volume 42, 1983, pp. 864-872.

A profound change has taken place in the consciousness of members of religious congregations in North America, a change with consequences still too far-reaching to see or assess. It has come about as a result of their careful and vigorous response to the mandate of the Second Vatican Council to rediscover their original charisms, to experiment with living those original creative impulses effectively in the contemporary world, and to shuck off encrusted structures and customs which did not serve that purpose. The ferment of the ensuing years, moreover, did not take place in a vacuum but in a dialogue with and active relation to the broad ecclesial and cultural worlds of which religious congregations are a part. Hence, liturgical, biblical, theological and structural renewal in the Church as well as civil movements toward human (including women's) rights, justice and peace, have all had input into the development occurring within these groups within the Church. Through the pain and the joy of ongoing renewal process, a new sense of identity and self-understanding has emerged, a new sense of direction which is coming to expression both directly and indirectly in written constitutions.

At this time it seems important to reflect on the need for a new envisionment of this particular way of life, for a new way of encapsulating the meaning at the heart of this commitment, for imaging the new pattern of individual and group self-understanding. There is a need for comprehending the life called "religious" as a whole in such a way that the gains of the past are safeguarded while at the same time the way remains open to meet the perhaps unimagined challenges of the coming future. There is a need on the part of individuals to

35

grasp their own lives in such a way that daily life patterns as well as major decisions make profound sense in the light of the whole. It is the suggestion of this reflection that the root model of discipleship or the following of Jesus Christ has the potential to serve this need, and in fact has already begun to do so.

Not that the following of Christ as the essence of religious life is a totally new category; in one form, in fact, it is quite traditional. On the wall of many novitiates in this country, before the renewal, could be found a picture of an ascetic-looking Jesus Christ, gesturing with one hand toward his heart and with the other toward the onlooker, while across the bottom of the picture were imprinted the words, "Come, follow me." Thus was inspiration offered to the young member to persevere in a vocation which was envisioned as a personal and deeply spiritual following of Christ. When the Second Vatican Council, then, declared that "since the fundamental norm of the religious life is a following of Christ as proposed by the gospel, such is to be regarded by all communities as their supreme law,"[1] the statement resonated in memory and experience. As a result of both biblical studies on pertinent New Testament texts and contemporary reflection on the nature of the Church, however, the content of the category of "following" or being a disciple has undergone incisive development, so that it now connotes a manner of life and consciousness quite different from the one indicated by that traditional art and the piety which it expressed.

The following reflection draws upon biblical and theological resources to explore the elements of discipleship as it has come to be understood, with the conviction that it is a key category for the interpretation of the lives of those in religious congregations. By delineating the original meaning of "following" in the New Testament and then bringing it to bear on the present situation, the significance and integrative power of the idea of discipleship may be illumined.

Origins: "They Followed Him"

Throughout his ministry Jesus of Nazareth formed around himself a band of disciples, people who were intrigued with what he was doing and left everything to "follow" him.[2] This group was a growing group, not limited to the number of the "twelve apostles" although they, of course, were members of it. To an external observer, the disciples spent time going around with Jesus on his itinerant ministry, listening to his preaching, witnessing his conflicts and his acts of power, enjoying his table companionship, at times helping out. During his tumultuous last hours, a good part of the band of disciples deserted him; by all accounts some of the women disciples kept vigil with him to the end and even after.

To get at the interior reality of what it meant to follow Jesus, it is helpful to compare it with the following of other leaders at that time. It was not unusual in first century Palestine for a rabbi to have disciples who attached themselves to him for the purpose of learning interpretation of the Torah. Nor was it unusual for a charismatic revolutionary leader of the Zealot party to attract disciples who joined him with the goal of liberating the country from foreign occupation. In both cases, the disciples were said to "follow" the teacher or guerilla leader. Following meant technically "walking behind," and was used of the pupil or fighter who literally followed behind the rabbi or military leader on the road, as a sign of the relationship between the one who had the authority of knowledge or arms and the ones who sought to share in it.

Comparing discipleship in the company of Jesus to the usual pattern of discipleship at the time surfaces what is truly distinctive and original about following Jesus. Five elements can be unraveled from the discipleship stories of the gospels which, taken together, form the paradigm for the Christian discipleship rediscovered in our own day.

- Being a disciple of Jesus depends first of all on his call. Unlike the custom of a pupil approaching a rabbi and asking to study with him, here the pattern is reversed. Jesus chooses his own disciples, often people with seemingly little to recommend them, and sometimes with obvious disqualifying characteristics. The person called is put in a situation where a response must be given in all freedom. Some, as we know, responded "no." Jesus' compelling call and the personal response of the one approached distinguish this kind of discipleship at the outset from other forms of the time. It is, from the beginning, a gift.

- Jesus' call to a person is a call to "follow *me*" (Mk 1:17), thus involving the disciple in a unique attachment to his person. Joining his band meant binding oneself to this person in a spirit of allegiance and concretely following him in the unpredictable ups and downs of his ministry. Even more deeply, it involved one in a willingness to share with him his uncertain and, as time went on, increasingly perilous destiny. This again is distinct to Jesus—the element of personal bonding and self-commitment to his person.

- Following Jesus brings with it an extraordinary demand: that the response be wholehearted and total. One has to abandon everything else in order to be a disciple. Parents and all family ties, nets and other means of livelihood, religious duties such as burying the dead, wealth, social status, pious customs—all are suitable payment for this pearl of great price. Nothing can come before the priority of following, and in the light of it all else becomes relative. This is something other leaders never dared demand, but is at the heart of the following of Jesus. Discipleship engages one in radical personal transformation, in a conversion process, so that one turns from egocentricity to letting go, dedication and self-gift.

- Discipleship in the company of Jesus brings the follower into association with Jesus' own mission, another non-rabbinic characteristic. That mission is to proclaim the nearness of God's powerful and loving reign and to reach out in a healing, liberating way to overturn oppression and to reconcile in the light of this reign of God already dawning. Jesus makes his disciples co-workers in this service of the coming God, even sending them out on their own to preach, to heal, to drive out the "demons" that hold people in bondage. Discipleship, then, carries a practical and critical edge. It means participation in the mission and authority of Jesus, and with him in the great eschatological event beginning in him and still to be completed.

- Vocation and personal following and radical freedom from all ties and mission, finally, introduce the disciple to a certain kind of open communal life. No one is a follower in isolation, but is supported and challenged by others with a similar commitment. For all of the inevitable tensions which arose, the ideal of their interaction with one another is mutual love, and the norm for the style of leadership among them is service, taking the last place, rather than the culturally prevalent mode of domination. Because of the orientation toward mission, they never become a circle of the elite over against the great unwashed "outside," but associate with all comers, sharing (sometimes to their chagrin) the joy and feasting of Jesus' table companionship with tax collectors and sinners.

The distinctive features which characterized the following of Jesus, namely, vocation and free response, personal commitment, abandonment of all other priorities, participation in mission in the light of the coming reign of God, and open communal life, all set this group apart from other bands of disciples engaged in scholarly or military movements of the time. The disciples of Jesus were brought into personal association with his person, mission, and destiny in the company of one another, an association which demanded (no more gentle word will do) *metanoia* or conversion and self-giving to an unparalleled degree. It is interesting to note that so dynamic is this following and so strongly is it connected with the person of Jesus and his history, that nowhere in the New Testament is there a noun corresponding to what we have been calling "discipleship"; the whole phenomenon is referred to simply by the active verb "to follow": the disciples followed him.

Disciples as Believers

After the events of the death and resurrection of Jesus, when the early communities of faith began to form and spread, being a disciple took on a new and broader connotation. No longer was it possible literally to walk with Jesus of Nazareth around the countryside of Galilee or to sit down at table with him. But his memory was alive in the communities and a new mode of his presence was known through his Spirit poured forth upon them. By the power of that Spirit and in his name, the name of Jesus now confessed as the Christ, people were still called to abandon everything and "follow" him, to proclaim the nearness of the power and mercy of God who acts on our behalf, to engage themselves in works of love and justice especially on behalf of the poor, and to gather around the table and break bread until he comes. Following Jesus began to mean living the life of Christian faith, being a Christian believer. Being a disciple took on the connotation of wayfaring though life in the manner of the one who is the way, following the "Way" as the Christian movement began to be called. All of the early Christians, not only the leadership personnel, were referred to as disciples (Ac 6:1; 9:19); collectively, the women and men of the Church were known as the "community of the disciples" (Ac 6:2).

Reaching into our tradition, creative thinkers have recently brought this ancient treasure of the idea of discipleship forth into the turmoil and challenge of the present situation. The Church of today can also be envisioned as a community of disciples, each one following Christ, gathering and being sent, sharing in effective action and suffering in the light of the coming reign of God.[3] This model can serve to integrate vastly differing experiences within the Church and provide a guiding vision of the whole. As recognized groups within the Church, religious communities can share in this ecclesial self-understanding. This means that religious communities can also be well-envisioned as communities of disciples, witnessing publicly and intensely in and for the whole Church to the vocation of following Christ which is the vocation of all Christian believers.[4] Once it is related to the discipleship of the whole Church, discipleship as the root model of life in religious communities serves as a potent integrative and inspiring symbol and a basis on which critical consciousness can rest.

Imitation or Following?

One extremely important caution needs to be raised in order to avoid any misunderstanding of what this model implies. Following Jesus Christ cannot be equated with literal imitation of his actions. Such imitation is simply impossible, since situations never repeat themselves exactly, and every person is likewise unique. But even more to the point, historical circumstances change from era to era, and doing the exact same thing in a different situation may result in an effect opposite to that of the original intention, or at any rate be ineffective. Creativity and discernment are called for as each disciple and group of disciples appropriates the Spirit of Jesus and responds in accord with the values of Christ in very diverse situations. Discipleship gives no easy assurance or quick security regarding behavior, since by its very nature it excludes simplistic or slavish copying. Rather, disciples get involved with Jesus Christ and his way, and go their own way in the light of Christ's directions. In one sense they are conservative, insofar as they persevere in the basic orientation of following Christ; in another sense they are progressive, since they creatively revise forms of response in accord with present historical conditions.[5] Following him, then, is a tremendously dynamic rather than static reality; the disciple reproduces the fundamental thrust of Jesus in new and undreamed of situations.

Taking discipleship as the chief model for envisioning the life of religious communities means that the elements which characterized the following of Jesus in his own lifetime and in the early Church are ingredient to this life today, in its very different circumstances. Within the context of the faith of the larger believing community there are the elements of call and free response, personal faith commitment, radical freedom from all ties, participation in mission in the light of the coming reign of God, and open communal life. All elements must be present for true following and, when they are, discipleship is seen at its best. From this perspective, exploring the relation of this model to the recent past, the present, and the future can further illumine its powerful implications.

After almost two decades of experimentation and change, discipleship provides a criterion by which emerging renewed structures can be measured and either welcomed or critiqued. In the light of this evaluation, they can be understood as leading to a deeper and more faithful following of Christ in the contemporary world or as weakening that fundamental direction of the life. Do growth in personal responsibility and wider zones of personal decision-making encourage personal discipleship? Are the practice of discernment in matters of importance, the adoption of a dialogic mode of obedience, explicit concern with justice in ministries (to mention some of the more salient changes) characteristics befitting the life-style of a band of disciples? The envisionment, design and acceptance or rejection of the developments of the recent past are well normed by the basic model of discipleship.

The idea of discipleship, furthermore, provides a way to bring traditional elements of this particular form of Christian life into new alignment, one which releases the possibility of more integrated life in the present. For all of the protestations to the contrary, there has traditionally been tension between the contemplative and the active dimensions (as they have been called), a tension which has grown more acute as the demands of the modern world have invaded the cloister. Weighting personal or communal choice toward the prayerful dimension can result in a privatized religious spirituality, disturbed by the need for strong action which is experienced as an interruption and as somehow less than holy. Tending overmuch in the other direction toward the public and practical dimension can also result in a truncation, a reduction of this way of life to a purely social pattern of behavior, lacking an explicit transcendent or religious reference. When filled with the content of New Testament following, the model of discipleship leads to the profound integration of the mystical (contemplative) and political (active) elements, undercutting the dualism so often experienced between the two.[6]

The disciple is one who receives the gift of being called to follow, experiences it as a transforming grace and responds freely. The disciple does not adhere just to Jesus' teaching or pattern of behavior but to his person, binding oneself to Christ in a spirit of personal allegiance and being faithful even in failure, even to the cross. Transformed by the grace of the call, the disciple forsakes all other security and in radical trust in God abandons everything else which might have a claim to first priority in life. These characteristics of lived discipleship insure deep personal spirituality as a non-negotiable dimension of life in religious community. Simultaneously and equally, the disciple is entrusted and charged with participation in the mission of Jesus, which means that one's whole life is oriented to the service of the coming reign of God. The disciple must proclaim it and must act on behalf of its coming, in particular (as a follower in *Jesus'* footsteps) by partisanship for the marginalized and the oppressed. This concrete practice of the reign of God, this working to recreate and liberate and reconcile all people and things with each other and with their loving and powerfully-coming God, is bound to put the disciple in situations of conflict and to necessitate the taking of unpopular stances. Ultimately, it demands a love fraught with suffering. The disciple is not a solitary individual in this, for one is bound with other disciples similarly giving themselves. These characteristics of lived discipleship insure strong and consistent action for the "other" as a non-negotiable dimension of life in religious community.

Both elements, then, the mystical and the political, worshipping praise of God and action on behalf of justice, personal conversion and critical engagement in oppressive situations, spirituality and the work of re-creation are profoundly integrated when the life called "religious" is imaged as the life of discipleship. It is then virtually impossible to exclude one dimension in favor of the other, for following Jesus Christ has always essentially included both, as indeed his own life included both.

Besides providing a criterion by which to create and evaluate renewed structures, and in addition to being a root model with powerful integrative force for actual living, the model of discipleship releases a powerful force for keeping the future open and for participating in the ever-coming, unknown and ultimately fulfilling future in the course of life. This again results from its being a category linked to the actual ministry of Jesus.

Jesus preached the dawning nearness of the rule of God and took bold stands in the light of the power of that wonderful and terrible event of the end, expected imminently. The approaching future, identified with the victory of the goodness of God crushing all evil, was the passion of his life. After Easter, the disciples realized and proclaimed that this rule had definitively arrived in and through his life and destiny, but it had arrived in advance of the ultimate fulfillment of the whole creation in all of its individual aspects. The final fulfillment for all was still to come.

Discipleship today involves the follower in that same realization. It evokes the far-reaching discovery that the ultimate reign of God, while begun, has not yet come, and thus no present reality or structure, ecclesial or social, may be allowed to be canonized. It engages the disciple in cooperating with the power of God's future as it seeks to transform the present. With the destiny of Jesus Christ as the pledge of future salvation, it impels especially the turn toward the poor in the firm hope that the present ostracism and alienation of their lives is not the final truth of their situation, for it is not the final possibility of the ever-coming God. At the same time, discipleship provides a continual spur toward greater individual fidelity and conversion of heart, for one is ever on the way, not yet arrived at the coming wholeness. This profound awareness of the "not-yet," of the incompleteness of the present with its concomitant orientation toward the coming future is, of course, and always has been the basis of the theological rationale of the vows. One vows a life of incompleteness in utter dedication to the fullness yet to be, in cooperation with God, the ever-coming power of the future, seeking to transform the present. In its original meaning, the idea of discipleship brings back to consciousness in a renewed and critical way the unfinished character of all things in time and the hope of future fulfillment. Drawn by God, the Absolute Future, communities of women and men, bands of disciples, participate in the work of tearing down and building up, of recreating hearts and structures, on the way to the blessedness to come.

In all of these ways—evaluating the past, integrating life in the present, inspiring life and critique in the light of the future—discipleship serves as a root model for the life of those in religious congregations. What is of crucial importance to note today is that it is the life of women for which discipleship is an appropriate model, not to the exclusion of its appropriateness for the life of men. Recent research is identifying evidence that women as well as men were disciples of Jesus during his ministry, were commissioned witnesses of the resurrection, were active believers in the early communities, leaders of house churches, and participants in the missionary effort.[7] Due to the androcentric (male-centered) nature of the traditioning process and of the ecclesial structures which evolved out of the first century, this discipleship of women was largely ignored or given short shrift in subsequent eras, although the experience and memory of it were still powerful enough to find their way into canonical written texts, at least as traces. Not that women ceased being followers of Jesus; there is a hidden history of the discipleship of women down through the whole Christian tradition. Uncovering that history in our present time gives added power to the idea of discipleship, leading women to reclaim their full heritage and identity as disciples. The fact that with this reclamation comes the challenge to the exclusion of women from certain ecclesial ministries should come as no surprise: it is inherent in the logic of the position, arguably based in Christian origins and principles.

Mary as Disciple

Waiting to be re-appropriated is the figure of Mary, mother of Jesus, whose key claim to attention lies in the scriptural portrayal of her as the model of the true disciple. In faith she heard the word of God and acted upon it (Lk 8:19-21 and 1:26-38). In the joy of her heart she worshipped God in gladness, and in her understanding of God's ways she is the singer of the song of justice for the poor and the oppressed (Lk 1:46-55). Not knowing how the journey would end, she kept faith with Jesus during his lifetime, and was part of the believing community after Easter waiting for his Spirit (Ac 1:14).

The Second Vatican Council reclaimed the early Christian idea that Mary is a type of the Church.[8] Mary and the Church, then, mutually reflect each other. The community of disciples which is the Church can gaze at Mary and see reflected back the ideal of its following in faith and mission, joy and prophecy. The image of this woman as the true disciple is an image around which regard for her can once again grow among committed disciples of Jesus Christ, who follow in her company.

A profound change has taken place in the consciousness of members of religious congregations in North America, a change with consequences still too far-reaching to see or assess. The lifestyle which is emerging can best be envisioned by means of the root model of discipleship, potent with consequences for understanding and action. In keeping with the non-isolated character of the whole renewal process in religious congregations, it is a category drawn from the Scriptures, gaining currency in contemporary theology of the Church, and able to be related in fruitful and critical ways to ecclesial and societal realities. In its full significance, it has the fiber to support commitment, to make it intelligible, and to challenge toward ever greater creative fidelity. As personally committed disciples, bonded into publicly vowed communities of disciples, members of religious congregations along with all other members of the *ekklesia* of God are wayfarers through line in the footsteps of Jesus by the power of the Spirit.

NOTES

[1] *Perfectae Caritatis,* n. 2, in *The Documents of Vatican II,* Walter M. Abbott, ed. (NY: America Press, 1966).

[2] For studies of discipleship during the ministry of Jesus, see Günther Bornkamm, *Jesus of Nazareth* (New York: Harper and Row, 1960), pp. 144-52; Martin Hengel, *The Charistmatic Leader and His Followers* (New York: Crossroad, 1981); Gerhard Kittel, *Theological Dictionary of the New Testament,* Vol. 1 (Grand Rapids, MI: Eerdmans, 1964), pp. 210-16; and Edward Schillebeeckx, *Jesus—An Experiment in Christology* (New York: Seabury, 1979), pp. 218-29.

[3] See Avery Dulles, *A Church to Believe In: Discipleship and the Dynamics of Freedom* (NY: Crossroad, 1982), especially "Imaging the Church for the 1980s," pp. 1-18.

[4] See Johannes B. Metz, *Followers of Christ* (New York: Paulist Press, 1978); and John Lozano, *Discipleship: Toward an Understanding of Religious Life* (Chicago: Claret Center, 1980).

[5] See Hans Küng, *On Being a Christian* (Garden City: Doubleday & Co., 1976), pp. 540-53; and Jon Sobrino, *Christology at the Crossroads* (Maryknoll, NY: Orbis Books, 1978), pp. 108-45.

[6] See the detailed reflection on this point in Edward Schillebeeckx, *Christ: The Experience of Jesus as Lord* (New York: Seabury, 1980), pp. 762-839.

[7] See Rosemary Ruether and Eleanor McLaughlin, eds., *Women of Spirit: Female Leadership in the Jewish and Christian Traditions* (New York: Simon and Schuster, 1979); Letty Russell, ed., *The Liberating Word* (Philadelphia: Westminster Press, 1976); and Elisabeth Schüssler Fiorenza, *In Memory of Her: A Feminist Theological Reconstruction of Christian Origins* (New York: Crossroad, 1983).

[8] *Lumen Gentium,* Chapter 8. See Raymond Brown, "The Meaning of Modern New Testament Studies for an Ecumenical Understanding of Mary," *Biblical Reflections on Crises Facing the Church* (New York: Paulist Press, 1975), pp. 84-108.

The Call to the Renewal of Religious Life

John R. Sheets, S.J.

Volume 43, 1984, pp. 175-190.

On June 22, 1983, the text entitled "Essential Elements in Church Teaching on Religious Life," prepared by the Sacred Congregation for Religious and Secular Institutes, was released. Accompanying the text was a letter of Pope John Paul II to the American bishops. In this letter the pope recalled the purpose of the Holy Year of the Redemption as a time devoted to special efforts for the renewal of the whole Church. In this context, he asked that religious, in particular the religious of the United States, review the experience of changes in their religious life over the past twenty years in order to consolidate the positive developments and to eliminate what was not authentic. As a means to facilitate this process of discernment and renewal, the pope set up a commission of bishops, chaired by Archbishop John Quinn of San Francisco.

Nearly seven months separate the time I am writing from the time of that intervention. The events that have taken place over these months have a significance for the future of religious life in this country (one could in fact say, for the whole Church in the United States) that cannot be overestimated. Before I speak about the significance, it is necessary to review these events so as to get a sense of the process that is at work.

The pope's intervention, as well as the text of *Essential Elements,* directed as they were to religious in the United States, caught them by surprise. It was unexpected, even though some said they sensed it was "in the air." Naturally the action prompted questions as to what lay behind it all. In particular, they asked, why were American religious singled out? The immediate and spontaneous public reactions were almost universally negative.

The negative reactions of some came from their perception that the intervention took place without warning and that the text was prepared without proper consultation, ignoring the years of work on religious life that had been done on this side of the ocean. Many found this unilateral way of proceeding inappropriate at a time when the importance of communication is so highly valued.

Other reactions stemmed from differences which were more substantial. These touched on understandings that concern the nature of religious life itself, whether and how it differs from lay life, and on the nature of authority within the Church. The contrast of "this-side-of-the-ocean" views was stressed, in contradistinction from "Roman" views, on the nature of law, of authority, of static and dynamic mind-sets. Where these objections were fueled with feminist positions the tone took on even deeper notes of anger, resentment, suspicion and defiance. The press in the United States in general reported the pope's intervention in a critical way, finding it "typical" of his continued practice of "picking on the Church in America."

The initial public reaction did not augur well for the plan the pope had in mind. If anything, the situation now seems worse than it was before because it surfaced prominently many latent differences (and some not so latent) between American religious and Rome, as well as among religious themselves. The fact that what could have been a catastrophe took a more positive turn in the subsequent weeks and months is due mainly to the tact, wisdom and courage of Archbishop Quinn and the members of his commission, together with their advisors, as well as the openness to dialogue that was demonstrated by representatives of the various religious groups. I would now like to give a brief overview of the work of the commission, then comment on the main thrust of the document *Essential Elements,* with particular reference to some of the problems facing religious life in the United States today.

The Work of the Commission

The exact purpose of the pope's intervention, as well as the nature of the commission's task, were not clear at the beginning, either to the members of the commission or to religious leaders. However, as the dialogue began and continued over the subsequent months, a sense of direction emerged.

The first step was to meet with the two groups who officially represent religious in the United States.[1] It is probably an understatement to say that the tone of both meetings was strained.

In August, Archbishop Quinn met with the Leadership Conference of Women Religious. In his talk to them, he spoke of the vision which the Church has of religious life, the sense of the paschal mystery in the history of religious life here over the past twenty years, the appeal that the pope was making to the bishops, and the charge given to the commission.

After his talk the archbishop listened to the reactions of the assembly. They can be summarized under three headings.

In the first place, many were highly critical of the document on essentials, finding it static rather than dynamic, monastic rather than apostolic, accenting vows rather than mission, embodying a "dubious ecclesiology," and being out of touch with the uniqueness of the American experience.

Others had problems with the intervention itself. What was behind it? Why were Americans singled out? Why was there no consultation? Was it in reality a devious way to get at religious women? How did this affect groups which were international in membership?

Finally there were reactions coming out of feminist issues, perceiving the whole affair as another instance of the male Church attempting to control women, a further evidence of paternalism, a continuation of the injustice of asking for service without granting full admission into ministry.

In spite of the strained nature of the meeting, it concluded with a loud round of applause as a sign of gratitude and appreciation to Archbishop Quinn.

Another member of the bishops' commission, Archbishop Thomas Kelly, O.P., met with the Conference of Major Superiors of Men, which also met in August. The problems voiced there had to do mainly with the manner in which the whole affair took place, its one-sided nature, without previous consultation, seemingly ignoring all of the work that had gone into these various questions already. There was questioning concerning the purpose and the worthwhileness of what was being asked.

In October, Archbishop Kelly met with the assembly of *Consortium Perfectae Caritatis*. Their response was overwhelmingly positive. There was a basic hope that steps could be taken to renew religious life and unite the various organizations. At the same time it was feared that the result might be an intensification of division. They felt that the easy categorizing of the differences that divide religious into conservative and liberal overlook the root of division, which comes from radically different notions of religious life, the vows, authority, law, the Church, and in particular the attitude to the Holy See. These discordant views are found even within one and the same congregation. The lack of unity within carries over then into recruitment of new vocations, as well as into the formation of young religious, compounding the existing divisions, as well as effectively discouraging new vocations.

Perhaps the most important step in this series of stages to implement the mandate given to the commission took place on November 14, when Archbishop Quinn gave a report to the bishops at their annual conference. Since his address is reproduced elsewhere in this issue in its entirety, I shall limit myself to its main ideas. Archbishop Quinn brought out that the bishops are not called to something extraordinary. Rather it was a particular concretization of their pastoral responsibility, rooted in their episcopal office as set forth in Vatican II, and as encouraged and fostered in other Vatican documents. He stressed the importance of what the Holy Father was asking from the bishops, not only for religious, but for the whole Church in the United States.

Archbishop Quinn commented on *Essential Elements,* stressing both its binding force and also the fact that it does not exempt those who would be guided by it from interpretation and application in a prudential way according to particular circumstances. The bishops are called to exercise their pastoral responsibility in a spirit of dialogue. This involves listening. It also involves the apostolic duty of correction and admonition when necessary. The particular contribution of the bishops by virtue of their apostolic office is to provide the discernment for what is consonant with the life of the Church, and what is not.

He called attention to the fact that the main concern is not numerical decline in the membership of religious communities, nor the fact that many worthwhile apostolic works will be lost. "But a far more important reason for concern about the decline in numbers of those entering religious life is the prospect of losing the public witness of the poverty, obedience and chastity of Christ which is their first and highest contribution to the Church."

In order to remove the carrying out of the mandate from the level of exhortation to concrete steps, in the course of that same meeting of bishops a packet of material was given out by Archbishop Kelly to the bishops, with suggestions for ways to set this pastoral responsibility into action. A "time-line" was set. The bishops were asked to make a report to the pontifical commission by May 15, 1984.

Attention was called also to the letter of Archbishop Mario Schierano, reminding all that February 2, 1984, was to be a Jubilee Day for Religious. On that day there will be a solemn eucharistic liturgy in St. Peter's Basilica, at which the religious who are present will renew their vows.

Reviewing, then, the events of the past seven months, we see that one of the most significant events in the contemporary Church is beginning to take shape. It could turn out to be the most important event for the Church in the United States in our time.

What are the prospects for success? The Pontifical Commission has demonstrated an unusual combination of qualities. It has a genuine sense for what the pope is asking. Though there are pressures to tone down the call for genuine renewal, members of the commission have shown theological depth, an openness that is non-threatening, and have transmitted to their brother bishops the importance of the task which the Holy Father is asking of them.

Up to the present most of the action has taken place among the religious who represent the various organizations; so far it has not reached down to touch the rank and file. But even on this level, after the initial edginess there has been a turn to a more positive approach.

The Pope Calls

In his talk to the *Consortium Perfectae Caritatis,* Archbishop Kelly told of an experience that took place when some of the American bishops made their *ad limina* visit. Someone, referring to the papal intervention, asked: "What is this all about?" The pope reflected quietly for a few moments, then said: "During the Holy Year every Christian is called to conversion. The bishops of the United States are to call religious to conversion." He paused, then added: "Let me refine this a bit. You are being called to mutual conversion. When two people are mutually converted they turn to one another. There is great possibility here."

There is no hidden agenda here. Pope John Paul is not asking for more studies or workshops. He is not asking simply for renewal, nor is he asking simply that the bishops do their job. He is asking that renewal be brought about through the experience of corporateness that is of the very nature of the Church. "There is great possibility here."

The intervention really should not come as a surprise. His pontificate has exhibited two main characteristics: an effort to carry out the directives of Vatican II, and a determination to exhort, in season and out, those who have leadership roles in the Church, bishops, priests, religious, to live up to the fullness of their vocation. The words of St. Paul can easily be applied to the pope: "There is the responsibility that weighs on me every day, my anxious concern for the congregations" (2 Co 11:28). "Even if I did wound you by the letter I sent, I do not now regret it. I may have been sorry for it when I saw that the letter had caused you pain, even if only for a time; but now I am happy, not that your feelings were wounded but that the wound led to a change of heart" (2 Co 7:8,9).

What the pope is looking for, then, is a change of heart. He describes as the occasion for his letter the call to renewal which has gone out to all the faithful during this Holy Year. "In this extraordinary Holy Year which has just begun, the whole Church is seeking to live more intensely the mystery of redemption. She is seeking to respond more faithfully to the immense love of Jesus Christ the Redeemer of the world" (Letter to the Bishops, April, 1983). This is the call to the faithful. Within that universal call, the pope has issued the special call to American bishops and religious to join in the common effort for renewal.

On September 5, 1983, at Castelgandolfo the pope spoke to twenty-three American bishops who were making their *ad limina* visit. He called the bishops once again to a consciousness of their role: as individuals, to be a living sign of Jesus Christ, and collegially to lead the Church as servant pastors. He returned to the theme of conversion. "We bishops experience the need for conversion— deep conversion, sustained conversion, renewed conversion. . . . And you . . . must call your people to conversion, especially in this Holy Year of the Redemption. . . . I pointed out its special relevance for religious in the letter that I wrote to all the bishops of the United States at Easter."

Reviewing these events over the past seven months, there is one inescapable conclusion: it is all of one piece. This inherent unity comes from the insight rooted in faith that through all of God's activity in time there is only one call; it is the call to conversion. While it is a call directed to everyone in the Church, those who have leadership roles have special responsibility to open themselves to this call. These are the bishops, the priests, the religious. In answering this call, we are to help one another, through the various gifts God has given to different members. In particular, the pope is asking bishops and religious to collaborate in this mutual call to conversion.

Essential Elements in Church Teaching on Religious Life

The call to renewal is situated, as we have seen, within the context of the Holy Year. This call is brought into sharper focus through two other documents: the pope's letter of April 3, 1983, and the text called "Essential Elements in Church Teaching on Religious Life" of May 31, 1983. Both of these were made public on June 22.

The call to renewal, however, at this particular point in our history takes the special form of discernment. Tremendous changes have taken place in religious life over the past twenty years. The purpose of *Essential Elements* is to provide the authentic norms for discerning what is genuine in those changes from what is spurious. There can be no renewal without truth. The document sets down underlying characteristics that by their very nature characterize true religious life.

Not everything in the document, however, has the same intrinsic weight. Since it is a compilation of earlier papal and conciliar statements, one has to go to the original sources to determine the relative value of each part. There are, therefore, all sorts of shadings in the very term *essentials,* ranging from what is intrinsically constitutive of religious life to what is highly appropriate.

The total range of meaning from intrinsic necessity to what is highly appropriate is thematized in one word, *consecration.* It is the theme that unites *Essential Elements* with the pope's letter in which he calls religious to renewal in this Holy Year when we recall the mystery of redemption. "By their very vocation, religious are intimately linked to the redemption. In their consecration to Jesus Christ they are a sign of the redemption that he accomplished." Because of its centrality, then I would like to comment on the scriptural and theological implications of consecration.

The word always describes a hallowing that takes place when some person or thing is enveloped by the power of the Holy Spirit to give the person or thing a totally new meaning. The primary meaning of consecration is the change in meaning that takes place in the very heart of reality itself when the unredeemed world is tranformed into the New Creation through Christ's redemptive death. The world may look the same before and after. But the very heart of reality has been changed. The paschal mystery through the power of the Spirit has enveloped the whole of reality to change it in its very roots. In the language of Paul, it is a "metamorphosis," a change of structure. "For anyone who is in Christ, there is a new creation; the old creation has gone, and now the new one is here" (2 Co 4:17).

In the first sense, then, consecration means the hallowed transformation at the heart of reality itself. "Through him God chose to reconcile the whole universe to himself, making peace through the shedding of his blood upon the cross, to reconcile all things whether on earth or in heaven, through him alone" (Col 1:20). Here we are on the level of ontology, of reality itself, as it undergoes a transformation, when it is enveloped by the New Being of the resurrected Christ through the power of the Holy Spirit. This is the most radical sense of consecration. Reality which has been desecrated through original and personal sin has undergone a radical consecration.

The transformation at the heart of reality finds its epiphany in the Church in a visible, tangible way, as the communion of those who have been consecrated. For this reason, St. Paul addresses members of the Church as "saints." But the Church is not only the manifestation of this mystery. It is the embodiment in time and space, in human flesh, of the paschal mystery itself, with its power to continue the mission of consecration. It is not only a hallowed community, but hallowing.

There is a second level of consecration, presupposing and flowing from the first. The radical change in the very heart of reality which gives us a share in the very consecration of Christ himself demands a change in the way we live our lives. Strictly speaking Christian conduct is not based on moral or ethical laws but on the implications that flow from the transformation that has taken place in the very being of Christians by the fact of their consecration. Paul speaks of the new way of life as based on their new mind. "Think of God's mercy, my brothers, and worship him, I beg you, in a way that is worthy of thinking beings, by offering your living bodies as a holy sacrifice, truly pleasing to God. Do not model yourselves on the behavior of the world around you, but let your behavior change, molded by your new mind" (Rm 12:1,2).

Finally the term consecration is used in Scripture to describe a special kind of vocation. It involves a special call by God to an individual to share in his redemptive design, and a free acceptance on the part of the one called, which can be given only in faith. It involves the recasting of the designs one might have for his own life in order to shape his life according to the designs of God.

Jeremiah describes his own call as an act of consecration: "The word of Yahweh was addressed to me, saying, 'Before I formed you in the womb I knew you; before you came to birth I consecrated you; I have appointed you as a prophet to the nations" (Jr 1:4,5). Paul alludes to this passage when he describes his own call. "Then God, who had specially chosen me while I was still in my mother's womb, called me through his grace and chose to reveal his Son in me, so that I might preach the Good News about him to the pagans" (Ga 1:15,16).

Jesus uses the language of consecration to describe his own role in the Father's redemptive design. He describes himself as the one whom "the Father has consecrated and sent into the world" (Jn 10:36). He prays that his disciples share this consecration through their own role in the redemptive design: "Consecrate them in the truth. As you sent me into the world, I have sent them into the world, and for their sake I consecrate myself, so that they too may be consecrated in truth" (Jn 17:17-19). Though the full act of consecration will take place at Pentecost, Christ, while still in the redemptive "moment" of his hour, performs the act of consecration through the gift of the Spirit. "He breathed on them and said: 'Receive the Holy Spirit. For those whose sins you forgive, they are forgiven; for those whose sins you retain, they are retained" (Jn 20:22,23).

In this last sense of the word, consecration exhibits the following characteristics. There is the overall sense of the mysterious counsel God has, his design for salvation. He deliberately chooses some to share in the effective realization of his design. In turn, when they respond with openness to God's will for them, their lives take on a meaning and orientation that relativizes their personal desires in order that they be completely dedicated to their role in God's redemptive design. In our contemporary language, their lives become symbolic, that is, weighted with a meaning and power that comes from the Spirit.

The word consecration, then, has three interrelated meanings. It refers to the radical reorientation of reality as it undergoes a tranformation through the redemptive death and resurrection of Christ. The community of those who through baptism and faith have been transformed is the Church. In the second place, this consecration at the root of their being overflows into a new mode of behavior, as "becomes the saints." Thirdly, the term also describes what is meant by devotion in its original meaning, that is, a life completely vowed to carry out God's purpose. Christian tradition, has used the term consecration in this last sense to speak of a life dedicated to God through the evangelical counsels of poverty, chastity, and obedience. This is the sense that the word has in the document *Essential Elements.*

In order to show the centrality of the theme of consecration in the document it would be necessary to give a summary of the whole text, which is not possible in this short paper, nor does it fit my purpose. "Consecration is the basis of religious life" (n. 5). Everything else in the document flows from that one sentence.

Each way of speaking of consecration in some way points to the New Creation brought into being by Christ's redemptive act. No aspect can be taken independently from the others. The mode of consecration which we call religious life presupposes and lives within the transformed, hallowed community, which is the Church. If it is taken outside the context of the hallowed community, it becomes desacralized, and takes on a secularistic meaning.

The consecrated life of the counsels is not of human origin, like other societies. It is called forth through the Spirit to be the symbol, or the epiphany, of a life lived in a redemptive mode, devoted, or vowed, to this redemptive mode. The redemptive mode envelopes the whole of one's being, but it crystallizes under the form of the three vows of poverty, chastity, obedience. In each of these, the paradox of the redemptive mystery is symbolized, a paradox of presence and absence, emptiness and fullness, death and resurrection, limitations that are freeing; a paradox of loss of self and finding of oneself, being set apart and being more deeply united. To develop these remarks would entail writing a treatise on the theology of religious life. It is enough for our purposes here to set them down as aspects of the rich meaning of the consecrated religious life.

Problems in Renewal

In the first part of this paper I described the circumstances surrounding the pope's intervention, and his call to religious to evaluate the experience of the past twenty years in order to benefit by what is genuine, and to abandon what is not. To give this program of renewal a definite shape he appointed a commission which was to animate the other bishops in the assumption of their pastoral responsibility, to foster dialogue of religious among themselves, and to act as general facilitator to oversee the whole process. The norms that form the authentic basis of religious life flow from the nature of consecration itself. The experience of the past twenty years is to be evaluated then against the intrinsic norms that flow from the very nature of consecration. To the degree that they deepen it, they are valid, or on the other side of the coin, to the degree that they evacuate the intrinsic nature of the consecration, they are invalid.

Reading the responses to the pope's call, I find there are mainly two points of view. Some stress the fact that the overall experience has been genuine, with minor deviations here and there. They feel that the negative picture comes largely from the media and from ultraconservative groups who have the ear of the Vatican. They feel that beneath the call to renewal is a negative view on the part of Rome of religious life as experienced in this country. As a consequence, they see the whole of the American experience as put on trial; for this reason, they tend to take a defensive and uncritical, even a triumphalistic posture.

Others feel that the experience of the past twenty years is very mixed. In fact they see points of view expressed regarding religious life which are incompatible with each other. These clashes are to be found in essential points such as authority, relationship to the Church, the nature of the vows, the purpose of religious life itself. For these the future of religious life in this country is beset with problems.

Perhaps each of these groups can learn something from the other. The first cannot ignore the obvious fact of destructive pluralism existing within religious life. The second has to make the effort to see the positive developments that have taken place. And both groups should be mindful of the fact that thousands of religious have already gone through this difficult process of evaluating changes, and have taken the path leading through the narrow gate as they carry out their mission in a redemptive mode of life.

In order to get some kind of a handle on the main problems facing the implementation of this call to renewal, I have divided them up into several categories.

1. *The Nature of the Call to Renewal*

The main problem of course, is that we are being called to a mode of *being,* not simply to some kind of program. It is the call on which all the prophets floundered, and which brought Christ to his death. If it were a call that could be easily translated into plans for building a society where peace and justice would reign, it would have a ring to it. But it is a call to "be still and know that I am God."

There is the problem of the various audiences to whom the call is addressed. Some will remain indifferent to it, others antagonistic, while still others will offer varying degrees of cooperation.

There are the practical problems also to be faced in the actual implementation of the process on the part of the bishops. In his address to the American bishops at their recent meeting in Washington, Archbishop Quinn called upon them to give *quality time* to this pastoral need. How can they find this "quality time" when they are already overburdened? How can religious leaders also find the quality time that *they* will have to devote to the process?

2. *The Faith Perspective*

The realities described as the New Creation, the New Being, Redemption, consecration, the Church herself as consecrated and consecrating community—these are realities that can only be perceived by faith. Thus the values involved in this call to renewal also belong only to the realm of faith.

Imperceptibly in the life of all of us, personally and collectively, norms and values that are based on the social sciences come in to compete with, and even conterfeit those that can be perceived only in faith. The mystery that is the Church is then reduced to social and political categories prevalent at this point in history. The notions of authority and obedience lose the meaning which Paul encompassed in his short phrase, "to obey in the Lord," and take on the pattern of mere social dynamics.

The talking at cross-purposes that takes place so often in this area of renewal comes from the fact that basic faith-assumptions are not shared.

3. *The Lack of Integration of Spiritual Life and Mission*

Some have brought up the objection that the document on essentials is "monastic," and thus not really applicable to apostolic religious. That is simplistic. The document, in fact, states that it is addressed specifically to apostolic religious. It stresses that unless mission is rooted in and energized by union with God, it remains sterile and lifeless as far as its ultimate value for the kingdom of God. The interrelatedness of consecration on the three levels we spoke of above is essential: a life that is transformed; its consequence in a transformation in behavior; and the special call to live the consecrated life in a redemptive mode. St. Ignatius, to whom many look as one of the founders of apostolic religious life, was convinced that there was only one source of apostolic energy: union with God. "The means which unite the human instrument with God and so dispose it that it may be wielded dexterously by his divine hand are more effective than those which equip it in relation to men" (*Constitutions*, 813).

In recent years mission seems to have been self-consciously directed mainly to concerns of peace and justice. Yet, without using those terms, these have been among the goals of all apostolic work from the beginning of Christianity. In our own American history religious have accomplished a moral miracle in the area of justice. In the course of a hundred years they have been the principle "agents of change" who enabled millions of Catholic immigrants, second-class citizens, to take their place within the mainstream of American life. There is nothing that parallels this marvel in the whole of Catholic history.

One cannot help but be struck by the emphasis given in the mission statements of so many revised constitutions in the setting of priorities for the pursuit of peace and justice. When such a pursuit is rooted in faith and animated by charity, it ought to have the highest of priorities. At the same time, do we not actually find here a subtle source of an actual separation of "mission" from the "spiritual life"? This can take place in two ways, both of which are devices of the infamous Screwtape portrayed by C. S. Lewis. In Ch. 6 of *The Screwtape Letters*, he points out that virtues grow through being in touch with concrete, particular realities. The effort of the devil, then, is to move the target soul from concreteness to abstractions, to push in the direction of "states of mind," generalities, imaginative constructs which have nothing to do with reality, which are only simulations of virtue and not the real thing.

In Ch. 7, Screwtape advises his apprentice devil to lead a person to religious idealism, and then, gradually, lead him to subordinate his religion to "the cause." Then Christianity simply becomes a means to accomplish "the cause." Once the devil can make a movement become the end and faith a means, then he has won. "Provided that meetings, pamphlets, policies, movements, causes, and crusades matter more to him than prayers and sacraments and charity, he is ours." The more noble the cause, the more subtle the counterfeit. It is possible that the spiritual life itself will be dried up, even as there is increased insistence on the mission of peace and justice—especially where these have become abstractions, or where they have become an end and faith a means.

4. *The Feminist Movement*

At our present stage of history in the Western world, we are caught in the strong winds of the feminist movement. It is so complex, has so many ramifications, is so fraught with emotion, so well organized, has such momentum, is so comprehensive in scope that it defies analysis and evaluation. One thing is certain. Its potential for good is matched by its potential to become yet another disastrous polarizing movement in the history of the Church.

The movement itself has undergone a transformation over the past two decades.[2] In its initial stages it concerned itself with violation of basic human rights. It worked to overcome the economic, social, and cultural injustices suffered by women. In very short order, it moved from those concerns to other demands that were far more radical, such as "control over one's body," the overthrow of sex roles in child nurturing, freedom from all coercion, whether biological or physical. Gradually the movement took on the character of an all-embracing philosophy, while still claiming to be a social and political movement. As a philosophy, it pronounces on every aspect of reality: the meaning of God, what it means to be human, the nature of language, the meaning of sexuality. Beginning as a movement aimed at the rectification of economic and social injustices, it assumed in the course of a few years the form of an ideology.

While the feminist movement has many repercussions within the Church, most visibly, perhaps, in the matter of language that is perceived as sexist, the most neuralgic area is surely the one concerned with ministry. It is not possible to untangle this problem here. But it is in this area in particular that the philosophical assumptions of the feminist movement come to the fore. Underlying the agitation for women's ordination, for example, is the assumption that all social functions are interchangeable, coming from a human nature that is, for the most part, undifferentiated according to male or female gender. Once that philosophical assumption is granted, then there is no intrinsic reason why any social role or function should be predicated on differences of gender. The fact that priesthood in the Catholic Church may be the one function that challenges this basic assumption makes the situation to be all the more polarizing. The problem, in the eyes of most of the people involved, is seen to be one of justice. In reality, the problem lies in basic philosophical assumptions.

Connected with the philosophical assumptions is the sense that difference in function can be changed by the pressure of political, social or economic measures. Yet the fact that priesthood is a sacrament, and as such does not come from human invention but from Christ, challenges the basic assumption that ministry is merely function attached to human nature as such. In fact, the question about ordination is a theological question about the nature of the sacramental sign involved in orders. Specifically, the theological question is whether the sign by its nature is exclusively masculine or not. Like all theological questions, it has to be resolved through theological method. It is not answered by administrative fiat, nor by increased agitation.

We are faced, then, with irreconcilable assumptions which go beyond the possibility of the simple rectification of social injustices. If all social functions are simply functional, and as such interchangeable, then there is no way to resist the image of the power-hungry, threatened, masculine clerics holding on, like beleaguered defenders of the castle, to their traditional status. If, on the other hand, the question has to do with a sacramental sign, not the product of human creation, then the question is theological, and has to be approached with the method proper to any theological question, and there is no way that the pope or anyone else, can short-circuit this process.

I have taken the time to comment on the feminist issues because they condition what is heard by so many when they hear this call to renewal. The conditioning is such that, for them, the call to renewal is only an aggravation of already open wounds.

Is there any way out of this stormy impasse? Not within the foreseeable future. Chesterton compared certain movements to a fast-moving train. The faster the train is going, the harder it is to jump off: "The very fact of some social or political or artistic movement going quicker and quicker means that fewer people have the courage to move against it. And at last nobody will make a leap for real intellectual liberty." This is true of the radical feminist movement. It accelerates so rapidly because it is fueled with what the philosopher Nietzsche has called *ressentiment*. This is group-emotion that is the fusion of anger, hurt, envy, resentment, the desire for vengeance. It is fed by the group-memory of a long history of injustice. At the same time, Nietzsche described the inevitable results of *ressentiment*. It leads to division, hatred, polarization. It desires, not equality, but the power to crush its enemies.

Only genuine conversion on the personal and collective level can take the poison out of a movement, can purify it and raise it to become a movement for justice animated by the Holy Spirit.

5. *"The Essential" and the "Highly Appropriate"*

As has been all too evident in media reports following the publication of *Essential Elements,* the question of religious garb remains one of the most sensitive issues. The term *essentials* is not to be taken univocally, as if everything in the document is equally constitutive of religious life. The range of the term is wide. It goes from the intrinsically constitutive, which belongs to the nature of consecration, to corollaries, which flow more or less from these constitutive principles. Even among the corollaries there are levels—from what is closely related to the intrinsic principles and inseparable from them, to those that are highly appropriate, but without the same intrinsic inseparability.

The matter of religious garb falls under the category of the highly appropriate.

There are two extreme positions in this question. One dismisses the need for an exterior sign such as the religious habit as irrelevant, or even as counterproductive. The other absolutizes religious garb to the point where its necessity is identified as intrinsic to, and inseparable from, religious life itself. Both positions are faulty. When we describe wearing an external sign of consecration as belonging to those aspects of religious life that are highly appropriate, this is not to be looked on as a compromise position. The term is used to point out that there is an inescapable logic in the progression from one level of consecration to another as it seeks its symbolic fullness.

The fundamental consecration that lies in the transformation of one's being manifests itself through deeds which are holy. The consecration that describes a special vocation to be the instrument of God's redemptive design shows itself in the concentration and centering of one's whole life around that role. The prophets, as well as Christ himself, performed symbolic actions to manifest in striking ways the total symbolism of their lives, brought about by their consecration.

Those who live consecrated lives may not be called upon to perform such isolated symbolic acts. However, religious garb becomes a sign that *all* their actions are clothed with a symbolic value. What to the public eye is a secular activity takes on the aspect of a sacred act when it is seen contextualized by a religious sign such as a habit.

While this is so, it would be a mistake to put this public sign on the same level as the intrinsic principles of religious life. There can be compelling reasons why the inner logic of the sign-value of consecration stops short of the full symbolism of the habit. These reasons can be justified, for example, from particular circumstances of the apostolate, or from personal reasons that have sufficient gravity. However, even those who for legitimate reasons do not wear the religious garb would surely grant that there is a consistency, at least in the abstract, in desiring that consecration manifest its symbolic nature as fully as possible.[3]

This issue continues to divide religious, both those belonging to different congregations and those within the same congregation. In responding to the pope's call to renewal, there should be a reassessment of the implications of symbolic fullness, and, at the same time, a willingness to recognize circumstances that can justify exceptions without making an individual to be any less a religious.

Toward the Future

What does the future hold for religious life in this country? There are some things which are predictable, and others remain in the realm of the unpredictable.

Among the predictable elements is a continued decline in numbers, especially in congregations of religious women. This comes from two factors: the present small number of novices entering, and the steady rise of the median age.

This decline will carry with it many side effects. Ministry will tend to be less and less corporate, and, at the same time, take on more and more diversity. Community life will also be affected, taking its concrete circumstances from the diversity of ministries.

Some religious congregations will surely disappear entirely, not because they have been unfaithful to their call, but because in God's providence they have served their purpose. While this prospect naturally evokes fear and sadness, there is also the ground for that joy which comes from the awareness of having been faithful to one's call.

At the same time that these predictable developments take place, we also face the unpredictable. With the pope's intervention, the setting up of the pontifical commission, and the implementation of renewal through the pastoral assistance of the bishops, a new process has been set in motion which is unprecedented in the history of religious life. In his own pastoral concern as Shepherd of the Universal Church, the Holy Father has called upon bishops and religious to minister to one another after the manner of the special gifts given to each. The goal is mutual conversion, which will overflow in its effects into the whole Church.

I quoted the words of the Holy Father when he spoke to some of our American bishops. He said, "There is great possibility here." But looking at the hard realities, can we say there is any reasonable hope that these rich possibilities will be realized to any significant degree? The answer to that question depends on many contingencies.

In the first place it depends on whether the bishops and the leaders of religious congregations are convinced of the critical nature of the present moment in religious life in this country, and of the high priority to be given to assisting in its renewal. Without that conviction, compliance will be either token or one of complete indifference. The significance of the present moment must also be transmitted to the individual members of the various congregations by those who have leadership roles. Then ways have to be found to bring together the two aspects of renewal: personal conversion, and discernment between authentic and inauthentic change in religious life.

It is unlikely that this "great possibility" will be accomplished through the multiplication of more meetings. Most religious, as well as bishops, could not bear the thought of another round of meetings in which they would repeat what they have heard a dozen times already. There is a need for a new format, one that would provide the setting to reach a genuine spiritual freedom in the Lord. Perhaps the bishops could make extended retreats with religious superiors so that together, in an atmosphere of faith and prayer, they could come to a better understanding of one another, as well as a sense of what the Lord is asking.

Conclusion

At this point in our history it is also important to recall the debt we owe to those religious who have served the Lord and the Catholics in this country so well, and who now, like Anna and Simeon, enter into the sunset of their lives. They were the educators, nurses, catechists, administrators who, more than any other single factor, brought the Church into the twentieth century, and allowed Catholics to take their place in the ranks of every profession. In those days sisters fostered vocations to the priesthood and brotherhood, and priests directed young women to enter into religious life. That partnership has been shaken, at times, even lost, and at this juncture almost always exists in tension. Could not our corporate response to the pope's call heal those relationships, and call us once again to mutual trust and collaboration?

If the pope's intention could be realized even to some partial degree, then could the shepherd's words in Shakespeare's *The Winter's Tale* be fittingly applied: "Now bless thyself; thou meetest with things dying. I with things new-born."

NOTES

[1]There are many associations of religious men and women in the United States. They are listed in the *National Catholic Directory* and in the *Catholic Almanac.* The two which officially represent religious are the Leadership Conference of Women Religious (LCWR), approved in 1962, and the Conference of Major Superiors of Men (CMSM), established in 1960. Other organizations with significant membership are the *Consortium Perfectae Caritatis,* dating from 1971, and *The Institute on Religious Life,* founded in 1974.

[2]See "The Place of Women as a Problem in Theological Anthropology," Karl Lehmann, *Communio: International Catholic Review,* Fall, 1983, pp. 219-239.

[3]Some additional observations are in place. In those congregations which have definitely opted as communities to keep the religious habit, exceptions would be less common and would be made in consultation with superiors. Also, considering the situation of so many religious today in the United States who do not wear the religious garb, it would seem that conditions are such that a return to the habit in the foreseeable future is practically impossible.

The Charism and Identity of Religious Life

Michael J. Buckley, S.J.

Volume 44, 1985, pp. 654-664.

Prenote: The limitations imposed by the nature of this conference do not allow for anything more than a fragmentary set of reflections upon a topic of such critical importance to the understanding of religious life. This paper, then, can do no more than attempt three of the many tasks which fall under so general a title: (1) To sketch something of the development of the magisterium's teaching on this subject; (2) to indicate some of the problems which this teaching entails; and (3) to suggest a manner in which these problems might be understood and moved towards resolution. The paper proposes the following three theses: (1) The fundamental identity of religious life must be grasped in terms of charism; (2) This understanding of religious life as charismatic raises profound problems that touch every aspect of its reality; (3) The office of the hierarchy is to discern an authentic charism from its counterfeit, while the exercise of this office is subject to the very real danger that excessive legalism will quench the Spirit.

One theme that contemporary philosophy and modern hermeneutics have insisted upon is this: Words have an effect like architecture. With architecture, you build the buildings, and then the buildings you live in build you. Similarly with language, you introduce terms into a discussion, and the language you admit either expands your perception of the issues or it hopelessly limits it. The concern of the early Fathers and Councils about language was not trivial: language forms our perception of reality. If our words are careless or precise, exaggerated or discriminating, we will have that kind of discussion. Even more, we will have that kind of perception of the very reality we are attempting to understand. Few contemporary Church leaders realized this better than Pope

Paul VI. He was painstaking, even scrupulous, in his selection of words. And it was this pope who introduced the vocabulary: "the charism of religious life" and "the charisms of the founders [of religious communities] who were raised up by God within his Church."[1] (ET II) The Second Vatican Council prepared for this stage of theological development, but Paul VI brought it into articulation and existence.

Charism and Religious Life

Lumen Gentium, in its critical second chapter, had spoken of the charisms given by the Spirit for the renewal and building of the Church (12). *Lumen Gentium,* had distinguished the hierarchical gifts from the charismatic gifts (4, 7, 12). But *Lumen Gentium* never applied its doctrine on charism explicitly to religious life, though much of the theology of the gifts is contained in its sixth chapter, the section that deals with religious life in the Church. Similarly, *Perfectae Caritatis* contains many of these same elements and even adds an essential note missing from the previous Dogmatic Constitution on the Church, namely, that the origins of religious life lie with "*Spiritu Sancto afflante* (under the inspiration of the Holy Spirit)" (1). But the word "charism" does not occur. It was Paul VI who took the Church's general teachings about charism and the charismatic and applied them repeatedly during his pontificate to religious life. And the documents and the *allocutiones* of the present pontificate have continued this application. This usage of the more recent popes, however, has not gone unchallenged. Very recently, some have objected to the use of this term on two grounds: the word, "charism," is very difficult to define, and the Code of Canon Law does not include this term.

Nevertheless, the present pope did use the term—and he did so specifically in his Letter to the American Bishops, charging them to "encourage the religious, their institutes and associations to live fully the mystery of the redemption, in union with the whole Church and *according to the specific charism of their religious life*" (LTTR #3). The American bishops cannot step over this term: it frames the perspective on their mandate. It occurs three times in that same section of the papal letter, specifying both the nature of religious life as a "proper ecclesial charism" and reminding the bishops that "in the local churches the discernment of the *exercise* of these charisms is authenticated by the bishops in union with the successor of Peter. This work is a truly important aspect of your episcopal ministry" (ibid).

Furthermore: This charge to the American bishops is not an isolated phenomenon. *Mutuae Relationes* places the most critical responsibility of religious superiors precisely in this same terminology which others have found so dangerous: "Religious superiors have a grave duty, *their foremost responsibility in fact,* to assure the fidelity of the members to the *charism of the Founder* by fostering the renewal prescribed by the Council and required by the times" (14c). The documents of the magisterium speak either of the charism of religious life in general or of the charism of a particular form of religious life. But two things should be noted in either case: First, when they speak about charism, they are speaking about what is fundamental to its identity. Second, this fidelity to charism involves change together with stability, a change demanded either by the conciliar documents or by the needs of the time.

What does "charism" mean, then, and why is the papal use of it so illuminative of the identity of religious life?

The classic description of charism is given in the second chapter of *Lumen Gentium* (12b): "It is not only through the sacraments and the ministrations of the Church that the *Holy Spirit* makes holy the People, leads them and enriches them with his virtues. Allotting his gifts as he wills (1 Co 12:11), he also distributes *special graces* among the faithful of every rank. By these gifts, he makes them *fit and ready to undertake various tasks and offices for the renewal and building up of the Church,* as it is written, 'the manifestation of the Spirit is given to everyone for the common good' (1 Co 12:7). Whether *these charisms* be very remarkable or more simple and widely diffused, they are to be received with thanksgiving and consolation since they are fitting and useful for the needs of the Church . . . . Those *who have charge over the Church should judge* the genuineness and proper use of these gifts through their office, *not indeed to extinguish the Spirit,* but to *test all things* and *hold fast* to what is good" (1 Th 5:12, 19-21).

From this text we can affirm that the term "charism" includes the following notes:

(1) The origin of every charism is the Holy Spirit—not the hierarchy nor human structures.

(2) Its impetus is distinguished from the action of the Spirit in the sacraments and in the habitual ministrations of the Church's ministers.

(3) Charism is by its nature a special grace, given to anyone of the faithful as an enabling gift for a specific ministry within the Body of Christ.

(4) Its purpose is the renewal and the development of the Church.

(5) The authenticity of a charism is to be tested and judged by the hierarchy— and the allusions to St. Paul's negative prohibition not to extinguish the Spirit indicates the danger that a charism can be destroyed by the bad judgment of the very ones who are to judge and support it.

Lumen Gentium and *Perfectae Caritatis* made two other significant contributions to the development of the identity of religious life as a charism. (1) Neither document discusses religious life in the juridical language of *status* or "the state of perfection to be acquired." Neither document uses the technical expression, "status perfectionis acquierendae"; while the word *status* is used six times in *Lumen Gentium* VI and only once in *Perfectae Caritatis,* it never becomes the principal or governing category. *Status* is recognized as a canonical term, but not given the position of being the organizing perspective through which religious life is understood. The history of the title of *Perfectae Caritatis* indicates how progressive and deliberate that exclusion was made. It is not that *status* could not be profitably used: its heritage can be traced from Pseudo-

Dionysius' *The Ecclesiastical Hierarchy,* to the profound treatment of Saint Thomas—distinguishing *officium, status,* and *gradus*—to *Provida Mater* of Pius XII. But the concept of *status* over these centuries has increasingly become static, and a fundamental juridical category.[2] Vatican II, by refusing to subsume religious life under this juridical heading as its primary category, was clearing the way for the further theological developments of Paul VI. These documents from the Council provided many of the elements in their description of religious life which would allow *Evangelica Testificatio* to bring them together under the general rubric of charism.

What the Church witnessed in *Evangelica Testificatio,* then, is a conscious and radical shift—to be very precise, a categorical shift: from religious life classified primarily as a canonical reality, one whose forms are set and understood fundamentally in terms of juridical, even constitutional, structures, to a charismatic reality, whose forms and constitutions themselves are judged by the classic signs of the Spirit and by the manner in which its members are configured to the life of Christ.

Both charism and law are obviously necessary. Religious life is not a variation of antinomianism. But the question is what is categorical. And Paul VI has said that the fundamental category is charismatic: *Charism* has been given a priority over *status.*[3]

What the deliberate choice of the term "charism" asserts is that religious life is directly dependent upon the Spirit, both for its origins and for its continually new forms. As Paul VI put it: "The charism of the religious life, far from being an impulse 'born of flesh and blood,' or one derived from a mentality which conforms itself to the modern world, is the fruit of the Holy Spirit, who is always at work within the Church" (ET 11). The various forms of religious life are derived from the charisms of the founders of these religious communities who were raised up by God through this gift of the Spirit. This charism of the founder does two things: It gives each religious community that dynamism which defines it—often called its particular spirit—and it provides for the future a "certain constancy of orientation" that allows for a continual revitalization and change in external forms (ET 12).[4] The development of a religious community, as opposed to its decline, lies with the organic growth of its original and defining charism.

Mutuae Relationes expanded this teaching, insisting with bishops that "they are entrusted with the duty of caring for religious charisms, all the more so because the very indivisibility of their pastoral ministry makes them responsible for perfecting the entire flock" (9c). Here the charism of the founder is stated precisely as "'an experience of the Spirit,' transmitted to their disciples to be lived, safeguarded, *deepened* and *constantly developed* by them in harmony with the Body of Christ continually *in the process of growth*" (11). It is this experience of the Spirit that gives the distinctive character to their religious community: "This distinctive character also involves a particular style of sanctification and of apostolate, which creates its particular tradition with the result that one can readily perceive its objective elements" (11).

Implications and Difficulties

Now, for rather pragmatic Americans, this discussion of charism seems sound enough, but hardly earth-shattering—hardly important enough to wonder whether it is or is not in the Code. But it is the implications that are found threatening, implications which *Mutuae Relationes* is at pains to point out: "Every authentic charism implies a certain element of (1) genuine originality and of (2) special initiative for the spiritual life of the Church. In its surroundings, it may appear troublesome and may even cause difficulties, since it is not always and immediately easy to recognize it as coming from the Spirit" (12).

Concretely and pragmatically, charism implies that religious life will always involve something that the Church has not seen before—or at least seen in this way. Because of its novelty and its presence as an unforeseen impetus within the Church, charism may well mean the presence of the "troublesome," and the presence of new difficulties and challenges to the Church. Call religious life a charism, and you have already said the Church expects to be continually challenged in many ways, and the hierarchy is bound by God to the difficult and nuanced discernment of the authenticity of these challenges. Unlike *status,* whose structures can be determined adequately by law, charism presages the new, the creative, and the troublesome. This has formed the history of religious orders over the centuries, and for the United States it has been the history of religious communities of men and women since Vatican II.

An Example: During this time, a radically new articulation of the religious life for women has come into consciousness and acceptance: many women are assuming both ministerial roles within the Church hitherto reserved for men and have adopted small and flexible community styles which have made these new missions possible. Women religious no longer necessarily dress in the same identical fashion, nor do they assume collective tasks independent of their particular orientations, skills, and experienced vocations. What is emerging in many religious orders is a thoroughly contemporary woman, as competent as her contemporaries in her accomplishments and in her extensive acquaintance with the issues and experiences of her times. This does not mean that either the initial spirit or the sound traditions of her order have been rejected. This may, of course, have occurred in some cases, but it has not been the rule.

What this new order means is that many American religious communities of women have transposed their heritage into a modern idiom. This neither discredits nor invalidates other forms of religious life and the charism of older forms of religious expression, any more than the active communities of the nineteenth century were a rejection of Benedictine monasticism or of the clerks regular. But it does mean that something new is here. These religious communities of women have begun, perhaps for the first time in the Church, a synthesis of religious consecration and an inculturation into the forms of contemporary life—a synthesis made in service to their mission.

If one looks at previous external customs or previous regulations or even some of the current mandates being stretched in the name of this growth—that is, if one looks at religious life primarily as legal *status,* one can wonder at this phenomenon and question whether we are dealing with decline or infidelity. On the other hand, if one sees religious life primarily as *charism,* a charism that needs constitutions and laws for its objectification and constancy of orientation, but not as the exhaustive or adequate statement of its nature, then one might wonder if we are not witnessing a new impetus of the Spirit within the Church.

Could it be the case that at a time in which women are assuming directive and leadership roles within all forms of contemporary culture, the Spirit of God is raising up within the Church renewed or new charismatic communities, religious who will be just as individually characterized and just as culturally coordinate as their contemporaries and impelled to this new inculturation by the very charism of their founders? If so, we may be witnessing a movement which will carry an importance to the Church similar to that of the rise of the mendicants in the thirteenth century. Quite new—perhaps radically new—but of enormous importance to the future of the Church. But how is one to judge this?

Another Example: Repeatedly *Religious and Human Promotion* encourages religious to be "enterprising in their undertakings and initiatives" because this is "in keeping with the charismatic and prophetic nature of religious life itself" (27; See 4a and 24). Placing the prophetic together with the charismatic and then asserting this hendiadys as characteristic of the nature of religious life, constitutes a significant challenge. Fidelity to the charism of religious life, then, could well involve religious in those activities which alienated many people in the Church from them: speaking out about the morality of American intervention in Latin America, writing about discrimination even within the Church, demanding fair hiring practices in local business, far ranging discussions within their national conferences of areas of injustice and oppression.

Indeed, this document foresees precisely such a development: "Conferences of religious, because of their more immediate knowledge of ecclesial and social conditions, are in a better position to identify the problems of different countries and continents. Through an exchange of experiences and study meetings, they could, in collaboration with the episcopal conferences and respecting the various charisms, find solutions and means more in harmony with the hopes for integral human promotion" (35). When religious bring these subjects continually to the fore in their discussions and in their activities, and when they ask for episcopal collaboration in the exploration and elimination of these evils, are we not dealing with something that issues from the very nature of religious life as a charism— even when this elicits irritation from good Catholics or results in picket-lines, protests, and imprisonment? How are the bishops to judge whether this is of God, however much it disturb expectations and social concord?

Discernment, Not Repression

These two examples raise the same question, as would many more that could be cited: How can one judge growth or decline? How can the hierarchy judge authentic charism, even authentic prophetic action — when *Mutuae Relationes* (19) taught that "a responsiveness rich in creative initiative is eminently compatible with the charismatic nature of the religious life"? How can one test the Spirit, not quench it?

Mutuae Relationes suggests three criteria by which this sifting of the genuine from the inauthentic can be done (51):

First: Charism has "its special origin from the Spirit." Consequently the leaders of the Church can legitimately expect that the signs which *Galatians* enumerates as present in authentic charismatic movement: "love, joy, peace, patience, kindness, goodness, faithfulness, gentleness and self-control. Against such there is no law" (Ga 5:22-23). If these are present, one has every reason to suspect that the claim upon our conscience is from God.

Secondly: "A profound ardor of love to be conformed to Christ in order to give witness to some aspect of his mystery." When I read this, I had to wonder what the Holy See had in mind here, and I think it is this: Charism always effects a particular configuration to Christ. This is especially true in the mystery of his cross. Authentic charism will always be costly, will always entail an inescapable element of suffering and of the cross as one attempts to bring to the contemporary world or into the contemporary Church something that is truly of Christ. Authentic charism involves a willingness (albeit with a sinking feeling) to undergo, to endure as did Christ. A previous paragraph in this same document put it this way: "The true relation between genuine charism with its perspectives of newness and interior suffering, carries with it an unvarying history of the connection between charism and cross, which, above every motive that may justify misunderstandings, is supremely helpful in discerning the authenticity of a vocation" (12).

Finally: "A constructive love of the Church, which absolutely shrinks from causing any discord in her." This does not mean that conflict can always be avoided, but that one spontaneously shrinks from causing it, that one does not revel in fights or get one's sense of identity from party divisions and dissensions. Charism leads to the building up of the Church.

Charism always involves three factors: It is an enabling gift of the Spirit which so conforms the recipients to Christ that they will build the Church. *Mutuae Relationes* has touched upon each one of these. This set of three criteria does not mean that religious women or men will be without the faults and limitations of human beings, but it does mean that even in sinfulness these three religious attitudes will be basically present.[5] Between the boldness of the new initiatives which the charismatic nature of religious institutes demands and the expectations of some members of the Church or of the hierarchy, there will be unavoidable moments of tension—tensions which are not resolved by eliminating either side of this dialectic: by quenching the Spirit or by disobedience to the hierarchy in the legitimate exercise of its leadership. Either would mean the destruction of the directive influence of the Spirit of God bringing the Church into this new age. It is possible for bishops (even culpably) to quench the Spirit, to fail to recognize the charisms given by the Spirit; it is possible for religious to become incapable of serious self-criticism and to reject the need to submit the charism of their lives to the Church for its discernment. Either of these spells out a disintegration of religious life, and both are real possibilities. This is the reason that *Mutuae Relationes* adds the following addendum to its three criteria: "Moreover, the genuine figure of the founders entails men and women whose proven virtue (see LG 45) demonstrates a real docility both to the sacred hierarchy and to the following of that inspiration, which exists in them as a gift of the Spirit" (51).

But these dangers become somewhat mitigated if all the members of the Church come to understand what Paul VI brought to expression: that what is most profoundly at issue here—demanding prayer and discernment and those sufferings which go with any struggle to recognize the Spirit of God—is the radical identity of religious life as developing charism. The present pope has insisted in *Redemptionis Donum* that it is out of this that the apostolic presence of religious comes; the charism of every religious order becomes a charism for the different needs of the Church: "The apostolate is *always born* from *that particular gift* of your founders, which, *received from God* and *approved by the Church,* has become a *charism for the different needs of the Church and the world* at particular moments of history, and in its turn it is *extended* and *strengthened* in the life of the religious communities as one of the enduring elements of the Church's life and apostolate" (15).

Both Paul VI and John Paul II indicate the dynamic nature of the charismatic: Fidelity to the charism of the founder will demand the changes indicated by the Council and required by the times (ET 12; MR 11). A static understanding of charism leads some to think that religious precisely in order to be faithful to their charism should remain just as they were before, even despite the Council, the magisterial documents, and the needs of the time. But charism is essentially a living reality, and like every living reality confronts continually the questions of growth or decline, of development or disintegration. External changes, even radical external changes, can mean either.

Stability and change are not opposed; they are coordinate. You can only change what remains the same; as Gilson remarked many years ago, the only way you can keep the same fence is if you paint it often! Change is a necessity if the same thing is to continue. Charism involves both change and stability. There is no more reason *a priori* to expect that the contemporary religious woman will look like the nuns from the middle ages or the sisters from the nineteenth century than to expect that the contemporary Church simply copy the primitive Christian community. The sober assessment of this change constitutes the continual discernment done in most religious communities. It is in a parallel ongoing discernment by the hierarchy that their own office will be accomplished. For the major function of the hierarchy here is not so often to discern the charism of a radically new community, but to recognize the development of a charism in terms of a Church and a world that is changing so rapidly. To be aware of the authentic presence of the developing charism within a religious community is to be conscious of its fundamental identity, found not in a static repetition of the past but in growth and continuity.

NOTES

[1]The following abbreviations are used for documents of the magisterium to which reference is made in this article:

From Vatican II

> LG   *Lumen Gentium:* The Dogmatic Constitution on the Church
> PC   *Perfectae Caritatis:* The Decree on the Renewal of Religious Life

From the Pontificate of Paul VI

> ET   *Evangelica Testificatio:* Apostolic Exhortation on the Renewal of Religious Life
> MR   *Mutuae Relationes:* Directives for Mutual Relations Between Bishops and Religious in the Church, published by CRIS/CB

From the Pontificate of John Paul II

> RHP   *Religious and Human Promotion*   CRIS
> CDRL   *Contemplative Dimension of Religious Life*   CRIS
> LTTR   *Letter of John Paul II to the Bishops of the United States. April 3, 1983*
> EE   *Essential Elements in the Church's Teaching on Religious Life as Applied to Institutes Dedicated to Works of the Apostolate*
> RD   *Redemptionis Donum:* Apostolic Exhortation on Religious Consecration in the Light of the Mystery of Redemption

[2]See Bernard Olivier, O.P., "Il carisma della vita religiosa nel Concilio e nei documenti postconciliari," *Vita Consecrata* 17 (1981), pp. 329-331. Father Olivier agrees with the previous evaluation of J. M. Tillard that the development within the Council ran as follows: "From the idea of *religious state (stato religioso),* thus from a perspective essentially static and juridical, from a consideration of the religious in their canonical situation which characterizes them in contrast with the laity and clerics, one arrives at the evangelical and dynamic notion of *life* with everything which this implies about charity and human involvement" (ibid. pp. 329-330). See also the article by P. R. Regamey, O.P., under the title, "Carismi," *Dizionario degli istituti di perfezione,* edited by Guerrino Peliccia and Giancarlo Rocca, Vol. II, columns 299-315.

[3]This primacy of charism over legal description is classic in religious rules. Witness for example the "Preface" to the *Constitutions of the Society of Jesus:* "Although it must be the Supreme Wisdom and Goodness of God, our Creator and Lord, which will preserve, direct, and carry forward in his divine service this least Society of Jesus, just as he deigned to begin it; and although what helps most on our part toward this end must be, more than any exterior constitutions, the interior law of charity and love which the Holy Spirit writes and engraves upon hearts; nevertheless, since the gentle arrangement of Divine Providence requires cooperation from his creatures, and since too the Vicar of Christ our Lord has ordered this, and since the examples given by the saints and reason itself teach us so in our Lord, we think it necessary that constitutions should be written

to aid us to proceed better, in conformity with our Institute, along the path of divine service on which we have entered" (*The Constitutions of the Society of Jesus,* translated and edited by George E. Ganss, S.J. [St. Louis: The Institute of Jesuit Sources, 1970]), "Preamble to the Constitutions," [#134].

[4]The last word has not been either said or assimilated in this development initiated by the Council and brought to terminological articulation by Paul VI—otherwise it would have been impossible for *Essential Elements* to claim that the doctrinal richness of the magisterial teachings over the past twenty years "has been distilled and reflected in the revised Code of Canon Law." (3) No external legal structure is adequate to a reality whose identity is primarily charism. Hence the papal letter to the American bishops modifies that claim substantially with the statement: "*Much of* this doctrinal richness has been distilled and reflected in the revised Code." (3) Beneath the papal claim and that of *Essential Elements* lies the fundamental difference between the understanding of religious life primarily as a charism of the Spirit or as a juridical *status.*

[5]*Mutuae Relationes* provides a more particularized list for the discernment of authentic charism. Though cited above, it deserves to be included in full: "The specific charismatic note of any institute demands, both of the founder and of his disciples, a continual examination regarding: fidelity to the Lord; docility to his Spirit; intelligent attention to circumstances and an outlook cautiously directed to the signs of the times; the will to be part of the Church; the awareness of subordination to the sacred hierarchy; boldness of initiatives; constancy in the giving of self; humility in bearing with adversities. The true relation between genuine charism, with its perspectives of newness, and interior suffering, carries with it an unvarying history of the connection between charism and cross, which, above every motive that may justify misunderstandings is supremely helpful in discerning the authenticity of a vocation" (12).

The Primordial Mystery of Consecration

John R. Sheets, S.J.

Volume 44, 1985, pp. 641-653.

It seems that among people with religious sensitivities, there is reawakening of the sense of mystery. This is taking place on every level of the Church, among laity, religious, priests. In spite of the technological milieu in which we live, there breaks through what Peter Berger once called "the rumor of angels." This is a sense of what lies beyond, beneath, and around the "manufactured" world that seems to dry up and suck out that deep source of life which overflows from the fountain of living water, through the mysteries of nature and of grace.

It is the sense of what Teilhard de Chardin called "The Divine Milieu." "The perception of the divine omnipresence is essentially a seeing, a taste, that is to say a sort of intuition bearing upon certain superior qualities in things. It cannot, therefore, be attained directly by any process of reasoning, nor by any human artifice" (*The Divine Milieu,* p. 131).

Perhaps this deepening sense of mystery is taking place not only in spite of the technologizing of our world, but because of it. When windows are shut and there is no fresh air, our lungs cry out for this freshness in a stronger way than we felt when fresh air was part of our normal life.

This milieu of the "freshness" at the heart of reality is the world of the sacred. It is the world where two worlds join and compenetrate, the sacred world, which is the "milieu" of the divine, and our created, spatial-temporal world. The overflow of the sacred into our world is con-secration. Etymologically the word means a "with-sacredness," or a "co-sacredness." In a manner that is pure gift, what belongs to God alone, his *milieu,* so to speak, becomes our milieu.

In what follows, I would like to take this notion of milieu as a way of speaking about consecration. In particular, I want to show how religious consecration, a life committed to Christ through commitment to the evangelical counsels of chastity, poverty and obedience, is a particular florescence of the sacred milieu into which we are drawn through baptism. Baptism is not only the "door of the Church," as it has often been called. It is also the way in which Christ's own consecration enters into us, and we are drawn into his. It is what has been described as the "*admirabile commercium*," the wonderful exchange. His *milieu* becomes mine, and mine becomes his. What Jacob said about the place where he had wrestled with the angel applies to the sacrament of baptism: "This is indeed the house of God and the gate of heaven." It is out of this sacred milieu into which we are drawn through baptism that religious consecration arises as a particular "art form" of the mystery of consecration.

The Milieus in Which We Live

Since the notion of milieu is central to the way that I want to speak of religious consecration, I shall begin with a brief description of its meaning: then, comment on the different milieus which shape our lives.

A milieu, according to the etymology, is a "middle place." I am not sure of all that is implied in that derivation. But in someway, everything, and every person in a milieu is always in the middle of it, no matter where the thing or person is. It is the mystery of the interpenetration of two levels of reality: that by which we belong to what is greater than we. Yet what is greater than any individual enters into the individual as though each individual is a center of convergence of all that is in the milieu. Undoubtedly one could speculate on this interdependence of individual and milieu at length. But this is not the place to do that. It is enough to call attention to the way that the whole exists in the part, and the part in the whole. The milieu is not merely something external to the individuals, but works to shape individuals, groups, nations, marking them with an identity which gives them a sameness even in their individuality.

For our purposes we can speak of three different milieus. The first is that of the world of things as they exist within the interdependence of the whole. Today we call that milieu, and the way that individual things interact with it, the ecosystem.

There is also the milieu in which we exist, not simply as things, but as spirit-embodied in the world of things. It is the world created by spirit-in-the-flesh, the world of culture. It is the world which is our home as persons, a world created by the power of the spirit—the world of language, art, literature, and the world of human relationships.

In the third place, there is the world of the sacred. By its very nature, every milieu is found in time and space, but has no limits or boundaries. Also, every milieu compenetrates, in a greater or lesser degree, everything that is within it. But in the realm of the sacred milieu this is even more profound. There is in every heart, as well as in communities of mankind, a sense of the more, the depth, and the beyond that surrounds, encompasses, sustains, every other aspect of our existence.

This sense of the sacred is found in the heart of individuals and in the collective awareness of all peoples. Augustine describes it as the restlessness of the human heart that thirsts for the fullness which cannot be satisfied by any limited good. "Our hearts are made for thee, O God, and they are restless, until they find their rest in thee." Rudolf Otto speaks of it as the sense of the numinous (*The Idea of the Holy*). Paul Tillich as "ultimate concern." Rabbi Heschel describes it as the "sense of wonder coming from the ineffable depths of reality." No matter how it is described, all the descriptions point to the milieu which is the source and sustaining power of the whole of created existence. St. Paul, in his speech to the Athenians, will speak of God as this milieu: ". . . he is not far from any of us, for in him we live, and move and have our being" (Ac 17:27).

It is this sense of the sacred that is at the heart of all the searching for meaning of life, the attempt to make some sense out of the problem of evil, suffering, death. It is the basis of all religious practice, in the attempt to enter into communion with this absolute reality, or to propitiate it.

It is here, then, for the first time that we find a new reality. It is the mystery of *con-secration*, a "with-sacredness." This boundless mystery, which is out of time and space, is concretized in time and space. Certain persons, places, things are set apart to embody this mystery, to be the "sacrament" which inserts the mystery into our lives, so that it can touch us, and we can touch it. For this reason, persons, places, things are set apart and assume the specialness that belongs to the mystery of the sacred. In other words, they are consecrated.

We have been speaking of the mystery of the sacred, and the consecration by which it takes on a certain sacramental presence in the world. This is the realm of what is called natural religion.

But with God's entering into the history of Israel through the call of Moses, and the whole of the Exodus experience, there is a new sense of the sacred. We are now in the realm of *dialogue*. In an incomprehensible way, the sacred is revealed as a person, who calls, chooses, sends. He has a name, "Yahweh." He has designs for the whole people, and the whole of history. He invites the people to enter into his own holiness, to share it. This is an entirely new dimension in the mystery of the sacred, as well as in the meaning of con-secration.

The mystery of the holy is not only the mystery of the numinous, but the revelation of a God who is also *will*. His will is that we might live. But his will, as well as our lives, are inseparable from keeping his word. "From this you know that now, if you obey my voice and hold fast to my covenant, you of all the nations shall be my very own; for all the earth is mine. I will count you a kingdom of priests, a consecrated nation" (Ex 19:5).

As we saw above, in the realm of natural religion, the sense of the sacred is incarnated in the world of persons, actions and things, which are consecrated, to be the meeting place of the sacred and the human. The same is true in Israel, but with a richer meaning that comes from revelation. Now, the consecration of persons, places, things serves to put the people in touch with what took place in the saving events of their history, whose meaning is revealed through the prophetic word.

Even within the consecrated people, the tribe of Levi has a special consecration to be the tribe to serve as priests. They would receive no part of the land allotted to the others, because God himself was to be their lot.

However, all these aspects of the sacred, from natural religion, to the historical religion of Israel, are only stages to the revelation we find in Christ. The Letter to the Hebrews describes the whole pattern of consecrating activities in the Old Testament as shadows and figures of what is to come. "For the Law contains but a shadow, and no true image of the good things which were to come" (Heb 10:1). "These are no more than a shadow of what was to come; the solid reality is Christ" (Col 2:17).

The entrance of God into history in a unique and unforeseeable way in the Incarnation is described as an act of consecration. Mary is to be overshadowed by the power of the Holy Spirit, and the one to be born of her will be called the Holy One. The terminology is reminiscent of the description of the consecration of the temple of Solomon. A cloud, symbolizing the consecrating presence of Yahweh, filled the temple (1 K 8:10). Jesus himself is the one who is consecrated, the one in whom and through the Father's redemptive love reaches out to us, and through whom we touch the Father. He is the fulfillment of the meaning of the ladder stretching from heaven to earth seen in Jacob's dream (Gn 28:17). "You shall see greater things than that. In truth, in very truth I tell you all, you shall see heaven wide open, and God's angels ascending and descending upon the Son of Man" (Jn 1:51).

The theme of consecration is in particular central to the Johannine thought. Jesus is at one and the same time the one consecrated by the Father, as well as the one who consecrates the world. He is lamb and priest. "I have been consecrated and sent into the world by the Father (Jn 10:36). He is the fullness of the Father's hallowing act, that takes place in his Hour, the Hour in which he is glorified. But this hallowing act overflows to consecrate the world, in particular the Church. "For their sake I now consecrate myself that they may be consecrated by the truth" (Jn 17:19). In the blood and water flowing from his open side, together with the gift of the Spirit, are symbolized the consecration, in the first place of Christ, and then the manner in which his own consecration reaches out to touch the world.

In Paul in particular, there is the sense of what we can call the Christic milieu. To be a Christian is to be put into Christ, incorporated in him. This is an insertion into Christ's own consecration. One of the favorite phrases he used to express the whole mystery of the faith is "in Christ Jesus," or "in the Lord." The Christian finds his identity as the new creation by being taken up in Christ's consecration.

This theme is central to the thought of Paul. I shall give only a sampling of the texts. In his farewell to the elders at Miletus, Paul told them: "And now I commend you to God and to his gracious word, which has power to build you up and give you your heritage among all who are consecrated to him" (Ac 20:32). The Corinthians "have been consecrated in Christ Jesus" (1 Co 1:2), "washed and consecrated" (6:11). His own ministry is described as a liturgical act: "It falls to me to offer the gentiles to him as an acceptable sacrifice, consecrated by the Holy Spirit" (Rm 15:16)

Hebrews stresses the identity which is established between Christ and the Christian through being consecrated by Christ: "For a consecrating priest and those whom he consecrates are all of one stock" (Heb 2:11). Peter speaks of the faithful as "consecrated by the Spirit to a life of obedience to Jesus Christ" (1 P 1:2).

A person who is consecrated by Christ and in Christ should live the kind of life that flows from consecration and brings it to fulfillment. "Let us therefore cleanse ourselves from all that can defile flesh or spirit, and in the fear of God complete our consecration" (2 Co 7:1).

The consecration of a believing spouse has inner power to draw the unbelieving wife or husband into the consecration of the believing spouse. "For the heathen husband now belongs to God through his Christian wife, and the heathen wife through her Christian husband. Otherwise your children would not belong to God, whereas in fact they do" (1 Co 7:14).

Paul parallels the sacrificial love by which Christ consecrated the Church with the way that a husband should love his wife: "Husbands, love your wives as Christ also loved the Church and gave himself up for it, to consecrate it, cleansing it by water and word, so that he might present the Church to himself all glorious, with no stain or wrinkle or anything of the sort, but holy and without blemish" (Ep 5:25-27).

The extension of Christ's power to consecrate is transmitted in the mysterious power by which his own power to consecrate is sacramentalized in his apostles. They are told to "do this in memory of me," that is, to repeat sacramentally the act by which Christ consecrated the world. They are empowered by being given the gift of the consecrating, or rather, re-consecrating Spirit." 'Peace be with you. As the Father sent me, so I send you.' He then breathed on them, saying: 'Receive the Holy Spirit. If you forgive any man's sins, they stand forgiven; if you pronounce them unforgiven, unforgiven they remain'" (Jn 20:21-23).

It is this sacred power sacramentalized in his apostles and their successors which is described by the world hierarchy. In popular understanding, the word is identified with power and bureaucracy. But its original meaning, coming from the word "*hieros*" and "*archia*," "holy principle," is the sacramentalization of Christ's power to consecrate the faithful.

Before proceeding on to the topic of religious consecration, I would like to sum up what I have said. At first it might seem as though I have a very long staircase, by way of introduction, to reach the place where I am going.

As I said above, it is important to recapture the importance of the various milieus in which we live. Each in its own way, on different levels, contributes to the shaping of individuals and societies. This is especially true of the milieu of the sacred. There is an analogy between the comprehensive force of the power of gravity in the ecosystem with the power of the sacred to sustain and give meaning to the whole of reality.

This sense of the way that the sacred permeates the whole of created reality is at the root of the symbolism in the Book of Revelation, ch. 4, where created reality acclaims the One who is on the throne, singing, "Holy, holy, holy is God the sovereign Lord of all, who was, and is, and is to come" (v. 8).

In the Old Testament, this milieu is described through images such as covenanted people, people of God. In the New Testament, the images abound: kingdom, city, temple, body, vine and branches, the New Creation.

We must, then, recapture the radical or primordial meaning of consecration. It is not something which touches us merely externally. To be "in the Lord," or "in Christ Jesus," means to be in a milieu which transforms the inner person into a new creature, while at the same time it draws him into a consecrated community.

The following passage, then, will serve as a summary of what I have said, as well as a bridge to the next section. "Let us then establish ourselves in the divine *milieu*. There we shall be within the inmost depths of souls and the greatest consistency of matter. There, at the confluence of all the forms of beauty, we shall discover the ultra-vital, ultra-perceptible, ultra-active point of the universe; and, at the same time, we shall experience in the depths of our own being the effortless deployment of the *plenitude* of all our powers of action and of adoration. For it is not merely that at that privileged point all the external springs of the world are coordinated and harmonized: there is the further, complementary marvel that the man who surrenders himself to the divine *milieu* feels his own inward powers directed and enlarged by it with a sureness which enables him effortlessly to avoid the all too numerous reefs on which mystical quests have so often foundered" (*Hymn of the Universe*, Pierre Teilhard de Chardin, p. 141).

Religious Consecration: The Florescence of the Divine Milieu

I would like then to apply what I have said above, about the way we are consecrated by being drawn into the milieu of Christ through baptism and the Church, to the consecrated life of the counsels. I shall do this by commenting on Pope John Paul's letter on the religious life, *Redemptionis Donum (The Gift of Redemption)*. It was addressed to religious throughout the world at the close of the Jubilee Year of the Redemption. It is dated March 25, 1984. But first I would like to give some of my own reflections about the letter.

In my mind it is most consistent, the most profound presentation of the theology of the religious life ever written. That is a bold satement. But I think it is true. In the first place it is a *coherent theology* taking in all the mysteries of our faith to bring them to converge on the meaning of the religious life: Trinity, incarnation, Church, sacraments, grace, Mary. What we have in Vatican II and other official statements about religious life brings out the meaning but not in the context of a coherent theology.

There is a *depth* to the treatment which undercuts the traditional dichotomies which often prevent us from getting to the central meaning of religious life. Such, for example, are the contrasts between "Pre-Vatican and Post-Vatican," "monastic and apostolic," "conservative and liberal," "American and Roman," "male and female."

The letter goes to what is permanent beneath all of the changes. It shows the principle of identity that marks the religious life wherever and whenever it is found. Perhaps one of the main reasons for confusion today among religious, and in the formation programs of so many congregations, is the lack of any permanent base which acts as a constant among the many variables which affect religious life as it emerges in different cultures throughout history, responding to new needs of the Church as these develop.

How many things have been written in the past couple of decades on the "religious life of the future," "changing religious life today," and more. Most of these are projections from a view of the religious life which is simply a recombination of variables, without any sense of a constant which gives them consistency. They are like the skywriting messages we see in the sky, which are there, lose their shape, disappear, to be succeeded by more skywriting. In this sense, to be current is to be always out-of-date.

To come then to the letter itself. There are seven sections to it. I want to call special attention to sections three and four. Section Three is entitled "Consecration," and Section Four, "Evangelical Counsels."

In Section One, "Greeting," the Holy Father describes the purpose of the letter, which is, first of all, in the context of the Jubilee Year of the Redemption, a call to conversion; and secondly, it is the opportunity for him as the Vicar of Christ to express in the name of the whole Church a message of love to religious.

In Section Two, he turns to the account of Jesus' dialogue with the rich young man (Mk 10:21 ff). "He looked upon him and loved him." He said, "If you want to be perfect, go sell what you have, give to the poor, and come follow me." The man went away sad. This gospel narrative, then, is applied to each of those whom Christ called. It puts vocation in the context of an ongoing dialogue with Christ. Christian religious life is not like, for example, that of the Buddhist monks. Their life of celibacy, together with their other commitments, arises out of what we spoke of above as "natural religion." Christian religious life arises out of a *personal dialogue* of Christ with the individual. It is not a call simply to asceticism. It is a call "to follow Christ." For this reason, it is a call to a *lived-communion*. The Holy Father speaks of this as *"spousal"* nature of religious life.

Then, in the part which concerns us in particular, Section Three, "Consecration," he describes religious life as a special form that our baptismal consecration takes, as Christ enters into dialogue with us, to draw us to a special form of baptismal consecration.

In the context of what I said above about the "divine milieu," this means that we are taken up into this milieu of Christ through our baptism, which at the same time draws us into the society of "saints" (Paul's word for members of the consecrated community of faithful). Within this milieu, through this ongoing dialogue of Christ with the heart of each of his faithful, he draws them to the particular charism which is their special way of consecrating the whole community. Paul speaks of the individual charisms (or graces, gifts) as "building up" the community. But in reality, there is no way to build except by drawing out all the implications of the radical consecration through our baptism.

Within the manifold of ways of living out the baptismal consecration, there is the vocation of the evangelical counsels. What is the uniqueness of this charism in respect to the other vocations that arise through the prompting of the Holy Spirit from our baptismal consecration?

The answer is found in the unique way that religious life bears witness to what is at the heart of the baptismal consecration. As the Holy Father says: "Upon the sacramental basis of baptism in which it is rooted, religious profession is a new 'burial in the death of Christ': new, because it is made with awareness and by choice; new, because of love and vocation; new, by reason of unceasing 'conversion.' This 'burial in death' causes the person 'buried together with Christ' to walk in newness of life. In Christ crucified is to be found the ultimate foundation both of baptismal consecration and of the profession of the evangelical counsels, which—in the words of the Second Vatican Council—constitutes a 'special consecration.' *It is at one and the same time both death and liberation*" (#7).

The clue that is at the heart of the Holy Father's faith-insight into baptismal consecration, and the religious consecration which is rooted in it, lies in two words: *paschal duality*. The paschal mystery has two different, but inseparable aspects, *death-resurrection*. This paschal duality can be expressed in other ways: sacrifice-communion, giving up in order to give to another, impoverishment-enrichment, emptying-filling, powerlessness-empowerment.

The uniqueness, then, of the charism of religious consecration lies in the way that it renders visible, tangible and operative, the paschal duality that lies in the very heart of the Church.

In Section Four, "Evangelical Counsels," the Pope points out how the life of the evangelical counsels is not simply a kind of private way of life. Such a life transposes what he calls the "economy of the redemption" into the here and now. The economy of the redemption is another way of speaking of the paschal mystery, and the paschal duality. The life of the counsels incarnates the redemptive pattern into the life of an individual and a community. In this way, such a life carries within it the very liberating power of Christ's own death and resurrection. This emphasis shows how the religious life, even if lived in a cloister, is by its very nature the most powerful liberating force in the world.

"In this way the economy of the redemption transfers the power of the paschal mystery to the level of humanity, docile to Christ's call to life in chastity, poverty and obedience, that is, to a life according to the evangelical counsels" (#10).

In Section Five, the Holy Father takes up each of the evangelical counsels in order to point out how they exhibit this paschal duality. On the one hand, the counsel of chastity for the kingdom of God means giving up marriage and the joy of having one's own family. But in this case, renunciation is not something negative. It is at the same time *annunciation* that the ultimate goal of all of us is a here and now possibility. With the power of the Holy Spirit it is possible to open one's heart and allow Christ to fill it completely. The intangible reality that Christ is the only spouse of the Church is made visible in the lives of those for whom he is truly spouse here and now through chastity for the kingdom of God.

"The evangelical counsel of chastity is only an indication of that particular possibility which for the human heart, whether of a man or of a woman, constitutes the spousal love of Christ himself, of Jesus the 'Lord.' To make themselves eunuchs for the sake of the kingdom of heaven' is not in fact merely a free renunciation of marriage, but a charismatic choice of Christ as one's exclusive spouse . . . In this way consecrated persons accomplish the interior purpose of the entire economy of the redemption . . . they bring into the midst of this passing world the announcement of the future resurrection and of eternal life: life in union with God himself through the beatific vision and the love which contains in itself and completely pervades all the other loves of the human heart" (#11).

Then he turns to the evangelical counsel of poverty. He develops the paschal duality involved in the counsel by his reflections on the way that Christ enriched us through his poverty. "For you know the grace of our Lord Jesus Christ, that though he was rich, yet for your sake he became poor, so that by his poverty you might become rich" (2 Co 8:9).

He continues: "For this reason he says to the young man of the synoptic Gospels: 'Sell what you possess and give to the poor, and you will have treasure in heaven.' In these words there is a call to enrich others through one's own poverty, but in the depths of this call there is hidden the testimony of the infinite richness of God, which transferred to the human soul in the mystery of grace, creates in man himself, precisely through poverty, a source for enriching others not comparable with any other resource of material goods, a source for bestowing gifts on others in the manner of God himself . . . . We see how this process of enrichment unfolds in the pages of the Gospel, finding its culmination in the paschal event: Christ, the poorest in his death on the cross, is also the one who enriches us infinitely with the fullness of new life through the resurrection" (#12).

He then turns to the counsel of obedience. He takes as the key text Paul's description of the *kenosis* (emptying) of Christ. "Though he was in the form of God, he did not count equality with God a thing to be grasped, but emptied himself, taking the form of a servant, being born in the likeness of men. And being found in human form he humbled himself and became obedient unto death, even death on a cross" (Ph 2:6-8).

He locates the inmost constitutive element of the paschal mystery in the obedience of Christ to the Father. "Here, in these words of the Letter of St. Paul to the Philippians, we touch the very essence of the redemption. In this reality is inscribed in a primary and constitutive way the obedience of Jesus Christ.

Other words of the apostle . . . confirm this: "For as by one man's disobedience many were made sinners, so by one man's obedience many will be made righteous" (Rm 5:19).

In living out the counsel of obedience, through which they place themselves at this disposal of the community and the Church through obedience to their superior, they cooperate in redeeming the world. Here in this redemptive mode of life, they echo both the words of Mary and of Jesus; "Be it done to me according to your will." "By living out the evangelical counsel of obedience, they reach the deep essence of the entire economy of the redemption" (#13).

Of course, every Christian must live out his life in obedience to God through obedience to legitimate authority. But the life of the religious should be marked in a special way with this duality, an emptying of self-will, which paradoxically constitutes an inner freedom. "And since this obedience of Christ constitutes the essential nucleus of the work of the redemption, as is seen from the words of the apostle quoted above, therefore, also in the fulfilling of the evangelical counsel of obedience we must discern a particular moment in that 'economy of the redemption' which pervades your whole vocation in the Church" (#13).

Throughout the letter the Pope stresses that the "treasure in heaven" promised to those who give up all things to follow him is not reserved for heaven. It takes place here and now. When the paschal mystery is allowed to "seed" the heart, which is constricted by the threefold way in which its inner instincts are twisted, the "lust of the flesh, the lust of the eyes, and the pride of life" (1 Jn 2:15-17), its power to love takes on the infinity of Christ's own love.

"Remember also, dear brothers and sisters, that the obedience to which you committed yourselves by consecrating yourselves without reserve to God through the profession of the evangelical counsels is a particular expression of interior freedom, just as the definitive expression of Christ's freedom was his obedience 'unto death': 'I lay down my life, that I may take it up again. No one takes it from me, but I lay it down of my own accord'" (Jn 10:17, 18) (#13).

In Section Six, he shows how the life of the counsels witnesses to the redemptive power of the paschal mystery, because it frees the heart, which is open to the counsels, to embrace that paschal duality in the whole of one's life. It touches us in the three most radical aspects of our lives: the need to have things, the need for human, intimate love, and the need to be master of our destinies. In this way, religious life is witness to the presence of the paschal mystery in our hearts.

"These counsels, each in its own way and all of them together in their intimate connection, 'bear witness' to the redemption which, by the power of Christ's cross and resurrection, leads the world and humanity in the Holy Spirit toward that definitive fulfillment, which man and through man, the whole of creation finds in God and only in God" (#14).

He stresses then the way that religious by their consecration share in the apostolate of the Church. But at the same time their most fundamental apostolate is found in being who they are. "And thus, even though the many different apostolic works that you perform are extremely important, nevertheless, the truly fundamental work of the apostolate remains always what (and at the same time who) you are in the Church'' (#15).

Finally, in the conclusion, he stresses that this paschal mystery which finds its special witness in the religious life is a mystery that can be penetrated only with the eyes of faith. "May the Holy Spirit—through Christ's cross and resurrection —'having the eyes of your hearts enlightened,' enable you 'to know what is the hope to which he has called you, what are the riches of his glorious inheritance in the saints'" (Ep 1:18) (#16).

Summary and Conclusion

It is probably a mixed metaphor to say that we have gone through light-years in this article. We have seen that the mystery of the sacred, the holy, is the mystery that sustains all things. It is the milieu in which all things have their being. Yet the mystery is so boundless that it has to be, so to speak, scaled down for us to be in touch with it. This "scaling down" is itself a mystery. We call it consecration. Somehow, what has all the opaqueness, earthiness of this world, imperviousness of the world of creatures, becomes charged with the infinite power of the holy. Through revelation, we are able to see with the eyes of faith, the inner nature of this milieu, the holiness of God. His mystery of holiness is also a mystery of love which seeks to share what one has and what one is. This sharing takes place through the redemptive love of Christ. The world, then, ultimately exists in a Christic milieu. It is a world washed with the blood of Christ, recreated, re-consecrated.

We enter this consecrated milieu through baptism. This radical consecration can never be lost, even though we might desecrate it. This is called in theological terms the sacramental stamp, or character.

Through the variety of gifts given by the Holy Spirit, the radical consecration flowers in many ways. In particular, it blossoms in the religious life. It is there that the fundamental character of the paschal duality is re-presented, in a way that parallels the re-presentation of Christ's sacrifice in the Mass. For in and through the consecrated life of chastity, poverty, and obedience, Christ says, "Here's what I am. Here's what I came to do."

This mystery of the way that the milieu of Christ enters into us to consecrate us by taking us up into himself finds some remote analogy in the images used by the poet William Blake in his *Songs of Innocence*.

> To see a World in a grain of sand
> And a Heaven in a wild flower,
> Hold infinity in the palm of your hand,
> And eternity in an hour.
> A robin redbreast in a cage
> Puts all Heaven in a rage.
> A dove-house filled with doves and pigeons
> Shudders Hell through all its regions.

II. Religious Vows

A. *Chastity*

Living Consecrated Celibacy Today

Consecrated Celibacy: Gift and Challenge

Poverty, Time, Solitude: A Context for Celibate Lifestyle

Vowed Celibacy and Human Sexuality

B. *Poverty*

A Christian is a Poor Man

Models of Poverty

The Center of Religious Poverty

The Price of Poverty

C. *Obedience*

Obedience to Mission

The Service of Religious Authority: Reflections on Government in the Review of Constitutions

Provincials as 'Cultural Revolutionaries': The Role of Provincials Today

Christian and Religious Obedience

Living Consecrated Celibacy Today

John Carroll Futrell, S.J.

Volume 31, 1972, pp. 931-936.

Т he meaning and value of consecrated celibacy as a Christian way of life has been severely challenged during the last few years, not only by Freudian or secularized mentalities, but also even by priests and religious who at one time made the permanenet commitment to a life of consecrated celibacy. It has been argued that a life of consecrated celibacy is unnatural and inhuman, and that, consequently, no celibate can attain true personal fulfillment and human maturity. The life of celibacy has been attacked as an at least implicit belittling of marriage as a Christian way of life, as contempt for a less perfect vocation for those who are incapable of living the "perfect" life of virginity. The law of the Latin rite which requires celibacy of its priests has been attacked as an unjustifiable act of tyranny denying the basic human right of human fulfillment through sexual union to men who wish to be ordained. Undoubtedly, these arguments have had influence upon some persons who have left the priesthood or the religious life in order to marry. These theories also brought about the aberrations of the "Third Way" a few years ago, which was a naive attempt to enjoy affective fulfillment in an exclusive relationship with another individual of the other sex through all the bodily expressions of love short of sexual union.

The purpose of the following reflections is not to discuss or defend the law of celibacy for priests in the Latin rite. This law has been studied and controverted in many books and articles during recent years. It is well to recall, however, that *any* community has the right and the duty to demand certain qualifications of those members of the community called upon to carry out specific functions within it. A "job description" always includes the qualities which the community feels the persons who are to serve it in particular capacities should possess. It is not, therefore, a violation of human rights that for historical reasons the Church decided that its priests in the Latin rite should be chosen from only those among the faithful to whom the charism of virginity has been given. Whether in the light of contemporary pastoral needs it is a wise decision to retain this law universally is another question. But the issue is one of pastoral discernment, not of violated human rights.

The following reflections are concerned, rather, with the meaning of consecrated celibacy as an authentic Christian alternative, a specific and valuable vocation within the Church both for individual persons and for those called to celibate communities. After recalling the basic motivation for celibacy as a Christian way of life, some practical considerations will be offered on the particular challenges in the contemporary world to those persons who feel called to live their lives as consecrated celibates.

First of all, it should be recalled that celibacy is a *charism*—a special divine gifting of the Holy Spirit to individual persons for the service of the whole People of God and of all mankind. Christ said that only those can make themselves "eunuchs" for the sake of the kingdom of heaven "to whom it is granted" (Mt 19:10-2). In his First Letter to the Corinthians, St. Paul, in his instructions on marriage and virginity, after remarking that he would be happy if all remained as himself celibate, adds that, nevertheless, "everybody has his own particular *gifts from God,* one with a gift for one thing and another with a gift for the opposite" (7:7). The Holy Spirit pours out a variety of charismatic gifts upon the members of the community of the faithful for the good of the entire body. The foot needs the hand, the hand the eye, the eye the ear (1 Co 12:12-30). Thus, those who receive the charism of celibacy are given a gift from the Spirit which is authentic and valuable for the whole people. To discern that one has been given this charism and to choose to accept it and to live out its consequences is not a priori to destroy the possibility of true human fulfillment and maturity. This depends upon the way a person integrates his celibacy into his growth as a person. Human maturity and fulfillment are no more automatically achieved through sexual union in or out of marriage than they are through consecrated celibacy. There is abundant human evidence to demonstrate this fact.

Human beings are totally sexual beings, and to come to human fulfillment we must assume our sexuality in our personal integration through a growing maturity of loving, finally leading us to the full expression of our deepest urge to love—totally self-giving love—which is also what gives human meaning to physical sexual union. But human sexuality is not identical with genitality. There are other authentic ways to express the deepest meaning of human sexuality, which is to enter into *personal* union with other persons through self-giving love. It is the experience and the expression of personal, self-giving love which is the fulfillment of human sexuality, whether this expression is through physical sexual union or through a life of consecrated celibacy.

To discern that one has received the charism of celibacy and to choose to accept it is not a belittling of marriage, whatever may at times have been the mistaken attitudes of certain individuals. It is not as a matter of fact to show contempt for marriage if one recognizes that consecrated celibacy is a Christian alternative (chosen by Jesus and by St. Paul also) and that one is called to it. Whether one Christian vocation is "better" or "more perfect" than another is at best a theoretical question, the answer to which depends upon the norms one uses to establish his hierarchy of values. For the individual person, this question is always concrete, existential, and relative: "What is better *for me?* What am *I* called to through the gifting of the Holy Spirit to *me*?"

The fundamental motive to live a life of consecrated celibacy is the experience through the charismatic gift of celibacy of being called to give all one's love totally and personally to Jesus Christ and to symbolize the totality of this love by foregoing the physically sexual expression of love during one's whole life. Consecrated celibacy, then, is grounded in an all-encompassing personal relationship of love with Jesus Christ, whatever other secondary values it may involve, such as mobility and freedom for apostolic service. The functional value of celibacy cannot be the fundamental reason for living it. For one thing, in certain circumstances good functional arguments can be given for non-celibate apostles. Furthermore, merely functional motivation will be inadequate for most persons to live consecrated celibacy authentically and deeply for a lifetime. Their celibacy must be experienced as the full exercise of their love for Jesus energizing their love for all other persons.

Only a celibacy which is the human expression of deep personal love for and identification with Jesus Christ, himself a celibate for the sake of the kingdom of heaven, can bring the consecrated celibate to true growth as a mature human person who gradually experiences progressive self-fulfillment through his personal relationship with Jesus and his life of witness and service to mankind. He grows to authentic personal development through the experience of being like Jesus and with Jesus a "man for others," who gives away his life in love to all other men and women through his celibacy. Consecrated celibacy, then, is a sign embodied in a human life of the true meaning of all personal love which in every case, including marriage, is realized only through self-giving to the other.

Consecrated celibacy also has a unique value as a striking, visible witness to mankind of the depth of the faith and hope of the People of God in the complete fulfillment of the kingdom of God when the Lord Jesus will come again and God will be all in all in the Parousia. Those who, following a charism from the Holy Spirit "bar themselves from marrying for the sake of the kingdom of heaven" (Mt 19:12), give the same testimony of their whole lives and of all their love to belief and hope in the Paschal good news of Jesus Christ which a martyr gives through his death. Through his life-time fidelity to his commitment of love, the consecrated celibate is a living sign of the Church's belief in the irrevocable promise of God, in his eternal fidelity. The celibate's renunciation of the physical expression of love is proclamation in one human life of the Church's hearing of the word of the Lord that love will never end. Consecrated celibacy is perhaps the most telling testimony of faith in Christ's promise of everlasting life, of life after death. Men can feel that the celibate is a fool, but they must confess that the faith and hope of Christians is powerful indeed, since it can inspire men and women to such a life, to such a love of Jesus who is encountered only in faith, to such a hope in God as the Absolute Future of man.

The first practical challenge to the person who feels called to the life of consecrated celibacy is to discern authentically that he truly possesses this charism, a discernment which must be confirmed by the community if his vocation is to enter a religious congregation. A charism is known by its visible effects. The presence of the charism of celibacy is discerned, therefore, by evaluating the psychological, emotional, and spiritual maturity of a person for indications that he is capable of living a life of authentic celibacy. At the beginning of such a life, it is necessarily a matter of judging the foundation within the young person for growth into a full life of consecrated celibacy. One important evidence of possessing this foundation is the fact that he has no great emotional or moral problems in living a chaste life already. It is necessary also to ascertain that his motivation for chastity is based upon a true appreciation of human sexuality at the person's level of human maturity and spiritual development and not upon fearful anxieties or false notions about sexuality.

Since the fundamental motive for freely choosing to respond to the charism of celibacy is personal love for Jesus Christ, it must be discerned that the person's desire for this life is rooted in his faith experience of the person of the risen Jesus. The growth and depth and permanence of this charism depends upon the growth and depth and permanence of his personal relationship with Jesus in love, which depends upon his continuing and deepening life of prayer. Thus, he must have initiated already an ongoing practice of profound personal prayer and be convinced of the need of continuing it and growing in it throughout his lifetime.

The second practical challenge to the consecrated celibate is the authentic living out of the consequences of his commitment. Each individual must possess a realistic recognition of the necessary consequences in his concrete lifestyle of commitment to consecrated celibacy. That is to say, he must conduct himself in his interior, personal life and in his external behavior and in his relationships with other people in a way that will guarantee constant and loyal authentic living of his celibacy. The individual exigencies of such a lifestyle are relative to the great variety of temperaments and the psychological and physiological conditions and experiences of individual persons. Therefore, it is impossible to give more than a few very obvious general prescriptions. What is required of each person is absolute honesty with himself before God in discerning his concrete actions in here and now situations, so that he does not permit himself to behave in a way that will "chip away" at his authentic celibacy, rather than in a way that will deepen it and strengthen it. To guarantee this honesty in such a delicate area of life, true openness with a competent spiritual director is of great importance.

Particularly, the celibate must be sensitive to "non-verbal" communication—the risk of sending messages to other persons which go counter to a relationship of truly celibate love, even when the verbal conversation is quite in accord with it. A truly honest person who prayerfully reflects upon the authenticity of his living of celibacy develops this sensitivity and will be aware when a relationship is beginning to be dangerous to his own celibacy or detrimental to another person. Most celibates will at times experience "falling in love" with someone. Perhaps even more often, at least after several years of authentically living celibacy, they will experience others falling in love with them, when this is not reciprocal. Here, the celibate's temptation may well be to a subtle form of seduction or manipulation of the other person because of the flattery he enjoys. Any of these situations must be confronted with the means honestly discerned as those demanded in order to maintain true celibacy and true charity. These means might range all the way from non-verbal communication, through discussing the situation with the other person, to the necessity for completely breaking off the relationship. Once more, true prayerful discernment and the help of a spiritual director are necessary to discover what actions are called for in each concrete situation.

The consecrated celibate must accept the fact that in freely choosing to respond to this charism he is deciding to live the rest of his life in tension with "the couple that might have been," just as any person who makes a life commitment to a specific personal identity must live in tension with what he might have chosen to become. The "couple that might have been" may be one face or a succession of faces. At certain moments of life, this tension will be felt as a heavy burden, a true cross, especially when one wants to share a great joy or a great grief with another person in the way of sharing that can only develop within the uniquely intimate relationship of marriage. It is perhaps in moments such as these that the celibate is aware of making the least falsified act of love of God that he will make until his ultimate act of love on his own death bed.

A third practical challenge to the consecrated celibate is to achieve true, human, affective fulfillment within his life of celibacy. Human, affective fulfillment is developed only through the self-transcending experience of love with other persons. Thus, the celibate must have truly complementary relationships of love with other human persons—celibates and non-celibates, men and women. The "incompleteness" that seeks completion through self-giving love relationships with other persons is at the root of human sexuality, and the integration of sexuality into consecrated celibacy requires such complementary relationships. What is renounced by choosing to respond to the charism of celibacy is the relationship of *exclusive* complementarity with one other human person, as happens in marriage. The celibate must experience the relationship of exclusive complementarity in his personal love relationship with Jesus Christ encountered in faith. This means that the celibate must have a deep prayer life bringing him into a communion of personal love with Jesus that gradually will permeate all his relationships and all his life, so that he finds God in all things.

Recognizing that sexuality is not identical with genitality and that it can be expressed in other than genitally-oriented ways, the celibate will express his sexuality in relationships of true love growing out of openness to all the persons he contacts. The day will come when he will feel great joy in his life of celibacy precisely because of the many relationships of love it has left him free to experience.

It would seem normal that the consecrated celibate would have affectively fulfilling relationships above all with other persons who share the same vocation, especially in his or her own religious community. Through their shared vocation, these persons share the same personal identity in Christ, the common identity of their own community charism. This provides them with a unique basis for developing deep interpersonal communication, true mutual understanding and support and love. In the contemporary world, it seems evident that religious communities have a serious obligation to provide an atmosphere where all the members truly feel "at home" and enjoy warm personal relationships which enable them to experience their own community as the human affective center of their lives and the support of their development as whole men and women.

Especially in some cultures the development of healthy relationships of human, affective love among the members of religious communities has been greatly impeded by an exaggerated fear of homosexuality. The old taboo about "particular friendships" was a manifestation of this fear. Particularly in the situation in the past of houses of formation cut off from the possibility of healthy relationships with persons of the opposite sex, it was possible for young religious to go into panic and to fear that they were abnormal when they experienced affectionate feelings towards their companions, especially if these feelings sometimes had sexual resonance. It was possible because of these fears to "condition" oneself into a kind of "homosexual box." But a person who recognizes that human affectivity will reach out to those persons one is in constant contact with, and that the experience of sexual resonance is a natural human phenomenon, will remain relaxed and at peace, knowing that contact with persons of the opposite sex in a more open situation will result in the experience of normal affectivity towards them. The expression of affection, then, is guided by the honest discernment in each specific situation of what is required in behavior in order to live consecrated celibacy authentically in every relationship. Should a celibate have truly homosexual tendencies, his discernment of behavior must be equally honest in his situation, just as his own relationship of exclusive complementarity with another person must be found in the experience of his personal love for Jesus Christ.

Consecrated celibates should be aware of the special kind of love that can exist between a celibate and a person of the opposite sex. Karl Rahner has expressed this very well in *Servants of the Lord* (p. 153): "True celibacy has nothing in common with the sexlessness of the eunuch but is possible only in a sound relationship between the sexes, where one recognizes oneself as a man and a woman as a woman." Rahner points out that we must understand "the purpose, nature, and limits of a very special kind of love, a real spiritual friendship between a priest and a woman . . . . Whatever it should be called—it occurs too in the history of the saints—it can perfectly well exist in many degrees. I need not explain to you that this is not to be grossly misinterpreted as a 'loophole'" (p. 171).

Finally, in order to achieve true fulfillment as a human being, the consecrated celibate needs to have the experience of parenthood, of being a father or mother who brings forth life. This experience is needed particularly as persons reach their middle years, when it becomes vital to them to have created something which they can recognize as a continuation of their own lives, of themselves. How this parenthood is experienced depends upon the temperament of individual persons and their own life situation. It may be through apostolic work, through spiritual guidance of persons, or even through writing or other tasks. It is essential, however, that this be felt and realized as the psychological fulfillment of parenthood—which is no more identified with physical generation than sexuality is with genitality.

As he authentically lives out his life of consecrated celibacy, the person who has received this charism should experience true growth and fulfillment as a human person, an ever-increasing delight in his celibacy and in the many relationships of human love that his state of life has made possible, and an ever-deeper communion of love with Jesus Christ. Consecrated celibacy finally becomes a mysticism, a unique form of experienced union with the Absolute, the Holy One, the *mysterium tremendum,* who has revealed himself in Jesus Christ to be a community of love: Father, Son and Holy Spirit, and who has reached into the vital center of the person he has called to celibacy and drawn the very springs of his love entirely to the Love who is God.

Consecrated Celibacy:
Gift and Challenge

Mary Anne Hoope, B.V.M.

Volume 40, 1981, pp. 902-11.

Contemporary research and reflection have emphasized various aspects of the vow of celibacy. Before considering consecrated celibacy (celibacy vowed to God out of love for him and for his people) as a gift and a challenge, it may be helpful to indicate something of the context in which celibacy is being, and has been, discussed within the last three to five years. Another way of getting at the same issue is to ask the question of "trends." Can one describe or delineate certain trends in the discussions and literature about celibacy? I believe one can.

As I see it, recent reflections on the vow of celibacy have emphasized the following:

1. The necessity of a certain degree of maturity—maturity in faith, psychological and emotional maturity, social maturity—if one is to respond to Christ as a celibate woman or man, to respond to him and to others in *authentic love for life*. Maturity, therefore, is important not only in relation to one's personal development in religious life, but in relation to ministry. We realize today that many so-called vocational crises are due to the fact that vocational decisions are often made at a rather young age, and commitment to celibacy is affirmed before questions of identity and intimacy have been resolved.

2. Instead of speaking of religious life as a "state of life" which seems to imply something static, there is an emphasis on the developmental or "process" nature of the vowed life. Thus we read about "becoming a celibate lover" or "becoming unmarriageable for the sake of the king-

dom." Ribando says: "The gift of celibacy cannot be presumed (that is, taken for granted) even by those who have lived it for many years." Don Goergen in *The Sexual Celibate* says that celibacy is "an ideal," and that celibate chastity "as an ideal is seldom perfectly realized in the concrete. Yet it must be continually sought and held up as an ideal."[1] Here Goergen's position has caused controversy, some feeling that his view is somewhat pessimistic, that some do achieve celibate chastity, even early in life.

3. The relation of celibacy to sexuality, genitality, and affectivity, and the distinctions among these. Sexuality refers to the fact that I am male or female. As a woman or a man I may choose to relate to a member of the opposite sex physically, that is, genitally. Genital relationship is the usual expression of one's sexuality within married love. All Christians, however, are called to express their sexuality in terms of affectivity, those qualities of gentleness and tenderness, care and compassion which I so admire in others and which I must continually strive to nurture in my own life.

4. The relational aspect of celibacy—the commitment to celibacy as a *commitment to love.* What does this imply in terms of today's world, a world in which millions are starving and oppressed? What does this mean in relation to friendship: with members of one's own sex, with members of the opposite sex?

5. The importance of community as nurture for celibate love. A warm, loving community is not only a support to the individual striving to live out celibate commitment, but such a community is a powerful witness to others, and often a means that the Lord will use to draw others to join us and to follow him in religious life.

6. The interrelationship of all the vows, with primacy given quite often to celibacy.

As we move into our reflection upon the meaning of consecrated celibacy, the above trends will be taken into account in my remarks. It is important to realize, however, that the meaning of the vow is not exhausted by these, nor are these trends necessarily to be accepted without question or revision.

The "Heart" of Celibacy: Invitation and Response

In attempting to get at the "heart" of celibacy, I would like to begin at the beginning, and that is with the notion of call or, if you prefer, invitation. Basic to any theology of celibacy is the understanding of the vow as call or invitation that is *gift,* a totally free and gratuitous expression of the Lord's own love. Celibacy-as-gift is also a *charism.* Therefore, it is a gift given to us not only for our own holiness but for the wholeness and holiness of the Church, the People of God. Because the Lord respects us as persons endowed with intellect and free will, with a heart and a deep capacity to give and receive love, it is up to us to accept his invitation, it is up to us to pledge fidelity, while always remembering that it is *his* fidelity that makes possible ours.

Most theologians today are speaking of celibacy as given and received within the context of religious experience, within the context of personal relationship. It is in personal encounter with the Lord, in a desire to follow Jesus, that I am drawn to commit myself to love in this way. In the past, we often spoke of the functional value of celibacy. Because I am not committed to a wife or husband and to children, I am more free, more able to go anywhere; I have more time to serve. To a certain extent this is Paul's argument in I Corinthians. While this may be true, and is still an important aspect in ministry, most today do not see this as the basic element in vowed celibacy. The heart of vowed celibacy is rather a special, unique, total consecration to Christ that involves an obligation to manifest that love in certain ways. (Both are essential—the total consecration and the obligation to manifest love in certain ways.) There is, then, a difference between the celibacy chosen by a young woman or man who wants to devote herself or himself to a career—whatever it might be—without any specific or explicit reference to Christ, and the celibacy of one who falls in love with Christ and wants to devote oneself totally to his kingdom.

There is a great deal of controversy today about the meaning of the saying in Mt 19:12 where Jesus speaks about those who make themselves eunuchs "for" or "on account of" the kingdom of heaven—whether it refers to married people who choose not to marry after their first marriage breaks up or whether, as has been traditionally taught, it refers to those who choose not to marry at all.[2] The one thing about which there is almost universal agreement, however, is the meaning of *dia,* "for" or "on account of." "On account of the kingdom of heaven" does not imply that one chooses celibacy *so that* one can devote oneself to the kingdom of heaven, but that it is *because of* the kingdom of heaven that one chooses to be celibate. The kingdom of heaven is not an abstract, summary term for some philosophy or some code of behavior, but refers to God's reign, his reigning. God's reign or his active presence has taken flesh in Jesus. So Christian celibacy is explicitly related to the person of Jesus. The relationship of any person to Jesus-as-person admits of different degrees. But without *any* relationship to him, there is no Christian celibacy, no consecrated celibacy, no authentic vow of celibacy.

As I said, theologians today are looking at celibacy within the ambience of religious experience. Edward Schillebeeckx speaks of celibacy as "an existential inability to do otherwise."[3] I am so grasped by God, by Jesus and his kingdom, that I cannot do otherwise. A simple analogy is that of falling in love. Have you ever wondered what some woman sees in the man she is to marry? Yet she is so attracted to him that she is willing to live with him, grow with him, work with him, share with him her total self—forever! Ann Goggin speaks about "becoming unmarriageable for the kingdom," growing toward that point when I am so captured by Christ that there is no point of return.

She writes:

> To make ourselves unmarriageable is quite a job. I love the line from the Rule of Taizé which says: "This work of Christ in you demands infinite patience." I think this is true. It doesn't happen in two years of novitiate. At the moment of final vows most of us aren't unmarriageable. It takes decades. If we look around we know that after many years of religious life some aren't.[4]

We see here idealism blended with realism, affirmation of divine love as well as the necessity of human response. We recognize that to say that celibacy is a gift does not deny the need for sufficient human maturity and growth if the decision is to be truly free and personal, if the full implications of the commitment are to be grasped. Celibacy is first of all a commitment to love Christ in a special and unique way. It is a promise to love him *totally*, in *all* ways for *all* of my days. To vow celibate love is to say that I *intend never to marry*, that the actualization of my covenant with the Lord, a covenant founded in baptism, will be such that it will not admit of the covenant which is marriage. Celibacy, then, is a challenge, a challenge to become the persons we are called to be, and thus to maximize our giftedness to others. Our call to follow Jesus as celibate men or women is at the heart of who we are as persons, and who we are as persons is a significant aspect of ministry.

Now one may say: "All of that is very nice. But what does it mean in my day-to-day living?" If celibacy is a commitment to love Christ totally, it is also a commitment to love as Christ loves, and *with* His love. The challenges of celibacy and the rewards of celibacy are the challenges and rewards of love. If celibacy involves love, it then involves relationship, my relationship to the Lord, to others, and to myself.

The Celibate Relationship to Jesus

We spoke of celibacy as a "being grasped" by Jesus, a seeing in his values and ideals, in his way of life, the "pearl of great price," the "treasure" where our heart is. Growth in celibate love, therefore, involves a continual deepening of our relationship to Jesus. It involves a nurturing of love—a constant "being with" him, a bringing to him of all my life experiences, my hopes and dreams, my disappointments and failures, my successes and gifts. It involves a pondering of his being, and pondering thus that I may likewise be and do, a "putting on" of his mind and heart, an involving of myself in those activities to which he devoted his time and energy. It is a searching with him to do only the will of our Father (and here especially we see a relationship to obedience). Celibacy is a commitment to growing intimacy with Jesus, an intimacy which, however, implies a deepening commitment to love others.

The Celibate Relationship to Others

Celibacy is a commitment to love others, to love *all*, to love unselfishly and authentically, to love humanly—which is to love divinely. It is a call to make present in time the Father's own love made present and experienced by us in

Jesus: "God so loved the world that He sent His only Son!"

The call to "love others" may conjure up for many of us different pictures. For some, family or friends may come to mind. For others, the members of one's own congregation or local community. And for still others, those with whom we work or those to whom we minister. To whom am I referring when I speak of celibacy as a call to love others? To these, but to more: to *all* our brothers and sisters. Celibate love is a love which is rooted in Jesus' own love, and therefore it is meant to be both *universal* and *sacrificial*. Celibacy is meant to stretch us, to call us beyond ourselves, even to the point of crucifixion. Through the gift of Jesus' own Spirit, the Spirit of love, we are progressively transformed and enabled to love as Jesus loves, to minister as Jesus ministers. Celibacy is a commitment to love others with the love of Jesus himself; it is a commitment to an affection and a concern that is universal, to a love that is *life-giving* and *without limit*. It is a commitment to "bring the good news to everyone."

Here we might ask about the social implications of the vow of celibacy. What does it mean, in our time, to love the other with the love of Jesus himself, when so many in our world are living in dire poverty, subject to the most oppressive, alienating, and dehumanizing social structures? Does not a genuine commitment to love, to love authentically and radically, imply a lifestyle and an apostolic involvement that address such issues, not only in their effects, but in their root causes? It is here, perhaps, more than any other area, that we need to see the relationship of celibacy to poverty. Our love requires a commitment to justice. Intrinsic to total consecration to Jesus is a commitment to his people that is also total.

In relation to those we know well, who are close to us, there may have been in the past a concern about what we called "particular friendships," friendships which were exclusive and therefore a violation of charity. Today there is a great emphasis on the importance of forming authentic friendships with both women and men. We believe that to be human is to be relational, and that to grow is to "encounter" a "thou." There is probably no area more singled out for condemnation in relation to celibacy today than the failure to love. This failure may manifest itself in aloofness, coldness, self-centeredness, or selfishness. Or it may be embodied in what one author calls "a protective partnership":

> a largely unrecognized conspiracy of two or more persons to maintain isolation and distance from others. . . . This relieves them of having to deal with the challenges of being intimate with others outside their clique . . . and protects those involved from psychic injury and threats of disconfirmation.[5]

It is often comfortable for us to isolate ourselves from those who think differently than we do, from those to whom we are not particularly attracted.

There is a tremendous need today for men and women vowed to celibacy to risk friendship, to learn how to enter into warm and meaningful relationships with others. Such relationships imply that I know and accept myself, that I am willing to share myself with others (this is the basic meaning of intimacy), and that I intend to receive the revelation of these others as gift. Although we cannot and do not relate to all in the same degree—neither did Jesus—no one should be excluded from our care and concern. This is especially true of the people with whom we live. We need to express our affection and care of one another in word, but most of all, in action. Our love must be embodied and enfleshed in a compliment, a look, a touch, an embrace. It must be expressed in the ordinary ways of day-to-day life. People must look at us and see "how much we love one another." Only then will celibate life lived in community be a prophetic sign of Christ's own love in its universal, unifying dimensions.

An area of special contemporary concern, and an area in which there are still many questions, is that of friendship between a celibate man or woman and a member of the opposite sex, celibate or non-celibate. With all that has happened within religious life in the past ten to fifteen years, the female-male relationship has taken on some new dimensions. I say "some new dimensions" because from my conversations with some sisters and priests, I realize that in the past there *have* been cases of close friendship, even ones in which there were frequent and intense physical expressions of love.

Today brothers, sisters and priests come into closer and more frequent contact with members of the opposite sex, and therefore it is only natural that friendships should be formed. What are the values of such friendships? What are the risks? A contemporary theology of celibacy must deal with both.

The value that I would like to emphasize first, and perhaps most strongly, is that of personal richness. If we truly believe that God created the human person in his image—"male and female he created them"—then we affirm a certain complementarity between the sexes. If that complementarity is manifest in the totality of relationship with members of the opposite sex, and not just in genital relationship, then there is a certain richness inherent in those relationships. That richness is not only a richness for those involved (and therefore possibly selfish), but it is a richness which can be gift to the Christian community and to the world-at-large. When Christ asked us to "love one another as I have loved you," he was asking us to love as he loved—not only Peter or John or the little children, but as he loved Mary and Martha, the prostitutes and sinners, the women who accompanied him (see Lk 23:49).

Because the friendship about which I am talking involves women and men who are celibate, the relationship must always be seen within that context, within the context of a unique and special love for Christ, which means that I intend not to marry another. If the love between friends is genuine and authentic, if it is truly self-giving and not selfish, if it is honestly Christian, the following dimensions must be present.

1. There must be a deep concern for the vocation of the other, a desire that the other continue to respond to the call of Jesus as that has been discerned. There must be the same desire for oneself.

2. The relationship must be Christ-centered. I must love the other in Christ or the other with the love of Christ which is my love. Here we see the absolute importance of honest, persevering prayer.

3. The relationship must be seen in relation to other, often prior commitments—my ministry, my community. Does my relationship with my friend nurture and increase my giftedness to my ministry, to my sisters or brothers in community?

4. The relationship must not take on those aspects of exclusivity and physical expression that normally lead to the exclusivity and physical expression *proper to marriage.*

Perhaps today, more than ever before, there is a need in our world for the presence of warm, affectionate, life-giving relationships with members of the opposite sex that do not involve genitality. So often the culture implies that all male-female relationships must end in genital expression if they are to find fulfillment. Authentic relationships between men and women are a needed counter-cultural stance! Our culture extols power, pleasure, and possessions, and therefore our vows of obedience, celibacy, and poverty speak a much-needed creative and liberating word. As one writer put it,

> . . . a reclaiming of the gestures of affection from the tyranny of genitality might well bring relief and encouragement to those who otherwise see no alternative but to choose between promiscuity and aloofness. It might also be of some help to people wrestling with problems of homosexuality.[6]

In no way do I want to deny the degree of wholeness and holiness or the discipline required for deep male-female relationships to continue within a celibate commitment, but I am hopeful that such relationships are possible today, and that our time might even have a Francis and Clare, a John and Teresa, a Jane de Chantal and Francis de Sales.

We have looked at celibacy as a commitment to love, a commitment to love Christ preferentially and to love others universally with warmth and affection, with genuine concern. Lastly, I would like to consider celibacy in relation to the woman or man who is becoming "unmarriageable for the kingdom," who is growing as a celibate lover.

The Celibate Relationship to Self

First I would like to affirm what I should have affirmed perhaps at the beginning, and that is that celibate love, or love in any case, is more than a matter of feeling. It is much more a matter of *intentionality,* an intending to give oneself to and for another, a determination to reach out in care and concern. There will be times when Jesus will seem far away, when one feels the loneliness of being without a husband or wife and children, when one feels that there are not that many significant others in one's life or that they, too, seem far away, when one feels the lack of possessions, the rootedness of one's own home. Such feelings are not an indication that we are not called to celibacy or that we are failing as celibate lovers, but that we are human, and thank God, normal. It is also important to realize that we are sexual beings, men and women, that we have bodies. There are times when we will want to have someone hold us, embrace us, perhaps even go to bed with us. There are times when we will desire genital pleasure. At such times it is important that we accept ourselves as we are, women and men with needs and emotions, with bodies, that we continue to accept ourselves as God himself made us.

What is important with such feelings and desires is not whether we have them or not, but what we do with them. Are we willing to use them as an opportunity for growth, for deeper commitment to celibate love? When I am lonely, am I willing to turn to Christ, admit my loneliness, and ask for his help? Am I willing to reach out to another who may have even greater need than I? Or do I take the easy way out and try to fill the gap—perhaps with more work or an accumulation of things? Here we see our celibacy related to poverty. To be truly celibate is to be willing to experience emptiness, dependence, loneliness, to be open to a fulfillment that Christ alone can and wants to give.

Renunciation is intrinsic to all Christian life and certainly to religious life with its vows. Renunciation, however, *if* it is Christian, must always be a participation in the death-resurrection mystery of Jesus. This means, therefore, that the dying we accept is never meant to be an end in itself, but a means to greater life and growth. God does not ask us not to feel pain or loss, but only to use them creatively and, with his help, to grow. The renunciation that is intrinsic to vowed life in community is meant to bring about life-in-abundance—for us and, through us, for others (Jn 10:10).

In talking to many sisters and to some priests, and in dealing with some in spiritual direction, I have found that there is a great tendency to look upon one's own struggles with celibacy as unique. "No one could possibly feel as I have felt, desire as I have desired, or done as I have done" (the latter may refer to a struggle with masturbation, a homosexual incident, or some heterosexual lapse). It is here, perhaps more than in any other area, where my trust in the Lord's unique love for me, the love and understanding of friends, and the support of a loving community are crucial. One contemporary writer comments,

> We search out a director to do what our next door neighbor could better accomplish if only she were not afraid or he were more sensitive, if only they would listen, care, share their own bent and broken dreams. In fact, it seems to me that the possibility of living out a loving celibacy is in direct proportion to a community's ability to talk openly about the subject. How few communities provide such support.[7]

Friends of mine who are heavily engaged in spiritual direction, both women and men, have told me that some religious have so few opportunities to share intimately with others that the spiritual director, with whom one naturally shares what is deepest and most intimate, is sought after as the continual confidant, the intimate friend. What a distortion of the direction relationship! And what a disaster for the director who might have thirty directees, all of whom want to have her or him for their closest and most intimate friend!

Celibacy involves growth; sexual and spiritual maturity involve process, a continual becoming the person we are called to be, through and with Jesus, through and with others. Celibacy is a call to wholeness and to holiness, and this involves discipline, patience and care. We are pilgrims; we are on the way.

The Eschatological Dimensions of Celibacy

This brings me to the final point and that is the eschatological dimensions of celibacy. As Karl Rahner points out, "renunciation is basic to the evangelical counsels" and it is

> renunciation that is meant to give unambiguous witness to a faith that transcends the present. The renunciation involved in accepting a call to live poverty, celibacy, and obedience is not only a sign of God's grace offered, but of that grace as received and manifested in concrete human lives.[8]

The celibate woman or man says in her or his whole being that *God is,* that in a deep love-relationship with Jesus there is possible a fulfillment which at least equals, if not surpasses, the fulfillment made possible in commitment to another human being. The celibate person by his or her commitment to love universally and sacrificially, authentically also points to the love of God made manifest in Jesus. By concretizing in our time and our history the love of Father, Son and Spirit, we point to a charity that is gift, a charity which, though ever maturing, is still to reach perfection. "And hope does not disappoint us, because God's love has been poured into our hearts through the Holy Spirit which has been given to us" (Rom 5:5).

The celibate man or woman, ever dependent upon the grace of God if his or her commitment is to continue and to deepen, points not only to the in-breaking of God's graciousness in time, but to a union still to come, to that moment when Christ the Spouse says to his Bride, the Church, "Come!" and takes each of us, and all of us to himself in love that is eternal. The celibate is one who says, not only in word but in *body,* "all things are mine, and I am Christ's, and Christ is God's" (I Co 3:22). Celibate love, rooted as it is in divine love, witnesses to a transformation that is to be corporately liberating and unitive, one in which, together with Christ, we bring about a new heaven and a new earth. Celibacy, in the depth of its charity, is an anticipation in time of a fulfillment yet to come.

NOTES

[1]Patrick L. Carroll, S.J., "Becoming a Celibate Lover," *Sisters Today* 50 (Nov. 1978), pp. 174-79; William Ribando, C.S.C., "Celibacy: Gift for Loving," *Sisters Today* 49 (Dec. 1977), p. 230; Donald Goergen, *The Sexual Celibate* (New York: The Seabury Press, 1975), p. 202.

[2]Th. Matura, "Le Celibat dans le Nouveau Testament," *Nouvelle revue theologique* 6 (1975), pp. 481-500; pp. 593-604 give an excellent survey of recent studies on celibacy in the New Testament. The key work in English which questions the presence of a call to celibacy in Mt 19 is that of Quentin Quesnell, S.J., "Made Themselves Eunuchs for the Kingdom of Heaven (Mt 19:12)," *Catholic Biblical Quarterly* 30 (1968), pp. 335-58. See Jerome Kodel, O.S.B., "The Celibacy Logion in Matthew 19:12," *Biblical Theology Bulletin* 8 (Feb. 1978), pp. 19-23, for a position contrary to that of Quesnell.

[3]Edward Schillebeeckx, O.P., *Celibacy*, trans. C.A.L. Jarrett (New York: Sheed and Ward, 1968), p. 105.

[4]Ann Goggin, r.c., "The Heart of My Days," *Encounter* (Spring-Summer, 1975), pp. 3-4.

[5]Philip D. Cristantiello, "Psychosexual Maturity in Celibate Development," Review for Religious 5 (1978), p. 655.

[6]Simon Tugwell, "Celibacy," *The Furrow* 28 (June 1977), p. 345.

[7]Carroll, p. 180.

[8]Karl Rahner, "On the Evangelical Counsels," *Theological Investigations*, VIII, tr. David Bourke (New York: Herder and Herder, 1971), p. 166.

Poverty, Time, Solitude:
A Context for a Celibate Lifestyle

Anthony Wieczorek, O. Praem.

Volume 41, 1982, pp. 655-659.

Celibacy is a dimension of a religious way of life. To be understood, therefore, celibacy must be seen in the *context* of religious life. The meaning of celibacy arises out of its relationship with the complementary vows of poverty and obedience, as well as out of the significance of communal life, prayer, and basic Christian virtue. Seen out of the context of all these elements, celibacy suffers a deprivation and a distortion.

From the outset, it is important to be reminded that celibacy is not simply an ethic. Taken out of its context, celibacy is often reduced to being a moral directive—a negative moral directive. Celibacy is much more than a set of specific sexual mores; it is an extension of Christian virtue, a continuation of it. The sexual demeanor proper to celibacy rests upon Christian virtues and values such as respect for human dignity, single-heartedness, the sacredness of human life, a deep appreciation for what friendship and love can be, compassion, selflessness, and service.

A discussion of celibacy must begin here. Before a decision can be made about living celibately, the question must be considered: What does it mean to live a Christian way of life? Am I willing to live with the restraints and limitations imposed upon me, not by celibacy, but by basic Christian values?

Only after a person is willing to try to understand, accept, and live a Christian way of life can the matter of celibacy be addressed. Without this prior realization and commitment, celibacy has no context, no depth of meaning, and is left to be nothing more than just another "Thou shalt not. . . ."

To see at least some part of the richness and potential of celibacy, it must be viewed as a *dedication to poverty*, a *devotion of time*, and a *dependence upon solitude*.

Celibacy as a Dedication to Poverty

The vow of celibacy stands nearest to the vow of *poverty*. Hence, it is an understanding of poverty that sheds the most light upon an understanding of celibacy. If poverty as a way of life cannot be embraced, neither can celibacy.

Poverty is precisely a way of living. It is much more than not having the money to buy something .To be poor means to be without many of the everyday options and opportunities that people who are not poor have. To be poor means, among other things, to live in a constant situation of restriction and limitedness.

A poor person has not the option of going to a movie or a ball game, of eating apple pie or cherry, of going to one restaurant rather than another, of wearing these shoes or those, this coat or that. Very often poor people do not have these options because they do not have the physical resources that allow for them. Yet despite being deprived of these "necessities" the poor can live happy and holy lives.

The fact of poverty, the force of its physical reality, compels people who are poor to live according to needs and not simply wants. Poverty can "cleanse" us of the unnecessary. It can put us into a situation where we are able to more clearly distinguish between a need and a want. Poverty can liberate us from the bondage of wants, leaving us free to pursue our true needs, those things without which we cannot fully live a human life. Poverty can be humbling by forcing us to face our needs but it can also teach us that happiness lies not in having every want satisfied but in having our true needs satisfied. Seen in this light, poverty is the paradigm for celibacy.

Celibacy is not simply a deprivation, it is a way of life. Therefore, it must be a way of relating. While we can be impoverished in some ways of expressing love, we can be rich in others. After all, intimacy does not depend upon sexual expression any more than a meaningful gift depends upon price. The very restrictedness of our expression can heighten the value of a poem or letter or a simple touch or smile.

Celibacy, like poverty, can teach true gratitude for the beauty and preciousness of relationships. Celibacy has the potential to "cleanse" us of what is not essential and let us see what we truly need to both give and receive from people—the trust, the sharing, the dreaming. Celibacy does not demand that we repress our needs. Rather, it points them out in bolder relief and challenges us to distinguish between the frustration caused by the deprivation of needs and that caused by the deprivation of our wants.

It sometimes requires just as much creativity to live celibately as it does to live in poverty. Do I have the grace to express myself creatively to others? If the limitedness of deliberate impoverishment can be willfully chosen and reason for gratitude in one's life still be found, if one can be satisfied to have needs fulfilled even if wants must go unsatisfied and yet remain appreciative and joyous, then perhaps such a person truly has the grace, the call to live celibately.

Such a call is a gift. It is the nature of gifts to be both given and received. Therefore, it is quite possible to refuse the gift of celibacy. One of the most common ways of refusing celibacy is by being filled with self-pity.

It is not uncommon to hear celibates of all ages bemoan their celibacy the way an amputee bemoans the loss of a limb. Like some amputee victims, celibates can easily become lost in the conviction that they are only half human, that they are not whole. The way to overcome such feelings is not by trying to prove manliness or womanliness. Rather, the challenge is to find worth and dignity in who we are, in the deeper and more lasting qualities of humanness like compassion, the ability to listen, to laugh, to be grateful, to stand outside ourselves at the service of others. Our humanness depends upon our ability to love. *That* we love and are loved is a need. *How* we love and are loved is a want. Celibates live in the poverty of not having all their wants satisfied. Celibacy means distinguishing between needs and wants, accepting what cannot be, and finding satisfaction, thanksgiving, and peace in what is.

Celibacy as a Devotion of Time

One thing that poverty does provide in abundance is *time*. Being bereft of options does free up large amounts of time.

Celibacy likewise provides an abundance of time. The challenge is how that time is to be spent, what our time is to be devoted to. Celibacy, for example, frees us from the time it takes to raise a family, but what does it free us *for?*

Ideally, perhaps, we are freed for prayer, reading, study, even the opportunity to take time to see and wonder and dream. Celibacy also frees us to serve, to be available for people. Yet if all we do is remain available for work and devote little or no time to prayer and reading, we are distorting celibacy by removing it from a critical dimension of its context.

A big danger for both celibates and non-celibates is that they give themselves more to their jobs than to God and their families or communities. It is this issue, the proper use of time, that causes one of the biggest consternations for celibates. The tendency toward entrenchment in work can be an escape from intimacy, but it is also true that many of the occupations engaged in by celibates are extremely time-consuming and energy draining. Moreover, it is work which simply must be done. The tension between giving time and taking time is not lessened by the fact that most celibates do recognize the necessity for being present to community and for entering into solitude with God.

A celibate lifestyle that does not allow for time not only to recreate but also to read and reflect cannot give life to the celibate. Such a lifestyle will consume that person instead. One of the challenges and disciplines of celibacy is the proper use of time.

While celibacy ought to provide time, in practice it often does not. Here, too, celibacy shows a connection with poverty. The poor guard and dispense their resources carefully. So too with the celibate's dispensing of time.

Workaholism is as much a threat to celibacy as sexual licentiousness—perhaps even more so. Our consciences are sensitive to the issue of sexual restraint but not to making mistresses out of our work. Our culture emphasizes efficiency, productivity, and frowns upon anything that hints of wasting time. Therefore, celibates who find even a little free time quickly and perhaps unconsciously fill it in by *doing* more.

Yet celibacy as a lifestyle requires time to be set aside not for doing but for being. Time is a gift many celibates refuse to accept because in part they are afraid to take it. Time only makes the loneliness echo more loudly. Time takes away excuses. It confronts us. Yet time in a celibate lifestyle is essential, for it provides the panorama that enables us to see what we are to move toward. It gives us the opportunity to see and address our needs. Time must be part of every celibate's life, for without that time celibacy loses its context and the solitude that nourishes celibacy cannot be obtained. While celibacy ought to provide time, it is a commodity which so few celibates seem to have. Yet time is an essential resource for the celibate for it alone can acquire solitude for us.

Celibacy as a Dependence Upon Solitude

Celibacy cannot be endured, let alone lived, without the time to enter into *solitude* with God. Only by freely and gratefully embracing solitude can a person find life in celibacy. Solitude is not loneliness but aloneness, time apart to be alone with oneself and with one's God. Solitude for the celibate is essential for several reasons. Solitude teaches surrender. It strips away the illusion of wants. It is a confrontation with what is real, of what is essential, of what is true. Solitude teaches sight. In the stillness of solitude we see what we would ordinarily have overlooked, assumed, or taken for granted. Through solitude, we are taught to appreciate, admire, and wonder. Solitude teaches sensitivity. Compassion comes from seeing with another's eyes. Solitude makes one hungry to enter into another's life deeply, personally, respectfully, and gently.

But often celibates do not embrace solitude. Instead we try to fill in our time with possessions, work, television, and peripheral friendships. Yet it is essential that celibates in particular spend time in solitude so as to spend time with God.

In solitude we take time to share in God's aloneness. It is in solitude that we can more deeply fall in love with God. If a celibate does not put an effort into being at peace with solitude, into making a friend of solitude, not only does God become a stranger, but we become strangers to ourselves, and celibacy becomes an empty taunt and an ache. Solitude is so important for celibacy because solitude is a quiet moment with God in the privacy and intimacy of one's own heart.

Solitude is the backdrop for the silence we need to hear the Word of God. Solitude is the setting for prayer. It directs our life back to God. There is something about solitude that draws us back to center. If we are afraid to spend time with ourselves in the aloneness of our center, we will not come to commune with the silent places of God.

The prayer that comes from solitude is the celibate's life blood. Without prayer, celibacy will not, cannot, endure. Without solitude spent with God we become strangers to him and so to prayer. Prayer may lead us out of a celibate lifestyle, but without prayer the apparent emptiness and futility will drive us out of it.

Solitude, far from removing us from relationships, prepares us for them. In solitude we have the setting in which to know ourselves, to see ourselves truly, to hear ourselves honestly. To enter into solitude is to venture into the truth of ourselves—be that what it may. With that knowledge we are free to interact with people as persons. With a sense of our own depths we can move toward the depths of others and together with them enter in faith into the depths of God.

Conclusion

For a full understanding of what celibacy is, it is important that a person move beyond the initial frustration and unnaturalness of living a life of Christian virtues and enter into the discovery of the real mystery and beauty of celibacy. Celibacy centers around accepting solitude, welcoming time, and living in gratitude. It is such things as these that make celibacy seem unnatural. It is not acceptable or typical to be poor, to have time for oneself and for prayer, or to enter willingly into the solitude of one's own soul. To so many, the "unnaturalness" of celibacy is reduced to sexual denial, the deliberate refusal to marry and raise a family. Yet these are only peripheral issues. The seriousness of these issues, however, underscores the deeper difficulty of celibate life. Celibacy is not only an orientation *away from* family and spouse (which is hard enough), it must be an orientation *toward* poverty, time, and solitude.

Celibacy itself is neither the sacrifice nor the offering. What we do with celibacy is. The beauty and fulfillment in celibacy is found not in what it moves us away from but in what it compels us toward. To find peace and sanctity in celibacy, it is not so important what we purposely and deliberately deny. Rather, it is much more important what we willingly and lovingly embrace.

Vowed Celibacy and Human Sexuality

M. Keith, O.S.F.

Volume 44, 1985, pp. 521-527.

There is no doubt that the mentors of our society today, probably at no time more so in history, have placed a great deal of emphasis on complete sexual fulfillment as the answer to everything. Heavy demands are placed on people for self-fulfillment via genital satisfaction. New patterns of sexual manners and morals arise constantly. This stress on genital intimacy makes it even more difficult to ignore. Media blitzes, which overtly and covertly proffer a barrage of sexual invitations to genital intimacy to the whole of society, at times overwhelm people. It can be said then, without a doubt, that our culture's emphasis on genital sex does provide at least subliminal seduction to all.

Therefore, in this age, with its stress on genital intimacy for self-fulfillment, celibacy seems an impossible contradiction to the expectations for life which most people hold as a value. Lifelong celibacy, deliberately and freely chosen in the face of one of the most sex-oriented of societies, seems like the ultimate madness.

To choose celibacy is a challenge to the cultural idols of hedonism and consumerism. Not only does our culture attack the value of celibacy, western attitudes also undermine even the previous supports that once were available for the celibate lifestyle. In fact, in some ways, ours is the most discouraging culture possible for a celibate option. Celibacy today demands the courage of a totally countercultural stance.

Today it is much harder to avoid coming to grips with sexuality than it used to be. We are more aware how much sexuality pervades a person's entire life situation. One's sexuality is seen to extend to every level of being: bodily, emotional, intellectual and volitional.

More specifically, human sexuality is a powerful stimulus to move toward others and away from self-centeredness. Human sexuality thus helps attenuate ego-centrism, which dehumanizes both self and others.

"Genital sexuality," of course, refers to acts, thoughts, fantasies, desires and feelings which involve or promote direct genital behavior. It is in this sense that today's society holds to the notion that humanity is impossible without full gratification of the sex drive.

Such, however, is not a universal truth. It is the purpose of this paper to show that a vowed celibate is and can become a fully integrated, psychosexually mature being without genital sex.

Human sexuality is a basic ontological determinant of who we are as persons, and personal identity is a prerequisite for sexual maturity/identity. This personal identity is, in significant ways, worked out within images of sexual identity and sexual complementarity. Such is fully attained only in the arena of human relationships.

Psychological research shows that the incidence of sexual difficulties and immaturity is neither greater nor less among celibates than among non-celibates. Psychologist Abraham Maslow (1954) pointed out that it is not sexual abstinence as such that is pathogenic, but the feelings or motivations accompanying it.

> It is now well known that many cases are found in which celibacy has no pathological effects. Clinical work with non-neurotic people gives clear answer that sexual deprivation becomes pathogenic in the severe sense only when it is felt by the individual to represent rejection by the opposite sex, inferiority, lack of worth, lack of respect, isolation, or thwarting of basic needs. Sexual deprivation can be borne with some relative ease by individuals for whom it has no such implications.

Religious celibates in no way deny or wish to reject their sexuality. In fact their understanding of their celibacy and of their sexuality matures as they advance in age and experience. Becoming an enlightened and responsible sexual being is always a lifelong challenge. This challenge involves, among other things, the development of psychosexual maturity. And the goal of psychosexual maturity is not orgasm; it is the capacity to love.

In the celibate, this maturity is evidenced in the fuller development and harmonious interplay of the individual's psychological and sexual capacities within an ordered value system. Dr. Menninger has stated that "Insofar as choice determines behavior, it stems from some consideration of values." Psychosexual development in the celibate quite evidently cannot be isolated from choice and values. There is no realistic way of doing so.

In choosing celibacy, then, what is at issue is not a negation of any human good or value. It is rather a relativizing of priorities in life. In choosing a celibate lifestyle, it is a tribute to the values in life that one chooses to celebrate. Celibacy lived means to the individual that: 1) the development of full humanity is more important than genital sexual expression; 2) that true generativity is greater than sexual potency; 3) that self-transcendence is more fully human than self-fulfillment.

Psychosexual maturity is not static; it is a dynamic, ongoing process. Whether a person becomes a celibate or marries, the same maturity, acceptance of self as a sexual being and the ability to live with impulses and integrate them into the self, is a requirement to achieve full humanity.

The bald fact of not being married, of not being involved in a sexual relationship does not constitute the celibate life. To be a vowed celibate means *to be empty for God,* to be *free and open* for his presence in many people and to be *available* for his service.

In the past, perhaps, it was not uncommon for some religious and laity to think of celibacy as a state of being asexual. In fact, though, vowed celibacy is not an asexual state, even though it precludes full genital intimacy. Taking vows does not snuff out personality. To say that a vowed celibate drops out of the sexual rivalry game doesn't suggest that the person is no longer a sexual being. It is normal to have sexual feelings.

Modern modes of expression would say that the celibate is still fully a sexual being, but without actual genital expression. As stated above, becoming an enlightened and responsible sexual being is a lifelong process; and the celibate, like all other humans, must redirect the tendency to regress into becoming selfish. Celibates need to realize that sexual abstinence does not automatically confer the capacity to love people in general any more than incontinence in marriage increases the love for anyone. As a matter of fact, though, one difference in the celibate lifestyle is that it does move toward a more freeing love than do other lifestyles.

The heart of vowed celibacy is rather a special, unique and total consecration to Christ. The true celibate is effectively head over heels in love with God. Vowed celibacy is a commitment to love Christ.

This is achieved by a genuinely mystical form of life. Without some grasp of mystical vision, the celibate is unlikely to remain celibate for long. The depth and quality of personal prayer manifests itself in the depth and quality of vowed celibacy. Without vision, there is risk of psychic damage. Ignace Lepp (1963) states that ". . . the libido cannot be channeled in a different direction without injury to sexuality, unless it finds itself entirely consumed in the service of a higher psychic activity."

This sublimation means to *redirect* the sexual drive. It does not mean to pretend that the sex drive doesn't exist, or to forget it, or to set it aside. Sublimation channels the sexual impulse; it does not stamp it out. But in attempting sublimation, the person must be free and sufficiently motivated by life-ideals which can actually utilize these sublimated energies.

The vowed celibate life, attempted without convictions and some form of mysticism, is an attempt at sexual suicide and self-destruction. If lived without an internal conviction, the response will be the simple negation of all the good of life and love and humanity in the individual. One's vowed celibacy cannot be a complete withdrawal of all involvement in human sexuality; such a step would be the denial of humanity.

Rather, consecrated celibacy must become a positive affirmation of beauty and strength. The vow of celibacy, lived with faithfulness, speaks out against the negative aspects and excesses of the sexual revolution of our time. It contradicts the contemporary attitudes where infidelity and failure to keep commitments is an accepted way of life.

Celibacy makes a positive contribution to life since Christian celibacy is an explicit affirmation that a person is *a person* first and not second to his or her sex function. It provides a deeper insight into the sexuality of persons themselves. Vowed celibates are seen as total persons, not as individuals dichotomized into body/spirit.

Authentic celibacy, then, is an enfleshed experience. Celibacy cannot be understood in isolation. It is experienced in a heterosexual society. It is a growing life experience in and with Christ. This means growing in love with Christ and growing in prayer with Christ. The effects of this lead celibates to a growth and deepening in their love for all people, especially for all those with whom they come into contact. Their response will grow, become actualized and manifest itself in time. And like all love, it defies description.

Mature love does not come easy; it is always a growth process. For the celibate, this entails a process of growing as a sexual being. It is a continual becoming of the person the celibate is called to be through and with Christ. Thus celibacy is a call to wholeness and holiness that involves patience, discipline and care. Far from lessening our need of the experience of love, celibacy offers a greater freedom in loving—a freedom to love, at times, without hope of returned love, and to love the unlovable. This form of unselfish love witnesses to the compassion and mutual respect which are integral to justice, and moral rightness.

Celibates live fundamentally independent lives; lives not directed to the well-being of the single destiny for two that is common to marriage, but directed by the demands of Christ and the Church. Religious celibacy is for loving and living.

Celibate love is primarily universal in character. It is a call to be constantly open to authentic relationships, to befriend any person met with a non-demanding love. It thus is a challenge to celibates to become the persons they are meant to be, to maximize their love and self-giftedness to others. The challenges and rewards of celibacy are the challenges and rewards of love itself. The celibate experience, in sum, is a way of making love, somthing everyone must do, and, like all lovemaking, it defies close scrutiny. Like all lovemaking, it is a relational experience beyond words.

Another great value of the celibate experience is that of availability. The vowed celibate belongs to no one person, hence to all persons. There is risk to this. Depending on how it is lived, celibacy can either render the individual sterile or productive. Unless there is a giving away of self, celibacy is supreme sterility. Lived positively, selflessly, celibacy can be distinctively and consciously creative. These creative powers can be termed "generativity."

Generativity is the ability to give, nurture, and sustain life. Erikson states that: ". . . to know that adulthood is generative does not necessarily mean one must produce children. But it means to know what one does if one does not produce children."

In Erikson's eight stages of the development of the person, generativity characteristics of adult life are met even in institutions committed to celibacy.

Celibates believe that they will attain a sense of generativity through loving relationships with people, thus creating life. The celibates' self-abundance and vitality and life-giving existence will be evidenced by their presence and participation in the world. Specifically, the generativity found in vowed celibacy is a commitment to a care and concern that is universal; to a love that is life-giving and without limit.

Although there is total and exclusive intimacy between the vowed celibate and Christ, this does not exclude other relationships. In fact intimacy with Christ depends on other relationships to make it possible. Friendship and support are necessary to the celibate, as is deep prayer and honesty before Christ. Religious celibacy has everything to do with interpersonal relationships. The celibate is a person firmly planted on earth for relating to others. Indeed, to be human is to be relational. And, of course, the psychosexually mature celibate loves individuals, not abstract humanity.

Today there is a great emphasis on the forming of authentic friendships among both men and women religious. Research has shown that good psychosexual development involves and demands relationships with a variety of people. Drs. Conrad Baars and Anna Terruwe, who have integrated psychiatry with their faith, note that masculine/feminine relationships, as well as same sex friendships, help to develop a wholesome emotional life.

There can be no genuine happiness without friendships. Friendships, however, are not easily acquired. They demand work, time and cultivation. Human relations are never finalized. Celibacy also requires the development of a capacity for deep and lasting relationships. Friendship in the lives of religious celibates takes many forms. As one moves across the spectrum from acquaintance to friendship, however, the reality of celibacy becomes more pertinent.

The love of authentic friendship is not easy, and there are those hurts and disappointments which are part of the "human condition" (Sr. Marie Dugas, S.S.A. 1983). But the benefits of friendship help make life worthwhile.

Jesus is the model for celibates. He loved all people. He also had several disciples and social friends. These friendships also developed through hurts, misunderstandings and disappointments.

The love experienced in celibate friendship is that of the giving and receiving of love. This experience introduces one into a new understanding of life and one's relation to life. It allows one to rid oneself of the unneeded, counterproductive defenses which hinder growth and integration. It allows one to be touched by the power beyond the self.

Research has shown that true growth and healing take place only in a relationship characterized by love. Celibates, then, should have close friends. The development of friendships in the celibate lifestyle is critical to internal/external integration which if properly pursued will result in an adequately mature personality.

Sexual urges will not put the celibate value system and behaviors out of sync in genuine friendship. The celibate friendship is less a response to physical attractiveness and more of a caring for what is good in the *person*. The celibate friendship is an attentiveness to the other in a flexible manner rather than in a fixation. Mutual love cannot mean mutual possession. Celibates are united in friendship only by the bond of their free will, a bond that is not indissoluble as is that of marriage. And celibate friendships normally do not simply happen. There is ever present the element of choice involved in who will be admitted, and to what degree of intimacy he or she will be admitted.

All people, not only celibates, fill their need for intimacy through friendships. Intimacy in human living is important for personal growth, self-esteem and for a feeling that life is worthwhile. The more we live in a mass society, the more important are intimate relationships to maintain our individuality and identity. For Abraham Maslow, in the self-actualizing person, the higher need is for intimacy. If this need is satisfied, the need for genitality is lessened.

Intimacy can be defined as unfeared self-abandonment, an unfeared self-disclosure and a dissolving of ego boundaries. In intimacy, one gives up control of what is seen by the other. It involves the sharing of one's real identity with others. Eric Berne (1974) calls intimacy a "game free" relationship.

Healthy interpersonal living always involves both distance and intimacy. A celibate person striving for universal love must realize that this does not mean universal intimacy. Intimacy requires disciplined living. Besides being grounded in one's own vocation, the celibate must affirm and desire the growth of the other. This non-possessive, non-exclusive love also encourages the growth of the other's relationships with people. The celibate is pleased when the other develops new, outside relationships and interests, knowing that they are the sources of life and growth. The celibate knows that it is important that people never stop growing in love.

One definition put it this way, "A friend is one who knows you as you are, understands where you've been, accepts who you've become and still gently invites you to grow" (Sr. Marie Dugas, S.S.A. 1983). This is the heart of intimacy for the celibate lover. If the intimate relationship is healthy, life-giving and creative, it will enhance the quality of the celibate's prayer life, of other relationships and the general well-being itself of the celibate.

Vowed celibacy is a viable lifestyle. Although the way of celibacy suits relatively few persons, it is in itself, and for those persons a "normal" way to be, a viable way to meet life and create it. Celibacy means distinguishing between needs and wants. It is a meaningful lifestyle. This life entails an act of radical rejection of some values in the culture that easily become idolatrous. Celibacy is much more than a set of sexual mores; it is an extension of Christian virtue. It is an act of affirmation about certain human and gospel values that easily become submerged in the culture.

The celibate lifestyle is thus prophetic in its witness. The celibate life lived in the Spirit of Christ can be a very profound and rewarding way of life. The celibate, by foregoing the type of mutuality found in marriage, is saying that no human efforts or human projects can ever achieve the full destiny possible for humanity. The celibate is saying that our full destiny is achievable, not by our own power, but through the power of Jesus Christ. Celibacy joyfully lived, presents an alternate vision. This lifestyle proclaims that the end of life is intimacy with God and others. Joyfully lived, this lifestyle points to what must ultimately be the end of any lifestyle, love of God and others for the "sake of the kingdom."

Far from being quixotic, celibacy simply is one way that some men and women find it in their heart to be worth following, a way to be fully alive in this world.

A Christian Is a Poor Man

Kevin O'Shea, C.Ss.R.

Volume 33, 1974, pp. 1019-1025.

Poverty is the most difficult dimension of religious life at present. It is the point at which the tension is greatest between spirit and institution. Institutional poverty is reasonable, moderate, and tolerable; in fact, it is argued if it should rightly be called poverty. Charismatic poverty is anything but reasonable, is beyond moderation, and is nearly intolerable; it takes its spirit from a new reading of the Scriptures and calls poverty by its real name. In this sense, poverty is in all likelihood the greatest ferment in religious life at present. What a renewal of chastity and of obedience have not achieved, may well be done, in alarming proportion, by this renewal of poverty. Paradoxically, it is not among religious alone that the renewal is coming. It is coming from men of the Spirit who are taking the gospel to mean what it says.

The position of the Gospels on poverty is strikingly clear. Christ's followers must leave all, and give it to the poor; they must leave the world, and become poor. It is all or nothing. It is not measured and calculated action. It is a form of divine madness. It is the foolishness of love.

The New Testament suggests three main motivations for such poverty. Poverty is a Messianic mystery; it is a kenotic reality; and it is an ecclesial communion.

Poverty a Messianic Mystery

A long Hebrew tradition pictured the Messiah (the Christ) as anointed by God to go among the poor, to be a man of the poor, to join the ranks of the poor, and to bring help and life to the poor. Jesus lived in the strength of this image; he shared the misery of the poor and did all he could to lessen it, and he waited there in it with the poor for God to come, in his own day, and remove

112

it. The poor were the people who had no resources of their own to assure them of a future and a hope. They were the dispossessed, the disappropriated, the displaced people of this world. They were literally the no-hopers, the have-nots, the forgotten people, the little people without a land. And it was to them that the Messiah came, and it was among them that he became one of them. Not because their misery was a good thing, but because it was a good thing to be among them and to share it, remove it, wait in it patiently till God would take away all tears from their eyes. To his disciples who followed him, the Messiah asked a Messianic lifestyle: the mystery of their incorporation in the ranks of the poor. A Christian, like the Christ, is a poor man.

Poverty a Kenotic Reality

The New Testament speaks of a disease of the Christian heart called dipsychia. It is a split psychology, a sort of spiritual schizophrenia. The Christian wants to give himself totally to God, yet he feels an attraction to the things that are easy and immediately in front of him. He is torn two ways. He lacks unity and integration as a single person. There is only one cure for this trouble in the New Testament: it is kenosis, the self-emptying of the person to the very roots of his human existence of which Christ gave him the supreme example of His life and death on the cross. It is only in that utter nothingness of kenosis that integrity is possible. There is no other "fulfillment." But this kenosis is not an attitude, a spirit, and a mentality of mortification, as the Greeks might have thought. It is tangible and real: a man leaves all he has, and becomes poor, nothing, empty, dead in the things he has prized. He knows the nakedness of the poor man. It is not poverty of spirit. It is poverty.

Poverty and Ecclesial Communion

There is a principle in the New Testament that what one gives up to become poor is given over to the poor, so that they are enriched by it. Christ was rich in laying a rightful claim to Sonship of God. Rich though he was in this respect, he became poor for us and did not cling tenaciously to this right for himself. Thus, through his poverty, we became rich in his very Sonship. In the Jerusalem community, the model and norm of radical following of Christ in the Church, no one kept his own things *(ta idia)*—shall we say that no one "did his own thing"—but each one's own things became thereby the things of all *(ta koinonia)*. It is poverty, then, in its genuine realism and in the self-emptying it implies, that constitutes communion and community. The Church is a community because it is a Church of the poor. Its common life is not a sharing of advantages each retains so that one complements the other; it is a giving of one's all to all and for all, so that in the emptiness of all there can be a truly communed life.

Emphases in New Testament Poverty

In these three New Testament motives of poverty, there is a strong emphasis on *all*—all is given, so that a poor man can be nothing and have nothing. There is no limit to the poverty that might be embraced. There is no poor man excluded from the reach of the gospel. There is no poor man that the Christian will not help, no poor man that he will not join. *Anawim* (the poor) is a plural word; and it has no limits of poverty. There is an instinct for the most needy, the most abandoned, the poorest of all.

In these motives, too, there is a new kind of consciousness inculcated in the Christian disciple. What he does, effectively, by external action, for the poor, is limited and, in the last count, not very effective; that does not matter. What matters is what happens to him, and to the poor, when he gets among them and joins them. It gives him a compassion, a self-forgetfulness, a tenderness, an ability to care that transforms him and communicates itself to the poor to whom he now belongs. In poverty, he has become an embodiment of love. He has begun to sense the reality of an incarnation. He has begun to learn to live as a "dropout" from the existence he might have clung to. He has gone to the castoffs from society, who will love him even if they know that he was not always one of them and is not so deeply rooted in misery as they are. He has gone away from the comfortable and complacent, who have struck him off from their lists. He knows the loneliness of the missionary among the *anawim*.

In these motives, again, there is an undreamt of realism and a stark simplicity. This poverty is not a philosophical theory; one does not muse that every creature is poor, or that man is a conscious beggar for his given existence from God. Nor is this poverty simply the acceptance of whatever limitations (or "poverty") are in fact in one's life, which for the moment cannot be removed. Nor is it the poverty of someone who equips himself to help others, and then looks around for needy people to help, and has to be content with less than ideal types to begin. In this poverty, one does not work out first the a priori conditions of poverty and then see how to implement them. There are really poor people before our eyes, and it is their poverty we must share, with them that we must become one in a self-forgetting and serving compassion. The poor are always with us. They are there, and we respond to them in an instinct of love, not in a calculation of reason.

The Gospel Poor Man

The lifestyle of the gospel poor man is then that of a worker among the battlers for existence, a struggler among the not-yet-assured, a sharer among the insufficiently endowed, humanly as well as spiritually. It is a simple life, frugal, hard-earned, frustrating, substandard, where one is not sure how one is to survive, where one lives with the poor on their terms, and on his own, where one lives well below the ordinary normal comfort one might have as the result of one's talents and energy. The gospel poor man gives his time and his self to the poor, and finds his place among them. He can say, "We poor."

The inspiration for this way of life is biblical. We could sum it up in slogan words that resonate anew today in the heart of the Church: words like Messiah, *anawim,* shalom, shaliah, diakonia, evangelion, eucharistia, the mercy of God.

Messianism, *Anawim,* Covenant, and Peace

There is a real resurgence of Messianism in the Church today. Christians are realizing that they are not Christians unless they fall in love with Jesus as Messiah and adopt his Messianic lifestyle. This means that they must fall in love with the poor of their own time, and adopt their lifestyle, for love of Jesus and the gospel of the poor. A resurrection theology, over two decades, has divested us of an exaggerated spiritualism in our spirituality. A poverty theology, stemming from a new Messian theology, will divest us of a remaining complacency in which we would persuade ourselves, if not others, that we share in the sufferings of the Lord without sharing the lot of his little ones.

The *anawim* are his little ones. Because they are the poor, they are the poor of God. God cannot help it—he must fill emptiness with himself. He cannot make a covenant except with the poor. It is to those who have neither a future nor a hope that he comes to make flow upon them a river of peace, and to bind himself to be in person their future and their hope. God laughs at those who would offer him their goods and their love, and, as it were, enter a two-way relationship with him: he loves one way, giving his all to those who have nothing and are nothing. After all, he must have his own way of, as it were, joining the poor, too, musn't he? For, to them, he gives his all.

This is what the *covenant* means, and this is the *shalom* it brings. Shalom does not mean peace, at least, if peace means a comfortable inner feeling of security, and no hostilities without. When God loves the *anawim,* and sends his Christ to them, he does not—immediately, at least—take away their poverty. They are still the poor, these poor of God. His shalom is not an anaesthetic so that they do not feel it. But it is shalom, and it is a trust and a faith and a certainty that he has not chosen the things that are, but the things that are not. It is a willingness to smile, even at death. For resurrection is assured, since the eschaton belongs to the *anawim.*

The simplicity of washing the feet of the poor and of serving them in their deepest human needs is itself a total lifestyle, and those who have heard the Messianic call have no option but to live it. It is not easy to wash a poor man's feet. They are dirty, they smell, and he will probably not thank you, but kick you in the face. You probably won't succeed, but you will know that there is a kind of happiness words can never explain in keeping on doing it. This is the diakonia of the gospel.

Gospel means good news. To proclaim the gospel means to speak, but much more to be good news to men. Some of my American friends have an unkind expression about a difficult and unattractive character: They say, "He's bad news." They also say of a genuine and real person, "He's good news." Jesus himself was this kind of good news to the little ones, to the poor. When he began his Galilean ministry, he read from the scroll of Deutero-Isaiah: "He has sent me to be good news to the *anawim.*" When we work in his name, in our apostolate, are we, ourselves, good news to men, to poor men? And do we realize that there is no such thing as a direct apostolate to the rich and the well-established, there is only a mission of Jesus and his disciples to the poor? The others get in to the extent that they, too, leave all and become members of the *anawim!*

Eucharistia and Mercy

Eucharistia—the giving of thanks, the celebrating of life, and saying now in Christ, for the past thanks, for the future yes. Shall we ever know the truth of that thanks for the past until we can bless the Providence that has made us poor men? Shall we ever say a total yes to the future until we can face it without any resources as the pure gift of our Covenanted Resource, the God of the poor? It is only then that we shall know him in the breaking of the bread of pilgrims, at the table of the poor, and discover in surprise that the Eucharist is the liturgy of the little ones.

It is true. God has no love that is not mercy. Mercy is his response, in his heart, to misery. To be among the first clients of his mercy, we must be his *anawim*. A vocation to his love is a vocation to our brother, the poor man. Recently, a student of mine at Fordham wrote these words as the conclusion of an assignment on the meaning of the apostolate:

> Are the people of the Word something special, or is it only their words? Will their lives speak to us? The eye and ear world is all sewn up by the talented admen of Madison Avenue. What is left to us? The heart world. The world where flesh speaks to flesh, heart to heart. Do not speak religious themes to me. Speak the Word that is in your heart, your experience of life, enriched, made more than human, by the saving power in it that is believable because you believe it. I do want to be told, not by hearing you but by knowing you. Or is that an issue? I ask you if you understand, and your answer is your life.

The Recovery of Messianic Man

This poverty of Messianic man we are beginning to see again in our time. It is the challenge of our conscience, this cry of the poor. We can no longer vaguely know that half the world is starving for food, and more than half of it for love, and write off the situation as bad luck, or permitted by providence, and promise to pray for it and count our own blessings. That is not the Christian life; indeed, it is not human life. The new global village is one parish. Every man is my neighbor, and it is a sin to regard a man as a stranger. The Church is beginning to challenge the reasonable moderation and balanced calculation of its stance before the secular reality of poverty in the world. Some would even speak of the end of a "Constantinian era" and the beginning of a new Messianic epoch where the Spirit shall anoint us and send us to the poor.

If this is true, it is but a beginning. We have yet a long way to go. When we try to relate this thinking with the established or recently adopted norms of institutional poverty among religious, the lines do not even meet. Juridic poverty had a place in the history of religious life, but it is not the same as evangelical poverty. Many, of course, in the name of realism, will remind us that just as we once spoke of "tending to perfection," an ideal we never reached, so here we must feel obliged only to tend to this perfection of poverty and Messianic life, not to reach it immediately. Yes, but the acid test of the new Christian conscience is that it cannot use this theological formula as an excuse from real and significantly new action. Formulated obligation cannot measure up to a charismatic spirit. Our conscience is telling us that we are suffering from compassion fatigue, that we have enjoyed the protection of our callousness, that we must now make a new option to be compassionate rather than honorable. Our skin must stretch around the globe, so that if any man hurts, we hurt with him, and do something about it.

The Cry of the Poor

Pope Paul has taken up this point in his apostolic exhortation to religious (*Il tempio massimo,* July 2, 1971). "Our contemporaries," he says, "question you with particular insistence about poverty." "You hear rising up, more pressing than ever, the cry of the poor." "Was it not to respond to their appeal as God's privileged ones that Christ came, even going as far as to identify himself with them?" It is a "pressing call for a conversion of minds and attitudes, especially for you who follow Christ more closely in this earthly condition of self-emptying." It calls for "a conversion of hearts, it is a call to love." What, in practice, will the cry of the poor demand of religious?

First, "It must bar you from any compromise with any form of social injustice."

Secondly, "It obliges you to awaken consciences to the drama of human misery."

Thirdly, "It leads some of you to join the poor in their situation."

Fourthly, "It calls many institutes to rededicate some of their works to the poor."

Fifthly, "It enjoins on you a use of goods limited to the requirements of your work."

Sixthly, "It is necessary that in your daily lives you give external proof of poverty."

Seventhly, "It is not normal to allow yourself everything offered to you."

Eighthly, "Earn your own living and help the poor by your work."

Ninthly, "You cannot purely and simply conform to your surroundings."

Tenthly, "Do not be excessively preoccupied with appearing to be poor."

All this is said in conformity with the patterns of obedience and specific apostolate in a given institute. It is a call from the needs of the times and the demands of the gospel. It is a vocation to discover Christ as a poor man.

Renewal and Poverty

Much energy has gone into the renewal of religious community. Sometimes one gets the impression that they are trying to be beautiful resident communities of loving relationships which might then, as an overflow, have something to contribute to the poor. This is heresy. The Church has no mandate to be a resident, domesticated Church. It is essentially missionary, a pilgrim, servant Church of the poor. It is only by living its vocation to poverty among the poor that it can discover the kind of community life Christ intended for it. Likewise, much work has gone into the renewal of authority and obedience in religious life. It will not fully succeed until authority becomes an initiation of new life among the poor, and obedience is a heeding of the cry of the poor. Again, much has been done to make religious life more human, more relational, more interpersonal, more affective. But the tenderness and the gentleness and the caring concern that we so desire, we must learn from our involvement with the poor. It is but another work for the meekness of the *anawim*.

Of the poor, it has been said, "Only he who sees the invisible accomplishes the impossible." Of the gospel poor man who goes to the poor, we might likewise say, "Only he who loves the unlovable is good news to the little ones."

Models of Poverty

Gerald R. Grosh, S.J.

Volume 34, 1975, pp. 550-558.

In his latest book, *Models of the Church,*[1] Avery Dulles elucidates five models[2] of the Church which he finds operative in the minds of the faithful. He analyzes each one in terms of the advantages and disadvantages that each model has in aiding Christian living. Ultimately, Dulles says that the Church is a mystery and that no one model can adequately encompass a mystery. Rather, he states that the models are mutually complementary like the different shades and colors that blend together to create a total picture. The book is very freeing since it allows for various models and opens up other dimensions of the Church—especially for those persons who are locked into one framework.

The aim of this article is to do for our notion of poverty what Dulles has done for our notion of the Church. In our time religious generally are uneasy about their practice of poverty. Often it seems that specific features of our practice of poverty can be amply justified if they are taken one by one. But the features taken all together, the total picture, clearly leave much to be desired. What is wrong? Where do we fail? Perhaps the failure in poverty, if indeed it is failure, results from a too exclusive concentration on one model of poverty, from our failure to let our own dominant model of poverty be balanced adequately by other models. It is the belief of this author that a clarification of the models involved would facilitate the discussion as well as the choices that are made.

I shall delineate seven models which I see operative in our discussions of poverty. I shall briefly describe each model, indicate the spiritual value which it strives to encompass, indicate its advantages and disadvantages, and list some practical suggestions which might be in accord with a given model.

1. Poverty as Communitarian Sharing

The call to religious life is a call to living the vows *in community*. Religious life witnesses to the experience of community as we share our lives together and work toward the common goal of preaching the good news of Jesus Christ. The vow of poverty, then, calls us to share not only our living together and working together but also our material goods. This is rooted in the experience of the early Church: "The whole group of believers was united, heart and soul; no one claimed for his own use anything that he had, as everything they owned was held in common" (Acts 4:32). This model of poverty as communitarian sharing points to the fundamental unity which we have as religious—namely, a unity of heart. We are all believers. We share a common vision of faith and hope. We are united in love. Each person's value is not what he owns or has, but who he is. So deep is our oneness that we live in community and share our possessions. The goal is the underlying unity of mind and heart.

One of the advantages of this model is that it aims at eliminating differences between "rich and poor" and focuses on the equality of all. It attacks the roots of ownership which can so easily foster vanity and greed. Thus whatever is given to one is given to the whole community and goes to "the common barrel." The spiritual foundation for this mutual sharing of goods is the mutual care that the members of a given community have for one another.

The disadvantage of this model is that it becomes more difficult to live as life becomes more complex. We know that we *need* certain things for apostolic use. How, then, does one regulate the quality and quantity of goods that are needed? How does one maintain the equality of all and the non-ownership of all? The traditional response to this dilemma has been to link the acquisition and use of goods with receiving permission for them from the superior. The underlying purpose of asking permission has been to aid our acting as non-owners and to help free us from the power that is present in ownership. But it has been difficult for individuals not to compare what they have with what others have and therefore to justify their own acquisition of the same thing or of something else. It has been difficult for a superior to say "no" to one where he has said "yes" to another. Furthermore, critics of the system have pointed out that an adult makes his own decisions and that this practice has often seemed infantile. Also, as superiors so readily grant permission, the requirement has come to be seen by many as a formality to be gone through or even ignored. It has also been difficult to draw a fine line between what one needs and what one wants.

In the judgment of this author, in so far as poverty has been linked to asking permission for goods, it has failed—whether one blames the notion itself or the persons who have failed to live it. However, the model of poverty as communitarian living does have something to offer us today. The essence of the model is the mutual sharing of material goods in community. It would seem to preclude the private appropriation of goods (personal TVs, personal cars, etc.). It would also seem to preclude the free disposition of one's salary, e.g., the buying of books or equipment, travel, relaxation, or even almsgiving.

2. Poverty as Simplicity of Life

The second model of poverty is that of the frugal lifestyle or "simplicity of life." This model focuses clearly on poverty as a fact, i.e., material poverty. The spiritual foundation of simplicity of life is that it aids to singularity of purpose and focus—namely on the Lord and His work. *Nothing* else matters that much. This model of poverty is easily linked with the model of poverty as union with the poor. Stated simply, this model of simplicity of life points to the fact that a poor man does not have a lot of material possessions or the free disposition of a lot of money.

The advantage of this model is that it can act as a deterrent or as a negative norm for how we spend our money. Does a poor person have a color TV or is he able to jet across the country, or have a stereo set? How often can the poor person or family afford steak? Lavish spending is seen as an insult to the poor who struggle for their food and their meagre existence. Such spending is also seen to imply contempt for human work and the dignity of man involved in working hard for a day's pay. Also, as with the model of poverty as communitarian sharing, this model takes away the sense of power that is involved in the possession of goods and in the lavish disposition of one's finances.

The advantage, then, of this model of poverty is that it keeps one mindful of his union with the poor Christ and honest in terms of what he spends. Its primary disadvantage is that it can cause one to be so absorbed in bookkeeping and penny-pinching that he loses the perspective of apostolic service.

However, there are also other possible disadvantages that can accompany this model. Too great an emphasis on material things can lead to a pharisaism which overlooks the more important poverty of spirit. It can also result in divisiveness and criticism within communities as some will need more things than others to carry out their apostolic work.

The particular way of living according to this model would call a person to be continually mindful of how his or her standard of life compares with the poor. Such things as careful personal and community budgets, economical automobiles, buying articles on sale, adjusting budgets to meet emergencies, are evidences of the living of this model of poverty.

3. Poverty as Apostolic "Disponability"

Another model of poverty is that of apostolic "disponability" and freedom, i.e., poverty as functional in the service of others. This model recognizes a wider dimension of poverty than just what involves material goods. Basically, one is poor in order to be at the disposal of others. Therefore, all that one has—in fact, all that one is—is at the beck and call of people in need. This model of poverty calls for total self-giving. Therefore, if a person has money or possessions, they are freely given away. One gives what one has freely received.

This also applies to one's person. One's knowledge, talents, energy, and time are also at the claim of others. The poor man, in this model, does not "own" himself or his possessions. Everything is at the service of others. Even security and safety are not to be clung to. This model is strengthened through detachment—the whole purpose of detachment being for selfless charity.

The advantages of this model are numerous. For one thing, the focus is outward and other-centered. The reason for our vows is for us to be of service to God's people. One does not love God without loving one's neighbor. One is free to use whatever will be helpful to others in their growing closer to the Lord. This model is very incarnational, taking seriously the use of material goods for apostolic purposes. It also acts as a corrective for a too introspective or too literal-minded practice of poverty. Another advantage of this model is its flexibility. It allows various practices of poverty depending on the persons to whom ministry is offered. Thus one might embrace the lifestyle of the middle class while working with them, whereas a much simpler lifestyle would be called for if one is ministering to the poor.

One disadvantage of this model is that its norm often becomes efficiency rather than apostolic effectiveness. Thus it is "more efficient" to drive to work than to take public transportation (after all, one's time is valuable and is at the service of others). So too one needs his own camera to make slides for a class in school or he needs a complete set of Aristotle to be a better teacher. The problem is not with this or that individual decision with regard to the use of goods. Each one can no doubt be justified. The problem is that the over-all impression which is given often bears little resemblance to the common meaning of "poverty."

Furthermore, in practice, this model is often very confusing since almost anything—even seeming contradictories—can be justified in the name of apostolic service. For example, this model has called many to spend themselves generously for others—even to getting "burnt out" at a young age. On the other hand, it is possible for another kind of person to come to the conclusion that he needs more leisure time in order to be more present and relaxed when he encounters others. And so in the name of "apostolic relaxation" he has his own stereo set or portable television and takes a winter vacation in Florida or a summer cruise in the Caribbean.

This model of poverty is lived out concretely in the prudent use of goods for apostolic service. Nothing is intrinsically useless for the apostolate. Consequently, the important thing is discernment and the spirit of detachment. Generally, if this model is to function successfully, it needs to be complemented by a corrective model which summons to material poverty.

4. Poverty as Visible Witness

This model of poverty calls forth a traditional value that has always been considered to be embodied in the vows, namely, the value of visible witness. In the traditional theology of the vows, they acted as a constant inspiring reminder that spiritual things are more important than material things. Thus poverty points to a freedom from the materialistic values of our society.

The advantage of this model is that it calls us to be contemporary in the living of our vows. Times change, but the need for the prophet is always there. We easily cling to possessions. Cultural values easily become absolutes. Being poor leaves us free to challenge our world with the radical message of love to which Christ calls us. This is especially true when our poverty is linked with some apostolic purpose. No one denies being touched by the simplicity of Mother Teresa or Jean Vanier and their work among the poor. In fact, they attract followers and co-workers, whereas many of our established religious communities have little attraction among the young. Current advocates of this model of poverty would see it linked with social justice. Through his lifestyle one can choose to go against the consumer-orientation of our American society. One can also let go one's need for security, thereby calling others to trust in the Lord as he does himself.

The disadvantages of this model are numerous. Our modern world with its scientific and technological advancement, is quite aware of the evils of poverty and, rather than freely choose it, desires to eradicate it. Furthermore, in an effort to be more fully apostolic, we feel called to use rather than to deny ourselves the fruits of today's progress. The result, however, is that the faithful are often scandalized rather than edified by our poverty. Such things as late-model automobiles (which are easier to maintain and bought at a discount "from one of our alumni"), new buildings with spacious grounds that often make our dwellings look like wealthy estates, nice furnishings, good food, and an open liquor closet—all meant to aid our apostolates as well as our psyches—give the picture of opulent living no matter how simply a particular individual might live. Expensive vacations, often financed by friends or relatives and meant to renew the spirit of the weary apostle, play havoc with the hope of portraying any similarity to the Christ "who had no place to lay his head." Far from challenging the materialism of our culture, our lives seem to be succumbing to it. The realization that our actual lifestyle may not be witnessing to material poverty has led some religious to desire to change the name of the vow to something like "detachment" or "gratuitous sharing."

A second disadvantage of this model is that, perhaps more than any other model, it is divisive of religious community. When one starts looking at "visible" witness, one *sees* many things and it is hard not to be judgmental. One can always justify one's own behavior; it is "the other" who is misguided. Thus, on the one hand, there is the person who calls for less use of material goods. Often, he becomes cynical, frustrated, and bitter if he meets with little response. It is also very difficult for him to avoid a pharisaical "I am better than you" attitude. On the other hand, there is the one who is challenged. This person has usually justified his or her way of life as necessary for apostolic service and consequently sees the challenger as someone who is idealistic and unrealistic. Sometimes this person also judges the challenger as hypocritical (calling to poverty in some areas but not in others) or pharisaical (judging self to be better than others).

If this model of poverty as visible witness is to work, it would seem that a radical conversion is necessary on the part of all—as every document on poverty in recent years has advocated. Furthermore, it would seem that, to function effectively, it needs to be united with other models, especially union with the poor and exploited.

Living this model of poverty is radical; it jars the lives of the people around us—as well as our own lives. It jars our desire for security and our adherence to the consumer-mentality. Living out this model of poverty might lead communities to sell their property and give the proceeds to the poor—as Jesus advised the rich young man to do. Such a model might also lead to getting rid of emergency funds that have been built up and to trust more fully in God's Providence.

5. Poverty as Union with the Poor and Exploited

Currently, the vow of poverty is being very much influenced by the theology of liberation which is emerging in the Third World. At the root of this theology is the recognition that economic and social freedom greatly affect one's spiritual freedom. In this context, a vibrant prophetic model of poverty has been emerging. It challenges the other models of poverty as being too narrow and limited. It recognizes that poverty has been embraced out of love for one's neighbor, but contends the meaning of "neighbor" has been limited, omitting the utterly poor and the exploited. The spiritual basis for this model of poverty is union with Christ as he is present in the poor and the oppressed.

This model treats poverty as an evil. Material poverty is a subhuman situation which was caused by man's sin, by his selfish economic and political exploitation. Material poverty is not a Christian ideal, but an evil caused by social injustice and therefore something to be eradicated.

In this model the religious embraces poverty as an act of love for the poor and exploited. He voluntarily choose solidarity with them in protest against the poverty which has been forced upon the poor. Love leads to identification with the other—in this case, with those who are oppressed.

The advantage of this model of poverty is that it does, in fact, witness to poverty. Furthermore, it is apostolic, attempting to respond to one of the most pressing needs of our time: the need to eliminate social, political, and economic injustice. It places the religious right in the center of the world "where the action is," trying to convert it. Furthermore, it treats man as a whole, recognizing the influence that social structures have on his ability to become free. It is also very contemporary: responding to the signs of the times, sympathizing with the struggles of emerging nations, recognizing the abuses within capitalism and colonialism as well as within totalitarianism, and acknowledging the unjust gap between rich and poor and the exploitation of the poor by those who hold political and economic power.

The disadvantage of this model of poverty is that it easily becomes one-sided. If one sides with people who are oppressed, then he stands against those who oppress them. He "loves" the oppressor through confronting him with his sin. It is difficult to take such a stance without becoming self-righteous, bitter, angry, and resentful. One should be certain first that he has seen the beam in his own eye, for no conversion or new life happens without compassion.

This model needs compassion as its corrective. It needs the realization that the oppressor is very often just as oppressed by sin—by greed, competition, loneliness, and unhappiness—as the one who is oppressed. The oppressor has often unconsciously "bought into" a system and social structure which hinders his own freedom and growth. This is an evil different from material poverty. Yet it is an evil that needs to be met. This model can focus too exclusively on material poverty and social oppression and miss the call to deeper freedom that comes to every person.

Obviously, one can live this model of poverty through living and working among the poor and exploited and embracing their lifestyle. But, in today's world, where our churches and institutions have become powerful, the expression of this model might well be political. Those in nations which exploit—and there is growing evidence of America's economic imperialism—will be called to challenge their governments and its economic foreign policy. In addition, a type of "over-seeing" of our larger corporations, and especially of multinational corporations, might be set up to ensure that they are just in their dealings with the poor. Our preaching and teaching might continually challenge the faithful to "repent" in the context of world injustice, as our bishops and religious leaders have been summoning us to do.

6. Poverty as Reliance on God Alone

Another model of poverty is spiritual poverty or poverty of spirit. This model cuts beneath material poverty to the root of all poverty—namely, the human condition. To be a man is to be poor in the face of God and to rely on God alone. It is to recognize that before God man of himself is nothing, he is powerless. To be a man is to be creature before Creator—to be utterly dependent on him for all.

This model of poverty takes the human condition seriously and sees it as the vehicle for happiness and grace. To be human is to exist in misery with needs. It is to be insecure in the face of death, change, and loneliness. It is to be plagued by doubts and a restless spirit. It is to experience the solitariness of human choice and the limitations of one's own potentialities. One is totally finite. Even to love is a gift from the other.

The spiritual basis for this model of poverty is the Incarnation where God accepts our humanity: "His state was divine, yet he did not cling to his equality with God but emptied himself to assume the condition of a slave, and became as men are," (Phil 2:6-7). The way to salvation, the way to freedom, is the acceptance of ourselves as we are in all our humanity.

The concrete embodiment of this model of poverty is usually expressed by detachment. One is detached from concerns about his own safety and goods and time and money. He seeks no security other than trust in God's Providence. It is the same goal that poverty as simplicity of life points to.

The advantage of this model of poverty is that it focuses one's attention beyond the material to the more ultimate situation of dependence on God and trust in his providence. It also serves as a basis for compassion when one accepts his union with all men and women in human weakness.

The disadvantage of this model of poverty is that it can easily be divorced from the concrete existential situation of time and space. We do live in a world which demands man's cooperation with divine grace. A false poverty of spirit can lead a person to non-involvement in the world, to a failure to engage in some of the apostolic exigencies of our time—especially in the struggles against the evils of social structures.

The concrete living out of this model will be a simple trust in God—neither seeking material goods nor avoiding them. The world is irrelevant. One uses material goods in so far as they help him find God; otherwise he avoids them. The spirit of detachment reigns. This might also lead to the abandonment of our financial stockpiling and of our acquiring salaries. We might see religious begging again. Also, as one sees one's person at the service of others, one comes to share one's weaknesses as part of living out this model. Perhaps, the "greatest" poverty of all is simply to be who one is—and to share his or her own weakness for the good of others.[3]

7. Poverty as Union with the Poor Christ

The final model of poverty is that of mystical poverty, i.e., poverty which is embraced simply out of desire to be one with Jesus, who had nowhere to lay his head and who emptied himself in becoming man. This is ultimately the most radical model and offers no other justification for itself than what is given from the perspective of faith.

The spiritual basis for this model is identification with Christ. Ultimately, this is at the root of all the other forms of poverty. Christ came to serve others and to be with them in love. In being poor, we choose union with Christ—the total Christ, head and members.

The advantage of this model of poverty is that it is compatible with all the other models whether they be apostolic, communitarian, or spiritual. The real reason why we choose to be poor is to be one with Christ who was poor and who loved the poor. This is a deep grace. Such a model reaches to the heart of the Christian revelation. It embraces the Paschal Mystery—the death and resurrection of Jesus and our own participation in it. It expects a "pinch"—some form of dying in our practice of poverty—yet it is deeply joyful. It clearly focuses on our living poverty as a response to love—the love Jesus showed for us in becoming man and dying for us.

It is hard to find any disadvantages to this model. Perhaps, the only disadvantage occurs if it becomes the exclusive model. Almost anything can be and has been justified in the name of Christ: excess in abstinence and excess in participation. It is difficult to make concrete suggestions as to how this model will be lived out. One hopes, ultimately, that every religious grows into having this as his or her motivation in being poor.

The first two models of poverty look to lifestyle, the next three to apostolate, and the last two to the interior spirit that underlies any external practice of poverty. Poverty as communitarian sharing points out that all the vows are founded in community and meant to help foster unity. Poverty as simplicity of life calls us to a fundamental material poverty that is shown in a frugal lifestyle. Poverty as apostolic "disponability" reminds us that community and frugality are not simply ends in themselves, but are meant to help us effectively to love our neighbor. Poverty as visible witness reminds us of the need to challenge contemporary culture and its consumerism-mentality. Poverty as union with the oppressed points to one of the most serious challenges in our contemporary world: social injustice and economic exploitation. Poverty as reliance on God alone is also a prophetic challenge to detachment and a crticism of a materialistic outlook. Finally, poverty as union with Christ calls us to the foundation of all Christian living: union with Jesus out of love for him and his people.

The various models of poverty are complementary and can act as correctives to one another. One can so focus inwardly on the spiritual life or on religious community that one loses sight of the apostolate. Or one can so focus on the apostolate that one's life of poverty becomes a charade. It seems that today there is a genuine call to a much simpler lifestyle—even a radically simple one—in the context of social injustice.

Many religious today suffer a malaise with regard to the practice of poverty. It is the opinion of this author that poverty as union with the poor and oppressed is meant to be the dominant model of poverty for the seventies. In our time—*now*—this embodies all the other models. It calls us to communitarian sharing, sharing our wealth and persons with the poor. Such sharing necessarily leads to a frugal lifestyle. It is fundamentally apostolic in terms of one of the most pressing problems of our times: economic and social injustice. It challenges contemporary culture to respond to this problem. It embodies poverty of spirit as we acknowledge our human sinfulness for our own part in the exploitation of the poor. And, finally, our emptying ourselves does not make any sense apart from Jesus who emptied himself out of love for us. One can only pray that we can begin to live out this model soon.

NOTES

[1] Avery Dulles, *Models of the Church* (Garden City: Doubleday and Company, Inc., 1974).

[2] A model is an attitude of mind or a mental framework. It is a way of looking at and understanding a particular phenomenon. It points more to a structure of the mind than to a particular content.

[3] See Cf. Johannes Baptist Metz, *Poverty of Spirit* (Paramus, N.J.: Newman Press, 1968).

The Center of Religious Poverty

Boniface Ramsey, O.P.

Volume 42, 1983, pp. 534-544.

At the origin of this essay rests the perception that in numerous religious communities poverty is greatly misunderstood. Paradoxically, this is perhaps especially the case in some communities that have opted to embrace poverty as a value of the highest priority. This situation is by no means restricted to poverty, however; it appears in the two other traditional commitments of religious life as well, namely chastity and obedience, and it may also be felt in the area of community life.

The situation in question is quite simply that very frequently the reason or motive for taking on poverty, chastity, obedience or the demands of communal life is something other than a Christocentric one. Such non-Christocentric motives may perhaps be classified most readily as either functional (one recalls the title of Donald Gelpi's book from the mid-'60's, *Functional Asceticism*) or, for want of a better term, edificatory.

Functional motivation sees the vow or commitment in terms of accomplishing an end that, under other circumstances, could really be accomplished without the vow; the circumstances being what they are, however, the vow renders the accomplishment of the end most practical. *Edificatory* motivation, for its part, understands the vow in terms of the upbuilding of a group or of the individual, and it commonly takes the form of a thrust toward witness. An example of a functional motive for chastity would be that it facilitates the apostolate or makes the religious "available" in a way that married persons supposedly cannot be. An edificatory motive would be, for instance, that by his or her abstention from certain sexual activities the religious offers a critique of a society that is pathologically absorbed in sexuality. The *Christocentric* motive for chastity, on the other hand, would be that of relating to Christ as friend or lover or bridegroom.

More instances of the functional and edificatory types could be given with respect to chastity and also with respect to obedience and community life. Poverty, however, is particularly susceptible of non-Christocentric motivation.

Non-Christocentric Motives

The loftiest of non-Christocentric motives should be mentioned first. It is that of solidarity with the poor. This motive is a noble one because of the seriousness with which it takes the persons of the poor, granting them not merely recognition but also the dignity that is theirs, and implying that the poor have gifts to offer and contributions to make to those who are not economically poor. Often a psychological urgency is operative here: as long as there are poor in the world certain sensitive personalities find it impossible to be anything but poor themselves, just as most people would find it difficult to be cheerful while a loved one was feeling pain. This motive is closest to the Christocentric because, of course, Christ identifies himself with the poor (see Mt 25:31ff). And it is in fact primarily in the poor that we can understand Christ's own poverty, so that the very inspiration to be poor for Christ's sake—which is a Christocentric reason—implies some realization of how people concretely experience poverty and hence how Christ must have experienced it as well.

Another non-Christocentric motive is that of witnessing to non-material reality and to the fact that spiritual goods really exist and are worth exchanging material goods for. This represents a kind of act of faith in Jesus' words in Mt 19:21 to the effect that if a person renders himself poor he will have recompense in heaven.

A third such motive is witnessing to providence in the sense that is spoken of in Mt 6:24ff. The divine care for all of creation, and in particular for human beings, is so encompassing that, as the religious implicitly says, we may thrust ourselves upon it utterly. Indeed, not to do so would somehow impugn providence. Here the ideal form of poverty is seen as mendicancy, which was a part of the life of many of the greatest religious orders in their beginnings.

A fourth motive seems related to the two which immediately precede. This understands poverty in terms of a critique of western materialistic society and as a witness to the fact (characterized to some degree by the expression "small is beautiful") that it is possible to have little and to be happy.

Facilitation of the religious apostolate constitutes a fifth motive. Possessing few things means that one is able to move about more freely and to be more available to others. In this latter regard the often-noted hospitality and generosity of the poor may be cited: the fewer things one has the less defensive of them and of oneself one is, and consequently the freer one can be with them and with oneself.

Very similar to this is a sixth non-Christocentric motive, namely the facilitation of community life. According to this point of view, poverty is perceived as a good because a peaceful life together is more readily assured when no one can claim anything as his or her own and when there are fewer material objects to interfere with community interaction. Material goods offer the powerful temptation to be thing-oriented rather than person-oriented, whereas when people are obliged to make do with relatively few things they are more likely to have to depend upon one another.

A seventh non-Christocentric motive is spiritual or psychological purification. Here poverty is seen as the indispensable means to detachment, interior freedom and especially self-knowledge, for possessions are distractions that turn a person away from the contemplation of his or her own true self. A remarkable passage from a letter of Paulinus of Nola, a contemporary of Augustine, well illustrates this understanding:

> Just as when a pile of rubbish is removed from the earth we can discern numerous tree trunks under great mounds of dirt or the remains of ruins or many dangerous creatures (and especially vipers' young), so when the possession of and solicitude for temporal objects is distant from our thoughts and we are freed from the preoccupation that drew us out of ourselves we discover within ourselves the knots of ancient sins and the lurking places of our spiritual enemies. Now the interior of the house begins to appear to us, as well as the creeping things that are without number. Now the whole darkness of our unhappy situation is evident. Now at last we see how far we are from God and how dead we are in comparison with the living.[2]

For Paulinus it appears that the voluntary renunciation of material goods has basically the same effect as does the sense of desolation and abandonment that occurs in the course of psychoanalysis: it destroys pretense and clears the way for truth.

An eighth and final motive can be listed—simplicity, or "living a simple lifestyle." There are sometimes both ascetic and aesthetic considerations at play here. To reduce what one has to a minimum, and correspondingly to be sparing even in one's words and actions, has always been seen as a form of asceticism whose ultimate aim, as in the seventh motive, is interior freedom and detachment. In addition, however, simplicity in and of itself is frequently perceived as beautiful. This is to a large extent a gift from Japan, where simplicity has been identified with beauty to a high degree, and it undoubtedly represents, at least in part, a reaction against the clutter of previous generations.

Critique

Of these eight non-Christocentric motives for religious poverty, some of which are more plausible than others, "facilitating the apostolate" and "facilitating community life" might be characterized as functional, while the six remaining ones would be edificatory. Other motives could be added to this list, but these are probably the most significant.

The fundamental criticism that can be leveled against all these motives, and against others that would be similar to them, is that not one of them is specifically Christocentric, and hence not one of them is specifically Christian.

Some of them are indeed religiously and spiritually oriented, as, for example, the second, third and seventh. But Christians are not the only people who believe in spiritual reality, divine providence or the value inherent in self-discovery. Nor is solidarity with the poor something peculiarly Christian: atheists are capable of this quite as well as the baptized, although atheists presumably do not see Christ in the poor. Even less claim in this regard can be made by the other motives. This is not to suggest that at least some of these motives *cannot* have profoundly Christocentric aspects, especially the first. It is to suggest, rather, that they *need* not be Christocentric, or specifically Christian, and that too frequently they *are* not. What is the point of Christian and religious life in this context if it is not somehow distinct from what is non-Christian? What is the point, rather, if Christ need not make a difference?

Moreover, these eight motives have in common the danger of some kind of misdevelopment or degeneration. Thus:

— Solidarity with the poor *could* develop into a false mystique of poverty, which could view poverty as a good in itself (which it most certainly is not) and the poor as invariably more virtuous than other persons. It could also tend to view the poor more in terms of class or group than as individuals, each with his or her own history.

— Witnessing to the excellence of spiritual over material goods *could* turn into a disdain for material reality, which seems to have been characteristic of the ancient Gnostic heresies and which is, in fact, a standing temptation to the Christian.

— Witnessing to providence or casting oneself on God's providential care *could* degenerate into irresponsibility or presumptuousness. One of the temptations of the mendicant is to think that he or she has somehow deserved an alms.

— The critique of a materialistic society *could* be turned into bitterness with regard to that society and a rejection of all aspects of modern culture— hence into a sterile romanticism and a glorification of other times and other places.

— The idea of facilitating the apostolate *could* fall into the service of an end-justifies-the-means mentality. In some cases, after all, prudence appears to dictate the possession and disposal of large sums of money, the wielding of influence and numerous other accommodations—all for the sake of accomplishing an undoubtedly good end. Why continue to be poor, then, when it seems that one can facilitate the apostolate better with money?

— The facilitation of community life is subject to the same danger. After all, there are times when it will appear that only certain large expenditures— made on behalf of the whole community, to be sure, in an area such as that of communal recreation or even communal liturgy—will maintain a desirable minimum standard of community life. If at such times money is available to the community, why not use it? What is the purpose of poverty if its observance is an occasion for the community to suffer?

— Spiritual or psychological purification *could* become mere self-centered self-development.

— Finally, simplicity *could* turn into aestheticism, or it could be no more than a romantic escape from the complexity of modern life, which must be faced up to and acknowledged, even if it need not be accepted in all its aspects.

Two further comments can be made. The first is that "witness," which appears explicitly in three of the above and implicitly in one other (solidarity with the poor), is of itself insufficient reason for taking on any religious commitment. Witness is the result, the by-product, of an action or a style of life. Thus, if a community lives poorly it must do so out of a profound inner need instead of for some didactic purpose. And if a community judges itself by the effect of its witness on others it is almost bound to be either disappointed or inflated.

The second comment is more important and has to do with the fundamentally non-personal tendency to which each of these motives is subject. Even solidarity with the poor, as has been mentioned, is in danger of failing to see the individual for the group. Several of these motives are idea- or self-oriented. One cannot, however, take upon oneself the admittedly burdensome profession of religious poverty without it being grounded emotionally or affectively, and only a love having the nature of friendship (as opposed to, for example, the love of a class or a group or the love of an idea, no matter how exalted) can provide this grounding. Only a love radicated in a person can make poverty bearable. For the vowed religious, Christ is the person. Even poverty "for the sake of the kingdom" smacks too much of a mere idea or a program, unless by "the kingdom" is understood Christ and life with him.

The overriding and central motive for religious poverty, then, and the one under which all other motives may be subsumed, is attachment to and love for the poor Christ—"naked to follow the naked Christ," as Saint Jerome put it in an immortal phrase.[3] The rest of this essay will pursue this motive.

The Christocentric Grounding of Poverty

The traditional scriptural locus of religious poverty, from the time of Anthony of Egypt[4] in the second half of the third century until the present, has been Mt 19:21: "If you would be perfect, go, sell what you possess and give to the poor, and you will have treasure in heaven; and come, follow me." We can begin here by remarking that this verse can be divided into five sections:

— "If you would be perfect." This is a call to make a free offering of oneself, and to go the limit in that offering. "Perfect," indeed, means to go beyond the limit of human capabilities, as Mt 5:48 makes clear: "You, therefore, must be perfect, as your heavenly Father is perfect." This perfection is what distinguishes Christians from tax collectors and gentiles, for they do only what is reasonable from a human standpoint.

— "Go, sell what you possess." This means the real renunciation of material goods, i.e., of things that are salable.

— "And give to the poor." Renunciation is hence not to be without some social ramifications: one does not simply throw away one's wealth as if it were useless or evil, nor does one give it away to family or friends, but one gives it to those who are in need.

— "And you will have treasure in heaven." The significance of this promise has already been suggested earlier in the present essay. There is here a kind of act of faith in the existence of eternal life and in the fact that there is a mysterious proportionality between what we do in this world and what we shall receive in the world to come.

— "And come, follow me." This is the climax of the verse as well as the motive for what precedes. It is by following Christ that one becomes perfect, and one can only follow Christ in material poverty.

The Fathers of the Church understood that this verse meant very little without the final call to "follow me." "Getting rid of money," Jerome writes, mentioning two pagan philosophers who practiced poverty, "is for beginners, not for those who are perfect. Crates the Theban did this and so did Antisthenes. To offer oneself to God is proper to Christians and apostles."[5] And Augustine, in one of his sermons, poses the questions as to whether it is enough merely to give one's possessions to the poor. After answering in the negative he continues:

> And why is that? [Because] He says: "Come, follow me." Do you love, and do you wish to follow the one whom you love? He has hastened on, he has flown on ahead. Look and see where. O Christian! Don't you know where your Lord has gone? I ask you: Do you wish to follow him there? Through trials, insults, false accusations, through being spat upon in the face and slapped and beaten, through the crown of thorns, the cross and death. Why do you hesitate? Look, the way has been shown you. But, you say, it is a hard way. Who can follow him along it?[6]

With this citation from Augustine we have touched upon the heart and center of religious poverty: "Do you love, and do you wish to follow the one whom you love?" Poverty is an essential part of, or at least an essential preliminary to, union with a Christ who is himself understood to be poor.

Poverty is in fact at the very center of the mystery of Christ, as is attested by both 2 Co 8:9 ("For you know the grace of our Lord Jesus Christ, that though he was rich, yet for your sake he became poor, so that by his poverty you might become rich") and Ph 2:6ff, the passage about Christ's self-emptying. The incarnation of the Word is nothing less than impoverishment— the impoverishment of the *kenosis* itself and the impoverishment of a somewhat poor, although not desolate, life situation. While it has been rightly pointed out that Christ was not born into a poor family and that he was in some sense a member of the middle class,[2] his life is nonetheless marked by continual options in favor of poverty and the poor, and he willingly chooses for himself situations in which he may experience those things that the poor experience: dependence on others, vulnerability, aloneness, being subject to scorn and non-acceptance, violence. Then at the end there is desolation, when in his suffering on the cross Christ seems to be abandoned not only by his friends but by the Father himself.

Why did the Word become human, and become a poor human, when it could have been otherwise? The only answer to this is that shattering and ineffable love which must always remain part of the mystery. It is a love that "drove" the Word not only to become a man but to become a poor man and thus to experience the depth of what it means to be in the flesh, to be human. For at the center of our mystery as human beings is poverty, and the poor, we may dare say, are more at the disposal of this mystery than others. If Christ emptied himself, it was to enter into the emptiness that we are—an emptiness that is defined by the fact that we have been created out of nothing, are poised on the razor-edge of existence and continually orient ourselves to the nonexistence of sin and mere illusions. This is an emptiness, moreover, that itself creates emptiness and desolation all around itself. From the full realization of this emptiness, about which J. B. Metz has written so beautifully (if also somewhat somberly) in his little book *Poverty of Spirit*, we try, alas, to protect ourselves, and this is a further illusion.

And from the implications of this emptiness we have throughout our Christian history tried to protect Christ as well. Hence the heresies of Docetism, Apollinarianism, Monophysitism and Monothelitism, each of which denies some aspect of Christ's humanity, whether his flesh and blood or his mind or his human nature or his human will—things that make him one with us in this fallen world. These are archetypal responses to the scandal of the incarnation. In the face of the great confession that Christ was like us in all things but sin (see Heb 2:17; 4:15) we are in danger of perpetrating a trivialization if we say: "Yes, but of course Jesus was really God." The intent of a remark such as this is ultimately, it seems, to provide him with some sort of "escape" from the human condition, with a secret consolation to which he might always have had recourse. This is the chief argument against the thesis that Christ on earth experienced his divinity in a conscious way: it detracts from his humanity. For in his human nature he was unlike us *only* in his sinlessness. Indeed, we may say that the sinless, the innocent, suffer more because they are ordinarily more sensitive and notice injustices more readily. In some mysterious way, too, they attract evil to themselves, for evil cannot bear innocence.

As we are in danger of trivializing the reality of Christ's humanity by too glibly calling upon his divinity, so we are in danger of detracting from his suffering and death if we too easily say: "Yes, but of course Jesus was going to rise again." We must let him endure his passion and his cross as the real things that they were and against which he did not seek to defend himself.

Once we have appreciated Christ's absolute defenselessness with respect to the human condition, we can agree with Metz when he writes: "Christ, the sinless one, experienced the poverty of human existence more deeply than any other man could. He saw its many faces, including those shadowy aspects that we never glimpse."[8] To this may be added the teaching of the Mystical Body of Christ, which tells us that he is still poor and suffering, albeit in a mysterious way. This doctrine is most clearly expressed in Mt 25:31ff, but it also appears in striking fashion in some lines from Paulinus of Nola:

> From the beginning of the ages Christ suffers in all his own, for he is the beginning and the end, who is cloaked in the Law and revealed in the gospel, a Lord always wonderful and suffering and triumphant in his saints. In Abel he was slain by his brother, in Noah mocked by his son, in Abraham a wanderer, in Isaac sacrificed, in Jacob in servitude, in Joseph sold, in Moses exposed and at flight, in the prophets stoned and cut to pieces, in the apostles cast about on land and sea, and frequently slain on the many and varied crosses of the martyrs. He, therefore, bears our infirmities and our sickness now as well, because he is the man who has always been placed in the snare on our account and who knows how to bear our infirmity, which we are unable to bear and know not how to bear without him. He, I say, now also endures the world for us and in us, that by bearing it he may destroy it, and may make strength perfect in weakness. In you too he puts up with opprobrium, and this world hates him when it hates you.[9]

All this may appear to be an overemphasis on the tragic aspect of Christ's life and of human existence. But these are simply the data of Scripture, which puts Christ's own life and the Christian's squarely under the sign of the cross. By emphasizing these truths we are not denying the divinity of Christ or his resurrection or, for that matter, the joys that he experienced in his day-to-day living. We speak rather of the stuff of the *kenosis*, which is the result of love and which is most manifest in the Incarnate Word's having drunk deeply of the cup of suffering. As to why this had to be so, only one who has been in love will begin to understand.

It is this Christ, or Christ under this aspect, that the vow of poverty has in mind. "Do you love, and do you wish to follow the one whom you love?" For the Christian and for the religious, poverty is a kind of psychological truth, a psychological necessity. That is to say, first of all, that a person in love desires with intensity to be like the one whom he or she loves and resists being unlike the beloved. Lovers wish in particular to suffer what the beloved suffers, to take the burden upon themselves as if by so doing they could remove it from the beloved. In the case of the Christian this burden of Christ's is something that must be embraced whether one wishes to or not: this is part of the definition of "Christian." But others who wish to penetrate the mystery more deeply, whether laypersons or religious, seek to embrace the burden with desire, as lovers do. They can, in effect, do nothing else. This desire for the beloved is formalized for some in the commitment of chastity, but the desire for the beloved precisely as human being, with all that implies, is more specific and belongs to poverty.[10] If Christ in his human nature is a poor man, then his lovers wish nothing less for themselves than to taste his poverty.

In the second place, a person who is in love is primarily interested in the beloved and subordinates everything else to that love. Certainly the lover is moved not to love what the beloved does not love, and even if he had loved something of this sort once he loses interest in it for the sake of the beloved: this is at least the case if the lover is convinced that the beloved is morally superior to him and has something better to offer him than he had previously known. If Christ, then, does not love those things that are associated with wealth, neither do his lovers, his disciples.

That poverty is a psychological necessity in this context is verifiable in the lives of the saints, all of whom have practiced poverty, even if, by reason of some high office, for example, they have felt themselves obliged to do so privately or secretly. It is a psychological impossibility to be rich—or more precisely to enjoy wealth unquestioningly—and at the same time to follow Christ wherever he may lead or to love him wholeheartedly. This is not a doctrinal impossibility, as it was for certain heretical groups in the early Church (such as, for instance, the Pelagians, who held that the rich could not be saved), but rather an experiential one: that is to say, it is the experience of being in love rather than a teaching of the Church which tells us this truth.

We can conclude by asking what loving the poor Christ may mean for us and what effects it may have for us.

First of all, it certainly means to experience the emptiness of one's human condition, which for Christ was climaxed in the abandonment on the cross. It means to know where we stand in the universe and in God's plan—frail objects that we are of God's tremendous love; and this means to eschew all pretense and self-importance and, indeed, to embrace that emptiness as the only possible receptacle for the divine love. The opposing temptation is superficiality, the unwillingness to come to terms with one's emptiness, which is in turn the result of fear.

It means, secondly, to experience Christ's alienation from the rulers of society and those who set the standards of society, symbolized for him in his continual confrontations with the typical representatives of his society. It means to refuse to be seduced by advertisements, propaganda and the like, and to submit to having one's own judgments formed by the Father's will. Opposed to this is an unquestioning comfortableness in society, with its injustice, its prejudice and its pretense, and a willingness to be seduced and to be "accepted." This society, it may be noted, exists in religious houses too.

In the third place it means to experience Christ's solidarity with the poor, the oppressed and the alienated. Always, to the scandal of those around him, he singles out Samaritans and sinners for his loving attention. Opposed to this example of Christ is a distance from and a disinterest in the poor, or the all too great willingness to posit ill of them and to assume that they deserve their poverty or their oppression.

Fourthly, it means to experience Christ's lack of power and, in fact, his rejection of the use of even legitimate power. This is the significance of his refusal to give in to the temptations in the desert (see Mt 4:1ff par.), as well as of his refusal to call upon his Father to send him twelve legions of angels when he is seized in Gethsemane (see Mt 26:53). Opposed to this is a love of power and, more subtly, a belief in the possibility that one can manipulate power for the sake of good ends without losing one's innocence thereby. To this fundamentally naive belief is related the idea that it is wise to have influence or to know influential people and cultivate them—once again for the sake of good ends, for accomplishing the Church's work in the world, and so forth. This mentality rejects the basic Christian truth love is the most effective and most transforming of all powers.

Loving the poor Christ means, in the fifth place, to experience Christ's dependence on others. He was himself dependent on Mary and Joseph, on the disciples to whom he entrusted his Church, on those who succeeded them, on his countrypeople, on the Romans who occupied his country. He continues to be dependent on us, for in no other way than through us is he explicitly present in the world. This dependence, often abject and humiliating, is the common lot of poor people. Opposed to it is the ability to act on one's own, to get things done without having to fill out too many forms or go through too much red tape. This ability implies having resources and influence of one's own, which is the foundation of the independence that the poor do not have.

In the sixth place, loving the poor Christ means to experience—on another level than that of his dependence on other human beings—his real independence and freedom with respect to human affairs, his detachment and his love without possessiveness.

Finally it means to experience his sense of dependence on the Father. Jesus is, so to speak, the greatest of the *anawim*, and his poverty casts him completely on the Father as his sole provider. Consequently the Father is everything to him.

From what has been said thus far it can be seen that poverty motivated by love for Christ includes within itself most, if not all, of the elements that we said could not serve as primary reasons for embracing poverty—solidarity with the poor, a critique of society, simplicity of life, and still others more implicitly. Love for Christ precedes and vivifies these other elements that flow from this one source and center. This love, moreover, of its very nature, prevents these elements from degenerating into bitterness or self-centeredness or the other perversions to which they are susceptible.

Conclusion

The point of view that has been expressed in these pages is perhaps a relatively austere one. But love, too, is relatively austere, or at least austere at certain moments in everyone's life, and Jesus chose to identify love for himself primarily in terms of the cross. Yet it is not for this austerity as such that we live, as if this were to be our ultimate goal. For our ultimate goal is not poverty pure and simple, not even Christ's poverty, but rather his resurrection and his life. As when we love someone who suffers, it is not that person's suffering that we love, although somehow we do love it because it is related to the sufferer, and so we desire it to be ours because of that relationship. Anything else would be masochism, not love. Our aim is union with the beloved, not suffering, not poverty. But: "Do you love, and do you wish to follow the one whom you love?"

Even here, however, this poverty gives us a glimpse of resurrection and life, for it is in the midst of the experience of one's own poverty and nothingness that one discovers Christ within oneself. And this Christ is no longer the poor Christ, but a Christ who is powerful indeed—powerful to transform sorrow into joy, suffering into glory, and poverty into wealth. But to know this Christ and this transformation it is necessary to have been poor for his sake.

NOTES

[1]The Christocentric aspect of poverty, which is the theme of this article, has recently been stressed most strikingly in David Knight, *Cloud by Day, Fire by Night II: The Meaning and Choice of Religious Poverty* (Ottawa: Canadian Religious Conference, 1979), pp. 155 ff. J.M.R. Tillard, *Religieux: un chemin d'evangile* (Brussels: Editions Lumen Vitae, 1975), p. 28, sees the highly Christocentric Phil 3:8-14 passage as the most characteristic text in the New Testament for all of religious life: "Indeed, I count everything as loss because of the surpassing worth of knowing Christ Jesus my Lord . . . ." Authors who understand religious life in this way, however, and who pursue its consequences seem somewhat exceptional.

I am grateful to Larry Donohoo, O.P., for having provoked this essay, and to him and Camilla Mullay, O.P., for their very useful suggestions in regard to it.

[2]*Letter* 24.20.   [3]*Letter* 125.20.   [4]See Athanasius, *Vita Antonii* 2.
[5]*Letter* 71.3.   [6]*Sermon* 345.6.
[7]See, for example, Albert Nolan, *Jesus Before Christianity* (Maryknoll, NY: Orbis, 1978), p. 27.
[8]J. B. Metz, *Poverty of Spirit*, tr. by John Drury (Paramus, NJ: Paulist, 1968), p. 18.
[9]*Letter* 38.3.
[10]The commitment of chastity need not imply Christ in his human nature, although it certainly can. Gregory of Nyssa, e.g., in his treatise *De virginitate* 2, speaks of chastity simply as a bond with a God who is himself pure and uncorrupt.

The Price of Poverty

Donald Macdonald, S.M.M.

Volume 45, 1986, pp. 3-14.

An elderly lady came to the sacristy after Mass and gave (for her) quite a large sum of money to the priest "for shoes for that poor man who read at Mass today." The reader was in fact a University lecturer with an income way beyond anything the lady had ever known, who chose to dress shabbily with down-at-heel sandals. He had more choices as to lifestyle than the lady who pitied him. Similarly, one has heard a religious conducting a seminar on poverty, forcibly arguing that if one is to be true to the Gospel and the founder's charism, rootlessness is really what is meant. The word poverty is too weak to enshrine the concept. He himself was enjoying a professional salary with his own bank-account, not one penny of which ever went to his congregation.

It is not just or even chiefly a matter of human fallibility, but of unreality which is an ever present risk in discussing evangelical poverty. So often the appearance bears no relation to the fact. Even the possibility of discussing poverty argues a degree of unreality, as most people are either born into or forced into the poverty trap by circumstances. One can see this in a third-world context where, paradoxically, evangelical poverty is almost impossibly difficult to live since the blistering reality is so obvious, and the main thrust of society is to race away from it. Perhaps G. K. Chesterton offers a way into the discussion in suggesting that humanity is the basis for understanding poverty. He believed that

> a man ought to know something of the emotions of an insulted man, not by being insulted but simply by being a man. And he ought to know something of the emotions of a poor man not by being poor, but simply by being a man. Therefore in any writer who is describing poverty, my first objection to him will be that he has studied his subject. A democrat would have imagined it.[1]

Statistics obviously have their place, but are no substitute for fellow-feeling. Religious, asked "to be poor both in fact and spirit" (*Perfectae Caritatis* 13) can, therefore, consider a genuinely poor person in the contemporary world as a touchstone of reality.

Contemporary Poverty

A young woman, a soldier's wife was counting the hours until her husband came home on leave. He did come. He had a woman with him whom he sat on a settee while he went upstairs and packed a suitcase. He came down and said to his wife: "Well, that's that then; I am off." Such was the end of her married life. The biblical type of weakness, vulnerability and poverty is often seen in a woman on her own. I cannot see that the pattern is fundamentally different today. The religious who wants the feel of poverty could do worse than examine her experience. Rather than spend days and dollars in meetings discussing the topic, much better surely to visit such people who, regrettably, are to be found within walking distance of so many religious houses. Why talk when we can walk and meet the reality in person? Poverty is first felt, not discussed.

That woman is truly poor. She loved her husband and wanted his children in a lifetime together, but she was told in the crudest possible way that her love was worth nothing. She was nobody to him. In practical terms she had ceased to exist. She did not even rate a letter or word of understanding or explanation. Yet *he* was everything to *her*. One can glimpse the emotional poverty in a person with an immense capacity for love who is unable to express it as she is unwanted and rejected. She is, therefore, poor in her very identity as her love, which is essentially herself, is apparently worthless.

As a married woman growing into the role, she knew who she was. It was no part-time occupation she had chosen, but a full-time life to which she had given herself. In view of her particular rejection, inevitably questions must surface as to her personal worth. Who am I now? Is the best I have to give worth nothing?

Failure of any kind can bring humiliation. Here is a woman who could not keep her husband. Friends who once welcomed her into their homes as a married woman are now less keen as she is on her own. People will talk about her, scarcely handicapped by knowing little of the true situation. The self she once saw and recognized is now seriously shattered, and it will take more than cosmetics to put the piece together again. Could she be worth less?

Clearly emotionally impoverished, she is, too, almost certainly economically poor. Can she continue living in her house? Once budgeting with her husband's income as together they tried to build a home, now the home which she helped furnish, and in which she may have expressed her own taste, has to be broken up. Perhaps even the physical fabric in which, to a degree, she had invested herself will have to go too. She has been literally uprooted. Her future is a lottery. Have her career or work prospects been handicapped in marrying? How and where is she to live? What is she to do?

Contemporary Questions

For anyone seriously wishing to understand poverty with a view to living it, inevitably the question must arise, if this is poverty what am I living? Arriving at that woman's house what would I say to her? Is the level of religious poverty such that, without giving a personal history, one can communicate with her at quite a deep level? Does the religious have experience of rejection and failure? Has the religious ever felt worthless? Ever lived in a loveless house? Ever been unable to express love? Has the religious ever been lost in the present and afraid of the future? By the same token, has one received such warmth, love, affection and security that one can only feel for someone who quite obviously has not?

Self-respect might suggest that if she is a poor woman what am I? On the deeper level of emotion where all of us function, does religious poverty suggest that I came from Sinai with a tract or from life with fellow-feeling? The religious who has attempted to live "poor both in fact and spirit" will speak the poor woman's language with an immediacy which is first felt rather than expressed.

Poverty means limitation. In a world where destitution is rampant the meaning of poverty may be obscured. Destitution means absolutely no choice, and is indefensible as a way of life. Poverty implies limited opportunity. The former has no choice, the latter has little.

Chesterton, in the essay mentioned earlier, felt it necessary to say that "a poor man is a man who has not got much money." This seems self-evident to the point of banality, but if it is such a truism why does it appear to have escaped the lifestyle of so many religious? If that was taken as a rule of thumb, possibly much of the rationalizing of evangelical poverty might go. "If a poor person can afford it I can consider it. If not, I can't." It may be that a limited budget with a need to count the pennies should be built into any realistic framework of poverty as a way of life, which, of course, is not the same as penny-pinching. If circumstances don't dictate it, those who freely choose such a life should.

With whom does one identify? Whatever "evangelical" means, it cannot mean unreal. The link between religious life and poverty should be progressively instinctive for the mature person. It was a young married woman caught in the poverty trap who summed it all up: "You get to the point that you don't think about things you can't afford." Horizons inevitably narrow. A poor person with limited opportunity has presumably little choice as to the people he lives among. He cannot choose his neighborhood, as many testify who would give heaven and earth to get out of a district if only to give the children a better chance, but cannot. For those who find work it is often a dead-end job. Educational and cultural opportunities, vacations and recreations are similarly limited. If such is not built into the fabric of evangelical poverty we seem to have missed much of the point.

Poor people tend to be marginal people in terms of status, influence and opportunity. One of the greatest tragedies of poverty, it has been noted, is the inability of so many people to make any contribution to society since so much potential is never given the chance to develop. This does not just disqualify many from competing in what is called "the rat race," where the prizes, however won, are strictly personal, but limits their contribution to life in general and their family and neighborhood in particular. Why, therefore, should the religious gibe at being subject to such limitations, perhaps in being ignored, used or patronized? Poverty feels like that. The very insecurity of contemporary religious life could be a chance to identify with such marginal people. There are so many marginal people even in the affluent societies of Western Europe and the United States, and surely the religious should not leave them behind. Insecurity is in the air. Living within such limits, the religious will be treated as such. In any case he can do no other. He has no choice. If his place in the pecking order determines how he is treated, in choosing poverty he has chosen to be last.

Why should anyone choose such a life? To play at it is one thing, but to choose to live permanently within such limits is something else. After all anyone who has ever lived in India, for example, will have seen there many "Mother Teresas," as no doubt they are to be found all over the globe, but it can still be puzzling as to why the average religious might *choose* that road. Most people, sensibly, want to widen their horizons, so why choose limitation in terms of relationships, lifestyle, dress, travel, opportunity? When poor people used to say that "poverty's no disgrace, but 'tis a great inconvenience," someone who grew up as one of them thought the comment too mild for what was in fact "a hampering drag upon them."[2] Most resist being pushed to the margin so why would anyone want to live there? It is hard to see anyone choosing this, other than as a voluntary short-term contract, yet, apparently, religious have chosen this for life.

Unless this choice is underpinned by an integrating vision which can give it worthwhile meaning, any such lifestyle will surely fragment under the age-old tension of catering to champagne tastes on a beer income. It is not in unredeemed human nature to choose less and be content. There is in much of religious poverty as lived today a close analogy with Parkinson's Law,[3] in as much as affluence expands and is seen to be necessary as goods and money become available. Yet if one lives on a fixed income in an economic climate of inflation, one cannot spend money as if there is no tomorrow. I cannot entertain as perhaps I would like. Nor can the main consideration of "travel abroad" be a valid passport. Limitation will be written into whatever I do.

Basically the choice of this lifestyle is made because the religious choose Christ who chose a stable in preference to a palace and consistently held to that even in death. It is said that the best fighter is the hungry fighter, and whoever really wants God in Christ must train to sacrifice anything that gets in the way. The point of poverty, then, is to remove the clutter and tension which would tend to crowd God out. The Methodist scholar Gordon Rupp underlined this in a general point: "Never had so many men so many great possessions as in our modern affluent societies, and what Jesus said about these things no Bultmann has ever been able to demythologize. If these things blind the spirit, and if the pure of heart see, then I should find a thousand within the Church on the road to perfection for every hundred outside."[4] The outlook of the consumer society can suffocate feeling for God.

The point of evangelical poverty is made more specific in an instructive misprint in my copy of the breviary, where St. Paul is made to say of Christ that "rich as he was, he made himself poor for your sake in order to make you rich by means of his *property* (sic)" (2 Co 8:9). This is undoubtedly the logic which appeals to the printer and the rest of us, but what St. Paul said, of course, was that it was in his total *poverty* that Christ enriched us. Here everything has been lost in translation. In an attempt to make sense of the text, nonsense has been made of the Gospel. To see the influence of this insight on St. Paul in that same second letter to the Corinthians can be of immense practical help in assimilating the reason for evangelical poverty and so nourishing its continuing dynamic.

First Put On Christ

Invariably Paul begins with Christ. Seeing him in his conversion, baptism and daily life—"even if we did once know Christ in the flesh, that is not how we know him now" (2 Co 5:16)—he is so enthralled by what he sees that he can only compare its effect on him to the creation of light: "For it is the God who said, 'Let light shine out of darkness,' who has shone in our hearts to give the light of the knowledge of the glory of God on the face of Christ" (2 Co 4:6). He knew his world and himself to be literally recreated anew in Christ. Reality, no matter how it presents itself, now comes to him in the face of Christ, so he comes to see what God is like in a sacramental world and, progressively, becomes like what he sees. Whatever happens to Paul is always in Christ. So illumined, life is shot through with Christ as he sees God giving himself in the happenings of every day.

The more he reflected on God giving himself to us in Christ the more he was possessed by what he saw: "For the love of Christ overwhelms us when we reflect . . ." (2 Co 5:14). To think that Christ had given his life for Paul in the absolute poverty of crucifixion and death! He could refuse Paul nothing. Living in such a world, he logically believed that the response of Christians should be "to live no longer for themselves but for him who for their sake died and was raised" (2 Co 5:15). In other words, the selfish, self-centered core in all of us, which can imprison us in self as cruelly as a child in a school playground without an adult present, has now been broken up. In Christ, one moves from self to selflessness. One lives now for Christ as the wholeness of his sacrifice registers, and one comes to realize what an enthralling discovery one has in this unprecedented gift. Even atomic calculations cannot quantify this.

So seismic is the effect on one who glimpses the reality that Paul can only see the person given that insight as a wholly new type of being, since, "for anyone who is in Christ, there is a new creation; the old creation has gone, and now the new one is here" (2 Co 5:17). One's outlook, value-system and life itself are now a response to God giving himself in Christ. That this can take place in the ordinary, everyday world of pagan Corinth Paul is assured, since "for our sake God made the sinless one into sin, so that in him we might become the goodness of God" (2 Co 5:21). In human nature at its worst seen in the crucifixion and death of the sinless Christ, our Lord plumbed the depths of human evil and weakness insofar as one person could, and so enables Paul to see that everything is redeemable in the death and resurrection of Christ. Nothing can hold us in Christ. Crucified as his Mother stood and watched, and buried in another man's grave, this it is that roots the experience of Christ in the humanity of every age, not least our own.

What of course was happening was "God in Christ was reconciling the world to himself, not holding men's faults against them . . ." (2 Co 5:20). Glimpsing this, Christians like Paul become "ambassadors for Christ . . . as though God were appealing through us" (2 Co 5:20). The message, of course, is simply to "be reconciled to God" (2 Co 5:20). Ideally the Christian reaches the point of so assimilating Paul's insight that he/she can do no other than share it.

For the religious, poverty is part of the price paid to preserve that insight. All else gradually falls away, no longer seen as having any real claim on us in the light of Christ: "And we, with our . . . faces reflecting like mirrors the brightness of the Lord, all grow brighter and brighter as we are turned into the image that we reflect" (2 Co 3:18). All of this takes place not in some Gnostic, esoteric enclave, but in the streets of wherever the Christian happens to be, since "this is the work of the Lord who is Spirit" (2 Co 3:18). The first and continuing step for anyone who would live genuinely evangelically poor, therefore, is to put on Christ. Contemplation is clearly primary. First recognize what it is to be christened, and poverty for the sake of Christ becomes a logical necessity. Whatever obscures that vision must go.

In Everyday Life

While it is true that Paul "was caught up into paradise and heard things which must not and cannot be put into human language" (2 Co 12:4), the second letter to the Corinthians makes it all too plain that he does not stay there. It is in the present, in the unpredictability of everyday life that he sees Christ, and this is marvelously encouraging for anyone attempting to live poor for Christ. Rich as he was in Christ, people and circumstances will so often combine to subject Paul to an experience not unlike that of the contemporary poor woman mentioned earlier. So often he will be stripped of everything but his faith (see 2 Co 1:8).

For some, Paul's all would not be enough. He invested not just the Gospel but his self in Corinth—"For my own part, I will gladly spend and be spent on your souls' behalf, though you should love me too little for loving you too well" (2 Co 12:15). The man who brought Christ to them at such physical and emotional cost is reduced to writing them a letter in an attempt to establish himself again (see 2 Co 3:1-3). "Someone said, 'He writes powerful and strongly-worded letters, but when he is with you, you see only half a man and no preacher at all'" (2 Co 10:10). It is not just gratuitous rudeness nor personal dislike, but Paul's nonacceptance as a genuine apostle that is at issue, so he is afraid that "your ideas may get corrupted and turned away from simple devotion to Christ" (2 Co 11:3).

Paul and his Christ are not accepted. His very identity, therefore, is questioned. In an attempt to try and reestablish some lost status he is humiliated into having to give something of his own record to show that he was not in it for himself, as was suggested—neither a naive, misguided convert nor a "con-man" taking advantage of them: "lashes . . . beaten . . . stoned . . . shipwrecked . . . false brethren . . . sleepless . . . hunger, thirst . . . cold . . . anxiety for all the churches" (2 Co 11:23-29).

Was all this for nothing? He gave everything, yet had not made first base with an influential, articulate group in the Corinthian church. He has deceived no one, yet if a man's good faith is questioned, as was Paul's, he is really poor, for, without that, he has no currency left. Corinth and life generally taught Paul that such paradox is of the essence of an apostle's life: "We are treated as imposters, and yet are true; as unknown, and yet well known; as dying, and behold we live; as punished, and yet not killed; as sorrowful, yet always rejoicing; as poor, yet making many rich; as having nothing, and yet possessing everything" (2 Co 7:8-10).

Read as experience and not literature, in these passages one will come close to the mind and life of a poor Christian man. Integrity, reputation, achievement, personality, wealth and so much more that can give a person self-respect and a worthwhile life are so often taken, and the individual is then dismissed as worthless. Even obvious achievement is seen as a mirage. To be poor feels like that, seemingly unable to make a contribution though one gives one's all.

Paul is so aware of the power of the Gospel and the powerlessness of the Christian as he tries to communicate it, that it would almost seem a contradiction in terms had not his life followed that pattern since first he gave himself to Christ. Perhaps he was never closer to his Lord than in this powerlessness. If the Christ he preached, the faith they received, the life he lived does not suggest integrity, he has nothing to offer except an appeal: "Open your hearts to us; we have taken advantage of no one" (2 Co 7:2).

To be reduced to speaking like that, one must be poor indeed. Against that background, too, incidentally, Paul is trying to collect money to help the impoverished Jerusalem church! (see 2 Co chs. 8-9). Part of the cost of becoming a Christian in those days may have meant, for many, broken family and community ties resulting in real poverty at so many levels.

Paul was also economically poor in Corinth: "When I was with you and ran out of money I was no burden to anyone" (2 Co 11:9). For whatever reason he judged it best not to accept help from the Corinthian church. This led to further misunderstanding, not least in leading some to assume that his message must be as cheap as its presenter. As so often with the really poor person it seems to be "heads you win, tails I lose," whatever way the coin falls.

Whenever he could not make ends meet, "I robbed other churches by accepting support from them in order to serve you" (2 Co 11:8). These were the other communities in Greece Paul had set up on his way south to Corinth, and it must surely have been an additional burden when he was aware of being helped by people who had little enough themselves, since "the troubles they have been through have tried them hard, yet in all this they have been so exuberantly happy that from the depths of their poverty they have shown themselves lavishly open-handed" (2 Co 8:2). Evidently poor themselves, they were so eager to help the poor in the Jerusalem church "begging and begging us for the favor of sharing in this service" that in so doing, "they offered their own selves first to God and, under God, to us" (2 Co 8:4-5). Such are the people helping Paul, so at one with the mind of their Lord that they, too, from their poverty, are helping to make others rich.

Think of the effect on Paul of such behavior—the bread he eats he owes to them, as also their faith builds up him and so many. They have learned much in a short time.

It must be the experience of so many religious across the world that it is largely because of the faith and generosity of such people today that they are able to live and work. Such support should have a marked effect on the way we live.

Personal Limitations

Emotionally and economically poor in a world in which any religious can find himself, St. Paul also works within the limits of a human frame. The most individual of men, he is always recognizably himself. Even those who tend to lay all that is wrong with Christianity at Paul's feet might acknowledge that there is something, much or little, in their own characters that they might wish to change, if only to be more effective witnesses to Christ. Paul knows this too.

One of the greatest benefits of time spent in Paul's company is to see him operate within the limitations of a genuinely human personality—which is just another expression of the intrinsic poverty which everyone shares. After each one of us was made they broke the mould. Paul is ever conscious of "a thorn in the flesh" which so bothered him that he pleaded with God to remove it (see 2 Co 12:7-8). Whatever it was, Paul knew he would be so much more effective if only he could be rid of it. His prayer was not answered. Instead, he was given one of his greatest, most encouraging insights, which can help anyone conscious of the poverty of his or her own resources: "My grace is sufficient for you, for my power is made perfect in weakness" (2 Co 12:9). Paul was fine as he was. The fewer his reserves the more must God supply. The greater his personal inadequacy the more pressing his claim on God.

So the ultimate paradox for Paul was that when he looked at himself in the mirror of his apostolate and saw much that he could wish changed, he saw what was really there, a poor man with all his limitations, loved by God in Christ. His obvious weakness was a claim on God's power. So he could relax and learn contentment at a very deep level: "and that is why I am quite content with my weaknesses, and with insults, hardships, persecutions, and the agonies I go through for Christ's sake. For it is when I am weak that I am strong" (2 Co 12:10).

The religious inevitably aware of some of his limitations would do well to assimilate that insight. As someone vowed to poverty, he can even integrate his own limitations within the comforting simplicity of that Gospel perspective, perhaps coming to see why Paul could say "No wonder we do not lose heart! Though our outward humanity is in decay, yet day by day we are inwardly renewed" (2 Co 4:16). As ever, the overriding belief in God giving himself in Christ in the present moment is the dynamic of evangelical poverty.

Repeated experience was to teach Paul this, even when he felt shattered as his identity as a genuine apostle is queried, pioneering a way for the Gospel, or facing the growing pains of an expanding Church. Often he finds himself as a leader without an army, let down by people from whom he had expected support.

Because of his fighting polemic Paul ran the risk, not always successfully avoided, of being unfair to others and no doubt had the chance to repent at leisure. The physical and emotional strain at times must have been severe, but it is again all part of carrying the treasure of the Gospel within the heart of a poor man. So he saw that "we are no better than pots of earthenware to contain this treasure, and this proves that such transcendent power does not come from us, but is God's alone" (2 Co 4:7).

What is attractive is that in circumstances which would have discouraged many of us, or have us return home to lecture, write our memoirs, or dine out on our experiences for Christ, Paul never gave up. He went forward into the situation, and there found God in Christ with a security given only to those who give up everything for him. His life as glimpsed in this letter shows that "human indeed we are, but it is in no human strength we fight our battles" (2 Co 10:3). He expresses this superbly when he admits that "we are in difficulties on all sides, but never cornered; we see no answer to our problems, but never despair; . . . persecuted, but never deserted; knocked down but never killed" (2 Co 4:8-9).

Again, one should not let the literary construction mask the human reality. Paul is not some superman (canonization is invariably posthumous), but a man in Christ, which is why problems, mistakes, anxiety and fear never ultimately crush him since they are seen as reflecting Christ. He is always in Christ and so in circumstances where our first move might be to the doctor, the bottle, the counselor or the return ticket, Paul's is always to Christ. So when he is in trouble, he sees what is happening to him: "Always, wherever we may be, we carry with us in our body the death of Jesus" (2 Co 4:9). He lives in Christ as Christ lives in him, not least in suffering and heartbreak. So real is this that "the sufferings of Christ, it is true, overflow into our lives," and in that very experience as Christ is there, "there is overflowing comfort, too, which Christ brings" (2 Co 1:5).

Up against it, seeing no way through, Paul believes Christ to be an indwelling presence not a distant model. He shares the experience, often nailed to Christ through people and circumstances beyond his control. So a man, who, like his Lord and so many on earth, knew much of failure, tears and poverty, at the same time, in the power and love of the risen Christ, sees that in his survival, though so powerless, "the life of Jesus, too, may always be seen in our body" (2 Co 4:10). The poverty-stricken Paul is enriched in Christ, even using suffering and failure to help reconcile him and his world to God.

Nothing in his experience, therefore, is pointless. Successive centuries have no doubt learned more from the failures of Paul and his Lord than from the successes of their commentators.

So a poor man, with at times scarcely a hold on life—"we were so utterly, and unbearably crushed that we despaired of life itself" (2 Co 1:8)—learned to rely on the richness of God. He must have found much time for prayer and reflection or he could never have read so much into the poverty of the human condition, these passages do not read as emotion recollected in tranquillity so much as the discovery of the presence of God in Christ when all seemed lost in a harsh, uncaring world. Under God, Paul learned that lesson well. And so, from his own experience of poverty at many levels, he was anxious and able to pass on what he had found, thanking "the God of all comfort, who comforts us in all our affliction, so that we may be able to comfort those who are in any affliction, with the comfort with which we ourselves are comforted by God" (2 Co 1:3-4). Paul seems hypnotized by the word *comfort*, since the experience was so real in the middle of his at times frightening poverty.

The religious looking for the vision and stamina to be "poor both in fact and spirit," would do well to spend time in the company of such a man who found so much of richness in his own poverty: "For what we preach is not ourselves, but Jesus Christ as Lord, with ourselves as your servant for Jesus' sake" (2 Co 4:5).

In any consideration of the vast topic of evangelical poverty there is both a community and an individual dimension. This article is simply meant as an aid to personal reflection. The Benedictine historian David Knowles, in the epilogue to one of his classic studies of English medieval monasticism, was of the opinion that property and wealth were contributory factors in its decline. No groups nor individuals could do much about it, as wealth "clung like pitch." This is surely a *human* development, not especially a medieval one. If a corrective cannot be found for the individual religious in the Gospel, a founder's manuscript rule, and a contemporary poor person, it is doubtful if legislation and discussion will make it real. It is for the individual to see.

NOTES

[1]G. K. Chesterton, "Slum Novelists and the Slums," in *Heretics* London 1905, p. 277.

[2]Flora Thompson, *Lark Rise to Candleford* Penguin Books 1973, p. 31.

[3]C. Northcote Parkinson, Parkinson's Law: "Work expands so as to fill the time available for its completion."

[4]Gordon Rupp, *The Old Reformation and the New,* Epworth 1967, p. 60.

Obedience to Mission

Sister Barbara Hendricks, M.M.

Volume 35, 1976, pp. 321-329.

Introduction

We live at a moment when the Church is approaching a fuller interpretation of its mission. We are beginning to understand that the Good News of Salvation in Jesus is neither deedless word nor wordless deed; it is rather an integral response to the many critical human needs. It is salvation which can pervade and heal the physical, psychological and spiritual wounds of the world. We are convinced that salvation begins now and that somehow we have to have an experience of it in our lives as persons and as communities. Salvation is not something that will only happen in eternity, but there must be a beginning of the kingdom here on earth. If this is true, then, holiness is not only a personal transformation but it is meant to flow outward into human relationships, both inter-personal and structural.

In the early sixties in South America we began to hear the word "evangelization" being used to describe the essential task of the Church. It was not a new word for those of us who used to call ourselves "foreign missionaries." It was sort of our "thing." It meant going out there beyond the Church community to preach the Gospel and plant the Church. Our articulated theology of mission put heavy emphasis on our "spiritual mission" but in actual fact, we spent a good deal of our time engaged in the corporal works of mercy. A lot of debate started then about what this Mission of Evangelization really means. It has been hot and heavy. The 1974 Synod on Evangelization and the latest Apostolic Exhortation, *Evangelii Nuntiandi,* are signs that the Church is indeed deeply concerned with Mission.

For some Christians "evangelization" has meant recruiting new members, religious instruction of converts, teaching catechism, cultivating an inner spirituality or preaching missions in parishes and dioceses. For others, especially in the 1960's, it began to mean serious social action: promoting civil rights and concern for human dignity, witnessing to justice and peace or liberation from all forms of economic and political oppression. In more recent years, for certain groups in the Church it has come to mean a closely-knit, mutually supportive inter-personal community of shared witness and prayer, highly alert to the presence of the Spirit, healing and reconciling. Our choice of definition depended a great deal on our own personal history, and the needs we experienced in ourselves and in the milieu around us. I think that the Holy Spirit has something to do with the recognition of each of these dimensions of the evangelizing mission of the Church, and although we engaged in heated debates during these last ten years as we struggled to live out and express an authentic contemporary theology of mission, most of us knew that somehow we had to bring it all together, that our mission had to reflect the mission of Jesus in its entirety.

The era of debate is subsiding as we move into the latter half of the 1970's. We Christians are beginning to listen to each other and to the Word of God spoken and still speaking in our midst. We are now more concerned with the message itself, realizing that method is only the secondary problem. Mission is both message and method; but without a clear understanding of the message, the method becomes a lifeless, meaningless exercise of communication skills. So our main concern, then, is what is the "Message of Salvation" and how are we as religious, as apostolic people, to proclaim it in life, in work and in word. More than ten years ago, at the close of Vatican II, we were left with three documents on the nature of the Church and its mission in the world; *Lumen Gentium, Gaudium et Spes* and *Ad Gentes*. I have a feeling that today we should put them together in a coordinated and harmonious integration. It was typical of the 1960's that three distinct documents were needed to describe the same subject—the Church. It will be typical of these next ten years that theology of mission will construct a synthesis of the many aspects of evangelization to be lived and articulated.

The Obedience of Jesus

In Saint Matthew's Gospel (3:13-17), we read: "As soon as Jesus was baptized, he came up from the water, and suddenly the heavens opened and he saw the Spirit of God descending like a dove and coming down on him. And a voice spoke from heaven, 'This is my Son, the Beloved; my favor rests on him.'" Jesus' mission comes from the Father, who confirms in him this mission of salvation for humanity. All mission is initiated by the Father, who consecrates and sends. This is the beginning of Jesus' public ministry—he is sent by the Father.

Immediately after his baptism, Jesus is led by the Spirit into the wilderness, where he is confronted by the demonic power. He is tempted three times and in his responses we have presented to us what I would call "guidelines for our mission." We can apply them to ourselves personally, to our religious communities and to the broader Church. They have to do with the means we take to proclaim the Good News:

First. Jesus is tempted to turn stones into bread. He responds, "man does not live on bread alone but on every word that comes from the mouth of God." To satisfy physical hunger without at the same time providing the Word of God, the Bread of Life, is to offer a partial salvation. Mission conceived of as promoting material well-being without the dialogue of faith and the sharing of the Word is not authentic Christian mission.

Second. Jesus is tempted to display his power and attract by the force of divine intervention. He replies, "You must not put the Lord, your God to the test." Jesus' mission is not to perform prodigies and thus draw to himself those who admire power and prestige, but rather it is to transform hearts and relationships. His miracles are reserved for those who are disposed to hear his Word and humbly ask his healing.

Third. Jesus is tempted to bow down before Satan—to lift up idols in place of the true God. He is told that worldly kingdoms will be thus at his disposal. He responds, "You must worship the Lord your God and serve him alone." Christian mission can never set up alliances with earthly powers or make arrangements for security at the cost of serving false gods. To accept the status quo and not to struggle for the realization of the kingdom of justice and holiness is to bow down before false gods.

These are the three temptations which persons, communities and the Church itself must confront and overcome both internally and in the world:

—seeking material well-being to the detriment of the spiritual dimension of life;

—using power by secret alliances, manipulation and oppression;

—setting up idols before the true God.

The disciple of Jesus consecrated for his mission is continually involved in an interior struggle against private demons while at the same time contesting the very same manifestations of evil in the institutional structures.

Jesus comes out of the wilderness and begins his mission with these words: "Repent, the kingdom of heaven is close at hand." His message is a two-edged sword; it names the evil, inviting closed hearts to open to love and it points to the signs of hope that salvation has penetrated the human reality:

He went around the whole of Galilee teaching in their synagogues proclaiming the Good News of the kingdom and curing all kinds of diseases and sickness among the people. His fame spread throughout Syria; and those who were suffering from diseases and painful complaints of one kind or another, the possessed, epileptics, the paralyzed, were all brought to him and he cured them. Large crowds followed him . . . (Mt 4:23-25).

Jesus Sends His Disciples

Jesus immediately calls and gathers disciples into the first community of apostolic followers. His recorded words are brief but they contain the essential relationship of "call" to "mission": "Follow me and I will make you fishers of men." They are called to be sent. He gathers them in his company so that they in turn will gather others in the company of mission. As he has been sent by the Father, Jesus will send them. His mission is to call human hearts and human communities to repentance of sin and to give them an experience of the nearness of the kingdom of God. They leave their concerns—their nets—and follow him. This is the first recorded response of disciples in obedience to the Lord Jesus' call to mission (Mt 4:12-17).

Having gathered his twelve disciples, he sends them in his name to the House of Israel: "And as you go, proclaim that the kingdom of heaven is close at hand, cure the sick, raise the dead, cleanse the lepers, cast out devils . . ." (Mt 10:7-8).

And after his death and resurrection, his last words to his disciples are clearly the universal mandate to mission: "Go, therefore, make disciples of all nations; baptize them in the name of the Father and of the Son and of the Holy Spirit, and teach them to observe all the commands I gave you. And know that I am with you always, yes, to the end of time (Mt 28:19-20).

> Repentance for the forgiveness of sins should be preached to all nations (Lk 24:47).
> Go out to the whole world: proclaim the Good News to all creation (Mk 16:16).
> As the Father sent me, so am I sending you (Jn 20:3).

What, then, do we perceive to be Jesus' obedience to mission?

—He is sent by the Father and he is obedient to the mission given him, even unto death.

—As he begins his public ministry, he confronts the demonic power of evil.

—He calls people to repentance, and announces the nearness of the kingdom of God. He explains God's plan for creation; the central figure of his concern is the human person for whom God wills the perfection of love. With his teaching, he completes the sacred history of the people.

—He gathers those who believe in him, calling each by name, and sends them as he, himself, has been sent by the Father.

—He travels through the land, proclaiming the Good News of

Salvation for all. His powerful word is heard and seen and felt because it is enfleshed in deeds of love and healing.

—He forms a community of faith, of service and of love in which he will continue his presence and prolong his mission until the time when he will return.

The mission of Jesus is both physical healing and spiritual reconciliation, liberation and fulfillment; the Lord's favor rests on the poor, the oppressed and the alienated. We have an image set before us of Jesus whose mission is lived out in absolute fidelity to his Father and in faithfulness to human persons and their critical needs. There seems to be no conflict of interest between building the earthly city and praising and glorifying God. This concern for the whole person—physical and spiritual dimensions—is the mission mandate, and it is also the criteria on which we will be judged at the end: "I was hungry and you gave me to eat, thirsty and you gave me to drink. . . ."

The Evangelizing Mission in the Acts of the Apostles

In the book of Acts there is a recurrent sequence of events which illustrate the continuous movement of Christian mission in the early Church. We recognize there, the essential elements of apostolic life. There is a constant flow of gathering and sending, healing and proclaiming, confronting and suffering, reflecting and celebrating.

The first few chapters concerned with the primitive Christian community in Jerusalem provide us with an outline of integral evangelization:

Gathering and sending: the disciples of Jesus having encountered the risen Lord and experienced his healing and saving love, come together to build a faith communion of love and sharing nourished by the Spirit. The community is bound together by prayer, by mutual service, by shared possessions, by the instructions of the apostles, and by the celebration of the eucharistic meal. The Spirit urges them to go outside the faith community and boldly preach the Good News of Salvation, challenging men and women to repent and to be converted.

Healing and proclaiming: the evangelizing mission thrusts outward beyond the community with a deed of mercy. "When Peter and John were going up to the temple for the prayers at the ninth hour, it happened that there was a man being carried past. He was a cripple from birth and they used to put him down every day near the temple entrance called the Beautiful Gate so he could beg from the people going in" (Acts 3:1-3). The evangelizers are led by the Spirit into the market place, outside the temple gate, and the Word, not yet spoken, is revealed by an act of mercy which responds to worldly agony and bodily need. In the name of Jesus, the man walks. In the midst of the deed, Peter speaks the Word. "Why are you so surprised at this? . . . it is the God of Abraham, Isaac and Jacob, the God of our ancestors, who has glorified his servant, Jesus. . . ."

He preaches the salvation of Jesus, incarnated, despised, suffering, rejected, yet resurrected and triumphant, active in the midst of the world.

Humans need to hear the Word of God spoken in faith and hope and addressed to their personal center, as well as see and feel the impact of the healing act of love. Christian mission never isolates the ministry of service from the ministry of the spoken Word. The evangelizing act is seen, felt and heard.

Confronting and suffering: there is the inevitable confrontation with the principalities and powers (Acts 4:3). The priests and the officers of the temple apprehend Peter and John. They are interrogated and harassed, told to be quiet, not to speak of Jesus and his message. The moment of confrontation with all the suffering it involves, provides the occasion for *kerygma.* Peter again proclaims the Good News even when it means resisting oppression. "You, yourselves, judge what is right in God's sight, to obey you or to obey God" (Acts 4:19).

Reflecting and celebrating: the disciples return to the community recounting their experiences, the healing act, the suffering they endured and there is rejoicing of all the members. They praise God, reflect together on Scripture, trying to interpret the events in order to discover God's plan and purpose in them. "As they prayed . . . they were filled with the Holy Spirit and began to proclaim the Word of God boldly" (Acts 4:31). The community of faith sharing and discerning together grows in creativity and valor.

A reflective reading of Acts steers us out of ourselves—away from a one-dimensional acting out of Christian life and mission. The continuous movement of evangelization in the Book of Acts links *diakonia, kerygma* and *koinonia*—deed, word and community are not three distinct ways of carrying on the mission of Jesus; they are three dimensions of one Christic process in which we are all called to participate.

Consecration for Mission in Religious Community

The invitation to follow the Lord Jesus is addressed to the personal center of the one who, in some mysterious way, has been chosen to announce the Good News of Salvation. The person thus "called" perceives the Word of God as an internal light or truth or warmth which presents an imperative to stop what one is presently concerned about, to turn to something new, to attend to a persistent urging and pursue a new direction.

The person who listens and responds to the invitation to follow this new inner direction finds herself (himself) caught up in a new relationship with God—a relationship which requires a commitment to his plan for the transformation of human hearts and human relationships. It is basically the same invitation addressed to the first disciples and many others in the history of the Christian Church: "Follow me and I will make you fishers of men." The call is for mission.

In the instance of a person called to apostolic religious life, there is an experience of deep significance, of the total engagement of one's being. It involves both a feeling of truth about oneself in relation to other human persons and a sense of well-being even when the commitment will require a difficult decision. A deep conviction arises from within the person that God is calling her (him) to a celibate life in community. What is important to note here is that the person called has indeed been "touched" by the Gospel and is motivated by that power from within. It should not be simply a matter of having heard about the power of the Gospel and being deeply impressed by what it has done for others. It has to be one's own experience of God beckoning.

Each of us at one point in our lives, before we entered our particular community, had a dream or a vision. This dream was the way in which we were able to express to ourselves the significance of our inner experience of call. It was about what we wanted to be and what we wanted to do with our lives. I believe that "call" and "mission" (the being and doing) are not two separate realities, but different aspects of the divine outward thrust of love; God breaking through to us and inviting us to participate in his mission, the mission of his Son, Jesus. God's desire to liberate and reconcile and, ultimately, transform all that he has created manifests itself in a special form of outreach to some chosen persons. He gathers these persons into communities for his special purposes in the historic process with its dire needs. None of us knows why his choice falls where it does, but we experience it and therefore, we believe it.

No one is "called" to be simply for herself (or himself) alone. We are invited by God to take part in a transforming mission which is the sharing of the Good News of Salvation in Jesus. We are called to proclaim the Word to our brothers and sisters who have not heard nor experienced God's powerful healing and reconciling Word.

Obedience: Listening to God's Word and Responding with "Yes"

Obedience is openness to God's designs and plans for the world. We do not have a blue print of his will and, therefore, obedience cannot simply be freedom to conform to what is already decided. It is not a passive acceptance of the way things are, but an enthusiastic search to discover the direction of the Spirit at work in hearts, in relationships and in institutional structures.

Obedience, then, means openness and attentiveness to the Word of God spoken and speaking in our midst. It means listening, consultation, study, dialogue and reflective prayer. Above all it means listening to one another in the local community, in our larger congregation, and to the different levels of Church in which we participate, especially our local Church, but also our universal Church, as it struggles to articulate its experience, its insights and its consensus. It means trying to read the signs of our times; listening and discerning the needs and aspirations of the society in which we are inserted, our neighborhood, our city, our nation and the new global world in which we live today.

As we listen, we need to analyze, consult and experience the pain and violence of our times, as well as its joys and aspirations. We need to name evil without despair and to point to the signs of hope with realism and honesty but with Christian faith in the resurrection and promise of the Lord. The Spirit is working in the events of history both within the hearts of all of us, within our communities and in the world itself. In the light of the Gospel message our task is to discover the purpose and plan of God taking place in our times and to discern our particular way of participating in the mission of Jesus.

We have to listen to the Word of God in Scripture and in our own hearts in prayer and reflection. We have to listen to his Word in our own local communities and articulate to each other the fruit of our reflection and prayer, so that spontaneously together we can share his Word and grow as a community of faith.

The main problem seems to be that we lack very often, the right structures and processes within our local communities and broader congregations which would enable a more enlightened obedience to mission today. Both personally and as communities we need an asceticism of consistent, well organized and faith-oriented "coming together" for dialogue, discernment and decision-making regarding our apostolic activities as well as for evaluation and growth in being communities of reflective faith-sharing. Our coming together should be characterized by the same belongingness which was typical of the early Church communities. They came back together after healing and preaching, confronting and suffering, and they shared their sufferings and joys, they reflected together to understand better God's plan for them, they offered common prayer and Eucharist. And, thus, they went out again with an even bolder enthusiasm to preach God's Word.

Obedience, then, consists in listening to God's Word, and growing in our ability to understand its deepest meaning for our life and our mission:

1. Growth in taking responsibility for community's life and direction.
2. Growth in developing meaningful ministries which try to meet the critical needs of today's world.
3. Growth in sharing the Word among ourselves and in the marketplace.

It seems to me that what we have traditionally called the "Vow of Obedience" is precisely the way in which each community agrees to live and work and share its faith together. It is the covenant we make with God and with each other in order to grow and deepen our consecration to the mission of Jesus.

Conclusion

It is imperative for our apostolic religious communities to intensify and deepen our humanization commitments of the 1960's and at the same time, to pursue our hungering spiritual quests of the 1970's. The Christian in mission to the contemporary world is called to struggle for both personal and social transformation in Jesus Christ. The realization of the kingdom which Jesus proclaimed is, in fact, the building of an ever widening network of relationships of justice, peace and friendship. The personal transformation each of us longs for is the holiness of the Gospel, and the social transformation which our world cries out for is our challenge to participate in the mission of the Gospel.

The cries of our contemporary global society are many—for bread, for freedom and justice, for truth and understanding, for peace and reconciliation, for independence and inter-dependence, for acceptance and friendship and for ultimate transcendent meaning.

Somehow, some way, the apostolic religious community must lift up a clear sign for all to see that the kingdom of holiness and justice which Jesus preached is possible in our world today and at the very same time we must effectively minister to the most critical social wounds in our milieu.

Our problem today in the Church and in our communities is not so much one of how to communicate the Good News of Salvation in Jesus but primarily how to live it.

The Service of Religious Authority: Reflections on Government in the Revision of Constitutions

Mary Linscott, S.N.D.

Volume 42, 1983, pp. 197-217.

Experience in recent years strongly suggests that religious authority, like most other kinds, is in a moment of crisis. A justifiable but over-vigorous reaction to some previous styles of operation has often been the immediate occasion of this. Other causes, however, have also contributed to the situation: the emergence of a strong culture-consciousness in certain areas; the introduction of new processes and patterns whether offered postively, negatively, or simply as a change from what existed before; the need to make values and structures correspond more evidently; the evolution of ideas about religious life itself and about the Church; and even the very fact of having lived since the late 1960's in experimental conditions which often did not provide clearly for the exercise of authority. The crisis is something which ultimately affects fundamental values in religious life: identity, apostolic efficacy, the nature and importance of consecration, the future form of religious life as such. Because of its potentially serious consequences, the crisis cannot be ignored. In fact, many institutes are facing it very honestly. Responses vary. A few follow the ostrich in seeming to assume that if no attention is paid to it, the situation will disappear of its own accord. Some tend to extremes: a holding to the *status quo* as if nothing had happened, or a leap into a pattern which involves the virtual dissipation, or at least the non-exercise, of any real authority. Some strive to keep the reality of authority but clothe it in a different language, often that of business management or politics. Some keep the concept in words but virtually shift the content to something else: usually participation, communication, consensus or leadership. None of these responses meets the situation but each indicates the realization that there is a situation to be faced.

More recent lines of development show a growing awareness of the need to relate religious authority to religious obedience, and both to the ecclesial dimension of consecrated life. Sisters are realizing that the authority question can only be handled adequately on the level of faith and of relation to the Church, and they are trying to find expressions which will simultaneously reflect faith, foster life and values, meet present realities, and be in accord both with the Church's common law and with the best traditions of their institute.

One such line of development is based on a better appreciation of the service rendered by authority. Current attempts to express this are frequently contradictory because the service of authority is taken to mean either authority *and* service or authority *as* service and the conclusions drawn are not wholly consistent with either one or the other. But if authority of itself is service—that is, if by the fact of being itself it serves religious life necessarily and fruitfully— we have a line with rich possibilities.

It is some of these lines which I hope to explore. Before doing so, I think that a few clarifications are in order. First, I will not be speaking about authority in general but only about religious authority: the authority properly exercised in a religious congregation because of its recognition by the Church. Secondly, since without it the religious congregation would not exist as such, I will be assuming that the reality of religious authority itself is not in question but that much of the crisis lies in the evolution of structures and the search for suitable styles of exercise. Thirdly, I will restrict my reflection to the experience of congregations of sisters of apostolic life. This is partly because it is in them that questions regarding authority and government are sharply presented, and partly because my own experience is extensively with them and my reflections are largely conditioned by their sharing.

The reflections fall into three main phases—a look at religious authority itself as it is seen in Jesus, in the Church and in religious institutes; then the service of authority in religious government; and finally some of the strengths, confusions and questions in the service of authority at present.

I. The Service of Religious Authority

1.1 In Jesus

Probably the most familiar scene associated with the authority of Jesus is the one at the end of St. Matthew's gospel (Mt 28:19-20). Mary of Magdala and the other Mary have been mandated, first by the angel at the tomb (28:7) and then by the risen Lord himself (28:10) to tell the disciples, "my brothers," to go to Galilee. It is a solemn convocation to the "mountain where Jesus arranged to meet them." There, before the adoration of some and the hesitation of others, Jesus makes his last, confident claim, gives his last command, and pledges his last promise in a setting which, for Matthew, recalls the old law of Sinai and the new law of the beatitudes. The claim is absolute—

"All authority in heaven and on earth is given to me" (Mt 28:19), and, to make this effective, he promises to be with them until the end of time (Mt 28:20). Therefore, in the work of evangelization—preaching, baptizing, teaching, carrying God's word everywhere and to all the ages—the inner strength, impulse and power are always that of Christ himself, to whom all authority is given.

To the disciples, this can hardly have been surprising. Many knew Jesus as one who had authority and who exercised it. He spoke with authority and not as the scribes and pharisees (Mt 7:28-29); he interpreted the law on no authority but his own (Mt 5:21-22 ff.); he ordered evil spirits to go forth, and they went (Mt 8:32); he commanded the winds and the seas, and they obeyed him (Mt 9:27); he had authority over sickness (Mt 8:14-15); blindness (Mt 9:29); deafness (Mk 9:7-35); dumbness (Mt 9:32-33); lameness (Mt 15:30); paralysis (Mk 2:11); sin (Mk 2:10); and death itself (Lk 7:15). The authority he exercised in regard to the disciples was unquestioned. So also was the fact that, when he chose, he could confer on others authority similar to his own. Sometimes the authority was for a short period, as when the apostles who had rejoiced exuberantly in it during their first mission (Mk 6:7, 30) found that they no longer had it when they tried to cure the boy possessed, at the foot of Tabor (Mk 9:18). Sometimes it was promised for a longer future, as to Peter after his confession of faith (Mt 16:18); and by the lake of Tiberias it was given in a definitive way (Jn 21:15-17). Jesus was Lord and Master, Shepherd and Teacher, King, though not of this world; Lord of the Sabbath, Messiah and Son of the living God. His authority was never in doubt.

According to his own testimony, however, this authority was neither assumed nor taken by acclaim, but given. Like his priesthood, it was not something that Jesus conferred upon himself or took of his own initiative (see Heb 5:4), nor was it something that he would accept from the acclamation of delighted followers who wanted to make him King (Jn 6:15). It was, as he himself said, "given" and given by the Father.

For this reason, his authority was unlike any other. Intimately connected with his person as Son and with his mission as Redeemer, it served a purpose which was the Father's business (see Jn 14:31), the "will of him who sent me" (Jn 5:30). It extended to all things in heaven and on earth. It was clearly distinct in its exercise from the authority of "the rulers of this world who lord it over their subjects" (Jn 22:25) and it was used to give life (Jn 10:10) and to heal (Mt 8:16); to teach (Mt 5:14); to save (Jn 12:47); to forgive (Mt 9:6); to sanctify (Jn 1:12); to unite (Jn 17:21); to bind and loose in heaven (Mt 18:18); to send in evangelizing mission (Mk 16:16); to found the Church (Mt 16:18).

1.2 In the Church

It is this authority, exercised for the same purpose and in the same manner, that Christ continues in his Church by his presence to the end of time. Peter's authority was something that was given as a matter of faith: it was Christ's authority invested in him. He knew it when he said to the man at the Beautiful Gate of the Temple: "In the name of Jesus Christ of Nazareth, get up and walk" (Ac 3:7). He knew it when he helped phrase the decision of the so-called Council of Jerusalem in the words: "It has seemed good to the Holy Spirit and to us" (Ac 15:25). He experienced it in the inner changes of values that he had to make in order to welcome Cornelius (Ac 10:34, 42) and to break with the Judaizers at Antioch (Ga 2:11-14). Exercising the authority of binding and loosing that Christ had uniquely given him (Mt 16:19) and confident in the Lord's prayer for him (Lk 22:32), Peter confirmed his brethren with a power which he knew was pure gift. It was at the service of Christ's mission. It depended for its efficacy on an intimate personal relation and loving obedience to the Master who had conferred it and it was exercised for Christ's purposes and in Christ's way even to union with him in martyrdom.

The same characteristics marked Paul's exercise of authority. "Be imitators of me as I am of Christ" (1 Co 4:1) was his cryptic summary of his own place in relation to the Lord who was his life (Ph 1:20) and the new Christians who were his responsibility. He could appeal, and did, to the moral authority of example which can result from the quality of life, of work and of prayer in someone who is fully living his or her baptism. But he had another kind, too: a personal authority given him by God for his work among the gentiles whereby, in union with Peter, he could inspire, instruct, encourage, correct, judge, and organize the Churches he founded in order to lead them to the fullness of Christ. In using it, he made a careful distinction between what was common teaching "from the Lord," as he called it, and what was his own opinion (1 Co 7:10, 12). He was particular not to profit from it in any way personally (1 Th 3:8-9 and 1 Co 9:15-18) and he was at pains to ensure that it was continued in his young Churches (2 Tm 1:6, 2:1-2). So we find him constantly instructing, correcting errors whether of doctrine in Galatia or of manner of life in Corinth, fostering order in the local Churches whether liturgical (1 Co 11) or organizational (Tt 1:15) or in the matter of interpersonal relations (Ph 4:2). When necessary, he appealed for material support from them (1 Co 16:1-4 and Rm 15:25). None of this was done without suffering, as the second letter to the Corinthians makes clear. The authority of Christ was only exercised in the way of Christ—through the passion and resurrection, and Paul's was a paschal experience.

Religious authority in both Peter and Paul was the power of Christ given them and acting through them to fulfill the purposes for which the Church was founded. From their time onwards, the essential authority of the Church has been the same. Her task is to save, to sanctify, to unite, to reconcile to the Father, and to spread the good news of Jesus Christ concretely to all nations and to the end of time. She is, in Vatican II's beautiful phrase, the sacrament of salvation. She therefore has to direct, judge and teach with an authority that cannot come from her members and which she cannot take upon herself but which is the authority of Christ whose presence she is. Her intimate union and identification with him ensure that his own authority is exercised in and through her. It does not, however, make her proof against human weakness in her style of exercising it, any more than it protected Peter from errors of judgment or Paul from the consequences of a volatile temperament. In the course of history much has occurred to condition the Church's structures in ways that needed later revision, and, on that level, she has been embroiled at times in uses and abuses of authority that had little to do with the authority of Christ. But the essential truth remains. The authority which is uniquely proper to the Church is a religious authority—that of Christ himself—to save, to make disciples, to preach the gospel, to bring all to the Father in every place and age.

This is the authority which is exercised in the recognition of religious institutes by the Church as a microcosm of her own reality. It is to this authority that they relate; and it is this authority which gives them theirs.

1.3 In Religious Institutes

There are several circumstances which require that the authority in a religious institute be an ecclesial or religious authority and not just one which meets functional or organizational needs. These circumstances touch the nature of religious life itself. Religious institutes do not originate of themselves nor do they continue entirely as a result of their own efforts and planning— they are the result of a gift of God and they depend on him for both their origin and their continuance. Their basic reason for existence is the closer following of Jesus Christ from which, for them, everything else must flow and to which everything else must be related. Moreover, they are in a special way God's gift to the Church: their way of life makes good sense only on the level of faith; they witness to realities and absolutes that are neither tangible nor visible, and it is only in virtue of the Church's recognition and approval that they exist. Their purpose is that of Christ and of the Church. Such institutes require an authority that operates on the level of faith, Christ and Church, and which corresponds to the obedience which the members have freely vowed as a value because of their closer following of the Christ whose love made him obedient even unto death.

All religious foundresses have become aware of the need for this kind of authority as God continued to act in their lives. A variety of providential circumstances can bring Christians together to do good—Pax Christi, the Christian Social Volunteers, CAFOD, the Catholic Women's Guilds would be random samples, and the members of these groups need no more than the authority that results from their own self-organization in order to operate well and to achieve their purposes. Their members give to each other whatever authority is necessary for the organization to function. They are related to the Church, not essentially or by nature of the authority which they exercise, but by the recognition of their common purpose and by the baptismal commitment of the individual members. Some religious institutes have begun in this way.

At some point in their development, however, came the realization that they were aspiring to something more than what a group of Christians, however well-intentioned, could give to itself. The desire for a total public commitment to God formally received, the need for perpetual vows, the call to follow Christ intimately and as community in his obedience, and the urge towards a particular insertion into his public mission, would be some of the reasons which would prompt a founder or foundress to ask the Church to exercise her proper authority and to recognize the institute as a religious family. The Church alone, in Christ's name, can establish a religious institute, can receive vows that are vows of religion, can give an ecclesial mission and can confer the specifically religious authority in virtue of which an institute can require its members so to live and to work as to attain the purpose for which the institute was erected.

This authority, which I will call religious authority, relates particularly to consecration, vowed life, mission, formation and government. It is specific to religious institutes and it is not the same thing as organization, responsibility, power or leadership. Given by the Church, it always involves an ecclesial accountability.

Moreover, religious authority is never absolute. It is invested in persons clearly designated but who for the most part may not operate alone, and it is mediated through structures, usually worked out by the foundress in dialogue with the Church, which express the charism, nature, spirit and purpose of the institute and which are approved in its constitutions. Such authority makes possible a life of vowed obedience. Moreover, it is necessary for it.

It is true, of course, that the structures by which religious authority is mediated can become outdated. They can atrophy, be abused or manipulated, lose contact with reality, or fail to function. They can reach a stage when they no longer correspond to or express the values that they are meant to foster. They then need to be revised and renewed. For this process, it is of the utmost importance to bear in mind the nature, purpose and source of religious authority, since models that are suitable to other forms are not necessarily appropriate to the structures of authority in religious life. It is also necessary to remember and respect the strongly ecclesial dimension of religious authority since this makes renewal of authority structures always a matter of dialogue with the Holy See and not simply the unilateral initiative of an institute. We further need to keep clear the correlation of authority with charism and life as expressed in the institute's own sound traditions, since this gives the best practical guidance for structures which will reaffirm the institute's identity in creative fidelity, continuity and openness. Where structures are renewed in this way, authority is a fruitful reality serving the purposes for which religious life exists. It is a witness to him who came not to be served but to serve and who used his authority at the service of the kingdom. Where the renewal of structures somehow loses sight of the unique nature, ecclesial dimension, and charismatic continuity of religious authority on the level of faith, it can ultimately betray religious life itself by secularizing it, in the negative sense, in what is fundamental to it. The various crises of authority at present lie at various points between these two possibilities.

II. The Service of Authority in Religious Government

2.1 The Model

The model of the authority that serves is Christ, the Servant of Yahweh. He to whom all power is given in heaven and on earth is also, and without diminishing either aspect, the one who came to serve, who emptied himself, obeyed even to the cross, and gave his life as a ransom for many. Clearly in Jesus authority and service are not in contradiction. One is not at the expense of the other and there is no tension of opposites having to be held in balance. He refers easily to both, as when he is washing Peter's feet (Jn 13:14), and he never attempts to justify either. Being at once Son and Servant, he exercises both authority and service as one, and this is of the essence of his incarnation.

As religious, the goal of our life is the closer following of Christ in all its fullness but there is no doubt that we have a certain difficulty with this aspect of his reality. This may be because we tend to separate the concepts of authority and service in a way which he does not. Jesus is concerned with the reality of each; he never confuses them, but they are one in his person. We tend to oppose them and to get involved in words to describe them. For example, we often think or speak of authority as an abstraction. Its synonym is power, with connotations of lordship, mastery, might and force that move easily into oppression and violence. Its implications are efficiency and the carrying out of orders. Its contrary is subservience. We think of service as a function accomplished or something done in view of helping another, whether this is a kindly individual act like giving a hand to an old person, or a public utility, like driving a bus, or the meeting of a national need like the operation of civil service. Its synonym is action in relation to something or action in view of something. It implies somehow being less or becoming less than another. Its contrary is command. We tend, therefore, to identify authority with the power and lordship which are the contrary of service and, because of the negative connotations which we attach to it, we try in fact to avoid its exercise in common life, to reduce or even to eliminate it, and we forego, perhaps too simplistically, the potential which it has for holiness and for fruitfulness in the apostolate. Yet Christ had authority, used it, and did not hesitate to speak of it and to confer it. It enriched, and in no way diminished, his capacity to serve. Perhaps we need to look more closely at why something which seems contradictory to us presents no difficulty in him.

The key lies probably in his total love of the Father. The Servant of Yahweh is also Son; all that the Father has is his (Jn 16:15); he always does what pleases the Father (Jn 8:29); he empties himself to do the Father's will in joy, in love and in complete oneness with him even to the cross and the resurrection. He is at once less than (Jn 16:28) and equal to the Father (Jn

10:30; 17:5), distinct from and one with him (Jn 1:1). The complement of Servant for Jesus is not Master but Father, even on the cross, and he is so one with the Father that all the Father's authority and power are his. He exercises them in union with the Father, in love, and specifically not as his own (Jn 10:37-38) but he exercises them all the more effectively because of that, and always for the Father's purpose.

It is into this mystery and reality that the exercise of authority in religious life has to enter. Only in close union with the person of Christ, dependent on the Father and missioned by him, can we find that simplicity, poverty of heart and generosity which has courage enough to exercise authority frankly as Jesus did, and to serve by the very fact of doing so. Government then becomes a process for fostering efficaciously the power and love of God in the lives of all the members of the institute. It helps to achieve his purposes in us and it enables us to carry out the mission he gives us.

Because the authority-service of Jesus is paschal, it can be continued in religious life only through a union with him which will also be a sharing in his passion as well as in his resurrection. There is no shortcut where this is concerned. If authority is to be service in the Christian sense, it will be so in union with the Servant who suffered. It can only serve from the cross. But it will also, therefore, know the joy of the cross and the fruitfulness of the cross and will be a source of hope and strength both to those who exercise it and to those who accept it. This dimension of faith, above all, is what distinguishes religious authority from all the other forms of power, leadership and organizational process with which it is so often confused.

Once the faith dimension has been grasped in Christ, there is no longer a problem as to how to combine an effective personal authority, needed to live the vow of obedience, with a genuine Christian service and freedom. Since to live is Christ, we find that he himself provides the solution, not by an external imitation but by an internal dwelling, action and transformation. It is not we who live but Christ who lives in us (Ga 2:20). He lives in us with both the authority and the service of the Servant-Son. We are therefore more likely to see our own authority-service situations on his level and become less inclined to solve them on levels that fall short of those of faith. We will be less prone to swing from a right rejection of authoritarianism to an over-egalitarian alternative which can only bring confusion and which endangers some basic religious values. We are less afraid of affirming authority, of indicating clearly those who will exercise it and of making the exercise effective. All this adds up to a growing spiritual maturity and, where it is found, the structures of religious government will be simple and rooted in faith. We will find ourselves free and peaceful in heart in living them, since freedom and peace are two gifts which the authority of Christ particularly gives, and they will call us constantly to the deepest values of our life. If they do not call us to these values, we have a responsibility to ask—why not?

2.2.1 Structures

It rests with each institute, in union with the Church, to determine what structures best express the value of authority in its own case. Structures are necessary because vowed obedience is more than a disposition of heart—it is that disposition expressed in action within an ecclesially approved framework. This is what distinguishes it from the Christian obedience required by baptism. The framework is provided by the structures of authority/obedience described in constitutions approved by the Church; and, in approving constitutions, the Church gives the authority which is necessary for the life of vowed obedience and which is meant to nourish the values of vowed living as a whole.

These values should be fostered through structures which are stable and which reflect sound priorities. Stability of structure is necessary for peace and growth and usually flows in continuity from the identity and lived tradition of the institute. Such stability is not stagnation. On the contrary, it keeps pace with life in organic continuity; it reflects a consistent identity but allows for necessary evolution. If it is too suddenly or too violently disturbed, balance is lost and both growth and identity suffer. They suffer, too, if priorities are confused. Religious life has its own clear priorities: the ongoing experience and following of Christ who called us, consecration to him, sharing his mission in community according to a given charism recognized by the Church. Structures of authority should reflect these and be Christ-centered not only in words but in reality. A religious institute does not have the structure priorities of any other kind of body. A bank is structured to be a good bank, not a good football club. A school is structured according to priorities of education; a business firm according to its requirements for commercial efficiency; a political party according to its goal and policies. Structures are determined largely by principles, history, goals and priorities, needs, concrete resources and actual circumstances as well as by a good many imponderables, but essentially they should correspond to priorities. In the case of a religious institute, structures are at the service of a group which exists for God, for the Church, for the life in Christ of its members and for participation in Christ's mission wherever it finds itself. This implies that, at all levels, structures of authority will promote unity, spiritual and human development in the members of the institute, and effectiveness in mission. They should do this in a unified and balanced way as the values are interdependent. Insistence on one at the expense of the others can be destructive. On the other hand, authority properly structured so as to promote well-balanced values is a highly effective element in the well-being of a religious institute and in the fruitfulness of its mission. The first priority of government is to ensure it. This means that at each level, general, provincial and local, there needs to be a clear locus of authority in *someone* whose primary responsibility is to foster the unity for which Christ prayed, to encourage the development of his life in all those to whom her authority extends, and to promote creative fidelity to his mission in her concrete circumstances, according to the spirit, tradition, and constitutions of the institute. In practice, the exercise of such authority involves a multiplicity of choices. There are demands for reflection, communication, representation, arbitration, discernment, endless listening, attention to details, information, accompanying dialogue and even occasionally a decision. Which comes first? how is one to act? and with whom? Good structures are a sound help in answering these questions, in keeping the priorities clear and in being a reminder that it is by keeping the whole reality of religious authority firmly in the context of Christ himself that one can come to a valid conclusion in any given instance.

A few short observations should be made at this point about structures in general. First, they should be determined and should be used in faith. It is a mistake to assume that faith can be taken for granted or that it does not need to be recalled in matters dealing with government. On the contrary! If it is not consistently presented, the Christ-element can disappear from this aspect of life more easily than from any other. The situation is then particularly vulnerable as the fundamental norm which gives religious life its identity is no longer available to evaluate and criticize other structure models which, though attractive, may have little to do with religious life itself. Another note would be that structures should be in conformity with ecclesial principles such as personal authority and accountability, the right relation of councils to superiors, the respect for integrity of conscience, and so forth. The Church's common law has a broad approach and gives wide latitude to individual institutes, but structures of government are a matter of dialogue with the Holy See both in their inception and in their ongoing modification. There is no *carte blanche* for an institute to go it alone in the matter, as this would be against its very nature as an ecclesial body. In the third place, authority structures appropriate for religious, while having a common simplicity, are a matter internal to each institute. In the process of shaping them, a pattern may evolve that has something to offer to other walks of life, but, where this happens, it is coincidental. The structure concerned is not necessarily deficient because this does not occur. The criterion for a good structure is its appropriateness to the promotion of religious life according to the charism and tradition of the institute adopting it. Finally, religious structures are personal in the sense that they serve a personal authority. Religious obedience is to individual persons entrusted with authority, and not to groups or to documents. We have to remind ourselves of this sometimes, remembering too that the best structure can be badly used, and that a dedicated and capable person can give good service despite a defective structure. The first does not make a case for dropping necessary structures, nor does the second justify the continuation of poor ones.

2.2.2 Style

Granted that structures are sound, there can be great liberty of style in operation and it is perhaps in this area that there has been the most marked progress since *Ecclesiae Sanctae* stressed the need for consultation and wide participation. The fact that religious authority is vested in individual persons has never meant that these individual religious act alone. It has never meant authoritarianism, however authoritarian certain individuals may have been, and may still be, even in today's changed circumstances. The Church has long insisted on the sharing of responsibility and the limiting of authority, as is evident from the necessity of councils and the enactments regarding general chapters. Religious have always been responsible for their own institutes but, depending on their culture and tradition, they often accepted this responsibility mainly through prayer, through exchanges of information on certain feasts and great occasions, and through participation in elections both provincial and general. The reiteration by Vatican II of the principles of shared responsibility and subsidiarity, however, coinciding as it did with new possibilities of communication and with strong grass roots movements in the more articulate societies, brought about considerable changes. Common prayer structures were often modified, informal exchanges of information gave way to more centralized and official publications, frequently of a less personal kind, and general chapters, for a time at least, assumed an importance that obscured their real nature as an ordinary aspect of an institute's responsibility for its own ongoing development and direction. They became a kind of public forum. At present, many institutes are moving towards a better balance where wide consultation is a steady feature but where it is recognized that, as a matter of common sense, not everyone does everything and that, in institutes of apostolic life, the involvement of the sisters has to be by an optimum, not a maximum, participation if the apostolate is to go on effectively. Mature institutes ensure such participation at the key moments of input, brainstorming, shaping of policy, expression of views before decisions on agenda that will direct the sisters' lives, and evaluation. But they leave those with authority free to act within the framework of constitutions and with a clear line of accountability. A participatory style needs the basis of effective authority, good structures and clear understanding of interrelationships. Where it lacks these, its effects are negative and tend to produce an uneasy erosion of values. Where it has them, it is one of the most positive developments since 1965.

Experience with different styles of operation, first by reaction in the early 1970's and then by evaluation at the end of the decade, is showing interesting results in currently presented constitutions. It seems clear that those now exercising authority can choose a style of operation that counts on a kind of collaboration that their predecessors did not have. It is not simply that many congregations are more at ease with the delegation of a certain authority to special groups for formation or finance or apostolate or personal development or communication, but that they are seeing the service of authority itself more clearly and are focusing it more on the priorities which are proper to it. Relationships are better defined, participation is more realistic and the level of trust is higher. Whereas a few years ago great emphasis was on style, particularly on team-style, group-style, or whole-style operation, sometimes at the expense of goals and structures, and in a way which could restrict true freedom of operations, the pendulum is now swinging in another direction. Constitutions are tending towards greater clarity and simplicity in their essential provisons. They are speaking more to fundamental principles and structures. In this way they leave much greater liberty of style.

2.3 Constitutional Expression

To support the service that authority renders to religious life, constitutions need clarity in three main areas: provision, process and terminology. Together with completeness and feasibility, clarity is a prime virtue in constitutional writing. Provided that an institute's goal is clear and that its members are united regarding identity and basic values, it can usually express its reflection of the Servant-Son in terms which reflect faithfully both the lived tradition and reality of the sisters and the common law of the Church. But the provision and processes need to be unambiguous.

2.3.1 Provision

Whatever the individual patterns may be, certain provisions for religious authority seem common to all institutes of active life. One is the assurance, at every level, of personal authority in accordance with the constitutions and in correspondence with the members' vow of obedience. This is what is called ordinary authority. It is exercised by designated individual religious—general, provincial and local superiors, while they are in office, for a specified length of time, and under conditions indicated in the constitutions. Ordinary authority cannot be wholly delegated. It continues whether a general chapter is in session or not and it ceases only when the sister exercising it ceases to hold office. Extraordinarily, and again according to the constitutions, authority is exercised by the general chapter when it is in session. It is understood that the general chapter is an ad hoc body representative of the whole congregation. Before it meets and after it is concluded, it does not exist as such, and for institutes of apostolic life at least, there is no permanent chapter. While in session, however, the general chapter exercises the highest authority in the congregation, though in an extraordinary way.

Other regional bodies, such as provincial or regional chapters, have whatever authority is given them by the constitutions as part of the congregation's particular law. Councils and councillors do not have personal authority by right of office, though the constitutions will indicate the occasions on which the superior whom they assist requires their deliberate vote for validity of action. Enlarged councils, inter-provincial meetings, assemblies and house-meetings do not have authority unless it is specifically delegated or unless the tradition of the congregation's particular law over a considerable period has provided otherwise. Given these general lines, provision is usually clear if the congregation asks itself who does what and for what purpose? for how long? in relation to whom? and with what accountability?

2.3.2 Process

Process deals with the "how" of authority as provision deals with the "what," "who," and "why." At present, "how" is particularly important with regard to forms of involvement and modes of operation. In a religious congregation, the motive for involving the members is a motive of faith. This does not touch the nature of personal authority, but it does ensure that it is exercised with belief in the truth that the Holy Spirit acts in all of us and can speak through any of us. The process by which major decisions are reached should therefore allow for that voice to be heard. This may need considerable time and patience, particularly in widely dispersed international congregations, but if our faith means anything to us, and this is the kind of process we have chosen, we have to be content to move at the Lord's pace rather than at our own. If we want the quicker decision, and we may be quite justified in doing so, we have to face the situation honestly in chapter and recognize that a complete consultation is not possible for us. The alternatives should be weighed and a choice made. This will avoid the confusion and distress which can occur when consultation is adopted as a principle, but is, in fact, found to be inoperable in practice.

Processes adopted should reflect the Servant-Son reality of Christ in the way that they are suited to the achievement of their goal and in their respect for religious values. They will, therefore, not become an end in themselves or assume an importance that they are not meant to have. They are a *means* to an end only. That is why, for the most part, they should not appear in constitutions. Apart from the key process of general chapter elections, their place is in a directory.

2.3.3 Terminology

Clarity of provision and process needs to be completed by clarity of terminology. Our vocabulary in referring to religious authority and government has changed enormously over the past years and it is hard to say how much the change has resulted from, as distinct from contributing to, confusion. Certainly confusion there is, and it seems to come from various sources: the use of jargon that is short-lived; the coining of words; the attachment of personal meanings to words which have another denotation in ordinary usage; imprecise language, and the substitution of inadequate terms for those which have an accepted, objective meaning. This is not the place to examine the effect of language on reality and of reality on language. It must be enough to remark that the influence works both ways—a fact which needs bearing in mind when revising constitutions. A constititutional text is a particular kind of document to be characterized by clarity, completeness and exactness of expression. This in no way diminishes its spiritual quality or its potential as a source of inspiration and encouragement. It does, however, determine the style which is appropriate to it. If we are writing poetry, we can be highly creative with language; if we are telling stories, we can be graphic with it; if we are making up cross-word puzzles, we can afford to be original; and, if we are writing constitutions, we need to be exact and univocal. There are three main reasons for this: the members of the congregation have the right to a clear and unambiguous text that means what it says and that is predictable in operation; the constitutions are not simply meant for the moment of writing but for a considerable time to come and they should therefore be expressed in a language that will wear well; the constitutions are a formal document agreed to by the congregation and approved by the Church, and they therefore belong to the body of writing which is technically affected by common law. Most professional bodies have an accepted terminology current in their communications—doctors for medicine, engineers for building, judges for law. The Church, too, in her Code and in communications connected with it has an accepted terminology whose meanings are exact. It is unwise, then, in a technical context, to substitute for this terminology one which is less clear or whose meaning is inadequate. For example, the words chapter, council, local community, election, appointment, consultation have each a content and meaning in ecclesial terminology that the words group, board, residence, selection, dialogue do not have. The second set of examples in many cases cannot replace the first without loss of clarity. Understandably, there is a reaction against certain words but, if a substitute is proposed, it should at least be as exact as the term it is replacing. We may not want a "Superior" at local level, even while we want the ordinary authority that a Superior exercises and the service of a Superior to the community, but we have to recognize that neither coordinator nor leader nor president nor person in charge nor representative denotes what "Superior" stands for in ecclesial terms. It would be a great help to many if a more acceptable word were found. In the meantime we are caught between an unpopularity and an inaccuracy!

Because a Superior General is required to govern according to the constitutions, it is necessary that these be clear and precise. However, there are many recurring examples in constitutional texts of imprecise language. Do we realize, for instance, that a *decisive* vote obliges the person with authority to act, and a *deliberative* vote does not? That a decision is hardly ever taken by the major superior *and* her council but by a major superior with the consent/deliberative vote of her council? that a council does not act *collegially* except on rare occasions that the constitutions indicate? that the Superior General is much more than the highest *executive* officer of the congregation? that the general chapter is not only a *legislative* body? that *consensus* alone does not imply decision? These and many others could seem over-detailed technical points but as a matter of fact they are the kinds of things that cause tension and suffering because in actual life they do not speak clearly about matters where clarity is needed. The exercise of authority, and collaboration with it, can be made painful because of them.

III. Authority in Religious Life at Present

3.1 Positive Developments

All this seems to have come very far from the mystery of the Servant-Son which is at the heart of authority in religious life and yet the very coming down to terminological details is a reminder that the Incarnate Lord does indeed come, as Julian of Norwich said, "to the lowest part of our need." Dreams and values; theological truths and practical dynamics; processes, structures and vocabulary itself are all involved in the living of the obedience to persons in authority that we have vowed. One of the most positive trends in religious life at present is that authority is increasingly seen as a sharing in the mystery of the paschal Lord which is at once a service and a responsibility. Where that is grasped, together with its implications of both cross and resurrection leading to the outpouring of the Spirit, the exercise of authority is fruitful. It is undertaken with simplicity in genuine poverty and openness of heart, and it is accepted with faith. This does not mean that there will be no mistakes. Only the dead are beyond that. But it does imply a willingness to learn, and an exercise of authority that is real. It is also an authority at the heart of community, not above or outside it. As this movement gains strength, there are more religious willing to accept the responsibility of authority than there were ten years ago. In several places, moreover, they are encouraged by a new appreciation on the part of fellow religious for the necessity of authority if consecrated life is to be properly lived. Another positive element in this development is the fact that in the final revision of constitutions, in which many congregations are now engaged, the role of the religious who exercises authority is much more clearly delineated than it was in the stormy seventies.

Positive, too, has been the stripping away from the concept of religious authority of the accretions which had become attached to it over the years and the singling out of its essential dimensions. This is reflected in the kind of qualities looked for in a potential superior and in the expectations listed for him or her. The days when the person exercising authority was virtually expected to do everything and know everything, "to be everything to everybody" in a sense that St. Paul never meant, are gone, thank God. There is still a lingering problem with regard to a confusion of authority with leadership, but on the whole, the concept of religious authority at present shows a marked improvement on what it was not too long ago. Fewer religious have real difficulty with it, fewer still reject it entirely, and those who do tend to have problems that are deeper than those of authority and obedience. I am not saying that because the concept is more readily accepted, authority and obedience are any easier to live: simply that the wider notional acceptance could well lead to a deeper acceptance in reality.

This means that religious authority has a better chance of achieving its purpose and that it is more likely to be appreciated for its efficacy than for its efficiency. As long as the criteria were largely functional, authority was expected to be efficient, to get things done, to ensure that all was running well.

Now that its true role is emerging more clearly, it is seen to be needed for its efficacity: the quality it has, because of its relation to Christ, to enable the congregation to achieve its purpose. Things will undoubtedly get done, all will run more or less well and efficiency is still a useful value, but we are coming to see that not for that do we need religious authority. We need it for religious life itself. It brings us back insistently to the dimension of faith and to the truth that the person of the paschal Christ is the reason for which religious life exists.

3.2 Some Weaker Areas

The effort to renew structures of authority, like any other human enterprise, has its weaknesses as well as its strengths. The ones which I indicate here are not an exhaustive list but simply three areas where weakness is specially apparent and specially risky. I base the observations on the study of revised constitutions, mainly those presented in English, and on work with the congregations who have produced them.

One area of weakness lies in a certain fear of authority itself. It can happen that the word authority appears in a text but that the reality of authority is conspicuously absent. Provisions are such that effective authority does not exist and that anyone who is called on to exercise it would find her effort virtually neutralized by a variety of counter-balancing groups. This type of thing is extreme and, fortunately, rare but it does exist, often as an unconscious reflection of a low level of trust rather than a desire for participation, mistakenly expressed. More often, the weakness comes from an identification of authority with service in a way which absolutizes the second without allowing for the true nature of the first. Authority is indeed a service but it can only serve by being itself; if there is no effective authority, there is no service either. A watered down authority, or one so widely diffused as to be inoperative, or one that is lost in excessive clutter of checks and balances, cannot be a service. What suffers in these cases is the living of vowed obedience, which is a basic value, and therefore also community effectiveness and mission.

A second area of weakness is a tendency to treat authority somehow outside the context of faith. It is notable sometimes that all references to faith and to spiritual values, to charism and to the Lord stop at the chapter on government. Texts of constitutions may have juxtaposed a fine spiritual-juridical expression of all other aspects of life and a provision for government which is purely organizational. This kind of secularism is often reflected in structures and language which are closer to the world of business or politics than they are to the values of consecration and religious life. This is not to say that the human sciences, the processes of business and the structures of politics have nothing to teach us. On the contrary. But in learning from them and adopting what is good we have to remember that they are oriented to goals other than ours and that they are meant to achieve other purposes. The broad values on which they rest are often very different from those of religious life.

In the third place there is a weakness of authority where there is confusion, whether it is confusion of models or confusion of relationships. Models of government are not like styles of dress which can be tried for size and changed with the fashions. Each is closely associated with the charism of the institute which it expresses. It corresponds to the deep and identifying values of that institute and it cannot be altered fundamentally without affecting these. Moreover, the type of government proposed by the congregation and approved by the Church in the acceptance of the constitutions will be all of one piece: that is, it will have a unified inner coherence; there will be a positive and balanced relation between its various parts and between each part and the whole. A congregation setting a high value on availability for mission will need apostolic mobility and will probably have structures with a considerable degree of centralization, an authority able to act promptly where necessary and a style which balances the need for consultation and involvement with the need for action. A congregation whose prior value is involvement of the members will structure its authority for wide consultation, accepting the slower pace and limitation of action that this necessarily implies. It will have less mobility and possibly a considerable degree of decentralization. Either model is acceptable provided that it is consistent and corresponds to the congregation's own character and spirit. Difficulties arise, however, when a congregation, in modifying its government structures, tries to achieve the purpose of one model with the means of the other. Apostolic mobility may be hamstrung by over-wide involvement, and a patchy and selective consultation is often worse for a congregation than none at all. On the other hand, involvement gets lost if a traditionally decentralized structure suddenly becomes over-tight in the name of apostolic mobility. The same principle applies in the use of processes such as appointment and election. They are not freely interchangeable, as they usually tie in with the whole structure and tradition of a congregation. If a general chapter wishes to make modifications on this point, it should do so in the context of an overall appreciation of its congregation's purpose and tradition, as well as of present needs. Consideration should be given to the implications for the values involved as well as to likely effects on the various government levels.

Confusion of relationships is a practical point and arises with regard to the relation of the major superior to the council, particularly at general level. Two basic principles should be recognized: that the major superior exercises personal authority; and that no person in a Christian organization should be in the position of being pressured, much less obliged, to act contrary to conscience. If the major superior and the council are clearly distinct, problems regarding these principles do not arise. The advisory nature of the council is respected and, if there is a deliberative vote, it is understood that the superior may not act against it, but is not obliged to act in accordance with it. She needs it for validity of action but, if the majority is against what she proposes, she is free not to act at all. She is not in the position of being required by council vote to do something of which she may not approve. If the major superior and council are not distinguished from each other, the voting on matters which constitutionally require a vote may be more decisive than deliberative. In that case, the major superior may be required to act in accordance with the numerical majority whether she is in agreement with it or not. Such a situation needs careful provisions. Otherwise, the superior's authority is not free and there may be pressure of conscience which should not exist. It might be noted in passing that while much business at present is done by discussion and agreement and while common law in the case of dismissal at least requires a collegial vote, there are still a number of topics on which a deliberative vote is asked for. This is to ensure that the richness of the councillors' opinions is at the service of the congregation.

A last popular confusion arises from the equating of authority with leadership. Despite the present tendency to use the two words interchangeably, authority and leadership are not the same. Religious authority is not a charismatic gift—it is a power ultimately given by the Church for a specific time and under certain constitutional conditions to religious who are appointed or elected to certain offices. It is subject to legislation. Leadership, however, is a kind of charism. It enables a person to influence others and to carry them in a particular direction whether by force of personality or intellectual ability or moral strength or professional competence or whatever. Most people have some kind of leadership ability which should be fostered for the good of the community, but the exercise of it in no way confers authority. Moreover, one cannot legislate for leadership. Some of the most charismatic leaders of this present century have led millions along some very doubtful paths. It is better therefore to avoid expressions such as "leadership" when authority is meant. The term also tends to depersonalize if used when referring to superiors, since leadership is abstract, and superiors are persons. Instead of saying "selecting leadership," it is therefore better to say: appointing or electing sisters to positions of authority, if that is in fact what is being done.

3.3 Questions

Questions arising with regard to authority are many but perhaps four need to be singled out. They do not seem to have satisfactory answers at present and they seem to be moving in different directions. The experience of the next few years may bring greater clarity. The first is—given the dimension of faith which requires that the authority of the institute be an effective support and encouragement to each religious, and given the new demands of the apostolate which are causing community situations not thought of twenty years ago, what provisions can we make for structures at local level which will efficaciously ensure the service of authority while meeting the needs of new communities? Larger communities seem to have less difficulty here since, provided the value of personal authority is not lost, they can usually either meet their need from among their own members or make that need evident to the province or institute. Small and scattered groups present a different picture. It is not the personal goodness or integrity or zeal of the members which is in any way in question, nor are doubts being raised here about the reasons for the small residences. Assuming that all this is good, as it very well may be, the question remains about the particular and necessary religious value of ordinary personal authority and vowed obedience. How is this lived, since without it there is a gap in religious life? Cluster and group superiors are one way of meeting it. Affiliations are another. Accountability to intermediate level is a third. Each poses its own problems and has its own ramifications but it is a good sign that so many institutes at present are keenly aware of the question and are concerned to find a valid response.

A second question and one which moves in another direction, though it is less often heard now than five or six years ago, is this: can it be said that authority is in the members of the institute or in the communion of its members? and if so in what sense? Clearly, religious authority as such cannot be in question here as this is not invested in all the members of an institute, nor do those who exercise it do so in the same ways or on the same levels. But if this specifically religious authority is not being talked about, the question really becomes: does there exist in a religious institute an authority other than that given by the approval of the Church in its erection? If so, what is it? and can it be distinguished from specifically religious authority? Only after these points are resolved is it possible to ask whether such an authority is in the members or in their union, and how. Time may clarify this point, too, as it is not something that can be taken for granted. However, we do not need to wait for a solution for it to agree to what is very clear: that the members of an institute both individually and as a community have responsibility for their religious family whether they exercise authority or not. In several discussions on this point, responsibility has been the real issue. This does not mean to say that the question regarding authority has no content. It means, rather, that it must be clarified and accurately focused if it is to be constructive.

A third question emerges from certain cultural areas: is a team form of government an acceptable structure for the exercise of religious authority? This is a difficult question to address in general as the meaning attached to *team* or *group* or *collective* differs according to the individual institute which is using it. Concrete team situations are also very diverse, sometimes even within the same institute. Some constitutional requisites, however, are clear. Religious authority, being personal, is exercised at each level of government by one person who has also the responsibility for exercising it and the accountability for its exercise. She is helped, advised, assisted, and occasionally slowed down, by other members of the institute who, though they do not have personal authority themselves, are named to collaborate with her as councillors. In their respective roles they work together during a mandated time in close contact with the whole membership and in accordance with the constitutions in order to promote the good of all. So long as the concept of team keeps the relation of superior and council clear, the resulting collaboration, like that which exists among the members of a good symphony orchestra, is a source of richness, strength and creativity. Team government in this sense can be very good: the team has a captain as the orchestra has a conductor; the locus of authority is clear; the individual gifts of the team members are at the service of the institute in all their uniqueness.

Team structure is less acceptable when it somehow inhibits the exercise of authority or depersonalizes it. There are difficulties, for example, if no member of the team effectively exercises religious authority; or if the members are virtually so many individual superiors instead of being one superior with councillors; or if they try to divide up authority among themselves in such a way that it is fragmented: no one takes entire responsibility for what is done, and the members of the team seem to be so many fractions of one group-superior. These models would be unacceptable because, in the long run, they would be damaging to an effective apostolate and even more to the unity in Christ which religious authority is meant to support.

Institutes exploring the possibilities of a team form of government have the challenge, without violating the charism and sound traditions of their evolution, to find structures which will incorporate the values of personal ordinary authority, shared responsibility, and clear accountability without overlaps or lacunae.

A last question probes still deeper and is in the order of reflection rather than of immediate practical decision. It is this: given that the structures of society are in evolution and its paradigms are shifting, should not the forms and structures which express religious authority be shifting too, and in similar directions? The question needs prayer and reflection as it touches the delicate relation between the essence of religious authority itself and the conditioning of its expression by time, place and culture. Basically, it is not a new question, though the formulation may seem new. Religious life has evolved as an action of the Holy Spirit in response to changing needs in the Church and in the human family. The nature and purpose of successive types of religious institute, corresponding to the charism of each, has led the Church to recognize differences and evolutions in the structures through which religious authority has been exercised. The new element in the contemporary question is that the reason given for possible modifications is not the nature and charism of the institute to which the form of authority corresponds, but the evolution and shifting paradigms of society in which the institute is serving.

The question therefore is: what determines the structures of religious authority? Does its unique nature and relation to the Church as a first priority predetermine its structures? or, this relation being safeguarded, can there be an evolution of style and of structures that reflects different cultures and social changes?

Inevitably style, approach and application of principles are affected by cultural and societal change, as every international institute knows. Structures as an incarnation of values, however, may be another thing. Religious authority is not simply a social or cultural phenomenon, although it exists in communities which have a social and cultural dimension. It will take time, discernment and a constant return to the source and reality of religious authority itself to see to what extent shifting paradigms should affect its structures.

It would seem that responses to this fourth question which are mainly based on social or political considerations aiming to meet a current situation will not go far enough and may well prove harmful. If we are to find a valid point of departure, we will somehow need to reach deeply into the essentials of religious life, into its theological and ecclesial reality, and into the dimension of community-in-mission which is essential to religious authority and obedience. Only then will we be in a position to work out the relation between the stable and constant values which identify religious life in history and the kinds of change necessary to the concrete evolution of that life in a society whose paradigms are shifting.

IV. Conclusion

I have focused almost entirely on one aspect of religious government: the authority, itself a service, which is particular to religious life as an active presence of the risen Lord who was obedient unto death. I have not tried to look at forms of government, or at the expression of government in constitutions, which would be a paper in itself, or at current experiences of government except insofar as they touch religious authority. The restriction of field has been prompted by a profound conviction: that much of the current difficulty about authority and government is connected with the unconscious separation of both from Christ, in whom and through whom we obey. We have to become again very sure, as our founders and foundresses were, that authority and government are an important part of consecrated living and that some of our basic values are involved in them. They belong to the mystery of religious life and to the closer following of Christ. Without them, religious life does not exist. That may explain why some of the great mystics and most zealous apostolic saints worked out some of the best provisions for religious authority through good government structures. Such authority and structures are service by being themselves and by being effectively used. In this they reflect the oneness of authority and service in Christ, Son and Servant. All good religious government brings us steadily to this: that the simple acceptance of the authority which enables us to live our vowed obedience, whether that acceptance involves the exercise of authority or collaboration with it, is an act of faith and of growth in the risen Lord whom we cannot see but who unites us, lives in us and sends us on his mission. This consecrated union with the Servant-Son, shared in community, transforming in its effects, and fruitful in witness and in action, is the very stuff of our religious life. It is a value on which it is worth spending time and effort.

Provincials as "Cultural Revolutionaries": The Role of Provincial Superiors Today

Gerald A. Arbuckle, S.M.

Volume 44, 1985, pp. 175-190.

Innovation is at the heart of survival and growth. Without innovation in response to rapidly changing conditions, human groups stagnate and die. This is true of business firms, of local and national economies. It is also true of religious congregations, of provinces within the congregations.[1]

Religious exist to serve the Church. They are to be concerned not just for the survival of their own province and congregation, but in particular they are primarily oriented to spearhead pastoral and spiritual growth within the Church. They are to be specialists in innovation: "Their whole lives are dedicated to God's service." Religious are to show forth "boldness of initiatives."[2] In quite expressive language, the document *Mutuae Relationes* emphatically insists on the innovative role of religious: there is need "to devise new, ingenious, and courageous ecclesial experiments under the inspiration of the Holy Spirit. . . . A responsiveness rich in creative initiative is eminently compatible with the charismatic nature of the religious life."[3]

Innovation is the generation, acceptance, and implementation of new ideas, pastoral methods or services, whatever can help develop within ourselves and in others the kingdom of God. Application and implementation are at the core of this definition; it involves the ability to change or to adapt.[4] Easy enough to define innovation. But how does innovation take place? What role do major superiors, especially provincials, have in stimulating change?

This paper is an attempt to answer these questions. I propose to approach this key topic by:

—summarizing recent management studies on how innovation takes place;

–summarizing relevant research conclusions of applied anthropology;
–applying these insights to the role of provincials within religious congregations.

I believe provincials today face challenges that their predecessors rarely confronted prior to Vatican II. They are called to be change-agents within their congregations; in fact, I believe the future of their congregations might well be said to rest in their hands. But, through no fault of their own, they often do not know *what* to do. If they do know *what* to do, they often do not know *how* to go about stimulating innovation.

Japanese and American Business Cultures

During the world's tough economic years after 1978, the picture on either side of the Pacific Ocean was remarkably different: soup kitchens in Detroit contrasted vividly with an apparent freedom from economic depression in Japan, where business firms exported more and more the things that Americans made once upon a time. Some people almost in a fit of hysteria have called for more protectionism against the "Japanese menace." Saner minds, however, do not blame the Japanese or the tardiness of the American government to build trade barriers, but they blame the limitations of America's managerial culture.[5] Recently I noticed a bank advertisement in O'Hare airport, Chicago, which stated: "In Chicago, nothing takes off faster than a Good Idea." This is not as accurate as it should be, simply because the American culture at large, and the management sub-culture, are not as conducive and supportive of innovation as is the Japanese cultural system. Several management experts, therefore, have concentrated their research not so much on the psychology of industry or business management, but on the anthropology of culture and culture change in relation to business action.[6] By culture we mean that network of common meanings and values that is deeply rooted in the consciousness/unconsciousness of a group of people. This network gives life to distinctive structures and institutions, myths and symbols. The symbols of a people have many meanings that are deeply real to those who share them; they give people a sense of identity, security, purpose. But since they are derived so much more from the heart than the head they are difficult for outsiders to grasp and describe.

What are the significant differences between the two business cultures? There are two key variables—the individual or potential innovator and the group—and both are given different emphases in the two cultures. Both cultures stress the importance of change-agents or innovators, that is of people who are gifted with the "art of anticipating the need for, and of leading, productive change."[7] In Japanese culture, innovators evoke change in and through the harmonious support and active participation of the group. Loyalty to one's group is a most respected personal attribute. The culture emphasizes harmony not for the purposes of maintaining the status quo but for innovation. Group leaders know this and hence concentrate less on the task of production than on the growth of good relations, morale, values that support innovators within the group. The innovators themselves do not seek to stand outside the group; they recognize that only through the active support and participation of the group itself will the ideas be implemented.[8]

But in Western business culture, reflecting the broader culture of the society, group leaders tend to stress the productive task to the neglect of group maintenance activities. Theoretically there is an assent to the need for building a supportive innovative culture, but "American managers don't quite realize that what they are creating requires a lot of energy and attention from them to sustain."[9] The Western culture, and in particular the American way of life, gives vigorous support and status to independence, to being "a rugged individualist." The American West may have been built by thousands of "rugged individuals spread over the vast frontier. But millions of lone rangers employed under a few thousand corporate roofs may not much longer prove workable."[10] In this system the rugged individual, the would-be innovator or change agent, must struggle and battle alone to prove the value of his or her insight. The group is assumed to have what really adds up to a negative or opposition role. The individual, as it were, stands outside the group; the group is not assumed to have any substantial role in helping to stimulate the innovative idea or in participating in its implementation. In the Japanese culture the innovative idea can truly be said to be the group's, though articulated at first by a particular person; in American, or Western cultures in general, that is not the case. The consequence for Western economies of course is unfortunate. It generally takes an extraordinarily tough individual to sustain his or her enthusiasm in the face of constant passive or open opposition. Little wonder that managerial researchers complain about the deadening restraints on innovation in Western business cultures.

The firms that are notably successful today in America are precisely those where the leadership recognizes that the primary task is to clarify, articulate and insist on key values: quality goods and services, the participation of all employees in discovering and supporting people who have new ideas for the maintenance of quality. This task of leadership is a tough assignment. If it fails, then the business culture becomes stagnant, oppressive of innovators and new ideas.[11] So, if American (and Western) businesses are to become truly competitive with Japanese enterprises, their leaders must become and remain *cultural revolutionaries*. Then the advertisement at O'Hare airport will be accurate!

Innovation and Innovators: Insights of Applied Anthropology

Anthropologists in general have the reputation of always aiming to preserve what is traditional. If they do take that approach, it is because the general thrust of socio-economic development programs, particularly in Third World countries, has been in the direction of what an expert on fisheries once called "bulldozing the tropics into civilization."[12] In the 1960s and 1970s (to a less extent) it was rare indeed for development experts to take into account the fact that people are human beings and also have distinctive cultures. The so-called experts descended as it were from on high with the "good news of development." The people had to listen "with gratitude," do what they were told and become "rich and good" just like Westerners! Since so many projects have failed or are failing, there is a greater openness to turn to anthropologists to help uncover why "the good news" became "bad news." The ignorance of the experts might have been bliss for them, but their lack of wisdom has meant immense suffering for the people.

The following general conclusions have emerged from the study of anthropologists into the success or otherwise of development projects:

1. *Changes will succeed only if they are in response to felt needs of the people.*

The discovery of what in fact are the real felt needs of a group of people is a long and difficult task. It is so easy for the would-be innovator to impose his own needs on people who for the sake of peace agree. I came across an example of two American volunteer development workers on a South Pacific island, who were worried by the fact that the ladies of the village had to go down a rough slope to a river to do the washing. So, they imported cement, "convinced" the ladies that the use of the village washing tubs would be far more convenient. After the tubs had been built, the good ladies used them for one day and back they went to the river. The volunteers were annoyed, but humble enough to ask why the tubs were not used: "We like to gossip about the men. If you wash at the tubs, the men will hear. Also, our backs are sore from standing at the tubs. We like to squat when we do the washing!"

In order to obtain the real felt needs, there must be lengthy and tiring dialogue based on the willingness to learn on all sides, considerable questioning and active listening by the change-agent.

2. *Innovative leadership must be encouraged to emerge from within the group and be supported by the group.*

A girl was taken from a Fijian village and trained in the capital city in how to improve the nutrition quality of village cooking. She went back full of enthusiasm; within a few days she was back to the old style of cooking. Why? No one in the capital thought it important to work with villagers on the spot to help them become accepting of change and supportive of the local innovator. The experts expected the impossible of one person.

This is a critical point. Innovators or change agents are "the *right* people in the *right* place at the *right* time."[13] The *right* people are the would-be innovators because they have ideas that look beyond the established ways of doing things. By the *right* places we mean that the people who have to be motivated to accept the ideas are willing in fact to be motivated and to participate in implementing the ideas. The would-be innovator and the group are not to be in opposition to each other, but are to be integrated into a team. The task of the main leader or main innovator—often one who holds an official position, e.g. government officer, town mayor, village chief—is precisely to help create space for individuals to "get the power to experiment, to create, to develop to test—to innovate."[14] This means that a tremendous amount of time and energy must go into disposing the group to be open to change, to be positively accepting of the innovator. There is no short cut!

The more the group is encouraged to become the agent of its own growth, the more in fact it will be sensitive to the need for the right type of innovators. Would-be innovators tend to fall into two broad types: those who are basically loners, uninterested in the group, possibly deeply bitter about being rejected by the group. Unless they can get over their spirit of excessive individualism, such people, because of personal reasons and/or the neglect by the group, can obstruct growth. There are others, however, who have been pushed to the margins of the group's life, but who still are deeply attached to the welfare of the group and who in their own way sorrow for the sense of blind conservatism and fatalism that the group expresses. These are the people that should be very specially spotted and encouraged by the main change-agent or change-catalyst.

3. *Development projects are more readily successful, if there is maximum delegation and involvement within small groups.*

For example, I found credit unions far more successful than large-scale business co-operatives in Fiji, because the former were village-peopled based, but the latter were firmly directed from the capital city by government officials. The people felt the credit unions were theirs; they "owned them" by participating daily in credit union affairs, their management, direction. But, this could be done only because credit union values of cooperation and honesty were constantly articulated by the official educational change-agents. And the people were called to the accountable by their own leaders on the basis of these values.[15]

4. *The innovators must not move faster than the group.*

The innovator can be so far out front that the people lose confidence in the project. The innovator in this case is equivalently demanding culture changes that require too many risks for the people; identity and security are endangered. So, the people retreat to old and familiar values and customs. They cannot be blamed for this. They have everything to lose, but the insensitive innovator with his skills and status may have little to lose.

By way of summary, there are three indisputable research conclusions: people definitely resist cultural changes that appear to threaten their basic securities; they resist changes they do not understand and they resist changes that are being forced on them.[16]

But these conclusions all sound so logical, so obvious. Why are they so frequently ignored in practice by even the most educated and intelligent of people? I can pinpoint four reasons in particular.

First, it is not easy for many of us to realize that all change involves in one way or another culture change, that is change in values, new security systems, and more. And culture change basically is *very* slow. We belong to a culture that has come to assume instant answers to instant problems! It is difficult for us to grasp the reality that the innovation process is a combination of technical and human or cultural factors, rather than being a purely technical or mechanical matter. The would-be innovator requires considerable patience and openness to learn just how change takes place.

Secondly, *leadership* is so often confused with *the use of authority*. It is assumed that change can take place simply by command. For example, it was decided in the mid-1940s that Fijians should have in their villages hygenic toilets of a simple design. The word went out from London, eventually reaching the district British officers in rural Fiji. The fine toilets were built by the villagers, under British direction, but not used! Officials "forgot" to involve the villagers in a decision that concerned them. True leadership aims to evoke participation. This is often more important than what is visibly done.

Thirdly, no matter how intelligent and educated the innovator may be, if he is insensitive to the dignity of the people the project will fail. People yearn to grow as people through participation in all that concerns their lives. If they are refused the chance to participate, or if they sense the innovator is out to manipulate them by going through the motions of participation, then they will withdraw from involvement and become passive and angry observers. When I was researching in Fiji into village development, I was frequently told by colonial officials that "Fijians simply cannot handle their own affairs." The tragedy is that the people had been told this so often that many had come to believe it. When the credit union movement was brought to Fiji by an American Jesuit, Marion Ganey, the people showed that the colonial officials were wrong. The people discovered that they *could* handle their own affairs. A major factor in this movement of self-growth for the people was the deep faith that the Jesuit expressed in the people and their potential. One Fijian in a village summed up what this meant for him: "When he comes into the village, even though he cannot speak our language, we feel ten feet taller and ten years younger!" Respect for people must spring not from fine words, but from the deep conviction in the heart. People sense whether it is there or not.

Fourthly, would-be change-agents can fall into what really is culture shock. People when confronted with a culture that is different from their own can feel so lost that they really cannot cope. They lose all sense of judgment and may well begin by acting in a thoroughly authoritarian manner in order to cope.

In brief, the findings of contemporary managerial and applied anthropology studies are the same. Innovation is the key to survival and growth. Innovation flourishes in those cultures in which innovators and people are positively interacting and participating together in implementing the new ideas. No matter what position the potential innovator holds, e.g. manager, village chief, government officer, church official, member of a group, to be ultimately effective he or she must be imbued with a philosophy of deep respect for the potential of the people to be masters of their own growth. As George Foster notes: "The ethic of helping people change their culture includes knowing what the culture is . . . what its processes of change are. It is not enough to be a competent technician, morally fortified with the unquestioned assumptions of goodness of one's profession. . . . The ethic involves restraint and caution in missionary zeal. It means . . . [being] careful not to plan for people, but to work with them in searching for realistic answers to their problems. . . . It means learning to be humble, to be willing to learn. . . . It means sympathy and tolerance. . . . It means a genuine and unselfish desire to help . . . in a realistic way based on full understanding of the nature of culture."[17] The warning of the wise Lao-tzu centuries ago remains universally true: "As for the best leaders, the people do not notice their existence. The next best, the people honor and praise. The next, the people fear; and the next, the people hate. . . . When the best leader's work is done the people say, 'We did it ourselves.'"

Challenges Confronting Contemporary Provincials

The Church's culture, prior to Vatican II, was highly structured and open to little change at any level. Its mission was clear and its pastoral methods were considered to be universally valid no matter what culture was being evangelized. Religious congregations reflected this type of culture. Major superiors gave clear commands, reminding people of the importance to maintain the rules of the community. They commanded; subjects were expected to obey. Certainly they did not expect to be consulted. It was assumed that superiors knew what was right, what God wanted. But with Vatican II superiors and their fellow religious were reminded that together they had to search to discover what God was asking of them. Pastoral methods that were once valid could no longer be considered so in a world subject to chronic change. These new emphases and values undermined the security and identity of the old religious-life culture. Questions replaced answers; clear and simple commands gave way to process. Sole authority yielded to rule by committee. We know well the malaise and confusion that hit congregations and individual religious.[18]

The role of the contemporary provincial is an unenviable one. How can a provincial stimulate a province to accept a culture in which the religious are open to change, effectively willing to participate in change, are supportive of innovation and innovators? In order to understand the complex nature of this challenge, I will construct a "typical contemporary province culture." I will then summarize various possible reactions on the part of a provincial when faced with such a culture. Since we are dealing with a cultural construct or type or model, it is inevitable that there will be oversimplifications, imprecisions. Readers can make their own additions or subtractions.

A Typical Province Culture

–Membership is aging; few, if any, recruits.

–A significant number of religious were trained under the pre-Vatican model in which creativity and innovation were discouraged.

–A significant percentage of religious are distressed, disoriented, by the theological, pastoral and spiritual emphases following Vatican II.

–The province, in whole or in part, denies that there are real manpower crises which demand positive planning and changes.

–Houses are closed, pastoral works put aside, not because of creative, forward-looking pastoral planning, but because the province has run out of manpower resources.

–A significant percentage of the province is spiritually uninspired and uninspiring.

–Small groups of religious or individuals are marginalized because of their innovative pastoral ideas and practices, or because they ask out of deep love for the Church and for the congregation challenging questions relating to renewal, or because their radical religious lifestyles are uncomfortable to the power forces in the province.[19]

–Religious strongly support decentralization of authority and personal freedom, but do not support a corresponding accountability to major superiors and to the province.

In this cultural model of course there are values and practices that are in conflict with each other. In fact, it can happen that in this model many religious find little of substance that they have in common. What happens when a newly elected provincial is confronted with a province that approximates this type? He can react in a culture-shock manner or accept the reality in an understanding way and, adopting the operational principles that should guide any would-be change-agent (described above), proceed to help cultivate a religious-life culture that is innovative, effectively open to change, a culture in which religious support innovation and participate in its implementation.

A brief look first at possible models of culture-shock reactions of the new provincial. Again, it is important to note that we are constructing models; it is necessary to indicate emphases rather than rounded descriptions.

1. *The Minister Provincial*: one who concentrates almost exclusively on the welfare of the individual religious; planning and animation are neglected.

2. The *Administrator Provincial*: one who keeps to his office desk, involving himself as far as possible in paper work; ministering and animation are neglected.

3. The *Preacher Provincial*: one who concentrates on preaching about the need for change; planning and ministering are avoided. He has an impact on no one.

4. The *Laissez-faire Provincial*: he opts out of all key functions. He assumes that kind words to all will produce lasting peace. Others assert leadership by default, but it is a leadership that builds up power for some strong sections of the province to the detriment of weaker power blocks.

5. The *Planner Provincial*: this is the dreamer who devises all kinds of plans for change, but avoids the nitty-gritty of organizing the implementation of the plans, the hard grind of administration and the demanding task of animation and ministering to the religious of the province.
6. The *Authoritarian Provincial*: this is the one who assumes he can minister to the religious, plan, administer and animate all by himself. Refusing to dialogue or to delegate, he believes "it is time that religious obeyed, put their heads down and got on with the job." He may set up a variety of committees, not to hear what they say, but to get things done that he decides should be done.

Given the pressures on a provincial today, we must not be surprised if some behave in ways that approximate to one or other of these models. So great can culture-shock be that individuals may not consciously be aware of why they react in these ways.

We are now in a better position to look at objectively what the functions of a provincial are today, how he or she should act in a reasoned way when confronted with the task of fostering a culture supportive of innovation.

The Provincial as a Cultural Change-Agent

Leadership has to do with meeting needs. Religious need a sense of spiritual purpose, they need to feel valued by fellow religious, they need to participate in decisions that affect them, they need to be stimulated to accept in an ongoing way the call to a deep union in Christ; the province has need to be clear as to its goals and how to realize these goals in practice, it needs a culture that is supportive of change and change agents. Provincials truly exercise leadership to the degree that they respond to these needs. We are here speaking of *transformational* leadership, as defined by J. M. Burns. For him: "Transforming leadership ultimately becomes moral in that it raises the level of human conduct and ethical aspiration for both leader and led, and thus it has a transforming effect on both."[20] It is a leadership that rarely uses the authority of the office, not a leadership that moves people to act "by the sheer overwhelming magic of his personality and persuasive powers."[21] The type of leadership the provincial should be exercising is described in the findings of applied anthropology given above. It is therefore a leadership that aims to help religious discover, individually and corporately, that they have within themselves the power and the commitment to enter into a process of innovative change in service of the Lord and his Church. Such a provincial is "influential by strengthening and inspiriting his audience. . . . The leader arouses confidence in his followers. The followers feel better able to accomplish whatever goals he and they share."[22] This is an extremely tough assignment.

A provincial has several definite functions as a leader: to minister in a pastoral way to the needs of individual religious, to plan for the future of the province, to administer the province by implementing the plan and to animate the whole province to be part of the planning and implementation of the corporate plan. Each function is related to each other function listed. How in practice are these functions to be realized so that no one function achieves a priority it should not have?

I believe a provincial can fulfill the mandate to lead the province by empowering individuals and groups to use their gifts for the common good; by helping the province to discover its common goals; by helping the province to discover the means of achieving the goals.[23] Let me explain the meaning of each of these statements:

1. *The Empowering of Individuals and Groups*

Individuals and groups need to be reminded that they are called to serve the Church as committed religious, placing whatever gifts God has given them at the disposal of others. In the post-Vatican Church this is a most demanding provincial apostolate, particularly when so many religious have been personally wounded or disoriented as a result of the cultural changes following the Council. Tremendous patience in listening is required. Religious in fact may need specialized help if their sense of self-worth and confidence is to be restored to them. However, the more religious are affirmed in the gifts given by God, the more they are open to participate actively in sharing their visions with others and in supporting innovation.

In his visitations the provincial is also able to discover individuals who are already change-agents or potentially so. They may need affirming in their role, particularly if there is opposition to their insights. The provincial, eventually using his authority, may then decide to place these change-agents in positions where these people can be the *most* productive. He can spot those religious who with further training are able to become change-agents, e.g. as spiritual leaders, administrators, pastoral leaders.

At the corporate and individual levels, he articulates the values that relate to the welfare and purpose of the province, e.g. values of Christian service, cooperation, participation, support for innovators. This role is called the "hands-on, value-driven" approach, an apt description that religious life animation should mean.[24] It is a role that requires the provincial to keep challenging the province, to keep raising awkward or difficult questions that others do not want to raise, e.g. what is the purpose of what you are doing? why are we in this particular apostolate—just because we have always been doing it or because this is what God wants us to do because people really need it? what ideas do you have to improve the quality of your apostolate? It is not sufficient to ask the questions; he must be on the spot, either personally or through a delegate, to hear the answers and to question further if the answers are not adequate. Remember, this is the only way for the real pastoral felt needs to emerge. The more religious are *forced* into responding to such questions, the more in fact they are being empowered to utilize their God-given gifts.

The word *forced* needs to be further explained. In order to be forced into reacting to realities, it might well be necessary for a provincial to cultivate in certain circumstances a "planned apostolic neglect or avoidance" of individuals or groups. Sometimes people will not respond to reality until they are *forced* to do so through suffering and the discovery of their own powerlessness. The discerning provincial will know just when this suffering should be permitted to occur.[25] For periods of time he may become the object of considerable anger from the individuals or groups in question who keep demanding that "he solve their problems." I recall meeting members of a credit union in one Fijian village that for several years had become inactive. They told me that for a long time they blamed outsiders for their problems. The founder, Fr. Ganey, kept away quite deliberately until the people finally realized that they were the source of their own inactivity. They expressed gratitude for the *skilled neglect* on his part. Paradoxically, this is an example of the "hands-on, value-driven" type of leadership.

2. *Helping the Province to Discover Common Goals*

Without common goals, a religious province will break up into many competing groups, struggling for ascendancy over one another and for control over ever-declining manpower or financial resources. Just as the discovery of what the province's felt needs are is a long and difficult process, so also will it be challenging to refine the common goals that relate to these needs.

A provincial might be able to discover the goals himself and articulate them to the whole province. Notionally the province might accept them, but in practice they will reject them for they have never had the chance to *own them* by participating in discovering them themselves.

How are these goals to be discovered and articulated? We all know from bitter experience how chapters so frequently end up with finely worded statements of goals for the province and for this or that apostolate. But, once the texts are published they are shelved and nothing happens, until the next chapter when the same procedure is adopted! Recall the anthropological insight above: projects are more readily successful if there is maximum delegation and involvement within small groups. If this is done in provinces and the information and experience of the groups are fed up to a chapter or provincial council, then the goals that emerge will more likely be *owned* by the whole province.

A provincial then will use interest groups and, if necessary, foster new groups to emerge that are close to where action is taking place. Delegation is insufficient; he must keep calling them to accountability. When this process is adopted, time-consuming though it may be, individuals with innovative ideas are more likely to emerge and their insights more easily owned by the group. From the point of view of a desk administrator, the approach is not particularly efficient as regards the use of time, but it will definitely be effective. It means, of course, that the provincial either directly or indirectly will be present to these groups, actively listening, challenging them to see their goals and objectives in light of wider corporate needs and goals. If he ignores them, they rightly become discouraged, bitter and angry, eventually either going their own way independent of the province's needs or becoming purely passive without any interest in innovation.

3. *Helping the Province to Discover the Means to Achieve Goals*

A province that denies it has a manpower problem, when in fact it obviously has, must be challenged to recognize this reality. I heard of one province of a congregation which expected at the very most to have three priests ordained for the coming ten years. The provincial chapter encouraged each apostolate to state their manpower needs; they did and they were accepted without question by the chapter. No one wanted to accept the fact that the total manpower requirements of the province as passed by the chapter were twenty priests beyond what the province could ever possibly field. A province that is really participating in its own growth at the grassroots would never have reached such an unrealistic state of denying the obvious. A provincial will work closely with various interest and apostolic groups, challenging and planning how to achieve the goals established by the groups and by the province as a whole.

Moreover, the provincial will aim to discover just what the criteria for manpower assessment is being used at the grassroots. For example, if the Church is defined in organizational or hierarchical terms, then low recruitment coupled with an aging membership in a clerical religious congregation is a severe crisis. On the other hand, if the Church is defined in community terms, the present search for new directions promises all kinds of possible theological and sociological variations in forms of ministry.[26] In addition, a province in which many members have been trained to be passive, uncreative, unsupportive of innovation and innovators will have a manpower crisis that is open to correction by a provincial. A provincial who has the ability so to empower religious to discover that they can be creative even in small ways and open to change will be developing resources within the province that were not able to be considered before.

In brief, therefore, the provincial's task is to stimulate the province through its own discernment process to an awareness of its own resources. The criteria—theological and otherwise—need to be spelled out and repeatedly articulated until owned by the province. They cannot be the criteria of the provincial alone.

Qualities of the Provincial as Cultural Change-Agent

In this paper it has been assumed that leadership is "the process of influencing the activities of an individual or a group in efforts toward goal achievement in a given situation. In essence, leadership involves accomplishing goals with and through people."[27] It means that the leader is concerned about tasks, but also human relations. A provincial will need to know what the mission of the Church is, the charism and mission of his own congregation, an understanding of the manpower and financial resources of the province. He will need to know the theory that relates to how to stimulate the province to discover the pastoral needs of the people they exist to serve, and how to go about setting and implementing policies. If he has little knowledge of these points, he can still turn to others for help. But he cannot turn to anyone else for his most basic and primary skill, the skill of working with people.[28] As applied anthropology points out with incisive clarity, this quality must flow out of his sensitivity to the innate potential in every human person for responsible self-determination. This sensitivity will inevitably produce empathy, which is the ability to accept people as they are, not to condemn, but also to accept them for their potential. The response of empathy is not necessarily verbal. In fact it is primarily an internal response wherein a provincial identifies with the feelings of the province and the religious members.[29] From this sensitivity there will naturally emerge also a gift of listening, a willingness to enter into dialogue with the province and its religious at a speed that is not insulting to the dignity of all concerned. A provincial of this kind is a humble person, aware of the immense riches of God's grace and power that he will discover even in the most wounded of the province's members.

Ultimately, for a provincial such qualities of openness and sensitivity will be maintained, despite the considerable testing, only if his own life is centered within the heart of Christ the Servant (Mt 20:25-28). Rather than command with the authority of status and appointment, the servant shows by example. Servants seek the free choice of those being led.[30] This is the model clearly evident in the new Code of Canon Law (618): "The authority which Superiors receive from God through the ministry of the Church is to be exercised by them in a spirit of service. . . . By their reverence for the human person, they are to promote voluntary obedience. They are to listen willingly to their subjects and foster their cooperation for the good of the institute and the Church, without prejudice, however, to their authority to decide and to command what is to be done."

Finally, what amount of time should a provincial give each of his functions? I believe the greater percentage of his time should be directed to ministering to the corporate body, that is the emphasis on planning and animating the province to become a culture supportive of innovation and participating in innovation. I believe the ministry to individuals should occupy less time.[31] This latter is extremely demanding of energy and it can be never ending. But, it is a vital ministry that can be shared with others in the province. If a provincial is not clear as to his role, he can so easily slip into one or other of his functions to the detriment of the other duties.

Conclusion

A provincial is the officially appointed chief change-agent for a province. Without his vigorously stimulating leadership, it will be most unlikely that his province will become or remain innovative and creative in the service of the

Church. I assume throughout the article that innovation in itself will not really be effective, unless it comes out of a province that is turning with renewed vitality to Christ, the Stimulant and Sustainer of all change. I also assume that there is a process of reappropriation of the founding charism, that is members of the province reflecting on the needs of the world around them on the one hand, and the gospel message on the other, have the same sense of shock at the gap between them that their founder experienced.[32]

However, I can almost hear a very committed provincial who is deeply disturbed by the type of problems we have listed in the model of the "typical province" above say: "What you write sounds good, but it is from an ivory tower. I see several houses in my province that have long since served their apostolic usefulness. I know which way the province should move to touch the real needs of people. I see good-meaning people who are in fact obstructing all change. Therefore, I see the need to move fast and decisively; I will close the houses and disperse the men to places of real apostolic need. One needs to be practical, not theoretical!" I fully sympathize with such a provincial. But, in this article I claim that the most practical way of changing a culture so that it is supportive of positive innovation, not just for the present but also for the future, is for a provincial to learn to work *with* people in the ways explained above. Neither people nor cultures are mechanical structures. By struggling slowly to encourage innovators to develop within the culture and to be supported by the culture of the province, the provincial will be acting in a *thoroughly practical* way. This is the lesson of contemporary managerial studies, of the findings of applied anthropology, and, of course, of a spirituality of growth within religious life in the service of the Church.

We spoke in the article of the virtues needed in this challenging role. Together they could be united under one virtue—the gift of humor. A common characteristic of dictators, revolutionaries, and ecclesiastical authoritarians alike is the refusal both to laugh at themselves and to allow others to laugh at them.[33] He who has a sense of spiritual humor recognizes deep in his heart that ultimately he can do nothing by himself. He needs God, he needs other people. When he tries to do everything himself, he plays God. And what could be funnier! ". . . See how the kings of the earth stand in array. . . . He who dwells in heaven is laughing at their threats [their pride], the Lord makes light of them" (Ps 2).

NOTES

[1]See Raymond Hostie, *The Life and Death of Religious Orders: A Psycho-sociological Approach,* (Washington: Cara, 1983, pp. 276ff, and Lawrence Cada, Raymond Fitz, Gertrude Foley, Thomas Giardino and Carol Lichtenberg, *Shaping the Coming Age of Religious Life* (NY: The Seabury Press, 1979, p. 60 and passim.

[2]S.C. for Religious and Secular Institutes and S.C. for Bishops, *Directives for the Mutual Relations between Bishops and Religious in the Church*, Rome, 1978, par. 12.

[3]Ibid.

[4]See E. E. Hagen, *On the Theory of Social Change: How Economic Growth Begins* (London: Tavistock, 1962), pp. 88-97.

[5]See Rosabeth Moss Kanter, *The Change Masters: Corporate Entrepreneurs at Work* (London: George Allen & Unwin, 1983), pp. 17-36 and passim; William H. Davidson, *The Amazing Race: Winning the Techno-rivalry with Japan* (NY: John Wiley, 1984), passim.

[6]E.g. see R. M. Kanter, op. cit.; Terrence E. Deal and Allan A. Kennedy, *Corporate Cultures: The Rites and Rituals of Corporate Life*, (Reading: Addison-Wesley, 1982); Thomas J. Peters and Robert H. Waterman, *In Search of Excellence: Lessons from America's Best-Run Companies* (NY: Harper & Row, 1982).

[7]R. M. Kanter, op. cit., p. 13.

[8]See Richard T. Pascale and Anthony G. Athos, *The Art of Japanese Management* (London: Allen Lane, 1982), pp. 116-140); also Chie Nakane, *Japanese Society* (Harmondsworth: Penguin, 1973), pp. 88f.

[9]R. T. Pascale and A. G. Athos, op. cit. p. 126.

[10]Ibid, p. 124.

[11]See T. J. Peters and R. H. Waterman, op. cit. p. 291 and passim.

[12]See Lucy Mair, *Anthropology and Development* (London: Macmillan, 1984), p. 13.

[13]R. M. Kanter, op. cit., p. 306.

[14]Ibid, p. 23.

[15]See Gerald A. Arbuckle "Economic and Social Development in the Fiji Islands through Credit Unions" in *Credit Unions in the South Pacific*, edited by Neil Runcie (London: University of London Press, 1969), pp. 90-108.

[16]See (ed) Edward H. Spicer, *Human Problems in Technological Change* (NY: John Wiley, 1967), p. 18 and passim; Ward Hunt Goodenough, *Cooperation in Change: An Anthropological Approach to Community Development* (NY: John Wiley, 1966), passim; William W. Biddle and Loureide J. Biddle, *The Community Development Process: The Rediscovery of Local Initiative* (NY: Holt, Rinehart and Winston, 1965), passim.

[17]*Traditional Cultures: And the Impact of Technological Change* (NY: Harper, 1962, pp. 268f.

[18]See Gerald A. Arbuckle, "Why They Leave: Reflections of a Religious Anthropologist" in REVIEW FOR RELIGIOUS, Vol. 42, No. 6, 1983, pp. 815-826.

[19]See Evelyn M. Woodward, "On the Grim Periphery: Reflections on Marginality and Alienation" in REVIEW FOR RELIGIOUS, Vol. 42, No. 5, 1983, pp. 694-711.

[20]Cited by T. J. Peters and R. H. Waterman, op. cit., p. 83.

[21]David McClelland, cited by T. J. Peters and R. H. Waterman, op. cit., p. 84.

[22]David McClelland, ibid.

[23]See Speed B. Leas, *Leadership and Conflict* (Nashville: Abingdon, 1982), p. 28ff.

[24]See T. J. Peters and R. H. Waterman, op. cit., pp. 279-291.

[25]For an analysis of "situational leadership" see Paul Hersey and Ken Blanchard, *Management of Organizational Behavior: Utilizing Human Resources* (Englewood Cliffs: Prentice-Hall, 1982), pp. 149-175.

[26]See J. Moore, "Some Aspects of the Sociology of Priesthood" in *Social Studies: Irish Journal of Sociology*, April 1979, p. 129; and William R. Burrows, *New Ministries: The Global Context* (NY: Orbis, 1980), p. 117ff.

[27]See P. Hersey and K. Blanchard, op. cit., p. 84.

[28]See T. R. Batten, *The Human Factor in Community Work* (Oxford: Oxford University Press, 1965), p. 181.

[29]See Robert K. Greenleaf, *Servant Leadership: A Journey into the Nature of Legitimate Power and Greatness* (NY: Paulist, 1977), p. 20f.

[30]See Lawrence O. Richards and Clyde Hoeldtke, *A Theology of Church Leadership* (Grand

Rapids: Zondervan, 1982), p. 107 and passim.

[31]See comments by Conleth Overman, *Current Issues in Provincial Leadership* (Washington: Cara, 1983), p. 76.

[32]See Finbarr B. Connolly, *Religious Life: A Profile of the Future* (Dublin: Reality, 1982), pp. 10ff; Diarmuid O Murchu, *The Seed Must Die: Religious Life—Survival or Extinction?* (Dublin: Veritas, 1980), pp. 35-40 and passim.

[33]See Conrad Hyers, *The Comic Vision and the Christian Faith: A Celebration of Life and Laughter* (NY: The Pilgrim Press, 1981), p. 24.

Christian and Religious Obedience

Brian O'Leary, S.J.

Volume 44, 1985, pp. 513-520.

Our whole relationship with God can be both experienced and understood in terms of obedience and disobedience. Obedience is not just one virtue among other virtues. It is not part of a relationship that is experienced in isolation, or that can be examined in isolation from the remainder of that relationship. It is an element in every virtue, or if one prefers, it is the soil in which all other virtues take root and grow. This, of course, is taking obedience in its widest sense as cooperation with the will of God, but this is also its most fundamental sense. There is an all-pervasiveness about obedience which reaches into every nook and cranny of our human existence.

Obedience as Listening

It is illuminating to reflect on the root meaning of the Latin word *oboedire* which means *to listen*. We are called to listen to God as he speaks, communicates, reveals himself in Scripture, in the teaching of the Church, in other people, in the signs of the times, in our consciences, in the stirrings of our hearts. Such listening can take myriad forms, from basic self-acceptance, through an eager following of one's special calling within the Christian community, to the final *Amen* in accepting the time and manner of one's death. Samuel's "Speak, Yahweh, your servant is listening" (1 S 3:10) is the basic, lifelong attitude and prayer of the devout Christian.

Since Christianity is a form of theism, its adherents are committed to a belief in the self-revelation of a personal God. Consequently much emphasis is placed on the supernatural modes of God's speaking, such as inspired and inerrant Scriptures, and the life and teaching of Jesus himself:

At various times in the past and in various different ways, God spoke to our ancestors through the prophets; but in our own time, the last days, he has spoken to us through his Son, the Son that he has appointed to inherit everything and through whom he made everything there is (Heb 1:1-2).

But we ought not to minimize the more ordinary, natural modes of God's speaking. God is the God of reality, and so every aspect of reality is a vehicle for his communication with us. Listening begins, therefore, with what is closest to us—our experience of ourselves. We listen to our bodies as they reveal their needs to us (e.g. for nourishment, rest, shelter). We listen to our affectivity with its constantly fluctuating attractions and revulsions. We listen to our souls yearning for ultimate meaning, for aesthetic experience, and for eventual immortality. To fail to listen to ourselves is to fail to listen to God.

As we move outwards from our own psyches there awaits us the invitation to listen to others. Men and women in their very humanity, in their interpersonal relationships and as constitutive of society, are mediators of God and his loving plan for us. We are called to listen, not just to the words people use, but to the experiences, the vulnerability, the fragility, the mute longings that lie behind the words. This mode of attentive, empathetic listening, this contemplative attitude towards people, involves encountering the other as *other* and not as a mere projection of ourselves and our own concerns. As the other speaks, so God communicates, whether we are meeting that other as individual or as societal.

Obedience as Faith

The all-pervasive, all-embracing quality of obedience is also underlined in Paul's phrase, "the obedience of faith."

> Through him [Christ] we received grace and our apostolic mission to preach the obedience of faith to all pagan nations in honor of his name (Rm 1:5).

> Glory to him who is able to give you the strength to live according to the Good News I preach, and in which I proclaim Jesus Christ, the revelation of a mystery kept secret for endless ages, but now so clear that it must be broadcast to pagans everywhere to bring them to the obedience of faith (Rm 16:25-26).

Here obedience is clearly not a particular moral virtue, but that total human response to the Good News which is proclaimed in the apostolic preaching. Paul's mission is to bring people to this surrender in faith to God. This surrender is not forced; it may be refused. It is a free acceptance of, and response to the Word. This is the radical experience of *metanoia* for which Paul's own conversion on the road to Damascus could serve as a paradigm. Ultimately, for Paul faith is obedience and obedience is faith, while unbelief is disobedience and disobedience is unbelief.

In the Old Testament Abraham exemplifies this faith-obedience both in his response to God's call (Gn 12:1-5) and in his willingness to sacrifice his son, Isaac (Gn 22:1-18). In the latter story Abraham is asked to take and offer as a holocaust not only "your son, your only child Isaac, whom you love" (which would be a natural and personal tragedy), the one person through whom the promises of Yahweh were to be fulfilled for the Chosen People (which would be a spiritual and national tragedy). The key to the biblical writer's interpretation of this complex story is found in the words:

> All the nations of the earth shall bless themselves by your descendants, *as a reward for your obedience* (v. 18).

But the primary model of Christian obedience is that of the adult man Jesus to his Father. Time and again, in St. John's gospel particularly, we see the deep fascination which the Father exercised on the human sensibility of Jesus. Much light is thrown on what it meant for Jesus to be Son, and how his personal sense of identity came from his experience of filial relationship. His mission appears, not so much as something entrusted to him from outside, but as intrinsic to who he is. "To be Son" is "to be sent" is "to be on mission."

> My food is to do the will of the one who sent me, and to complete his work (Jn 4:34).
>
> I can do nothing by myself; I can only judge as I am told to judge, and my judging is just, because my aim is to do not my own will but the will of him who sent me (Jn 5:30).
>
> When you have lifted up the Son of Man, then you will know that I am he and that I do nothing of myself: what the Father has taught me is what I preach: he who sent me is with me and has not left me to myself, for I always do what pleases him (Jn 8:28-29).
>
> The world must be brought to know that I love the Father and that I am doing exactly what the Father told me (Jn 14:31).

The cumulative effect of such texts powerfully communicates the obediential attitude of Jesus into which the Father wishes to draw all Christians.

Obedience within the Church

The Father sent his Son to carry out a saving mission which culminated in the Paschal Mystery, the death and resurrection of Jesus. The Father and the Son sent the Holy Spirit to carry out a sanctifying mission which inaugurated the community of the New Israel at Pentecost—the community that is Church. Through baptism each person who is initiated into the Church is at the same time inserted into this two-pronged saving/sanctifying mission. Every Christian is not only saved and sanctified but called to share in the saving and sanctifying of others, to be sent into the world as was the Spirit-filled Jesus. But the primary subject of this sending or mission is not the individual but the community or Church itself. It is by being in communion with the Church that the individual receives his/her mission which has its ultimate source ("author") in the Father. Hence the need for authority.

Without authority and the means to exercise that authority the Church could not maintain itself in unity nor fulfill its mission to the world. Since the Church is of divine institution and part of God's plan for humanity, the only authority which can legitimately exist in it is God's authority. When we reflect on Scripture we see how God reveals himself, communicates his message, and exercises his authority through intermediaries or mediators. Moses mediated the Old Covenant to Israel in the Old Testament, while Jesus in his humanity mediated the New Covenant in New Testament times. Now the risen Christ through his Spirit shares this mediated authority with the Church as a whole and with its duly-constituted leaders. How such authority is exercised need not concern us here; enough to recognize that it exists and that it is coextensive with the needs of the community for its internal well-being and its saving/sanctifying mission. Much can be learned from the final logion in St. Matthew's gospel:

All authority in heaven and on earth has been given to me. Go, therefore, make disciples of all the nations; baptize them in the name of the Father and of the Son and of the Holy Spirit, and teach them to observe all the commands I gave you. And know that I am with you always; yes, to the end of time (Mt 28:18-20).

Christ's presence through the ages guarantees the reality of the lifeline linking the Church with the source, the author, of all authority—God the Father.

Religious Obedience

There is a parallel, although not an identity, between the authority which exists in the community that is Church, and that which exists in the community that is a religious institute. In both, the ultimate source of authority is God; in both, that authority is mediated; in both, an obediential response is required. Such authority within a religious institute is recognized in faith by a person making a vow of obedience, and then responded to existentially through the daily living out of that vow. Although both the authority and the obedience are mediated, the vow itself can only be made to God. More precisely, it is made to the Father. As with Christian obedience in general, of which religious obedience is a particular expression, our response-pattern as religious is that of Jesus who "emptied himself to assume the condition of a slave" (Ph 2:7), yet knowing that he is the Beloved Son of the Father.

Furthermore the religious state constitutes a closer imitation and an abiding reenactment in the Church of the form of life which the Son of God made his own when he came into the world to do the will of the Father (*Lumen Gentium,* 44).

A question, however, can be raised about the legitimacy of my (or any Christian's) making a vow of obedience in a particular institute. There is a presupposition that the will of God for me is to be found with more certainty and clarity in the context of this specific group of people. Both logically and chronologically, before the vow, and necessarily underpinning it, is an act of faith. How can such an act of faith be justified? The answer is twofold.

Subjectively, there is my own inner experience of call which is leading me, not into marriage, nor into the single lay state, nor into some other religious institute, but into this concrete grouping of likeminded and vowed Christians. It is presumed that this subjective experience has been prayerfully and realistically discerned with the aid of competent spiritual direction.

Objectively, there is the guarantee of the Church which, in approving this institute, has recognized it as a milieu in which the Holy Spirit is present and active. When the institute in its turn decides to accept me as a member, I can be sure that the Holy Spirit will speak to me in the context, and through the authority structures, of this grouping. Within such an institute ongoing discernment is possible, and such discernment brings together harmoniously the interdependent realities of authority and obedience. The vow implies that never again do I discern anything merely as an individual.

Religious obedience is primarily the attitude of the whole institute seeking the will of God through living out the implications of its charism in the contemporary world. At any particular time this communal attitude may be more or less faithful, and so more or less obediential, more or less Christlike. (A barometer, in psychological terms, is often that of morale.)

The individual member, in turn, may be more or less in harmony with this communal attitude. If I have a strong sense of belonging, then I will actively and enthusiastically participate in the institute's communal search for God's will, striving together towards viable and relevant apostolic choices. On the other hand, if I feel alienated from the institute, living on its fringes, I will tend to opt out of the communal search. I will become passive in regard to discernment and forward planning, at best adopting a privatized approach to obedience—doing what I am told, perhaps, but otherwise abandoning my responsibility to play an active role in the discerning and decision-making process within the institute. This is a form of disobedience and a failure in faith.

Four Aspects of Obedience

Christian and religious obedience involves the whole person and calls for a radical stance which can only originate at the core of a person's being. If that core has not been touched, obedience remains superficial if not inauthentic. Because of its all-pervasive nature, obedience is multi-faceted and needs to be examined from different points of view if its reality is not to be distorted. With religious obedience especially in mind we will now take up four of these aspects or dimensions.

Ascetical

The human person is not obedient by nature. There is both a positive and a negative reason for this. Positively, autonomy or self-rule is the mark of the mature person. The journey from childhood to adulthood is in large part a growth in desire for, capacity for, and exercise of autonomy. But since a person lives in a human community, this autonomy has to be balanced by the demands of interpersonal, social and political realities. Accepting the need for such balance, and integrating the corresponding limitations of one's autonomy, are also parts of the maturation process.

All of this already presupposes an ongoing asceticism. Limitations imposed on one's autonomy by external factors and forces invariably provoke resistance, anger, pain and yet eventually they have to be recognized as inevitable. This process of growth is sometimes presented as moving through the stages of dependence, independence, and interdependence. This last is the mark of the mature, socially-integrated adult: an autonomy which recognizes the corresponding autonomy and rights of others.

Negatively, there are the realities of sin and disorder. The healthy drive towards autonomy is seduced and vitiated by an unhealthy drive towards egoism and pride. While human autonomy can never be absolute, yet we are constantly beguiled by Satan's promise: "You will be like gods" (Gn 3:5). It is surely significant that the sin of Adam (humankind) is presented in Scripture as disobedience arising from an overweening desire for autonomy—the autonomy of God himself.

Against this background the ascetical aspect of religious obedience becomes clearer. Obedience is a human virtue, an attitudinal habit which must be learned through its exercise. The aim is never to break a person's will, but to lead the religious to a genuine inner freedom which will prevent manipulation either by outside pressures or by disorders within the self. Such freedom will express itself not only in docility and availability, but also in creativity and initiative.

Mystical

This second aspect of obedience consists in that contemplative gaze towards Christ which enables one to discover him in the interplay between authority and obedience. Given this contemplative attitude a religious actualizes an increasingly intimate union with Christ in two ways. Firstly, the person recognizes in the authority of the superior the authority of Christ, and in the person of the superior the person of Christ. Secondly, the religious enters into and continually enfleshes the obediential attitude of Christ himself. The Risen Lord does not hand over, as it were, our obedience to the Father as something extrinsic to himself. Rather, since we died and rose again with him in baptism, our obedience is part of his obedience, a prolongation of it in today's world, just as our prayer is part of his prayer and is offered to the Father as the prayer of the Whole Christ: the Body— head and members. Religious obedience, therefore, is both *obedience to Christ* present in the superior, and a sharing in the *obedience of Christ* as he responds filially and radically to his and our Father.

> He was humble and walked the path of obedience all the way to death—his death on the cross (Ph 2:8).

Our obedience and that of Christ are co-terminous. They both lead to Calvary. Obedience, therefore, can be compared with martyrdom, as indeed it has been in the tradition. Martyrdom may either be that total, instantaneous and violent handing over of ourselves to God through other-inflicted death, or the piecemeal, gradual, daily handing over of ourselves to God through the self-inflicted consequences of the vow of religious obedience. The latter is experienced as continued self-emptying which builds up to that final and inevitable self-emptying of our natural death when we shall hopefully say with utter freedom and love, "Father, into your hands I commit my spirit" (Lk 23:46).

Apostolic

Insofar as religious obedience is a union with the obediential will of Christ, so far is it also a union with the salvific will of the Father who "wants everyone to be saved and reach full knowledge of the truth" (1 Tm 2:4). As such, along with every other expression of Christian obedience, it is truly apostolic. Nevertheless, in specifically apostolic institutes the link between obedience and apostolate is much more explicit and direct. Here obedience is primarily in function of mission, a spiritual tool of mission. The reality of authority-obedience is the channel through which mission, which originates with the Father, is mediated to the institute and to the individual members. Since mission is constitutive of the basic charism of such institutes, and is not an optional or subsidiary dimension, obedience as apostolic has an enormous importance and centrality.

Under this heading comes the whole area of apostolic discernment, both personal and communal. Apostolic choices—the selection of ministries and plans for running and evaluating them—become a major issue. A deep level of trust and openness between the members of the institute, and especially in relations with superiors, is necessary. Underpinning this, a spirituality which closely integrates contemplation and action is required. Authority calls forth and harnesses the good will, talents and energies of all, directing them with zeal and in the spirit of the institute, towards mission. In such an atmosphere of faith and serious purpose one dare not trivialize obedience, for example, by seeing it merely in terms of discipline, good order, or even of asceticism. If mature adult obedience does not flourish, neither does the charism of the institute, and neither does the mission which is that of the contemporary Christ.

Unitive

Obedience leads to a union of minds and hearts. However, this is true only when its ascetical demands have been accepted, its mystical dimension has been experienced, and its apostolic thrust has become a powerful dynamic in one's own life and that of one's fellow-religious. This unitive aspect emerges almost spontaneously as the result of religious obedience which is lived authentically and faithfully. It is not the direct purpose of obedience, but rather a side effect which can be gratefully recognized and received as part of the hundredfold promised by Christ to those who have left all for his sake.

III. Religious Community

Individual Apostolates and Pluralism in Community Identity

John T. Ford, C.S.C.

Volume 35, 1976, pp. 829-848.

Not too long ago, as our history is measured, the apostolic endeavors of American religious communities almost invariably took a corporate or institutional form. A typical example is the religious house all of whose members work in an adjacent school. Though there may be considerable variety in the occupations of individual religious (e.g., administration, teaching, counseling, maintenance, etc.), the work of each is seen as contributing to the overall functioning of the institution. This corporate pattern is frequently paralleled in hospitals, parishes, and other works religious communities undertake.

An important consequence of this familiar pattern is a pervasive identification of religious community with its institutions. For example, this identification is commonly reinforced through a schedule that melds communal and institutional activities: if religious aren't working in the institution, then they usually can be found together at some communal activity in the nearby residence. The result is practically a "total institutionalization" that the more cynical have compared with imprisonment; however, as will be noted later, a more apt comparison is with the communal life of the "family farm" or the "cottage industry" in agrarian societies. In brief, then, an "institutional apostolate" is a particular activity that members of a religious community undertake as a corporate effort; it is both a means of livelihood and a means of realizing the goals of the community.

The melding of communal and institutional activities also affords a means of self-identity for religious. For example, the fact that religious (with appropriate humility) speak of "our school" is but one indication of the influence of merged communal-institutional life on individual religious. Recently, when it has become necessary to close "our school," this identification has sometimes become painfully apparent. In other terms, the American tendency to identify a person with his occupation (e.g., John Smith *is* a carpenter, Mary Doe *is* a teacher) reached sort of a zenith in the case of religious; indeed, religious may be so identified with a particular institution that "outsiders" may not even know the proper name of the community whose members work there (e.g., "the sisters who teach at St. Mary's").

The liabilities of institutional apostolates are all too familiar. Perhaps the most burdensome is the tendency to subordinate the personal life of religious to the consuming demands of the institution. Illustrations are legion: frequently requests of a personal nature are refused if they are seen as interfering with the work of the institution (rather than as being alien to community life). Another burden is an unrealistic subordination of communal life to institutional demands. While the acceptance of an institutional apostolate necessarily demands coordination with the life of the community, sometimes this is done by an additive process, as in the case of a community that fulfilled its quota of religious exercises, one rapidly following another, after closing school for the day. Occasionally, the reverse happens: the requirements of an institutional apostolate are over-ruled by community procedures. An obvious instance is the appointment of religious to institutional positions for which their major qualification is membership in the sponsoring community.

While post-conciliar renewal has (presumably?) caused the disappearance of the more conspicuous malpractices, still an inherent and recurring problem in institutional apostolates is to maintain an appropriate balance between institutional work, living in community, and personal life. Any notable imbalance in these relationships is likely to occasion friction or dissatisfaction within a community.

In addition to this perennial problem, there are other factors that have brought added pressures on institutional apostolates in recent years. For example, as a result of the post-conciliar decrease in the number of active religious, many communities have been unable to staff their institutions in the same measure as formerly. Maintaining institutional commitments is seemingly so burdensome that some religious doubt the wisdom of institutional apostolates at all—even if their community would have sufficient personnel in the future. This feeling is frequently shared by those younger religious who are disenchanted with institutions in general and have entered religious life in view of a more personalized type of service. While this anti-institutionalism is sometimes naively exaggerated, the fact remains that some communities have accepted members who simply do not identify with institutional apostolates.

Simultaneously new options have become available. For example, the closing of some schools has made it possible or necessary for religious to seek positions outside the educational institutions conducted by their own community. Again, recent developments in the Church have led to the creation of new positions that previously didn't exist—directors of religious education representing a common instance. And in some cases, religious have found employment in government agencies or public interest firms.

An interesting relationship has emerged in many institutions of higher education. In order to qualify for governmental assistance, a legal separation has been effected between institution and sponsoring community. While the same religious may continue their apostolate within the institution, legal separation makes it incongruous for a community to continue to consider the institution "ours." The legal status of religious working in the institution is also changed; for example, many religious now have contracts with institutions that were formerly controlled by their communities. Apparently, institutional apostolates are being "individualized."

Individual Apostolates

Such recent developments have led to the emergence of a variety of "individual apostolates."[1] Here an "individual apostolate" is taken to mean a particular occupation that a religious undertakes as a personal effort and responsibility; it is to some degree independent of the administration of the community as such; it depends more on the particular personal qualifications of the religious, not on membership in this or that community.

The degree of individuality, however, may vary considerably: religious who continue to work in what were formerly their community's institutions may find that legal separation is a more or less nominal change; other religious, however, may find that they have to qualify competitively for their positions. In the latter case, when a particular religious leaves an individual apostolate, the community can not expect and is not expected to furnish a replacement (as is frequently the case in institutional apostolates). An important characteristic of individual apostolates is that the religious community as such can not determine whether its members will be able to obtain specific positions.

Speaking of an apostolate as "individual" does not imply that it is independent of church or community; rather (if it is to be considered an apostolate) it must be conceived in some way as a service that witnesses to Christ and reflects the spirit of a particular community. Moreover, there is a sense in which every apostolate is "individual," insofar as religious are individually responsible for "personifying" the Gospel in their particular occupations.

However, one must admit the arbitrariness of classifying practically any occupation as an "apostolate." For example, practically any occupation—from farming to fine arts, from physical education to theoretical physics—has been placed under the generic umbrella of "apostolate" in various institutions conducted by religious. Given this precedent, it seems rather arbitrary to attempt to restrict "individual apostolates" along rigid lines.[2] In addition, individual apostolates have long-standing precedents in most active communities: the missionary stationed alone, the student religious living outside a community residence, the traveling retreat-master or fund-raiser, etc. Again on the basis of precedents, it is hard to disqualify individual apostolates on the ground of separation from daily community life. Or is it justifiable to consider these instances "temporary," when in fact they last for years? Or is it realistic to consider these cases exceptions or experiments, if they involve a relatively large percentage of a community?

The point in raising these questions is *not* to object to the legitimacy of individual apostolates in active communities.[3] Insofar as religious rules are guidelines, not absolutes, exceptions are allowable or, at times, necessary; there does not seem to be any *a priori* reason why individual apostolates can not be a justifiable exception. Likewise, communities have always had to experiment in their apostolates; accordingly, individual apostolates can be seen as a new type of apostolic venture attempting to respond to contemporary needs.

Still, it is hardly adequate to treat individual apostolates merely as exceptions or experiments. First of all, a more positive view is necessary. Individual apostolates should be seen as a development that is appropriate, perhaps necessary, if the Church is to witness to Christ in the contemporary world.[4] Indeed, individual apostolates have already proved beneficial in some communities; for example, their existence has occasioned a much needed delineation of lines of community responsibility in relation to all apostolates. Moreover, individual apostolates are a means whereby communities, instead of being constrained to fill various slots, can utilize their personnel in more creative ways. Perhaps the most attractive aspect of individual apostolates is their challenge to religious to develop fully their talents in the service of Christ.

On the other hand, since individual apostolates have seemingly arisen more by indirection than by intention, it is easy to continue the pattern of temporary expedients or ad hoc experiments without facing broader issues. For example, it may be tempting to presume that individual apostolates are only a passing fad that will eventually go away; yet what if they are really introducing a new and distinct form of religious life?[5] Again, it is tempting to assume that there is little difference between religious life for those in individual apostolates and those in institutional apostolates; accordingly, the same model of religious life should prevail in both. But what if there is need for a new type of balance between occupation, religious life, and personal lifestyle in individual apostolates?

The implications of individual apostolates for religious life have been emerging, like the apostolates themselves, only piecemeal. Though only partially apparent, these implications need to be examined, for they potentially constitute the raw material for either crisis or creativity—or more likely, a bit of both.

In other words, a pattern is being established that affects not only the individual religious involved, but the community as a whole. For example, a relatively high proportion of members in some communities is currently engaged in individual apostolates; even were it desirable to withdraw members from individual apostolates, it may no longer be feasible to do so without serious disruption (*viz.* problems in re-assignment, budget, residence, etc.). Somewhat incongruously, individual apostolates seem to have reached a point of institutionalization! On the theoretical level, what is at issue is a community's self-vision and self-identity. On the practical level is a complex of questions relating to the implementation of this vision and the fostering of community identity.

Theoretical Level: A New Vision?

Whatever the imbalances in institutional apostolates, they offer religious a sense of identity: "our community working in our institution." Quite commonly this sense of corporate identity is reinforced by a vision of religious life as a continual harmony of prayer and work, of work and prayer. Indeed, the identification of community and institution suggests something of an equation of communal prayer and institutional work.

If this vision of religious life was once convincingly painted in the novitiate, such an interlocking matrix of prayer and work seems alien to many religious today. The loss of this vision may occasion feelings of nostalgia for a vision now blurred and a rhythm of activity now disjointed. Yet before indulging guilt-feelings about visions lost, it would be well to ask whether the vision is worth recapturing at all.

The vision of religious life as harmonious integration of prayer and work seems to presuppose a double model: a sociological model of an agrarian society coupled with a theological model of a divinely regulated universe.[6] While an agrarian model may seem medieval, perhaps the proximate influence is the American frontier ideal of the self-sufficient family farm. Questions of historical origin aside, an agrarian model seems more influential in religious life than is commonly acknowledged. For example, most religious communities were originally founded within agrarian societies; more importantly, an agrarian ideal of community seems to survive in the expectations of many religious. Indeed, one may suspect that efforts to "return to the spirit of the founder" may on occasion be similar to the flight from urban life and its mounting frustrations: a yearning for a simpler life may be nostalgia for the benefits of an agrarian society. Or again, the once common practice of establishing houses of formation in rural settings ("where religious life could be lived at its ideal"), reflects something of the ideal of a self-sufficient family farm. Examples could be multiplied; variations on the agrarian model could be added (e.g., religious community as "cottage industry" or "ethnic village," etc.). It seems worth noting the similar melding of work and communal life that characterizes both agrarian societies and institutional apostolates.

Fitting neatly with an agrarian model of religious community is a theological model of a well regulated universe: just as the universe is harmoniously ordered in every detail by an inherent set of laws enacted by a provident God, so too is the religious community harmoniously regulated in every detail by a set of rules provided by a divinely guided founder and subsequently administered by omniscient superiors.[7] While this is blatant caricature, it should be remembered that every caricature hits uncomfortably close to life.

Both models have become theoretically untenable. The agrarian model is insufficient in view of the complexity of urban, technological society, while the theological model of a systematically directed universe is inadequate in the face of historical consciousness and philosophical pluralism. Accordingly, neither of these models provides a suitable framework for a vision of religious life. Nonetheless, there is one reason for their tenacious survival: they undoubtedly furnish a sense of security. It is spiritually reassuring to devote one's entire day in a harmonious blend of prayer and work dedicated to God: could a fervent religious want more?

For some religious, then, the harmonious vision is quite satisfying. For others, the vision may be feeble, but they are willing to live with inconsistency, because they are unable or unwilling to search for a new vision. If a few have discovered a new vision, many others are still searching. Aside from the fact that it is far easier to criticize a vision-become-problematic than to construct a replacement, visions are elusive and difficult to verbalize. More than likely, discussions within a community do not debate visions but center on practical issues: traditional procedures versus new approaches. It is tempting, for example, to treat individual apostolates merely as another practical problem. Yet much more is at stake: competing visions of community and apostolate that stand at the heart of personal and corporate self-identity.

Not surprisingly, the response to new visions has been varied. First of all, some would prefer to re-upholster the traditional vision by discarding out-dated elements and super-imposing sundry modern touches. Change is then cosmetic: the superficial appearance is different, but the fundamental vision remains the same. Nevertheless, there are definite advantages to this approach: it affords continuity with the past—a matter of concern to older members; it accommodates itself to new circumstances—a matter of importance for younger members; and it introduces changes gradually so that there is sufficient time to become accustomed to one set of changes before more are introduced—a matter of expediency in all social changes. Yet such an option carries with it a notable liability: it relies on a vision that is basically unattractive and unacceptable to many.

Nonetheless, the *right* of a community to take this option must be respected, for it may be the only option that a particular community can really live with.[8] To follow an out-dated vision may not be wise, but it need not be wrong. In fact, the attempt to jerk away an apparent Linus blanket from those committed to a traditional vision is likely to be disruptive of both community and apostolate.[9] Without arbitrarily precluding the possibility of future change, a community may decide very realistically and very honestly that its capacity for renewal can only accomplish so much at a given moment of its history.

Communities that decide to retain a traditional vision of community and apostolate would be well advised not to engage any of their members in individual apostolates that require a lifestyle that is basically incompatible with the community's traditional vision and thus threaten its corporate identity. The predictable result would be serious dissension that the community may not be prepared to bear. Yet this need not imply that such communities need to exclude every type of individual apostolate; what *is* implied is that each proposed individual apostolate must be carefully examined for its concordance with the community's self-vision and self-identity.

The Problem of Pluralism

If the traditional vision is unattractive or untenable, what is the new vision of community and apostolate? The option would be simple, if a compelling new vision were at hand; then at least the choice would be clear-cut: traditional or new. Unfortunately there is no one unifying vision that demands acceptance. If it is quite clear that modern life is technological not agrarian, pluralistic not uniform, it is not clear how such aspects can be synthesized in a new vision. Instead of one new vision, there are any number of competing visions—each with advantages, all with their respective liabilities. The way to the future seems to be: may the best vision win!

It is then quite understandable why many religious prefer to hold on to the vision they have, whatever its deficiencies, rather than risk the vague uncertainties of some apparently more problematic replacement. It is equally understandable why many other religious tend to hedge their options by tentatively exploring new possibilities, while keeping a firm grasp on a traditional vision.

Still, just as a diversity of liturgical practices and theological viewpoints has emerged in the post-conciliar Church, so a similar diversity in lifestyles and visions of community and apostolate has emerged in post-conciliar religious life. This variety is rooted in a greater theological awareness of the diversity in the mystery of Christ, the uniqueness of each person, and the temporal and cultural plurality of mankind.[10] Where formerly uniformity was prized as exemplifying the unity of the Church, now pluralism is seen as reflecting the Church's catholicity.

Yet if it is easy to pay lip-service to pluralism, it is much more difficult to cope consistently with its implications. For example, some religious have adopted new lifestyles, but have not related these to a new vision; and vice versa, new visions have been officially adopted in constitutions and rules without subsequent implementation in a community.

More importantly, the transition from uniformity to pluralism is both threatening and enticing. Those who were trained for, or are congenitally inclined to, a life of uniformity and regularity can be severely confused by a superabundance of choices and the burden of responsibility inherent in a pluralistic situation. For example, obedience seems to furnish an excuse for some religious to become over-dependent on their superiors; or vice versa, obedience seems to allow some superiors to pre-empt most decision-making from their subordinates. If some religious pale at pluralism, it may be the threat of responsibilities that they are unwilling or unable to bear; similarly, if some superiors resent pluralism, it may be through unwillingness to share their authority with former subordinates.

Another dismaying aspect of pluralism is the potential loss of community support-systems; when familiar practices vanish, religious may feel themselves ostracized from the group or isolated in their work. Change in any form is unsettling to creatures of habit, but clinging to a traditional pattern may result in isolation. Since the prospect of losing the respect and understanding of one's companions is unnerving, pluralism can prove to be just as formidable to younger religious as to older. In the case of the younger, it can be the refusal to adopt the vision currently in vogue among their peers.

Yet if pluralism is threatening, it is also attractive. In place of the enervating burden of predictable routine there is the prospect of flexibility and variety in both communal and apostolic life. Religious life is more easily seen as a challenging opportunity for personal initiative and creativity in the service of Christ. For example, obedience may be seen as a commitment to Christ that takes the form of submitting one's proposed activities to the critical encouragement and the charismatic evaluation of one's colleagues; authority is primarily that of competent advice; ultimate responsibility is one's own before Christ and community. But such a revised view of obedience has to be accepted, not only by the individual but by the community, which may have to ask whether it can function with a number of different and divergent views of obedience.

Another attractive aspect of pluralism is the atmosphere which the community provides religious for developing their self-potential both in their lives as Christians and in their apostolates; this implies a willingness and openness in sharing insights and successes, failures and feelings; indeed, the diversity of apostolates undertaken by their colleagues can become an incentive for religious to work at maximum capacity.

The preceding contrast exemplifies some of the positive and negative aspects of pluralism. The examples may also help explain why individuals react quite differently to the prospect of pluralism: some feel threatened; others are attracted; still others would like to have the advantages of both uniformity and pluralism without the liabilities of either.[11]

Insofar as pluralism seems to have emerged within religious life more as the result of a series of individual decisions and external trends than through precise planning for pluralism, its implications need attention. Earlier, pluralism in religious life tended to exist more as a collective phenomenon: different communities constituted a diversified spectrum of "catholic" religious life, but any one community tended to occupy only a section of this spectrum; each community enjoyed a fairly well specified corporate apostolic identity.

The importance attached to this identity-via-apostolate is illustrated by the fact that some communities (even when personnel was available) refused to undertake certain apostolates, as incompatible with their constitutions; as a result, some communities originated as off-shoots of others, when a new apostolate was needed which the parent community felt unable to enter.

Of course, some communities have always allowed greater internal diversity than others. For example, if some communities have restricted their endeavors to one or two specific apostolates, others have undertaken a variety. At first sight, individual apostolates appear to be simply an extension of this variety. And in fact, this seems to be the way most individual apostolates have come about: superiors have allowed individual religious to accept experimental apostolates as exceptions to accustomed practices. In fact, these exceptions have gradually reached the point in some communities where a comparatively high percentage of members is involved; in some instances, proportionately more members are now in individual apostolates than are in some traditional ones.

In effect, the exceptions appear to be constituting a new rule, though there is not always a new vision to accompany it. Thus, the introduction of individual apostolates may precipitate a re-orientation of a community's self-vision and self-identity. In other words, individual apostolates seem to imply the acceptance of a plurality of visions, only some of which are compatible with traditional vision(s). The basic question then is: to what extent is a community really willing to accept the implications of pluralism?

Practical Options

A community's vision of its apostolate(s) is a vital element in its corporate identity; presumably its apostolic vision is an important factor in attracting applicants and in training younger members; presumably too, apostolic vision is an essential motivation for the special spirit and dynamism of a community. Moreover, apostolic vision is necessary if a community is to avoid being victimized by the needs of the moment and to plan its activities on a long range basis. It is crucial, then, for a community to delineate its apostolic vision as clearly as possible, while recognizing that every option involves risk.[12]

A first option is for a community to continue its institutional apostolate(s) as its primary and (probably) exclusive commitment. Presuming of course that its institutions are really viable, the most compelling motive for this option can be found in the fact that this is what the membership recognizes as its proper charism and commits itself to do. The evident risk is that this option is not particularly appealing to those who want to work in a more personalized setting; thus, recruitment of new members and dissatisfaction among present members could well be problems. Moreover, this option may yield to the temptation to abandon the struggle to live a religious life in the modern pluralistic world.

The polar opposite is the option to make individual apostolates the primary and presumably exclusive emphasis in a community. As a means of responding to challenges facing the Church in the modern world, this option presupposes considerable flexibility in community structures as well as considerable self-reliance on the part of individual religious. These presumed strengths may be dissipated through excessive individualism on the one hand or through lack of traditional support-systems on the other. While a few communities, or at least some segments of communities, appear to be headed in the direction of this option, what may really be at stake is the creation of new communities (even though the present may not seem a particularly auspicious moment for new foundations).

A compromise between these two options is the attempt to juxtapose institutional and individual apostolates. In greater or less degree, this is the present option of many active communities in the United States. Indeed, it seems to be a typical bit of American pragmatism for a community to allow its members to dream different visions, to work in different settings, and yet to unite together as members of one family. If such diversity defies theoretical alignment, American religious will presumably be content, as long as their community lives and works harmoniously, however diversely. Compromise will tend to succeed as long as religious are genuinely tolerant of the inevitable tensions that diversity introduces. The unavoidable risk is that such a compromise will become unglued—for example, through a widespread failure to fulfill responsibilities both in apostolates and in religious life, through favoritism or factionalism introduced when one group attempts to impose its views on others, or through the difficulty of attracting new members to a pluralistic life.

If compromise is to be successful, it is important for the members of a community explicitly to recognize the terms of the compromise. In other words, if the tensions arising from diversity in visions and a variety of life-styles are not to be divisive, a community needs to recognize and to accept a spectrum of variant models of apostolic endeavor and of community life. A community should specify the extent of pluralism that it is capable of tolerating. For example, some communities may be open to any type of individual apostolate; others may wish to restrict themselves to select types. Without prior specification or evaluation, there is potential for arbitrary decision-making, either real or imagined; there is also the likelihood of disillusionment among members if their expectations, whether realistic or idealistic, are not met. (Disillusionment can affect both those who expect the traditional apostolates to be maintained, as well as those who want individual apostolates to be introduced.)

The acceptance of pluralism should eventually be expressed in both the constitutions, which describe a community's apostolic vision, and in the rules, which attempt to concretize this vision in the life of a community. Such formulation is a difficult endeavor, as the revisions undertaken after Vatican II amply confirm.[13] Moreover, the emergence of individual apostolates adds to the complexity: first, since the vision is pluralistic and personal, constitutions apparently can do little more than generalize about the limit-points of the pluralism that is acknowledged in principle; secondly, if rules presumably reflect the lived experience of a community over a period of time, individual apostolates, in their present form, are both recent and still experimental.

Accordingly, different communities may choose to accept individual apostolates in rather different ways. Some communities may find it feasible to consider them as extensions of existing apostolates; for example, a community whose apostolate is in education may decide to restrict the acceptance of individual apostolates to educational endeavors. Other communities, which have defined their apostolates in terms of specific groups (e.g., poor, unevangelized, ethnic, etc.) may allow individual apostolates as a broadening of their ministry to these groups. Still other communities may encourage any type of new individual apostolate that displays some relation to witnessing Christ in the modern world.

At least as crucial as express recognition of individual apostolates in constitutions and rules is the way religious regard such formulations. For some, rules are principles that must be uniformly applied in particular instances; others would view rules as determinations that are to be supplemented and emended according to actual experience. This contrast is given visual form, in the first case, by those rules that are published in leather-bound, red-edged volumes resembling miniature Bibles; in the second case, rules might well be mimeographed on loose-leaf sheets and placed in folders to facilitate periodic revision and up-dating. At least this illustration may indicate that attempting to specify rules for a diversity of individual apostolates is a tenuous enterprise. In addition, it suggests that traditional rules, however well suited to institutional apostolates, should not simply be used as an umbrella to cover the new situations encountered in individual apostolates. Since uniform rules for individual apostolates tend to be anomalous in theory and impractical in fact, it seems necessary for communities whose members are engaged in individual apostolates to develop new approaches. It may well be that a community may decide to formulate guidelines for community or procedures for administration or standards for professional life for those members in individual apostolates. In so doing, a community will need to face squarely both the advantages and the drawbacks that are encountered in attempting to live and work with quite different types of apostolates and lifestyles within the same community.

In any pluralistic situation, it is obviously impossible to list all the variables; yet it may be helpful to sample a few problem areas: administrative procedures, community life, and personal freedom.

Administrative Procedures

In the halcyon days of institutional apostolates, administration may have been tedious, but it frequently had the advantage of following a standard pattern of applying general norms to particular cases. This view of administration is inadequate for dealing with individual apostolates (and, it should be added, with most institutional apostolates as well). On the one hand, individual apostolates tend to elude uniform norms, unless these are extremely general; on the other hand, individual apostolates necessarily change the roles of and relationship between superiors and subordinates. This change in roles is graphically illustrated by the religious who occasionally employed the provincial superior on a part-time basis.

A prime factor in the reorientation of roles is the fact that in most individual apostolates, religious need a fair amount of latitude to negotiate with prospective employers and that, once employed, their work is not under the direct supervision of community superiors. As a result, a superior's role tends to be narrowed to antecedent approval (for it is frequently unfeasible, if not counterproductive, for a superior to become involved in negotiations) and subsequent ratification, which may be tantamount to rubber-stamping a *fait accompli*.

Some superiors may find this process quite congenial; they have plenty of other problems and are quite relieved if some religious can successfully pursue their individual apostolates without supervision. Other superiors may feel more or less frustrated at wanting to be helpful yet not being needed or at wanting to give daily directives yet being powerless; they may subconsciously resent the apparent diminution of their authority. All of these reactions manifest a lack of appreciation of the change in roles in the superior-subordinate relationship.

If it is unrealistic to expect to transfer a set of relationships en masse from institutional to individual apostolates, what then is the role of the superior in relation to religious in this context?

First of all, a superior has to take seriously the individuality of each apostolate as well as the personality of each religious; in effect, each apostolate must be considered as a separate and somewhat unique case, just as each religious is a unique individual. Instead of applying general norms to individual cases, a reverse process is needed: whether and how general principles apply needs to be discovered through an evaluation of each apostolate. The latter task can only be carried out as a joint effort of superior and subordinate, acting as colleagues.

Accordingly, the role of the superior is less a matter of issuing commands and more a matter of fostering dialogue, discernment, and discretion.[14] Dialogue is necessary if the superior is to understand different apostolates from the viewpoint of participant religious; though this does not necessarily imply that a participant's view is always the best, still it should at least be the point of departure for productive discussion. Discernment, in the sense of raising appropriate questions to evaluate the potential and performance for an individual apostolate, must also be a joint endeavor if the merits and disadvantages of a particular apostolate are to be appreciated. Discretion, which aims at deciding on an appropriate course of action among a number of alternatives, should also be shared; it is pointless to impose a decision that one cannot or will not be implemented.

Obviously, such an approach to community administration requires a more personal type of communication than may have been customary in the supervision of institutional apostolates. Where a large number of individual apostolates are involved, such an approach may require that supervisory responsibilities be divided among more than one superior. Effective use of such an approach demands that superiors be skilled in interpersonal communication; in practice, this may mean that other administrative tasks, such as financial management, may have to be delegated to others.

If a new administrative approach is required for individual apostolates, no approach is a panacea. While a more personal approach may be more human and hopefully more productive, both superiors and subordinates should realize that there is no advance assurance that their discussion will prove fruitful: if dialogue can result in agreement, it also may make any disagreement painfully evident; if discernment can raise crucial questions, it may also end in self-contented deception; if discretion can aid in determining appropriate action, it is also an arbitrary selection among alternatives. There is no method that as such will guarantee success. For example, one question that dispels any roseate view of this process is: can a community really accept various interpretations of obedience? In answering this question, two facts need attention: first, different views of obedience exist within communities; secondly, a community that insists on a single view of obedience has not really come to grips with pluralism.

In general, then, acceptance of individual apostolates presupposes the willingness of a community to accept additional tasks and to allow a plurality of visions whose diversity tends to make management more elusive and administration more complex.

Community Life

The assignment of religious to an institutional apostolate usually includes both work and residence at the institution. This combination offers religious a sense of personal identity through corporate involvement: religious share collectively in the achievements of their institutions; institutional problems are faced through group action; the concern of the group encompasses both the occupational and personal life of each religious, and so on.

Obviously, a portion of this total support system is lost in the transition to individual apostolates. If some would go further and blame individual apostolates for an erosion of community life, their accusation is over-simplified insofar as all communities tend to disintegrate as a result of urbanization and industrialization.[15] In any event, individual apostolates should not be allowed to become a casual means for avoiding the responsibility of Christian community. Yet if individual apostolates are to be creative of community, religious need to face candidly the inevitable separation between occupation and community that accompanies most individual apostolates.

This separation is apparent in the variety of living arrangements that have accompanied the emergence of individual apostolates: some religious live at the nearest institutional residence; several religious working in different apostolates in the same locale may reside together or, variantly, with members of other communities; some religious may live with families or alone. More often than not, the particular arrangement is determined by such practical considerations as convenient location, availability of accommodations, or congenial companionship—all of which undoubtedly have their respective importance.

Yet it is at least worth raising the question whether pragmatic considerations alone should be the determining factor. For example, if some might contend that living alone in an apartment is not religious community, others might reply that it is quite possible to live alone in a community residence. The issue then goes beyond arguments whether apartments can be metropolitan hermitages or whether community residences are motels for church functionaries.

One, of course, might propose that if religious are responsible for contracting their own employment, they should be able to arrange their own living accommodations. While this reply has the merit of consistency, is it sufficient? If the raison d'être for individual apostolates is that they are a means of more creative and personalized witness to Christ, is this witness entirely a matter of occupation? If an individual apostolate is more than a particular occupation, can living accommodations be considered a purely pragmatic option?

Or, in another vein, if the basic criterion for the occupational aspect of individual apostolates is not so much *what* a religious does, but *why,* the parallel issue in regard to lifestyles is not so much what are the physical accommodations and the like, but why.[16] Accordingly, in undertaking individual apostolates, it seems important, not only to ask to what extent is the occupation really a means of giving Christian witness, but also to ask to what extent is a particular lifestyle compatible with the witness and really a means of fostering religious life.[17]

In response to this question, it would be deceptive simply to transfer quantitative criteria from institutional apostolates, where community life may be presumed to depend upon the degree to which a religious is totally involved in a group or even upon the amount of time spent within the group. Another way of evaluating community is by the quality of Christian relationships available. Accordingly, a religious entering an individual apostolate should evaluate its potential for fostering community (in the broadest sense of Christian community) and for giving witness.

Although individual apostolates admittedly present hazards to community life (yet noting that institutional apostolates cannot insure genuine community either), one need not conclude that individual apostolates are incompatible with religious life. What should be concluded is that individual apostolates need qualitative evaluation on a continuing basis. Indeed, it might well be conjectured that the long-term success of religious in undertaking individual apostolates may well depend upon how well they manage to create an environment of Christian community.

Personal Freedom

One of the most prominent features of individual apostolates is the increased opportunity for personal freedom—a practical necessity if religious are to perform the work required. This is not to imply that freedom is not a major concern in institutional apostolates. What is implied (even should one prefer to argue that the pattern of freedom should be identical in both apostolate and community) is that the dimensions of freedom tend to be contextualized differently. In other words, just as individual apostolates effect a separation of occupation and community life, there is frequently an attendant differentiation of freedom into two rather distinct spheres. Accordingly, religious engaged in individual apostolates may experience some tension or encounter some problems if they expect the exercise of freedom to follow an identical pattern in both apostolate and community.

At first sight, it might appear that freedom is more restricted in institutional apostolates; this is indeed the case in those communities that regulate daily life in considerable detail. Yet along with institutional restrictions of freedom, there is commonly a pattern of familial reassurance that encourages religious in their work and supports them in their difficulties. When, for example, a religious finds the institutional schedule over-taxing, a sympathetic superior will usually allow some break in the routine. More importantly, an institutional community is usually aware of the work of individual religious, whose exercise of freedom is appreciated insofar as it contributes to the institutional apostolate and community.

In contrast, religious may find the occupational requirements of an individual apostolate more demanding than those experienced in many institutional apostolates; in effect, freedom may be more restricted. For example, some religious may be surprised to find that their new employment demands longer hours on the job in order to meet deadlines. Yet such demands are relatively minor matters; what is more likely to cause dissatisfaction is an apparent lack of community interest in and support of religious in individual apostolates.[18]

First, it should be recognized that it is difficult for a community to furnish the same type of support that exists in institutional apostolates whose members obviously share many interests in common. Where an institutional community can readily appreciate the contribution made by each religious to the community's institution, a community will likely have scant awareness of most of the work and little appreciation of either the successes or failures of religious in individual apostolates. Unfortunately, this lack of communication may leave religious in individual apostolates feeling cut off from their community.

If it is axiomatic that freedom has its price, that price for religious in individual apostolates may be a sense of loneliness. On the one hand, such religious need to make greater effort in deepening their association with their community. On the other hand, communities might well be encouraged to take more interest in the individual apostolates of their members; still the fact of the matter is—any community is basically limited in the concern it can express for any one member; this is particularly true of religious working outside community structures. Accordingly, those religious who need the constant support of a communal atmosphere for both living and working should presumably not enter individual apostolates. The freedom available in individual apostolates can be deceptive. Individual apostolates are not for those religious who need the environment of community structures to give shape and form to their religious life.[19]

Obviously, it is tempting for religious to discuss the amount of freedom they should have in individual apostolates. Such discussions can quickly degenerate into arguments about such details as religious garb versus secular apparel, or professional expenses versus community poverty, or the enticements of freedom versus the benefits of discipline, and so forth. However real and important such discussions are, they basically concern matters that can be as individual as the apostolates themselves. If such details need to be determined in practice, they cannot be determined in the same fashion as they are frequently determined in institutional apostolates.

Unfortunately, such discussions may cause religious to by-pass the more substantive issue of suitability for individual apostolates. Many communities presently offer their members some sort of option for engaging in either institutional or individual apostolates; if such an option is offered, it should not be implicitly rescinded by attempting to impose institutional norms that cannot realistically be observed.

A particular problem confronts those communities that are currently moving away from institutional apostolates toward individual apostolates as the pattern for the future. A community in such a phasing-out process may have an increasing problem in utilizing personnel who are not inclined toward individual apostolates; there will likely be a certain amount of tension and dissatisfaction even if the phase-out is gradual; an institutional vision is not relinquished without a struggle. It is also important that the decision to change to individual apostolates be explicitly accepted by a community; otherwise, for example, a community might continue to admit applicants whose inclination is basically towards an institutional style of life and work.

Another pertinent axiom is that freedom can be misused. Individual apostolates have had and presumably will continue to have their share of mistakes: sometimes the particular occupation or the particular living situation is unsuitable for nearly any religious; more likely, there is a mismatch between an individual religious and a particular type of work. Neither of these negative occurrences are really arguments against individual apostolates; these problems have institutional parallels. At most, one might maintain that it is easier for an institution to cover its mistakes, than it is for religious in individual apostolates to cover theirs.

The real problem is the very individuality of these apostolates and the challenge they present to personal maturity and responsibility. In most institutional communities, there is some idealized model of religious observance; indeed, some communities speak of certain members as "model religious." In general, an institutional community furnishes some conventional model of the way it expects its members to witness to Christ. In contrast, the individuality of an apostolate implies that the situation, and thus the witness, is more or less unique. A religious in an individual apostolate must have not only the freedom but also the maturity to work out a responsible mode of life that is uniquely appropriate both to the individual occupation and as a personal witnessing of Christ. In this endeavor, religious can not simply utilize a pre-fabricated model imported from an institutional setting; their solution must be personalized, individualized.

In other words, the need for freedom in individual apostolates is not simply occupational; more basically, it is the freedom necessary to integrate that work within a religious life. This integration needs to be accepted as a personal responsibility; new models are necessary, not simply models transposed from an institutional setting. If this implies considerable discretionary freedom, it also presupposes a level of maturity and responsibility that may be beyond some religious.[20]

Finally, the question of freedom in individual apostolates is an implicit challenge to the self-identity of religious communities. Those communities whose idealized vision of apostolic religious life is incompatible with such personal freedom should presumably not allow their members to engage in individual apostolates, unless the community is also willing to recast its corporate identity. Even those communities whose self-identity allows the necessary scope for freedom may find that in fact not all of their members possess the necessary maturity and responsibility for individual apostolates. It would be a travesty of both freedom and apostolic witness if communities "used" individual apostolates as a way of freeing themselves of immature and irresponsible members.

Until recently, the apostolic endeavors of active communities were normally centered in institutions, which both constituted the corporate commitment of and furnished the corporate identity for individual members. For a variety of reasons, religious are increasingly engaging in "individual apostolates," where occupation and community are more or less separate and which thus pose a problem for communal self-identity. Accordingly, individual apostolates, which seem to have emerged as exceptions or experiments, need to be examined in terms of a community's vision of itself and its apostolate(s). On the one hand, the traditional vision of religious life as a communal integration of prayer and work is inadequate; on the other hand, there is a plurality of competing visions, no single one of which compels acceptance. As a result, communities are faced with basic alternatives: retention of the traditional vision, acceptance of one or other new vision, or a compromise allowing a plurality of visions. Since each option has both advantages and disadvantages, no particular option can be unequivocally recommended for all communities. However, each community should recognize its responsibility to specify its option explicitly and should, of course, be willing to live with the incumbent disadvantages of its decision. In particular, those communities that opt for pluralism must be willing to live with the resultant diversity, both in theory and in practice. For example, pluralism in individual apostolates implies a change in the traditional superior-subordinate relationship, and, correspondingly, demands a new style of leadership. Again, the separation of occupation and community life will result in a diversity of living arrangements, which, however, should not be determined merely on a pragmatic basis but in terms of their potential for creating community. Thirdly, if individual apostolates necessarily require greater personal freedom for their fulfillment, such freedom is not simply a matter of occupation but presupposes the personal maturity and responsibility to live a religious life according to a new model.

In sum, the general thesis submitted is that individual apostolates challenge religious communities to take seriously the implications of pluralism in their vision and creation of community and apostolate.

NOTES

[1]Just as some may prefer terms such as "mission" or "ministry" in place of "apostolate," some may prefer terms such as "special" or "experimental" to "individual." Whatever the merits of one or other term, the concern here is with the implications of the *individuality* of these occupations in relation to community life.

[2]The question of what constitutes appropriate occupations for religious parallels that of appropriate occupations for priests; cf. G. Murray, "The Hyphenated Priest," *RfR* (=REVIEW FOR RELIGIOUS) 25 (1966), 693-702; D. Hassel, "The Priest-Expert," *Chicago Studies* 3 (1964), 201-225.

[3]Whether individual apostolates can be defended in contemplative communities is a different question; the example of Thomas Merton suggests that the possibility should not be peremptorily rejected.

[4]Cf. M. Rondet, "Choices of Religious Life in a Secularized World," *RfR* 34 (1975), 574-579.

[5]Cf. R. Faricy, "Change in the Apostolic Religious Life," *RfR* 34 (1975), 413-414, for a description of the "demonasticization of apostolates." Should individual apostolates be seen as the cutting edge of this centrifugal movement away from monasticism?

[6]Many different models have been used to explain the transition from one vision or world-view to another: for example, T. Nuij, "New Forms of Community Life," *RfR* 32 (1973), 59-64, contrasts community in primitive, rural or pre-technological, and technological or industrial cultures. Among the abundant literature on this transition, cf. T. O'Meara, *Holiness and Radicalism in Religious Life* (New York, 1972); G. Moran, *The New Community* (New York, 1970); L. Schaller, *Impact of the Future* and *The Change Agent* (Nashville-New York, 1969 and 1972, respectively); R. Wegmann, "The Catholic Clergy and Change," *Cross Currents* 19 (1969), 178-197. The well-known works of C. Reich, *The Greening of America* (New York, 1971) and A. Toffler, *Future Shock* (New York, 1970) offer additional models and numerous illustrations.

[7]The influence of another model, the church as institution, is also evident; on the advantages and limitations of this and other ecclesiological models, cf. A. Dulles, *Models of the Church* (Garden City, New York, 1974). It would be helpful to have a similar analysis of models of religious life.

[8]It might be well to develop a declaration of rights for religious similar to Vatican II's *Declaration on Religious Freedom.*

[9]The hazards of adopting a new vision are forcefully, though stridently, indicated by J. Hitchcock, *The Decline and Fall of Radical Catholicism* (New York, 1971); without accepting his viewpoint, one can still admit the need for facing straightforwardly his criticisms.

[10]Cf. E. Carter, "Pluralism in Christian Life," *RfR* 31 (1972), 22-26; K. Rahner, "Pluralism in Theology and the Oneness of the Church's Profession of Faith," *Concilium* 46: 103-123; A. Dulles, "Dogma as an Ecumenical Problem," *Theological Studies* 29 (1968), 397-416 (reprinted in Dulles' *The Survival of Dogma* [Garden City, New York, 1971], pp. 152-170).

[11]The reaction of any person to pluralism seems to involve a number of intertwined factors—personality, intelligence, education, age, occupation, etc.—so that it is impossible to predict an individual's receptivity to pluralism. Nor is receptivity merely a matter of age; the contrast "traditional-pluralistic" is not identical with older versus younger. Also, one may doubt whether it is possible to foster pluralism simply through instruction.

[12]Cf. the interesting interview with a superior general, C. Buttimer, "Is Religious Life Viable Today?" *America* 128/4 (February 3, 1973), 86-90.

[13]Cf. J. Lozano, "Revision of the Constitutions: Meaning, Criteria, and Problems," *RfR* 34 (1975), 525-534.

[14]One of the reasons that dialogue, discernment, and discretion have become major concerns in post-conciliar renewal is linked to increased recognition of religious as persons; an added reason for the importance of these means here is the *individuality* of apostolates.

[15]Cf. T. Nuij, *RfR* 32 (1973), 62.

[16]Cf. V. Branick, "Religious Life: Style or Culture?" *RfR* 33 (1974), 29-34.

[17]R. Faricy, *RfR* 34 (1975), 418, has posed the problem pointedly: "So it is possible for an individual religious or even for many members of an apostolic religious congregation to live in a way more suitable to members of a secular institute. And this is a danger, for it is part of the charism of the apostolic religious life to give a witness that is public, both on the part of individual religious and on the part of communities."

[18]As V. Branick, *RfR* 33 (1974), 29-34, points out, emphasis on personal life-style with de-emphasis on community environment is conducive to loneliness; yet this can also occur in institutional apostolates; W. Sexton, "Dealing with Resistance to Change in Community Development," *RfR* 34 (1975), 783, observes that the trend toward treating individual religious as "the basic building block," i.e., "concentration on the individual—can produce a feeling of loneliness among individual members which is intolerable."

[19]In terms of D. O'Rourke's "Three Models for Viewing Religious Life," *RfR* 31 (1972), 27-32, one may conjecture that those religious who rely on a "life-style" model seem unsuited for individual apostolates; those inclined to an "intellectual" model may or may not be suited; those religious inclined towards a "service" model would seem most suited.

[20]Cf. E. Carter, *RfR* 31 (1972), 22-26, who specifies the qualities requisite for coping with pluralism as discernment, maturity, and tolerance.

The Character of a Religious Community

Edward A. Malloy, C.S.C.

Volume 37, 1978, pp. 748-752.

In the Catholic tradition there has been a strong stress on the importance of moral *character* for individual Christian persons. At times, especially in the practice of moral casuistry which was preoccupied by decision-making, this central insight was obscured. Yet the best theology from St. Thomas Aquinas and those to follow has taken seriously this concern about habitual dispositions and practices. This theology suggests that we tend to act according to our being, according to the kind of person we have become. To attribute a good character to someone is to inspire implicit confidence in the choices he is likely to make.

I want to suggest that this sort of analysis can also be done on groups as well as individuals. By highlighting those pervasive qualities which seem to characterize a group's common life we move beyond description to certain normative judgments about what gives meaning to the members' collective life and work. We claim that they are worthy, as a group, of praise or blame. And we effectively decide whether we might be attracted to participate in similar groups ourselves, or at least to pursue these same qualities.

Congregations of men and women religious are one form of Christian grouping. While they have a canonical status and usually a definitive statement of purposes and rules in the form of a constitution, some of the most important aspects to their life together may elude such legal formulation. Hopefully, these diverse expressions of the Christian life have common roots in the Gospel and in the cumulative wisdom of human beings about the nature and function of social institutions. Perhaps by thinking about the common values underlying Christian community life, we can make better choices about alternative patterns

225

available to us.

I will suggest five qualities which seem to be especially important for religious communities in the contemporary context. By the type of formation that they provide, by the leadership that they generate, by the openness to reform and criticism that they embody, religious communities signal to their membership and to those who observe them what kind of Christians they aspire to be. It is not necessary that each religious exemplify all of these qualities. That would be an unrealistic expectation. Rather it is the group as a whole which provides a complementary context where the strengths and weaknesses of individuals can be balanced out; not in the form of some static compromise or situation of religious inertia, but through a collective dynamism that challenges each person to transcend his own limitations through God's help.

The following five qualities constitute a pattern, a structured form of common life. They give a community character.

1. *Consistent Prayerfulness*

In most religious communities the attempt is made to organize a prayer schedule so that private prayer and liturgical prayer might be an integrated whole. At the level of theory, few would dispute that prayer is important and that some minimal degree of regularity is desirable. Yet, religious today have many competing demands placed upon them and even well-regulated communities often experience a dissatisfaction with the vitality of their common prayer.

Perhaps it is the rhythm of prayer through the cycle of the year which best reveals whether the group achieves consistency in prayer. The first test is surely having a willing group present day by day. But vacation periods can also be revealing. Do they become an opportunity for a spiritual renewal and refreshment or a yearned-for break from all customary activity, including prayer?

In each local house some religious sustain the life of prayer more vigorously than others, sometimes because their work situation is not as demanding. But if these carriers of the tradition of prayer are written off as excessively pious and unrepresentative, then the group must ask itself from whom it will derive its standards. Another opportunity for honesty is when strangers live in our midst. We might well ask them how they perceive the spirit of prayer of our community. If it becomes embarrassing to explain away the non-observance of some or the lack of vitality of the whole, we must begin to face the truth about ourselves.

Some people impress us as deeply spiritual. And some groups measure up to similar criteria. One factor is the sheer physical presence at prayer—what might be called conscious attendance. But in itself this seems nothing more than a starting point. We are too aware of human duplicity and self-deception to be unduly swayed by mere performance. A second factor would seem to be personal integration. When there is an experienced connection between a person's participation in prayer and his everyday attitudes, responses and activity, we begin to discover a kind of integrity. Third, we may find that crisis situations call forth a depth of prayer in some that is linked to a sincerity of faith and a great confidence in God. Those who can pray well in the midst of pain, misfortune and tragedy have passed the ultimate test of consistency.

Today various movements of spiritual renewal have energized the prayer of countless Christians. As a result it is even more appropriate that religious communities take seriously the necessity for consistent prayerfulness in their common life. It is not a matter of conformity to rule. It cannot be subsumed under the category of moral sinfulness. Rather it flows from the gospel exhortation to "pray always."

2. *Spontaneous Generosity*

Recently, there has been much discussion in ethical writings of so-called "Good Samaritan Laws." What kind of obligation do we have to give aid to a stranger in distress? In response, some would hold that no one is bound to be a Good Samaritan or even a minimally decent Samaritan. All we can legitimately be asked to do is to live by standards of justice defined by equity of treatment. In a setting where religious appeals are considered unacceptable, it is hard to debate this point. However, the modeling for Christians that we find in the gospels is quite different. The Good Samaritan parable is in harmony with Jesus' foot-washing at the Last Supper and the parable of the Last Judgment in Matthew 25. These all suggest that Christian service is both concrete and without limits.

In examining the life of a religious community we can, therefore, have certain expectations for the kind of mutual service we would expect to find. By spontaneous generosity I am referring to the uncalculating involvement in the lives of others which is sensitive to basic needs and quickly responsive. At times it may appear primarily in the attitude with which inevitable, tedious tasks are done. But at other times there will be creativity present, a perceptivity to the challenges of the moment, which enables the person or persons to move beyond conventional service.

What we hope to find in any religious community is a mutual regard and loving concern which overcomes differences of personality and the tensions of the common life. Spontaneous generosity is one quality which builds bridges and elicits the best from other people. When it is missing, religious tend to compute carefully the value of all service and honor reciprocation as their highest ideal.

3. *Affectionate Support*

It is possible to live a celibate commitment in the religious life by sheer willpower or the avoidance of challenging situations. Yet normally we expect much more of each other than mere survival. We want to be known and appreciated and loved, at least by enough of our fellow religious that we are rooted in the community to which we belong. Some are better than others at expressing what they feel. Still a group can establish certain patterns of inter-relatedness such that concrete symbols of support are available to all.

The indispensable condition for belongingness is that we be befriended.

Despite the suspicion attached to warm and affectionate friendships in the recent past in religious life, we are courting a shallow and desiccated existence if we avoid the investment of self that is required for friendship to start up and grow. The wonderful thing about friendship is that it knows no barriers of age or temperament. Often we become closest to those with whom we seemingly have the least in common. It is as though true friends make up for each others' deficiencies.

One way that our fellow religious can support us is to recognize and prize our uniqueness. By giving us the latitude to develop our own gifts we are enabled to make contributions to the common life that would otherwise be impossible.

A second means for creating an environment of affectionate support is the ready articulation of the obvious. Words of thank you or consolation or encouragement do not always come easily, especially among those who live at close quarters. Yet they are important, for they make tangible what can easily never get communicated. Just as married couples are rediscovering the importance of love letters and other expressions of feelings, so religious must strive to develop comparable signs of affection.

4. *Diligent Labor*

In an age when technology and bureaucratic process have dehumanized many forms of work, it becomes increasingly necessary that religious develop an attitude toward labor, and a manner of personal participation in it, which preserves a Christian sense of its worth. We work of necessity, but we also make many choices about the specific work we do and the competence with which we engage in it. Preaching, teaching, counseling, administering and healing are typical kinds of apostolic involvement. We certify them in the Christian context by calling them *ministries*. They are forms of service in the wider Church and world. Yet they can be done well or poorly and for a wide variety of motives.

In the feudal social order with its organic understanding of everyone's place and role, it was possible to highlight complementarity. In our day we need to discover new possibilities for rediscovering the sustaining links between one kind of work and another. In religious communities the danger of competition and pettiness of vision needs to be offset by conscious efforts to blend our talents into common projects. Historically, we have achieved this by specific institutional commitments. In the more flexible situation of the present, we still must find common visions and ways of implementing them.

Diligent labor also involves an endurance in the task at hand. Some religious have spent a life-time in unspectacular kinds of service—doing repairs, organizing events, nursing the elderly, teaching the young. Part of the power of their witness is that their work, faithfully done across time, has made manifest their spirit of dedication and genuine readiness to use their talents productively. When religious communities no longer have such people available, they can easily degenerate into unreliable groups of individuals who are merely vaguely affiliated pursuers of careers.

5. *Leisurely Presence*

Those of us who are preoccupied with making efficient use of our time may employ questionable standards to determine our priorities. We may in fact point with scorn to religious who have become addicted to television or golf or travel or some non-apostolic pursuit. Yet, there are other religious who have so structured their life that community is more a general identification, relating one to a common formation experience and collective history, than a real event in the present.

An indispensable condition for leisurely presence is availability. If we are not physically present, with sufficient psychic energy to interact, then those moments we can prize together will never occur. Which is not to say that one must live in suffocating intimacy or make leisure a matter of forced routine. Instead there seems to be sufficient flexibility in most religious groups to allow for high-quality time together according to the rhythm of the groups' life.

Conclusion

When we point to certain individuals as personifying particular combinations of Christian values and virtues, we can appropriately describe them as people of character. In some instances the Church presents them in a formal way for emulation, as in the canonization of saints. However, when we speak of groups of people who are bound together by some common allegiance, we tend to hesitate to employ this same kind of language. What I have been trying to show is that groups also have a "character," at least in an analogical sense of the term, and that we can specify the kinds of qualities of the common life which create and sustain this character. I have suggested five qualities which seem especially pertinent to the nature of contemporary religious life—consistent prayerfulness, spontaneous generosity, affectionate support, diligent labor and leisurely presence. Any community which embodies these qualities in its own unique fashion may be said to have developed a spiritual character that makes manifest the Christian gospel.

Models of Community

Barbara Glendon, O.S.U.

Volume 38, 1979, pp. 206-216.

Ask several religious to tell you what the word *community* evokes within them and you will receive a variety of responses. Some will recall particular experiences of community such as special liturgies, celebrations, shared sorrow, work on a common project, table fellowship, forms of death and resurrection. Others will speak of their feelings associated with community: despair, fear, hope, joy, threat, growth, thanksgiving, support. Others still will tell you what community *should* be, entirely bypassing their own experience. Another group will want further specification: "What do you mean by community? My living group? My congregation? The parish in which I live? My co-workers in ministry? My friends? My neighborhood? My country? My world?"

These reactions indicate the many different ways we understand community, and these varying understandings, in turn, have created both anxiety and barriers whenever dialogue has begun on the subject of *community*. In fact, each of us functions within the context of some model of community which has been constructed either consciously or unconsciously. I further believe that it is an unawareness of the existence of these models and their differences that contributes to the breakdown in communication when we address the subject of *community*. It is my hope that this article will bring some new insights to our differing ways of viewing community and hence contribute to a renewal of dialogue among members of communities.

For many years we have operated on the assumption that we only had one model of religious community. Although the model tried to include many aspects of community, there was basically one pattern which was generally understood to be community. Community was assumed to be sisters or brothers living in the same place, sharing common meals, apostolate, prayer and recreation. However, in recent years we have seen communities come into existence which apparently do not follow this pattern. We have tended to lump them together as "new" communities. The older communities then became labelled "traditional" communities. This categorization, based primarily on date of origin, is a rather simplistic approach to the very complex reality of community.

A less simplistic approach might well lead to growth in our understanding of community. I have chosen to apply the method of "models" to the concept of community. By using this method, I hope to provide a tool which will enable us to comprehend better the differences in our convictions, commitments and hopes in regard to our life together. I share Avery Dulles' belief that "the method of models or types . . . can have great value in helping people to get beyond the limitations of their own particular outlook, and to enter into fruitful conversation with others having a fundamentally different mentality."[1] This article, then, is intended to contribute background for such a "fruitful conversation."

Definition of Terms

Before proceeding to the presentation and development of some models of community, I will define the two terms *model* and *community*. A *model* is basically an approach to, or an analogy of a reality which defies easy understanding. Models are used when dealing with complex realities which can best be comprehended by the simultaneous espousal of many different approaches. Thus, it is accepted as true that no one model need be better than another, that no one model can lay claim to the truth. Each model contains truth—but only partial truth. It should also be said that no one model exists in a pure state, and that, consequently, no one of us should identify with only one model. It is assumed here that, to understand community, we will need to develop several models, each explicating some aspect of the complex reality we call community.[2]

To define *community* is a much more difficult task. To aid us, we turn to the science of sociology. Traditionally, three characteristics have been used by sociologists in defining community: "locale," "common ties," and "social interaction." Some literature would suggest distinguishing the terms *the community* to emphasize "locale" as the basic component; *community* to emphasize the components of both "common ties" and "social interaction"; and *unities* to emphasize the component of "common ties," viewing "locale" and "social interaction" as relatively unimportant. Thus "unities" are organized primarily around a common intellectual or professional bond, or, for our purposes, a common religious understanding or spiritual bond.[3]

Though details may be disputed, it is urged by some that "locale" is no longer an essential aspect of community. Historically, they say, the rise of agriculture marked the advent of *the community,* with its emphasis on "locale." But today modern technology and mobility have marked the demise of this concept. Members of the post-industrial society have very minor ties to any particular place. Even now, the modern housewife is often more familiar with the locale of some soap opera than with her own town. Peoples' social worlds are not the same as their spatial worlds. The entire cities of Chicago and New York have more in common as a basis for decision-making than do the physically proximate neighborhoods of Harlem and Wall Street. A person is more apt to say, "I'm with IBM" than "I'm from New York." Consciousness-raising among minority and ideological groups has made ties stronger among the "enlightened," even if separated by continents, than among neighbors who do not share the same philosophy. As one pastor has said, the basic concept of the parish system is territorial, and "nothing but sewer districts operate that way today."[4]

In spite of these arguments, others remind us that the concept of *the community* with its emphasis on locale still has validity. Physical boundaries *are* still meaningful to residents. Many people do say "I'm from St. Ann's parish" or "I'm a New Englander" before identifying their work or other interests. There *is* a continual quest for community on a local level where, for most human beings, interaction takes place. Intimacy and confrontation are found primarily on the local level no matter how emancipated from spatial barriers the on-the-move modern may be. Today people feel rootless and are looking for closeness, physical as well as psychological. The new independence in locale and space relationships made possible in today's mobile world do not substitute for a high degree of personal intimacy nourished by continuity in time and space.[5]

Ask yourself, "How important is locale in my concept of community?" The answer may indicate the model of community with which you identify. These reflections on just one component of community, locale, give evidence of the complexity of the question: What is community? To carry the debate to the other components of the definition ask yourself: "Are both "common ties" and "social interaction" important to me? Or is a "common bond," with relatively little emphasis on "locale" and "social interaction," sufficient for community to exist?" Once again your answer may indicate the model you prefer.

A further clarification is necessitated by the many different *levels* at which we deal with community. Family is community, neighborhood is community, Church, city, state, nation, world are all communities. It is, in other words, a truism to say that we are all members of several communities. Actually, multi-community membership is one of the issues that the models will view differently.

Acts of the Apostles

I turn now to the first fifteen chapters of the Acts of the Apostles as an aid in discovering some aspects of community which will help delineate the different models I will develop. Prayer and fellowship played an important part in the life of the early Church. Emphasis is given to this importance by such lines as "Every day they continued to meet as a group in the temple, and they had their meals together in their homes, eating the food with glad and humble hearts, praising God, and enjoying the good will of all the people" (2:46),[6] or, "The group of believers was one in mind and heart" (4:32), or, "They strengthened the believers and encouraged them to remain true to the faith" (14:22).

The many miracles which took place in the early Church had far-reaching consequences on the community as well as on individuals. They no doubt played a part in the Church's growing understanding of itself. I have in mind the miracle of tongues at Pentecost (2:4), Peter's cure of the lame man (3:6), the miraculous release from prison on two different occasions (5:19; 12:7ff) and the scenes of general cures: "And crowds of people came in from the towns around Jerusalem, bringing their sick and those who had evil spirits in them, and they were all cured" (5:16). Other examples are Paul's striking the magician Elymas blind (13:9ff) and his cure of the lame man at Lystra (14:10ff).

Certainly the proclamation of the Word also predominates. Peter is continually preaching: at Pentecost (2:14ff), after the cure of the lame man (3:12ff), before the Jewish leaders (4:8ff; 5:29ff). Stephen's speech before his martyrdom (Chapter 7) and Saul's preaching after his conversion (9:20ff) and at Antioch (13:16ff) suggest this.

The dynamic that is involved as the early Church came together to make necessary decisions as a group also catches interest. The process to select a successor to Judas is one incident of this nature (1:15ff). Another example is in Chapter 6 where the apostles called the whole group of disciples together to find a solution to the problem of caring for widows, an action which resulted in the appointment of deacons. Again, the determination not to require circumcision of gentile converts gives an insight into how the group operated in decision-making (Chapter 15).

Another impression regarding the early community concerns the sharing of material possessions. "No one said that any of his belongings was his own, but they all shared with one another everything they had" (4:32). "They would sell their property and possessions and distribute the money among all, according to what each one needed" (2:45). Thus, with all this sharing "there was no one in the group who was in need" (4:34).

Finally, the influential role of the Holy Spirit draws special attention. A rough estimate of the number of times the Holy Spirit is mentioned in the first fifteen chapters of Acts is thirty. Indeed, the power of the Spirit, the witness of the Spirit, the reception of the Spirit, the initiatives of the Spirit appear throughout the Acts.

Would your thoughts have centered on one of these areas mentioned above, or several of them? Perhaps in reading the same material yourself, you would have noted an entirely different aspect. Such reactions may be indicative of the model of community you prefer.

The Models

The models I will present tend to emphasize one or other of the sociological components mentioned earlier. They choose among the aspects of the life of the early Church their dominant mode of understanding community. The models are not to be considered exhaustive; they are the ones that I find helpful in explaining the reality of community. You may wish to suggest others. The distinctions are made in an attempt to show that different models evoke different viewpoints on issues regarding community. Our purpose is to try to understand where the other person is coming from, to see how agreements and differences are related to models, and hopefully to allow ourselves to be enriched and brought closer to one another by an understanding of the models.

The Traditional Model

In the traditional model of community, the concept of "locale" is important. Place or geography is thought to be constitutive of community, corresponding to *the community* concept mentioned earlier. Furthermore, *the community* is a primary community.[7] Fellowship is the scriptural theme that is emphasized. Membership in other groups is tolerated insofar as it does not detract from presence and contribution to *the community*. Thus there is a strong claim for physical presence. There would be little outside socializing since the needs of the members would be met by the common exercises of meals, prayer, recreation and apostolate.

Prayer, although intrinsically important, is basically seen as one way in which the community comes together. Similarly, the apostolate is seen as an important element for common life. Hence the emphasis would be toward a single apostolate rather than diversity of ministries. As a matter of fact, common life would be seen as threatened by a diversity of ministries. The major factor in decision-making would be the common good. Change would come slowly in this model since stability and commonality are high values. Formation for new members would be geared to helping individuals to learn to live common life, to adjust their needs and expectations to those that *the community* could satisfy and accept.

The basic conviction in this model is that to live common life is to live community. Commitment is seen primarily in terms of physical presence and involvement. The goal is a smooth running community that can pray, work, and play together in peace and harmony, to accomplish the work of the kingdom.

The Social/Psychological Model

In the social/psychological model,[8] "locale" is not as important as "interaction"; an emphasis on "place" is replaced by an emphasis on "person." The group is still viewed however as a "primary community," but not so much for the sake of the community as for the sake of the individual. In this model the nurturing and growth of the individual is *the* important concern. Thus there would be a strong claim for psychological presence. Going out would not be seen as incongruent with community unless the individual began to draw more support, nourishment and growth from outside sources than from the community. Thus, sociologically, this model approximates the *community* concept, while also being influenced by the scriptural ideal of fellowship.

Prayer in common would be seen as a support and a challenge, helping the individual to grow by following his insights and gifts. It would also be viewed as an aid to the individual in living through hard times. Diversity in apostolate would be an inevitable consequence of this emphasis on the development of each individual's gifts and talents. The major factor in decision making would be how the community could aid each of its members to realize full potential as a religious. Thus change would be recognized as a normal growth-process, and mechanisms to support change would be a part of the practical planning in such a model. It follows that formation would be geared to helping the individual discover, develop and direct his or her gifts within the context of a strong community-type of "interaction" dynamic.

It is clear then, that the basic conviction in this model is that community exists to serve the individual needs of each member. Commitment is basically understood to be psychological presence to one another. Each member hopes for personal growth and development and a share in and a contribution to the growth and development of the other members.

The Service Model

"Locale" is even less a factor in the thinking of those who espouse a service model of community. Even group "interaction" is relatively unimportant. The major consideration is service to the needs of the larger society rather than of one's own community members. Thus membership in other groups and communities would be welcomed as one means to serve. It would not be unusual for some of the members to experience their "primary community" even outside the group. We see here the development of a *unities* model. The outreach manifested in the early Church by the miracles and the proclamation of the Word as well as the attitude of sharing material possessions would be a basis for this model.

Going out would be expected. A community member who was home a great deal of the time would be looked upon as not ministering to the demands of the larger society and hence not living this model of community. Prayer in common would be only an occasional happening, and the times for private prayer would be highly individualized. From what has been said so far, it should be clear that the active apostolate is of "primary" importance in this model. Other elements of community life would be means to the end of serving the larger society in need of the gifts and skills, of the members. There would be diversity in apostolate, but some limitations would be in effect. The major factor in decision-making, though, would be, "How will this decision provide greater availability and efficiency in serving the needs of others?" Change would be dictated by the changing needs of the society. As a result of this outlook a member in formation would be expected to experience the pull of service as a "primary" component of his or her religious life. A certain independence from the expectations of the "traditional" or "social/psychological" models would be cultivated.

This model is based on the conviction that community exists to aid the individual members to serve the needs of the larger society. Commitment to this service-apostolate is the criterion by which members are evaluated. The hope is to build a better world in which all people can live freely, justly, humanly.

The Witness-Community Model

In the witness-community model, the community itself and its manner of life and interaction would provide witness of the value of community life to the larger society. In a sense, the community exists for the sake of its witness value and hence the community is a *means* to an end. At the same time the community could not have witness value unless in some other very real sense it be also an *end* in itself. Both the fellowship of the early Church and its prophetic stance manifested in the proclamation of the Word would be integral to this model. It is not easy to distinguish in this model whether the "primary" commitment is to the community or to the witness value of the community. This ambiguity in the very nature of the model permeates each of its elements.

Perhaps going out would be necessary in order to project the witness, but it would also be apt to interfere with the community life which is itself the basic witness. So a solution may be found by bringing people in to share the life of the community. This would be particularly true in regard to communal prayer. Communal prayer is a necessity to sustain a model of witness since it would be hard to measure other tangible results. To invite the presence of "outsiders" at communal prayer would itself have witness value. But this could also be problematic as the group at prayer would be ever changing and thus strong community bonds harder to achieve. Thus a rhythm of inclusion and exclusion of outsiders may be developed in order to achieve the goals of this model.

Since in this model, the life of the community is itself the apostolate, other ministries would be chosen so as not to detract from this primary apostolate of witness in community life. The individual then has to live with the tension that may come when he begins to experience the demands of the ministry taking more time and energy than he feels able to devote in the light of his primary commitment and witness in community. Thus decision-making can also become a difficult task. The need to balance community as an end and community as a means is a constant reminder of the tightrope kind of situation this model presents. Change would come about as the group-members in their attempt to maintain the balance, choose to follow one emphasis for a time and then later choose to take up those other aspects that they had been neglecting. Consequently, the goal of the formation program in this model would be to aid the new member to integrate the two thrusts of this model: community and witness through community.

The basic conviction of the witness-community model is that the Christian community as a whole is a witness to the yet larger society of men regarding God's action in the world today. To live one's life as a witness-in-community, then, is the commitment that is expected in this model. The hope is that the group will live community in such a way that the larger society will be drawn to a greater understanding and desire for the ideal which is community.

The Witness-Word Model

The witness-Word model has a much different thrust from the "witness-community" model and is also more easily articulated. In fact a witness-Word community may have more in common with the "service community" than with the "witness-community." To focus the difference between the two witness models we can say that, sociologically, the "witness-community" model appears to be a *community* whereas the witness-Word model is a *unities* similar to the "service" model. For in the witness-Word community the emphasis is not on "locale," the local community, nor even on "interaction" in the group. The important factor is witness to the Word of God. Hence the primary commitment would be to preaching the Word in the larger society. The difference can also be seen by the elements of the early Church it would choose to emphasize. While the "witness-community" model strives to maintain a creative tension between fellowship and proclamation, the witness-Word community would tip the balance in favor of proclamation.

As in the "service" model, so in the witness-Word model, the "primary" commitment could not be lived unless the members go out. Community prayer would take a form which would enable the members to understand, absorb and integrate the Word in their own lives, so as to be able to witness to its call and power within the contemporary world. Clearly, this model would give privileged status to those apostolates or ministries which most directly involve preaching the Word. Decision-making change would be determined in the light of service to the Word. Hence, the formation of a new member would engage the individual in rigorous studies of Scripture and its message for today's world, as well as those communication skills which would allow him to give effective witness to the Word.

The basic conviction then would be that community exists to aid its members to witness to the word and its saving power in today's world. To live one's life preaching the Word is the commitment expected of each member within this model. The hope is that by witnessing to the Word, the members of the community would make the Word present and influential in the larger society.

The Spiritual Model

Once again, in the spiritual model of community, "locale" becomes an important factor. *The community* life centers around a place—the place or places of worship. This is reminiscent of the disciples gathered in the Upper Room where "they all joined together in a group to pray frequently together with the women, and Mary the mother of Jesus, and his brothers" (Acts 1:14). However, in this model the place is not as important as the fact of worship, the fact that each person, and the community as a whole, is called to holiness, to a deep commitment to prayer, to a rich love-life with God. In a sense, in this model of community, the "primary community" is that which is shared with the Trinitarian community. The ties each one has with the Lord are to be respected even if this might mean developing into a community of solitaries.

Going out in this model would depend a great deal on how the individual and/or community has integrated his spirituality with the needs, concerns, and life of the "world." Communal prayer would have a high value in this model, since it would serve to nourish the "primary" commitment of each individual and of the community as a whole. Common prayer, faith sharing, Eucharist would be the communal expressions of each one's commitment to the Lord. There would be a strong pressure for each member to the present at this prayer. The active apostolate, although important, would be to some extent less important than prayer. Prayer itself would be seen as a highly valued apostolate. If one were forced to choose between the active apostolate and prayer, the choice would be in favor of prayer. Thus the major factor in decision-making as well as in initiating changes would be, "How will this decision affect the prayer life of the individual and/or the community?" It follows that formation for a new member would emphasize the development, nourishment, and growth of a rich prayer-life both individually and communally.

The basic conviction of this model is that each member is called to a deep love-relationship with God, and that community exists to nourish this relationship in prayer throughout one's life. A commitment to prayer would be a prerequisite for this model. One's hopes would center on the Lord and his unfathomable love for all his people.

The Pneumatic Model

The last model I will develop is the pneumatic. In this model as in the "witness-Word" model, "locale" and "interaction" are not the major factors. The community gathers as a *unity* because of its attentiveness to the Spirit. The tie is their common openness to and the following of the Spirit. Hence community exists wherever the Spirit gathers two or three together. Some may choose to localize this community in a place, but the option exists for community to be as broad as the Spirit's influence. That, too, was the experience of the early Church. The Spirit impelled the disciples on.

Going out or not then has no particular meaning: the Spirit is continually calling forth community in different times and places; one is in community whenever the Spirit is present. Prayer is seen as "primary" inasmuch as prayer is a waiting upon the direction of the Spirit. Prayer and discernment are daily experiences for those whose model of community is pneumatic. In this model there is no set expectation either of common apostolate or of diversity in apostolate; the Spirit might lead at times to a common work or at other times to diversity. Certainly there are unlimited possibilities because one is living at the beck and call of "the Giver of all good gifts." The major concern in decision-making would be to discern the movement of the Spirit and to implement his inspirations. Change, or perhaps more accurately, spontaneity, would also be a daily experience in this model. The Spirit is alive and constantly calling forth a response. In light of this emphasis, formation would be primarily the work of the Spirit himself. It would be the task of those helping new members to teach them the ways of the Spirit and to listen and discern with them.

The basis for this model is the conviction that the Spirit permeates all life and thus community exists in many places. A commitment to allow the Spirit to direct one's life would be required in the pneumatic community. The hope of the members is that the influence of the Spirit will be ever-widening in their own lives, in the life of the community, and in the society at large.

Conclusion

In summary we see in these seven models varying approaches to community. In sociological terms, we see that some models place emphasis on "locale," *the community;* others, on "interaction" and "common ties," *community;* and still others emphasize the "common ties," bond, or vision almost to the exclusion of "locale" and "interaction." Due to this choice of emphasis, those espousing the models of this last category, *unities,* might be more comfortable describing themselves as "living groups" rather than "communities." The implication of such a choice of vocabulary might be worth pursuing. Finally we see that emphasis given to specific aspects of community life in the early Church also leads to differentiation among models.

It should also be clear that no actual group totally identifies with any single model, though each actual group does have varying degrees of affinity with each of the models. You probably experienced this as you were reading. If this be valid, then it should also be clear that a "true" attitude toward, and understanding of, community must involve the simultaneous embrace of several models. Each model raises legitimate questions which we would do well to address.

Hopefully, after reflecting on the models presented in this article, it will be easier to understand the nature and source of our difficulties in conversations and in making decisions about community and some of the issues in community. Perhaps, too, we will see better the need to broaden our own models, to get beyond their limitations by entering into "fruitful conversation" with others who espouse different models.

NOTES

[1]Avery Dulles, S.J., *Models of the Church*. Garden City, New York: Doubleday & Company, Inc., 1974, p. 10. In preparing this article, I am also indebted to Sr. Eileen Fane, O.S.U., for her ideas on conceptualizations of community.

[2]Dulles, pp. 7-8.

[3]Jesse Bernard, *The Sociology of Community*. Glenview, IL: Scott, Foresman and Company, 1973, pp. 3-5.

[4]Bernard, p. 183.

[5]Bernard, pp. 180-188.

[6]All Scripture quotations are taken from *Good News For Modern Man,* American Bible Society, 1966.

[7]I am using the term to refer to the place where the individual's energies are focused and/or to the place where one feels at home, rather than to Cooley's sociological concept of primary group.

[8]This term for one conceptualization of community was suggested to me by Sr. Eileen Fane, O.S.U.

Religious Life Is a Communion

Ernest R. Falardeau, S.S.S..

Volume 43, 1984, pp. 65-68.

At this time the very nature of religious life is under investigation. What is religious life and how are religious to live it? Since the end of Vatican Council II much study and experimentation emerged to answer that question. While the study goes on, a valuable contribution would be an investigation into the concept of communion to describe the Church, the Eucharist, and religious life itself.

The Church as Communion

A number of studies exist which explore the idea of the Church as communion, but the richness of this concept has not been exhausted. Like a mine whose deeper recesses reveal even greater treasures, the notion of communion unveils an ever deeper understanding of the Church.

Paul's epistles, especially to the Ephesians, and the Acts of the Apostles (see Ep 4:1-16 and Ac 2:24-27, and 4:32-35) underscore that the Church is a communion (*koinonia*), a fellowship of Christians who live closely united to Jesus Christ in faith, hope and love. This union with Jesus leads to communion with God and a unity with other Christians in the Body of Christ.

Ecclesiology today recognizes that far more important than the Church-as-institution is the concept of the Church-as-communion. Indeed a tunnel-vision of the Church as institution could impoverish our understanding of what the Church really is. People of God, family, servant-community, these are part of the total picture. *Communion* begins to say it all.

More than a matter of membership, to belong to the Church is to espouse a way of life. Through baptism we are incorporated into the Body of which

Jesus Christ is the head. We become the friends of Jesus and learn to love all who are part of his fellowship (*koinonia*). Friendship tends to make people who are alike drift together, or makes people who come together to be of one mind and heart.

The Church is a way of life. Inspired by the Gospel, members of the Church walk in the way of Jesus Christ. To be a Christian is to be another Christ. Faith is the root of this way of life, hope is its strength and love is its power.

The Acts of the Apostles, which describes the life of the early Christian community, indicates that there was oneness of faith (teaching of the Apostles), oneness of worship (fidelity to prayer), friendship/fellowship (*koinonia*) and a sharing of goods. No one was wanting or in need because there was intense sharing among the first Christians. People sold their possessions so as to be able to share the proceeds among the community of believers. Indeed sharing of faith and life ultimately leads to sharing of goods.

The Church is struggling today to recapture not only the notion of what the Church is, but also to realize its ideal in practical life. Fellowship with Jesus Christ means being concerned about our brothers and sisters. Thus the Church cannot ignore the burning social issues which face our world.

The Eucharist as Communion

The Eucharist is not only a symbol of what the Church is in its deepest reality (communion). The Eucharist is also the sacrament by which the Church, the Body of Jesus Christ, is built up. Source of the life of the Church, the Eucharist is also its ultimate goal (union with Jesus and the Trinity in glory). What the Eucharist is above all else is communion with Jesus Christ, and through him with the Father, Son and Spirit.

> He who eats my flesh and drinks my blood lives in me and I live in him. As I, who am sent by the living Father, myself draw life from the Father, so whoever eats me will draw life from me . . . . Anyone who eats this bread will live forever (Jn 6:56-58).

After instituting the Eucharist at the Last Supper, Jesus called the apostles his friends. He had given them the perfect means of developing this friendship: the Gospel and the Eucharist. Sharing a meal has always been the best way of making friends. Jesus went a step further and gave his Church an effective symbol, a divine reality, by which communion with him would grow:

> *Manducat Dominum pauper, servus, et humilis* (The poor, humble servant eats his very Lord).

But the communion achieved by the Eucharist is more than something of the moment. By the Eucharist we are made to share the agony and the ecstasy, the death and resurrection of the Lord. His "way" is the way of the cross, leading to resurrection and glory. In the Eucharist we share all. Hence the importance of the Eucharist to living the Christian life:

> I tell you most solemnly, if you do not eat the flesh of the Son of Man and drink his

blood, you will not have life in you. Anyone who does eat my flesh and drink my blood has eternal life, and I shall raise him up on the last day (Jn 6:53-54).

The Eucharist is communion with Jesus Christ and through him with the Trinity. It is also fellowship with all Christians. Paul in First Corinthians explains why:

The blessing-cup that we bless is a communion with the blood of Christ, and the bread we break is a communion with the body of Christ. The fact that there is only one loaf means that, though there are many of us, we form a single body because we all share in this one loaf (1 Co 10:16-17).

Because we are all united in Jesus Christ and form one Body of which he is the head, we are united to each other as members of one body. The diversity of gifts, talents, personalities serves the richness and well-being of the Body, as Paul explains in detail later on in the epistle (see 1 Co 12:4-30).

The Body is not in competition with itself, member warring against member, but is built up by the very diversity that exists in each member. Therefore, while the Eucharist builds up each of us as individual Christians, it also builds up the unity of the Body of Jesus Christ which is the Church.

Religious Life as Communion

As a microcosm of the Church and a witness of the kingdom of Jesus Christ, religious life must be a communion. It must reflect the kind of fellowship with Christ and his members that is described in the New Testament. The basic ingredient in this fellowship is not human compatibility or geniality. Rather this communion is rooted in faith and baptism and life in Jesus Christ. In the past, religious life tried to develop *koinonia* by uniformity. Novitiates were places where men and women learned to conform to a pattern and detail of life spelled out in constitutions and custom books. "Singularity" was the great sin of religious life. Common life was identified with doing the same thing at the same time. *Aggiornamento*, common sense, and a better theology have made us realize that such a road to perfection is actually opposed to God's creative power to diversify, and the Holy Spirit's action to develop members of the Body which are different and distinct. The genius of Christianity is to create unity in diversity, oneness in pluriformity.

. Friends need not do the same thing at the same time. They can be and often are different. The Gospel tells us we should be friends. It does not command uniformity. Jesus respected the diversity of his apostles. He never asked Peter to be like John. He had a wide range of men from Peter to Judas. Each had his distinct personality and contribution to make to the college of bishops.

The Eucharist is the center of religious life as it is of the Church. Its purpose is to unite each religious to Jesus Christ and to the holiness of God the Father. Jesus, the Risen Lord, gives us the gift of his Spirit who unites us to God and to each other. The Spirit is the creative power of God and develops the distinctness and variety of the members of the Body while bringing together in peaceful harmony the unity of the whole Christ. The Spirit transforms bread and wine into the sacramental Body of Christ. The Spirit also transforms each of us into the Mystical Body of Christ as its members. Peace and harmony and unity are the signs that the Eucharist is effective, and the Holy Spirit is at work.

Like the Church, religious life has suffered from an overemphasis on institution. Just as the Church must return to a concept of communion to de-institutionalize itself, so must religious life. Obviously we cannot do away with institutions in life. Governments, churches, institutions of all kinds are absolutely necessary for society to survive. Religious institutions have rediscovered the need for administrators, chapters and authority. However, the context in which these functions are created and operate must be one of communion. Fellowship should be the goal of our *aggiornamento*; friendship, the purpose of our reform. Finding our oneness in Jesus Christ and his Spirit should be the aim of our future efforts to update and renew religious life.

Communion is a sharing of one life not at the superficial level of schedule, dress, and living habits. It is oneness in fellowship and life with Jesus Christ at the deepest level of one's soul. Communion is sharing eternal life with Father, Son and Spirit. Communion is prayer and Eucharist. Communion is sharing faith, hope and charity. And this deep *koinonia* is the basis of our sharing of goods and lifestyle.

Communion of faith, life and goods leads to concern for social needs. In the updating which followed upon Vatican II, religious communities have become more aware of the problems of people in the Church and in the world. New ministries have been created and old apostolates diversified. Some religious feel this is a loss. The multiplicity of works undertaken is perceived as an obscuring of identity. Yet in virtually all religious communities there is a deep concern for tradition and distinctness. Diversification of ministries has brought new life to religious groups and new possibilities of service to the Church and human needs. As J.M.R. Tillard, O.P., points out in his *A Gospel Path: Religious Life** the task of adjusting religious life to the needs of God's people today requires an intense study of the charism of the religious community and such diversification. The heart of the matter is working toward a new unity at a deeper level, and allowing religious life to blossom with new growth.

Communion is unity in diversity. This unity is required of the Church. It is the fruit of the Eucharist. And it is the essence of religious life. Understanding this communion and realizing it in daily life is the challenge to us all.

---

*Tr. Olga Prendergast (Brussels: Lumen Vitae, 1978). See especially ch. 4, "Opening Out to Life," pp. 127-158.

IV. Religious Apostolate

A Theology of Social and Political Involvement for Religious

Philip S. Keane, S.S.

Volume 32, 1973, pp. 1338-1357.

Since the time of Vatican II and the publication of Harvey Cox's *The Secular City,*[1] large numbers of Roman Catholic religious have moved into full or part time apostolates involving a great deal of commitment to social and political reform and renewal. During this same period many religious communities have given institutional backing to their members' social projects, endorsing these projects in chapters, constitutions, and so forth. While all of this social involvement is an extremely good thing, the present writer does have the impression that some of the individual religious and religious communities who have become socially involved have done so in a somewhat rushed fashion, without giving much forethought to the questions of why Christianity should be involved in social and political renewal and what exactly Christianity, drawing from its traditions, might have to contribute to the social and political renewal of our troubled world. In other words, many religious and many communities in their official documents have simply taken it for granted that Christianity should be involved in social questions and that she has something unique to offer in answering these questions. It can be said further that the recent involvement of religious in social matters has not been as effective as it might have been precisely because so many religious have failed to take a sober theological look at both the potentialities and the shortcomings of Christianity as an agent of social reform.

Thus the purpose of this article will be to evaluate theologically the possibilities of Christianity in the social field, looking in particular to the meaning of religious life and what it may have to offer in reforming society. The first several sections of the article will apply to all Christians; the latter portions of it will focus on the specific theological resources of religious communities for social and political renewal.

Limitations of Christianity as Social Change Agent

It seems essential to begin any theology of Christianity and social reform by insisting that Christianity is greatly limited as a program for social change. This point, which is made by Karl Rahner and many other theologians today,[2] needs to be said especially to those Christians and religious who take it for granted that Christianity by its very nature offers us a concrete program for the renewal of society. Christianity simply does not offer such a program. On the contrary, from the very beginnings of Christianity there have been widely divergent views on social matters. In the Scriptures some passages give a seemingly total affirmation of the existing social order (for example, Romans 13:1-7: "You must obey all the governing authorities"). But other Scriptural passages appear to totally condemn the social order (for example, Revelation 13 wherein the State is called a "beast from the sea"). And still other Scriptural passages are more cautious about the State, neither totally condemning it nor totally affirming it (for example, Luke 20:25: "Render to Caesar the things that are Caesar's and to God the things that are God's"). Thus there is no uniform pattern in the Scriptures for Christian social action. We do not get clear answers to social problems from the Bible.[3]

Moreover, if we look to the whole history of Christianity, we find the very same thing. There is no one Christian pattern for social reform or renewal. Perhaps this has been best shown in recent times by H. Richard Niebuhr in his highly significant book, *Christ and Culture*.[4] Therein Niebuhr shows that over the centuries there has been a whole series of partial and divergent Christian answers to social questions rather than a uniform Christian response to society. Niebuhr cites five great types or motifs into which Christian responses to society have fallen: Christ against Culture, the Christ of Culture, Christ above Culture, Christ and Culture in Paradox, and Christ the Transformer of Culture. One might quibble about the exact accuracy of Niebuhr's five types. Maybe they do not include every single category, or possibly some of the types could be combined with one another. But there is no gainsaying of Niebuhr's main point: Throughout history there simply has been no one Christian way of facing social problems.

This whole matter is further complicated by the fact that even the partial answers to social issues which Christianity has offered have never been an exclusively Christian possession. Rather these same types of solutions to social dilemmas have been offered by other segments of society. In fact there have been times when other segments of society have offered solutions to society's problems better and more effectively than have Christians. These considerations have led some of our more prominent theologians today to conclude that in the final analysis there is no such thing as a distinctively Christian social ethic, no solutions to social problems possessed by Christians and no others. Such a position is held by Charles Curran.[5] Not all theologians agree with Curran on this matter, but there is a very wide-spread theological consensus today that Christianity finds itself in a severely limited position when it comes to the area of social ethics.

Hence it would seem that the first and most basic responsibility of any Christian or religious who wishes to enter the social field is an honest admission of his or her limitations in this field. It is decisively important for Christians to put an end to triumphalism when they enter the social field,[6] to stop thinking that they in their Christianity have inherently superior solutions to the specific problems of society. The fact is that the specific problems of society have about them an autonomous dimension of secularity which the Christian gospel cannot fully penetrate. With this in mind, Christians must enter the social field with a great deal of humility and with a real willingness to learn from others in society. With such an attitude of humble openness, Christians can surely share in the building up of society. They will be far more effective in renewing society if they admit the Gospels' limitations as a specific plan for social reform than if they ignore these limitations.

Radically Humanizing Nature of Christianity

The position just taken on the severely limited character of Christianity as a program for social involvement immediately raises profound and disturbing questions: If Christianity has no concrete program with which to approach the social problems of our world, why should Christianity be involved in social and political reform at all? Might it not be better for Christians, especially religious, to abandon social reform and keep to an apostolate of prayer if we have so little specific to offer in the social field? To answer these questions we must move to a deeper level of reflection than we have employed so far. Up to this point we have seen that Christianity does not have concrete solutions to the social problems of our times. But what about the deeper nature of Christianity? In its essence what does Christianity mean and how does its meaning relate to social concern?

Many definitions of Christianity have been proposed. All these definitions however have one thing in common: They all concern Jesus Christ who as man had a singular and unique relationship with the transcendent, with the divine. Different types of Christianity explain the relationship of the humanity of Christ to the divine differently. Most traditional forms of Christianity explain the relationship in terms of the hypostatic union, of God becoming man. While some modern theologies do not use this method, they still relate Christ's humanity to the transcendent or divine. The question which thus emerges about Christianity in our context is as follows: What effect does the fundamental humanity-in-relationship-with-divinity thrust of Christianity have on humanity, on the human situation? There seems to be no other answer but that Christianity, with its junction of the divine and human in Christ, teaches and urges upon us a radical ennobling of the human situation. Christianity, because of its belief in Christ as the human person totally open to God, is deeply committed to the value of humanity. Indeed, in the mind of a theologian like Karl Rahner the most basic fact about Christ is that he calls all of us to be totally open to our humanity so as to receive God's grace. Thus for Rahner Christianity becomes the ultimate humanism, the "ultimate radicalizing of the worth of man."[7]

The very nature of Christianity, therefore, makes it deeply humanistic, deeply concerned with human development. Christianity, of course, does not have an exclusive corner on the market when it comes to human concern, nor does it have specific solutions to the problems of human society. But in its very basis it is radically concerned for humanity. As this implies, social and political issues related to the development of man are truly issues about which Christians, both lay and religious, should care very deeply. Christianity's essence gives it solid reason for involvement in social and political renewal. There is no reason why social and political concerns should be ignored by religious on the basis that prayer is more related to their vocation. Building the human is of the essence of the generic vocation of all Christians, and therefore it is part of the vocation of religious who are called to the deepest living out of the generic vocation of Christians. The very fact that religious life is not a separate sacramental state suggests that religious life is not distinct from the fundamental vocation of all Christians. Instead it is the highest intensification of this vocation.

Christians and religious thus must humbly admit that they are very limited when it comes to finding specific solutions to social problems. But at the same time they must admit that the very nature of their Christianity impels them to be concerned about such problems. Christianity is basically humanistic. It ultimately radicalizes the worth of man.

Possible Stances for Christians in the Social Field

At this point the reader might well feel a bit uncomfortable. For the article has asserted that Christians must care about society and insisted in almost the same breath that Christians are really rather restricted in solving society's problems from a specifically Christian basis. Is this all that can be said? Or are there perhaps certain elements of the Christian theological tradition which might help to give at least some indication about specific stances which Christians might take in the social field? The present author feels that there are some indicators for social action in the Christian tradition, indicators which, while they are only partial answers, at least hint at the direction Christians might take in regard to social matters. Four of these indicators will be discussed herein: the eschatological nature of Christian humanism, the tradition of discernment of spirits, a balanced Christian anthropology which faces up to a theology of power, and a Pauline theology which places love over law.

Eschatological Nature of Christian Humanism

Probably the most striking thing about Christian humanism is its eschatological nature, its view of man as a being who is radically on the way, a being whose institutions and structures are imperfect and will be so as long as man lives in this world. The Scriptures are filled with passages which depict man as an eschatological or future oriented being. The discourses about the end of the world in Matthew, Mark, and Luke clearly tell us that man in this world has not reached his final state, that he is going somewhere. St. Paul's Eucharistic formula that we proclaim the death of the Lord until he comes (1 Cor 11:26) and his assertion that the world as we know it is passing away (1 Cor 7:31) suggest the same thing. So too, do the closing words of the Book of Revelation: "Maranatha, Come, Lord Jesus." The whole history of the Church over the centuries is filled with this idea that man and his communities are still on the way. Vatican II's characterization of the People of God as the Pilgrim Church especially shows forth this "on the way" approach to man and his world.

It must be admitted that in her history the Church has often forgotten her pilgrim nature and gotten stuck in the present instead of goading man to move on to his future which is beyond anything this world has to offer. Usually when the Church has forgotten her pilgrim or eschatological nature, individual Christians or sometimes even atheists have risen up to call the Church back to her future directed orientation. Thomas Münzer in the 16th century is one example of a person who challenged the Church in this way. In our own times Pierre Teilhard de Chardin and the Marxist Ernst Bloch have challenged the Church to face up to her eschatological nature.[8]

Especially as a result of Bloch's challenge many members of the present generation of Christian theologians (Moltmann, Pannenberg, Alves, Pieper, K. Rahner, Metz, and others)[9] have sought to rearticulate Christianity in a more eschatological or future oriented fashion. Rahner, for instance, holds that the very essence of man is to be a hoper and that the best way to describe God is to call him man's absolute future.[10]

Implications of This Attitude

Now what does this idea of Christianity as radically future oriented imply for Christian involvement in social and political activities? It implies that Christians as they look at society, must view it as something limited, something imperfect, something which is constantly in need of reform. In other words the eschatological nature of Christianity means that Christians must constantly be critical of society and social programs, ever looking for the wrongs of society and urging improvement. We hear a good deal these days about the term "political theology." In its essence political theology really means critical theology, it means that Christians, ever conscious of man's ultimate future in God, must refuse to let any merely human solution to a problem be considered absolute.[11]

Such a viewpoint on Christians as critics of society is hardly a new idea. The Old Testament prophets were profoundly critics of their society. So was Christ. So were many of the great religious over the centuries. So too are the Berrigan brothers, whether or not one agrees with them. Social criticism, therefore, or political theology, has been part of the Christian tradition. Working from present day theology, it can and must be said that *an attitude of social criticism is the most basic specific stance to be taken by Christians vis-a-vis the problems of society*. Thus when any Christian, any religious, asks what he or she can do as Christian, to specifically face the social problems of today's world, the most fundamental moral obligation to be cited to such a person is his or her primary Christian responsibility to criticize the evils of the social world. People will never begin to reform the world until they see its wrongs. Christianity can always bear witness against these wrongs, no matter how limited it is in finding concrete ways to overcome them. Social criticism may not be the only service Christianity renders the social world, but it is her most basic service.[12]

Consequences of the Christian as Critic

Some interesting consequences follow from Christianity's role as a critic of the world. For one thing, Christian social criticism requires that the Church and communities in the Church must criticize the world for shortcomings we ourselves bear unless we are willing to root these shortcomings out of ourselves. As an instance of this, what about the low wages which Catholic institutions pay those who work for them? Also, Christians who criticize the world must be willing to constantly criticize the pet social and political projects in which they become involved. They must face the fact that any positive structures for social renewal which they set up will need to be regularly scrutinized for shortcomings. Some post Vatican II Catholics, including religious, have forgotten this point and fallen into a naive uncritical humanism which baptizes all reform projects as Christian, no matter what limitations such reform projects have.

The Tradition of Discernment of Spirits

One might want to ask at this point whether the Church is limited in the social field to proclaiming general principles about human development and to criticizing things which are wrong. Is this all the Church can do? Hasn't this been precisely the problem of the Church in the social field in the past, that she has been general and critical, but never really offered any positive solutions to problems? Haven't many Church leaders, knowing their shortcomings in solving social questions, opted to avoid mistakes by doing nothing? Thus, granted that the Church does not have in her specific traditions clear answers for society's problems, and granted that social criticism is her most fundamental task, might there not be some way in which the Church could offer positive proposals on today's social dilemmas even if these proposals turn out to be mistaken? How can the Church criticize society without offering such proposals?

Various attempts might be made to explain how the Church could take a positive role in renewing society. However, the single best way in which to theologically ground positive Christian proposals for specific social problems is by appealing to our tradition of discernment of spirits. The whole point of this tradition of discernment is that God's presence to us, His light in our lives, goes beyond what we can find explicitly in the Scriptures and in other Christian sources. In other words, when we as Christians do not find direct answers to problems in Christian sources, our tradition of discernment, of the Spirit's presence to us, calls upon us to open our subjectivity to the persuasive power of the Spirit, to let his light guide us in making decisions.[13] Our decisions may not be perfect since we may not be perfectly discerning in the Spirit, but surely approaching any kind of difficulty or uncertainty on the basis of discernment is part of the Christian way of doing things. One of the most refreshing things which has been taking place in the Church in recent years has been the revival of a concern for prayer and the life of the Spirit. Yet it has seemed somewhat sad that this growing concern for prayer and the Spirit has not been more integrally related to moral decision making in general and to the matter of social action in particular. Often, for instance, in a religious community there has been one group greatly concerned with a revitalized life of prayer and discernment and another group deeply concerned with social reform, with the two groups seeing relatively little connection between one another's interests. They simply must get together. An integral connection must be seen between the social moral decisions of Christians and their lives of discernment. No longer can our traditions of prayer and discernment be relegated only to the personal lives of Christians.

Social Discernment

If we make this fuller juncture in our lives of discerning prayer with the area of decisions on specific social problems, it should be clear that with the gift of discernment, Christians can and must propose specific solutions to social problems. They will not claim that their solutions are the only ones or the most perfect ones since they know that God's Spirit works in other ways as well as through explicit Christians. Acts of social discernment on the part of Christians should spring from many levels. The whole Church at times can make acts of social discernment.[14] Bishops who know full well that such and such a political stance cannot be fully verified in Christian sources should be willing to boldly take that stance if they discern it to be in the Spirit. Surely such a stance taken by a group of bishops would have about it a different identity than a similar stance taken by the board of directors of one of our huge banks. Bishops have perhaps been hesitant about discerning solutions to social dilemmas in the Spirit. They must do more and more of this in the future.

Further, the whole Church and her leaders are not the only ones called to discern the social scene in the Spirit. Christian groups, both lay and religious, are also called to do this. Thus, the discernment projects being undertaken by some religious communities today should surely include a corporate effort to formulate positions on the social and political problems of the areas in which these communities live and work. Communities may not always be able to agree on such matters but in the Spirit they should try.

The individual Christian is also called upon to discern social problems in the Spirit. The fact is that if we look to the history of discernment, of the charismatic action of the Spirit in the Church, we see that such charism has almost always begun with individuals[15] and worked its way up through various lay and religious groups to the point where it has finally been accepted by the bishops and the whole Church. Only very rarely has the process of charismatic discernment run the other way, from the top down. It customarily begins with individuals.

This implies that individuals in the Church and in religious communities are very uniquely expected to recognize social evils and to act upon them in the Spirit. This task falls to individuals more than to anyone else. The role of individuals in discerning and acting on social matters also requires friends and associates of such individuals to show them a great deal of respect, even when the friends and associates cannot fully understand what the individuals are doing or why they are doing it. This kind of respect for the social charism of another is especially needed in religious communities whose members should not be made to feel like outcasts for their social convictions. Bishops, pastors, and religious superiors should also respect such social charism when it occurs.

One important observation which must be made regarding Christians charismatically discerning courses of action in the social sphere is that God helps those who help themselves. If what we are called to do in discernment is to let various options resound in our subjectivity, then the more our subjectivity has attuned itself to careful study in the social field, the more likely it is to discern correctly. In other words the charism of the Spirit in the social field should not be for Christians a substitute for disciplined research in that field.[16] Thus it seems essential that religious and lay people who wish to work for social reform full time be given an adequate professional preparation. Our Christianity does not give us an excuse to rush into the social field ill prepared as some have done. But in this field as elsewhere Christ has promised not to leave us orphans (John 15:18).

The Church and its members can therefore propose action on specific social matters even when they do not have definitive answers. They do this by discerning in the Spirit.

Christian Anthropology and a Theology of Power

A new type of question arises at this point. What might a Christian anthropology or view of man contribute to the style with which Christians criticize the world and charismatically seek to improve it? Traditionally Christian anthropology has included three elements: man as created, man as sinner, and man as redeemed or graced. Over the ages those Christian anthropologies have succeeded best which have included a good balance of all three of these elements of creation, sin, and grace. On the other hand those anthropologies which have so stressed one of these elements of man's life that they have forgotten the others have done less well.

Especially in regard to politics the Catholic anthropology which has predominated in recent centuries has been so creation or nature oriented that it has tended to lose sight of other aspects of man and society. In particular, it has tended to overlook man's sinfulness. Catholic anthropology's main point in recent centuries has been natural law, that is, that human nature was created good and therefore that human society can be established on the basis of justice and rights, on the basis of man's good will. Pope John XXIII's encyclical *Pacem in terris* is one of the best recent official Catholic statements of the natural law mentality.[17] It begins by appealing to all men of good will.

Now this Catholic natural law approach to society has tremendous value and it should not be forgotten. But is it the whole picture? Are all men of good will as *Pacem in terris* suggests? Many of our Protestant brethren who have traditionally paid more attention to human sinfulness would say no. Many of them would tend much more to follow Martin Luther and see human government and society as something God created because of man's wickedness in such a way that civil rulers become "God's jailers and hangmen . . . to punish the wicked and preserve outward peace."[18] Without doubt such a view could go too far, but it does say something many Catholics ought to hear once in awhile.

One of the greatest social theologians the United States has ever produced is the late Reinhold Niebuhr. For thirteen years in his early adulthood Niebuhr worked as a pastor in Detroit trying to face the social problems of that city, largely on a love and brotherhood ethic. He finally decided that such an ethic all by itself would not work because it ignored the sinfulness of man and even more so the sinfulness of society. Hence Niebuhr left Detroit and took up a teaching career. His first great book, *Moral Man and Immoral Society*[19] insisted that Christians who would do social ethics must face up to the sinfulness of society and he continued to write for the rest of his life in a similar vein.

It strikes the present author that some of the Catholics who work in the social field can very well stand to hear what Reinhold Niebuhr is saying. Otherwise, such Catholics may run the risk of being naively overoptimistic about what can be accomplished in society and how it can be done. It is true that Catholics should avoid the guilt complex about sin found in some strains of Protestantism. But Catholic social ethics would be building on a more effective basis if it blended its natural law thinking with a Niebuhrian concern for man's sinfulness, especially as this sinfulness is found in human societies.

Power as a Strategy of Social Action

The theological-anthropological category for strategies of social action which emerges when one thinks about sin is power. Of course, power would exist even if man were not sinful. The very fact that space on this planet is limited creates a power exertion situation since two people cannot occupy the same space at the same time. However, man's sinfulness makes him much more conscious of power, much more aware that to build up society in our world he must use power.

Many Catholics who venture into the social field tend to forget about power because they are so reliant on the natural law ethic with its stress on the goodness of man and society. Religious are sometimes especially guilty of this sort of naïvete about power. Catholics must be more open to the political thought of a theologian like Reinhold Niebuhr whose estimate of man clearly calls upon Christians to use power to bring about social change.

Three Theological Truths about Power

Theologians who write about power often cite three main theological truths about it.[20] First of all, power as it now exists in our world is the result of sin. Power would exist even if man were not sinful but were that so, power would not be as corrupting as it now is. Based on this first truth about power those Christians who exercise power to reform society must be aware that it can weaken them and tempt them to sin. The sinfulness of power in the existential order does not mean that Christians should shy away from power, but it does mean that they must be aware of the dangers it involves. Karl Rahner's famous articles on the sinful Church are a good testimony to the fact that power can corrupt those Christians who use it.[21]

The second theological truth about power is that even though it exists in man in a sinful manner, power in itself was created by God and is therefore a good thing, a gift which man can use creatively to build up his world. Power in other words should be used for social reform. The third truth about power reinforces the second one. It asserts that power can be used by men as an occasion for their redemption (or their damnation for that matter). Power, then, can be a tool for building the kingdom of God. Christians who are squeamish about power, about lay people or religious using it in the social field, simply must face up to the fact: power can be used redemptively.

Violent Use of Power

As far as specific power tactics which might be used by Christians to advance the social institution of mankind, the vast majority of the Christian tradition has held that violent uses of power cannot be absolutely excluded as a moral good for man in extreme and oppressive circumstances.[22] Thus it does not seem that we can totally exclude the violent use of power today when extraordinary circumstances call for it. Perhaps some of the problems of the Third World might be a case in point. This position on the possibly moral use of violent power in some cases implies no disrespect for the tremendous importance of the pacifist tradition in Christianity.[23] Its witness value has been very great, especially with regard to the Viet-Nam war. But absolute pacifism has not been the more common position of Christianity on power.

Regardless of how they feel about violence in extreme cases, all segments of Christianity would agree that violent power is immoral in cases which are not very extreme or oppressive. Thus when we speak of Christians using power for social reform we are almost always considering non-violent forms of power. Such was the position of Martin Luther King who drew significant facets of his inspiration from Reinhold Niebuhr.[24] The non-violent power which Christians might use for social reform in the Gospel spirit would certainly include confrontation tactics (boycotts, demonstrations, and so forth) and community action programs aimed at getting at and taking over the political and economic sources of power. Civil disobedience should also be considered as a power tactic to be used on some occasions by Christians. It has a long standing acceptance in some elements of the Christian tradition.[25]

Another point of note is that Christians and religious using various forms of power to bring about social reform should be granted at least a general climate of support by their peers and their communities. Also, as implied earlier, Christian social reformers should be given adequate professional training on how they might use power most effectively to bring about socially worthy objectives. Finally, Christians who use power to renew society must be willing to accept open criticism of their uses of power, realizing that power does have a corrupting element to it.

Political Office Holding

On the subject of office holding as a means of using power to redeem society, this would surely be theologically acceptable and very important for lay Christians and secular priests (granting that it is legally forbidden to secular priests at the present time). For religious, however, the matter is more complicated. A religious vocation is so close to the primal Christian political vocation of criticizing society's wrongs that it is at least questionable whether religious should take part in a limited structure such as political office which has its necessary shortcomings and associations with human sinfulness. Might it not be that the protest of religious against the limitations of society would maintain a higher witness value if religious did not hold political office? Religious over the centuries have claimed exemption from military service, not because such service is completely wrong in all cases but because it is never free of all association with wrong. Similarly, while political office is good, not bad, it is not free from all association with wrong. In fact some of the greatest revolutionaries in the history of the world have become corrupt once they came into political power and office. Should religious run this sort of risk? No one can say for sure and thus no one should propound an absolute theological prohibition against religious holding political office. There may be exceptional cases. In general, however, there is much to suggest that religious might do better to retain their primal role as critics of society and thus to reform society by exercising other less institutional forms of power than public office. But whatever they decide on public office, religious must use some kinds of power to reform society if they are going to admit to a balanced theological anthropology. Power is part of that anthropology.

The Pauline Theology of Love over Law

The realism or cynicism of the past section with its insistence that Christians must use power if they wish to bring about social reform may be disquieting to some. In this section, therefore, the main point is to note that power, while important and not to be ignored, should not be viewed as a final or ultimate Christian reality. Thus man should seek ways of reforming society without power when this is possible. Man as Christian should keep in mind that in the Christian vision power is not to be part of man's final state. This would suggest that in the world, power should be used to gradually eliminate itself as humanity moves closer to the eschaton.[26] Power will never be completely eliminated in this world, so the challenge becomes to find more loving ways of using power based upon a Christian viewpoint which sees love as transcendent over power.

Probably love's transcendence over power has been most clearly expressed in the Christian tradition by St. Paul and those who have followed his thinking. Paul's ideas on this point show up especially in his statements on the order of law. For Paul, while Christians are in this world they are "under the law" and therefore under power. But Christianity's whole purpose in Paul is to free men from the law and make them the adopted children of God (Gal 4:4-6). Thus when Christians come to full life in the Spirit no law can touch them (Gal 5:18). They live instead on a new basis, the basis of a loving relationship with God.

Paul should not be interpreted as meaning that law never serves a positive purpose for men, as some have interpreted him. He does not mean that we can simply get rid of all law and power here and now.[27] But he challenges us as Christians to live in a higher order, the order of love. Practically this means that when we as Christians set out to reform society we must work towards the higher ethics of love and brotherhood even though we face the facts of our world and soberly use power. A Christian or religious who becomes so wrapped up in a power ethic that he or she fails to manifest Christian love to society is guilty of a greater distortion of the gospel than the Christian whose emphasis on love is so unnuanced and naive that it forgets the reality of power.

Religious Life and Social and Political Reform

The possible approaches to Christian social action so far considered—political-critical theology, discernment of social strategies, power, and love—give clues to methods of social action relevant for all Christians, not just for religious. Hence at this point our horizons are shifted somewhat as we ask whether there are any factors in the theology of religious life which can serve as specific suggestions as to how religious might function in the area of social and political renewal. Three factors of some possible help will be cited herein: the sociological nature of religious communities, the theology of religious vows, and religious poverty.

The Sociological Nature of Religious Communities

Around the beginning of the twentieth century the great German theologian, Ernst Troeltsch, developed a sociology of Christian religious bodies, doing this especially in his book, *The Social Teaching of the Christian Churches.*[28] Much of what has transpired since in Christian social thought finds its roots in Troeltsch. In general Troeltsch's work distinguished two main sociological types of Christianity: the Church and the Sect.

To describe these two types of Christianity briefly, it can be said that the "Church" type of Christianity (exemplified by the Roman, Lutheran, and Calvinist branches of Christianity) tends by nature to be a large scale or institutional type of Christianity. As part of this large scale institutionalism, "Church" Christianity regularly has obligatory membership. It wants to take everybody in, usually doing so through infant baptism. Institutional Christianity relies heavily on objective structures to perpetuate itself. Such structures may include a hierarchy, sacraments, and, notably in Protestant "Churches," an authoritative interpretation of the Bible. Institutional Christianity usually has close ties with secular society. After all, it wants to take in the whole of society. Thus Catholicism and Lutheranism were especially close to Medieval feudal society, while Calvinism has been notably close to modern capitalist society. Some would even say that Calvinism created modern capitalist society.

Throughout its history, institutional Christianity has had several weaknesses. Perhaps its main weakness has been that is has often had so much at stake in maintaining the status quo of secular society that it has been completely impotent in criticizing the evils of secular society. A second weakness of institutional Christianity is that it has had relatively low standards for membership, that is, in its desire to take in all of society it has tended to accept as members persons only shallowly committed to the gospel or not committed to it at all. Finally, institutional Christianity has on frequent occasions been sensitive to the needs of minority groups. This fault too has come from institutional Christianity's close association with the status quo or in groups.

The second great sociological type of Christianity, the Sect (for example, the Quakers, the Mennonites, and the Baptists in their original form) differs greatly from the Church type. Christian Sects do not emphasize the need to be institutionally organized; they are not concerned with establishing themselves as large scale organisms. Instead Christian Sects function as free associations. They have voluntary rather than compulsory membership and they typically accept only adult members. They are greatly concerned for the moral asceticism and perfection of their members and they almost always expect their members to live a life of real prayer and mysticism. They simply will not accept as members the lax Christians often accepted by institutional Christianity. While not denying objective structures of salvation (sacraments and so forth), the Sects are far more concerned with the subjective role of the Holy Spirit in Christianity.

Another earmark of the Sect type of Christianity is that it regularly separates itself from the status quo of secular life. It has historically done this by adopting distinctive modes of dress, lifestyle, and so forth. The ethos of the Amish and Hütterites still persists in these separatist practices today. Related to its separatism from society, sectarian Christianity has tended to be highly critical of society. The leaders of Christian movements for social reforms have usually been sectarian Christians. Perhaps the Quakers are the best example. The point is that in their separation from society, sectarian Christians are free to criticize it. They are not heavily committed to the existing order whereas institutional Christians often are.

Weaknesses of sectarian Christianity include an occasional parasitism on society. For example, sectarians are often pacifists, but they could not maintain their pacifism if there were not some institutional Christians around to protect them. Also, and more seriously, the Christian Sect can be guilty of an esoteric perfectionism and self-concern, being taken up with the perfection of its members that it ignores the world around it. Historically the greatest difficulty of sectarian Christianity has been that in spite of its critical spirit it has been irrelevant in solving social problems because it has been so taken up with improving its own religious experience. Prayer groups and charismatic groups which are growing up in Christianity today would do well to pay attention to the history of some of the Sects and thus not to develop their prayer life in a fashion which will make them irrelevant for social reform.

With these characteristics of the Church and the Sect in mind, what can be said about religious communities and social action? The key point which must be noted right away is the unique position of religious communities vis-à-vis the Church and Sect types of Christianity. For perhaps more than any other single unit in Christianity, the Roman Catholic religious communities combine both of Troetsch's types of Christianity. In spirit the Catholic religious communities are purely sectarian. They take only voluntary adult members. They stress prayer and personal holiness. They tend to have a lifestyle distinct from that of society at large and they are often critics of society. But at the same time, the Catholic religious communities are clearly part of an institutional Church, a Church with hierarchy and sacraments, a Church heavily involved with the institutions of society. Religious communities are thus in the singular situation of bridging the two main sociological types of Christianity.

Fascinating and Frightening Prospects

The prospects of religious communities for the reform of society based on their sociological bridge position are both fascinating and frightening. The prospects are fascinating (and also challenging) inasmuch as it may be possible for religious communities to use the Sect side of their heritage to overcome the main fault of institutional Christianity (overinvolvement in the social status quo and inability to criticize this status quo) while at the same time using the Church side of their heritage to overcome the main fault of sectarian Christianity (excessive distance from the real problems of society and consequent irrelevancy). If Catholic religious communities were to accomplish all this, their bridge position in Christian sociology would be a tremendous resource uniquely equipping them to reform society.

On the other hand, the religious communities' bridge position is a fright as well as a fascination. The fright comes because of the danger that religious communities' immersion in both Church and Sect mentalities may result in their succumbing to the weakness of both mentalities rather than using the strength of one mentality to overcome the failings of the other. The upshot of a possible giving in to this double weakness would be that religious communities would have a naive uncritical involvement in society (like "Church" Christianity) while at the same time not really being close enough to the world to grasp society's real problems (like "Sect" Christianity).

A definite answer cannot be given as to how religious will use or fail to use their dual sociological structure in future efforts for social reform. But without doubt religious communities' sociology is one of the most challenging and exciting issues which such communities must face when they consider their prospects for renewing society. One would only hope that religious communities will use their sociological position advantageously in the social field.

A Theology of Vow

Another unique resource of religious communities for social action is the vowed life of their members. The effect of this resource is to reinforce the social role which was earlier described as Christians' primary role in society: the role of constant criticism of society in the light of the gospel. By their vary nature religious vows imply a protest against the absolutization of partial values. They witness that the world's ways of doing things, while good, are never quite good enough. Thus by their vows religious acquire a theological identity as critics or protestors against the shortcomings of society. Much of the psychology of religious life stems from this vow centered theological identity meaning that religious have a very intense affinity with Christianity's primal task of criticizing society. It is to be expected, then, that the efforts of religious at social reform will fit especially into the protesting or critical mode. The great freedom which religious gain through their vows equips them for a lifestyle critical of society.

Practically speaking, the nature of religious vows as symbols of protest suggests that religious who work for the renewal of our society might do so through symbolic gestures of criticism and confrontation: boycotts, demonstrations, fasting, working with outcast groups instead of with establishment people, civil disobedience, and so forth. These kinds of activities are close to the spirit of the vowed life. The stress given them does not mean that religious should never engage in social reform activities which have a more positive and less protesting nature, but it does not mean that the vows of religious are basically a strong resource supporting the critical or protesting style of social reform. This point about vows and strategies for religious social reformers is the basis for the remarks previously made about religious holding public office.

Poverty

While all the vows of religious are a theological resource for social renewal, the vow of poverty can be cited more particularly as a resource for religious who seek to renew society. One of the most talked about books of recent years is *The Limits to Growth,*[29] a research project done at MIT at the commission of a group of European community leaders. The conclusion of the book is that the most pressing social problem facing man today is the resource crisis. The book holds that modern man simply must cease consuming the goods and resources of our world at so fast a rate. If man does not turn from his consumerist lifestyle, *The Limits to Growth* finds that our world will collapse in a fairly short period of years. Many other voices in society are also talking about the consumer crisis. Possible shortages of gasoline and boycotts of meat due to high prices are two recent examples of the consumer crisis. The idea of meat boycotts is in one sense particularly intriguing because its gesture of protest about the consumer crisis is a point of asceticism which was followed by Catholics for generations (Friday abstinence). Perhaps society is finding a need to do things the Church has stopped doing.

In any case the vow of poverty, while it does not call upon religious to absolutely renounce the use of all material goods, establishes a religious lifestyle based on a notably limited consumption of goods. Our world today is especially in need of the witness of religious poverty, that is, the world needs leadership in cutting down on the consumption of goods. Sadly, religious poverty is probably not giving that clear a witness today to the ascetical use of goods: religious impress many people as living rather well. But if religious can succeed in recovering their traditional spirit of poverty, that spirit could be effective in providing sorely needed social renewal, in creating a society concentrating not on the consumption of goods but on human services and development. Religious poverty, then, can be a great theological resource for social reform.

Brief mention can be made of another aspect of the social reform potential of religious poverty, namely that such poverty will give religious a lifestyle very close to that of poor and socially oppressed people. This closeness of lifestyle should help religious to understand and effectively serve poor people, and it should help the poor people to accept religious as persons truly dedicated to serving them. None of this, of course, will happen if religious fail to live their poverty in an existentially meaningful way.

Conclusion

In conclusion, then, it can be said that from a theological viewpoint Christianity, while honestly and soberly admitting its limitations as a source of social reform, does have a variety of possible partial approaches to social questions. Some of its partial approaches cited herein apply to the whole Christian community (criticism, discernment, power, love). Others mentioned apply uniquely to religious communities (their sociological form, vows, poverty). All the approaches, because they are theological, may seem somewhat abstract. Readers may well wish to move on to more concrete techniques for working on society's problems. If, however, we seek to renew our world in an explicitly Christian way, we simply must begin by taking stock of the possibilities of Christianity in the field of social action. We cannot ignore these possibilities. Hopefully, this article has clarified at least a little what Christians and religious as such might do in rebuilding human society.

NOTES

[1] (Rev. ed.; New York: Macmillan, 1966).

[2] Examples of statements by Rahner on the Church's limitations in solving social problems include: "History of the World and Salvation History" in *Theological Investigations,* volume 5, p. 110 (Rahner's *Theological Investigations* have been published in 8 volumes; volumes 1-6 [Baltimore: Helicon, 1951-1959], volumes 7-8 [New York: Herder and Herder, 1967]; hereafter references to *Theological Investigations* will be by the abbreviation TI followed by the number indicating the volume number); *The Christian of the Future* (New York: Herder and Herder, 1967), pp. 53, 63-4, 70; "What is Heresy?" TI 5, pp. 511-2; "Theological Reflections on the Problem of Secularization," in *Theology of Renewal: The Renewal of the Church Centenary of Canada, 1867-1967,* ed. by L. K. Shook, v. 1, p. 172; *Sacramentum Mundi,* v. 1, p. 352; "The Changing Church," in *The Christian of the Future,* p. 28; "The Dignity and Freedom of Man," TI 2, pp. 254, 257-8.

[3] A good source discussing statements of the New Testament about the State and secular society is Oscar Cullman's *The State in the New Testament* (New York: Scribner's, 1956).

[4] (New York: Harper and Row, 1951).

[5] "Is There a Distinctively Christian Social Ethic?" in *Metropolis: Christian Presence and Responsibility,* ed. by Philip D. Morris (Notre Dame: Fides, 1970), pp. 92-120. For some other explorations of this question with somewhat varying viewpoints see Josef Fuchs, "Is There a Specifically Christian Morality?" *Theology Digest,* v. 19, pp. 39-45: Karl Rahner, "Christian Humanism," *Journal of Ecumenical Studies,* v. 4 (1967), pp. 369-84; Karl Rahner, "Christianity and the New Earth," *Theology Digest,* sesquicentennial issue, February 1968, pp. 70-7; James Gustafson, *Christian Ethics and the Community* (Philadelphia: Pilgrim, 1971); and Richard McCormick, "Notes on Moral Theology," *Theological Studies,* v. 32 (1971), pp. 73-6. The last item is a direct response to Curran.

[6] On this point see Karl Rahner, "The Church's Limits." *The Christian of the Future,* pp. 49-76.

[7] "Christian Humanism," *Journal of Ecumenical Studies,* v. 4 (1967), p. 371. The entire article is an excellent statement on the relationship between Christianity and humanism.

[8] See especially Bloch's *Man on His Own* (New York: Herder and Herder, 1970).

[9] Works on Christian eschatology by these authors include Jürgen Moltmann, *Theology of Hope: On the Ground and the Implications of the Christian Eschatology* (New York: Harper and Row, 1967); Wolfhart Pannenberg and others, *Revelation as History* (New York: Macmillan, 1968); Rubem Alves, *A Theology of Human Hope* (St. Meinrad, Indiana: Abbey Press, 1972); Joseph Pieper, *Hope and History* (New York: Herder and Herder, 1969); Johannes Metz, *Theology of the World* (New York: Herder and Herder, 1969).

[10] Perhaps the best sources in Rahner for man as hoper and God as absolute future are respectively "The Theology of Hope," *Theology Digest,* sesquicentennial issue, February 1968, pp. 78-87; and "Marxist Utopia and the Christian Future of Man," TI 6, pp. 59-68.

[11] J. B. Metz's, "The Church and the World in the Light of a Political Theology," in *Theology of the World,* pp. 107-24, is one of the best single articles on political theology.

[12] On this point see Karl Rahner, "Die Gesellschaftskritische Funktion in der Kirche," *Schriften zur Theologie,* v. 9 (Einsiedeln: Benziger, 1970), pp. 570-3.

[13] For a technical study of this point see Karl Rahner: "The Logic of Concrete Individual Knowledge in Ignatius of Loyola," *The Dynamic Element in the Church* (New York: Herder and Herder, 1964), pp. 84-170.

[14] Rahner develops this political discernment concept in detail in "The Nature of a Pastoral Constitution: Theological Considerations," in *The Church Today: Commentaries on the Pastoral Constitution on the Church in the Modern World,* ed. by Group 2000 (Westminster: Newman, 1968), pp. 283-300.

[15] On this whole matter see Karl Rahner, "The Charismatic Element in the Church," in *The Dynamic Element in the Church,* pp. 42-83.

[16] Karl Rahner, "The Nature of a Pastoral Constitution: Theological Considerations," *The Church Today,* pp. 294-6.

[17] For an uptodate critique of Catholic natural law thinking, see Charles E. Curran, "Dialogue with Social Ethics: Roman Catholic Social Ethics—Past, Present and Future," *Catholic Moral Theology in Dialogue* (Notre Dame: Fides, 1972), pp. 111-49.

[18] Martin Luther, "On Secular Authority: To What Extent It Is to Be Obeyed," in *Martin Luther: Selections from His Writings,* ed. by John Dillenberger (Garden City: Doubleday, 1961), pp. 388-9.

[19] (New York: Scribner's, 1932). Some of Niebuhr's later works (for example, *The Nature and Destiny of Man,* 2 v. [New York: Scribner's, 1941-143], and *Man's Nature and His Communities* [New York: Scribner's, 1965]) are more nuanced, but *Moral Man and Immoral Society* is probably the best introduction to the power of Niebuhr's thought.

[20] See, for example, Karl Rahner, "The Theology of Power," TI 4, pp. 381-409; Tex S. Sample, "Towards a Christian Understanding of Power," in *Towards a Discipline of Social Ethics: Essays in Honor of Walter G. Muelder,* ed. by Paul Deats (Boston: Boston University, 1972), pp. 117-41. There are many similarities between the two articles. Rahner's articles is especially significant because it is one of the few Catholic statements on the theology of power.

[21] "The Church of Sinners," TI 6, pp. 253-69; "The Sinful Church in the Decrees of Vatican II," ibid., pp. 270-94.

[22] Rahner teaches that war will be an existential necessity of the human situation as long as man endures in this world; on this see his "Der Friede Gottes und der Friede der Welt," *Schriften zur Theologie,* v. 8 (1967), p. 698.

[23] A good study of the pacifist tradition is Roland Bainton, *Christian Attitudes toward War and Peace: A Historical Survey and Critical Re-evaluation* (Nashville: Abingdon, 1960).

[24] Niebuhr virtually predicted the non-violent coercive strategy which King would have to use to advance the Biack cause, making this prediction in 1932, *Moral Man and Immoral Society,* pp. 252-6.

[25] A good source summarizing civil disobedience in the Christian tradition is Daniel Stevick, *Civil Disobedience and the Christian* (New York: Seabury, 1969). Former Supreme Court Justice Abe Fortas' *Concerning Dissent and Civil Disobedience* (New World, 1968) and Howard Zinn's *Disobedience and Democracy: Nine Fallacies on Law and Order* (New York: Random, 1969) are also helpful on this matter. Careful nuance is, of course, required in considering when civil disobedience is justifiable, but there is no doubt that at times civil disobedience can be a genuinely Christian act.

[26] Karl Rahner's "Theology of Power," TI 4, p. 406.

[27] Stanislaus Lyonnet, "St. Paul: Liberty and Law," in *Readings in Biblical Morality,* ed. by C. L. Salm (Englewood Cliffs, New Jersey: Prentice-Hall, 1967), pp. 62-83, offers an excellent summary of St. Paul's teachings on law, love, and freedom.

[28] 2 v. (New York: Harper Torchbooks, 1960)—the original German edition was in 1911. This is a massive and important work. No one today would claim that all religious bodies fit purely into one or the other of Troeltsch's two types, and it would probably be more accurate to say that different religious bodies contain varying admixtures of the two motifs Troeltsch describes. Nonetheless, Troeltsch's analysis can surely help us see the social strengths and weaknesses of different religious bodies.

[29] *The Limits to Growth,* ed. The Club of Rome (Washington: Potomac Associates, 1972).

A Theology of the Local Church and Religious Life

Ladislaus Orsy, S.J.

Volume 36, 1977, pp. 666-682.

Saint Thomas Aquinas introduced one of his famous works with the sentence: "A small error in the beginning leads to a great one in the end."[1] In the same spirit of wise caution we can say that the wrong question in the beginning is likely to lead to the wrong answer at the end.

Let us transform, therefore, the terse words of the title, "A Theology of the Local Church and Religious Life," into a question rightly construed, that can lead us securely in our inquiry toward the answers that we do not know at the point of our departure.

Indeed, the title breaks up quite naturally into three queries:

1. What is our understanding of the local church? (By understanding we mean *fides quaerens intellectum;* faith seeking understanding. Here we mean the knowledge of the local church that is given through faith, and is deepened through our reflection on the data of faith.)[2]

2. What is our understanding of religious life? (Understanding means, here again, knowledge through faith and reflection.)

3. What is, and what should be, the right relationship between the two?

The questions spring quite naturally from the title. Yet, I am still not satisfied with them. They should be focused with more care, sharpened with greater precision. Also, they should impose a limit on our rather broad topic, and thus make the discussion of it more manageable for our specific purpose. Let us try again to set the right questions.

1. *What is our understanding of the fact, of the event, of a particular church?*

265

There are two significant changes in this new formulation. We seek a better understanding of the fact or event of the church; that is, our focus is not on an abstract concept, but on an actually existing community of Christians who form a church, although not the universal Church. Our focus is concrete and existential. Our understanding will develop more from the observation of the living body than from the analysis of texts.

Also, we substituted the term "particular" for "local." The reason for this is that local church has a geographical connotation and tends to point to a parish or to a diocese, hardly to more than these. The term "particular" allows greater flexibility; it points toward the natural unity of a group of Christians inside the broad universal community. Such unity may well emerge in a diocese, but it may well go beyond it and extend as far as an ecclesiastical province, a region, or a country. It may even spread over several countries. To seek the understanding of a "particular" church, instead of a "local" church, frees us from narrow boundaries and will allow us to examine the issue in a broader context.[3]

But we must impose a restriction on ourselves. We do not intend to exhaust the mystery of a particular church by investigating all its dimensions. We want to understand its life in relationship to religious communities. That is all; but, it is a lot.

2. What is our understanding of the fact and event of religious communities?

Here, too, our focus is concrete. Our primary interest is not in the concept of religious life, but in the real life of religious communities.[4] With a well-defined limitation: we seek the understanding of the life and work of religious communities in their relationship to a particular church in which they exist, and where they give themselves to the service of the universal church.

3. What is, or what should be, the relationship between the two, a particular church and religious communities in it?

We intend to reflect on the living relationship that exists, or should exist, in the body of the church between two diverse members. We seek this understanding in view of intelligent Christian action, with the intention of finding norms and guidelines for such action.

Let us turn now to the first question.

First Question: How Can We Come to a Better Understanding of the Particular Church?

All understanding begins with the perception of facts. For facts about the particular church we must turn to the awareness of Christians throughout the centuries, from the beginning to our days.

Some historical pointers about the development of the particular church;

or, how did the Christian community perceive the particular church throughout its history?

In the early centuries, Christian communities developed mainly along the great commercial routes of the Roman Empire. Soon they structured themselves; the bishop presided over the congregation. The local communities were closely knit; those were the times when Christians knew each other by name. While they were aware of the universal dimension of their religion, they enjoyed a certain amount of local autonomy. Yet, right from the beginning, there was a movement to bring the smaller communities around the bishop into a larger unity, either under the supervision of a traveling bishop, or under a metropolitan residing in a larger city, usually the capital of a province. Particular churches with their own language, liturgy, discipline and customs, developed, not so much in each city, but in larger territories that represented a natural cultural unity.

They developed different understandings of Christian faith; they created different practices. Of course, those differences did not go so far as to deny or contradict the unity necessary for universality, but they certainly went far enough to give a different character to each of those particular churches.[5] Such trends are clearly discernible well into the Middle Ages. Individual dioceses in most places were too small to give a specific expression to their faith, to create their own discipline; culturally, they were absorbed into a larger unity, into the ecclesiastical province or the national church. Thus, the Irish church, from the beginning, was quite different from the continental churches, yet there was not much difference from one diocese to another. The English church, too, had its own characteristics under the leadership of Canterbury. On the Continent, the legal customs of Germanic peoples gave a certain unity to many churches.

In Spain, the Mozarabic rite developed and united many dioceses in worship. In France, churches around Lyons formed again a vital unity, distinguished by their liturgy.

We could continue the enumeration of such developments, but for the purpose of this article, let us content ourselves with a general statement, that I believe is historically correct. If by particular church we mean a church that has its own specific charisms, its own mind and its own heart within the universal Church, then only a few dioceses were truly particular churches.[6] Differences in theology, liturgy, and discipline could be found much more between ecclesiastical provinces, regions and territories of nations, than between dioceses. The source of such variety is much more in human culture than in the understanding of faith.

With the waning of the Middle Ages, a change takes place. The power of the metropolitan see in the Western church is reduced to a minimum. Liturgical worship, preaching, and discipline become strongly unified in the whole Church, even to the point of exaggerated uniformity. The role of particular churches, be they dioceses, regions or provinces, is reduced to a minimum.

Vatican Council II wanted to restore the dignity of the particular church and the bishops stressed its importance repeatedly.[7] Yet the council was not in a position to do much reflection on the nature of the particular church, on what it has been throughout different periods of history; it did not tell us how the term should be understood in the future.

Indeed, the developments after the council reflect some confusion, even some contradiction in these matters. In many theoretical writings and commentaries on the council, it is assumed that the particular church is the diocese. Its unity, its specific character, its distinctive vocation are emphasized. Yet recent developments in liturgical and disciplinary legislation do not give much importance to individual dioceses; they give much more power to larger units represented by national or regional episcopal conferences.

While differentiation on the diocesan level is virtually impossible, except in insignificant and minor matters, privileges, exemptions, special permissions are easily granted to a larger unit such as a region or a nation.

It is clear now that the term "particular church" can be used in two distinct ways. It may refer to an individual diocese, to one congregation around its bishop, or it may refer to a larger unit that comprises several dioceses and possesses a unity that springs from human factors such as culture, history, national inheritance, and so forth. Both uses are legitimate and important. But the meaning ought to be clarified in each case.

Reflecting on the relationship of religious communities to the particular church, we cannot sweep away this problem of meaning, calling it purely semantic. The issue of relationship is alive on both levels and brings up different problems that we must face.

There is the issue of the relationship of religious communities to a diocese. But there is also the issue of the relationship of religious communities to a larger unit, e.g., to the national church, that has its own particular characteristics. In the United States, both issues are alive.

Theological reflections on the fact or event of the particular church, or, what is our understanding of a particular church?

1. Christian people throughout their history were aware of belonging, as it were, to two communities: one, universal, the other, particular. The universal community is world-wide; it springs from the action of the one Spirit of God, who was poured out on the face of the earth. The entrance into it is through one baptism that is the same everywhere.

The particular community is the local one. For some, the local church means the parish, for some others the diocese, for others again, it may well mean the church in a country.

2. The temptation always existed, and will probably never leave us, to

oppose the two to the point that one is considered important at the expense of the other. But any such consideration is wrong because it tears up the visible body of Christ.

When we speak of the universal Church and the particular ones we do nothing less and nothing more than to describe an existing differentiation in the social body of Christ. His body is one, but it is composed of parts; the whole could not exist without the parts; and the parts have no life in themselves. Any separation means death for all; any destruction of natural harmony brings sickness to the whole organism.

3. Paradoxes can be helpful in our attempt to understand such complex differentiation. It can be said that there is both autonomy and dependence in each member of the body. The particular church is autonomous and yet it depends on the universal Church. The universal Church is itself the source of life for all other churches; yet its vitality comes entirely from the local churches.

We may think of the autonomy of the heart in our body. It will not perform well unless all the other organs let it do what its specific task is; any unwarranted intervention with the heart may bring subsequent disaster for the whole body.

Yet the heart is totally dependent in its function on the whole body. The rhythm of its beat, the strength of its action, are carefully regulated by numerous other factors and agents present in the living body. If they cease to function, no life-giving blood will flow into the heart.

We may not be able to reach a precise definition for the local church, but reflection through symbols and images can give us a great deal of understanding.

4. If we ask now what precisely the source of differences is among the local churches, we find that it is mainly in the humanity of those Christians who form them, that is, not so much in any specific Christian belief, but in the human traditions, history and culture of those who believe. Thus, initially, the Jews and the Greeks and the Romans all received the good news equally, but they built up churches that were marked by their own culture, national customs and characteristics. Thus there were soon Jewish churches, Hellenistic churches, and churches of the Romans, all part of the same universal Church, yet all different.

Later, the inhabitants of Ireland, of England, of the Iberian peninsula built their churches on the universal elements of Christian faith, worship, and discipline, and on the particular elements of their own inheritance.

5. The situation is not much different today. Here and there, an isolated diocese may be found that has its own distinctive life *as a diocese*. The Christian community of a Pacific Island may well develop distinctive traits that no other diocese in this world can possess. But such cases are rare today. More often there is a regional unity. The dioceses of Alaska form a natural unity that is quite different from their sister churches in the South.

There might also be a national unity. The dioceses of Japan are not mark-edly different from each other; the strong unity of the culture and traditions on the four islands is manifest in the particular church of Japan. Even a whole continent can display a unity. How many times in recent years we have heard the churches of South America speaking with voices that were strikingly similar to one another. There are foundations in South America for a specific particular unity that embraces the Christians of many dio-ceses, numerous provinces and several nations.

6. Such reflections and considerations do not leave us with a clear concept and definition of what a particular church is; but they leave us with a good working understanding of the complex nature of our Church that is both universal and particular at the same time. Our understanding reflects the true state of things and we do not become captive of romantic ideas that are definitely present in the post-conciliar writings. Father Karl Rahner himself stresses that there is *church* whenever the bishop celebrates the Eucharist, surrounded by his community. Such a vision certainly corre-sponds to our earliest traditions, but it is simply not realistic today. Few of the faithful ever partake in the Eucharist celebrated by the bishop, and the size of the dioceses geographically or numerically makes any such cele-bration virtually impossible. Our understanding is not in adopting clear theories. It is much more the perception of the changing, shifting realities of the Church. That is how it should be.

The duty of Christians to uphold the particular church; or, how must we confess in word and deed our belief in the particular church?

At this point, two facts stand out. One is that there is no Christian Church without particular churches, as there is no human body without members. The other is that there is no Christian who does not belong, somehow, to a particular church, as there is no individual cell that does not belong to a distinct organ in the human body.

No one can, therefore, belong to the Christian Church without assuming the duty to uphold a particular church, although this duty may well be differentiated according to the condition of each one, as we shall see. There is no direct and immediate entry into the universal Church, since it is the *communio* of local churches. Interestingly enough, not even the pope him-self, who traditionally has been called the "Bishop of Rome," or the "Uni-versal Bishop," belongs exclusively to the universal Church. He is not residing in a territory detached from all particular churches, as the Presi-dent of the United States resides in the District of Columbia, detached from any allegiance to any state. The pope is the Bishop of Rome and belongs to that particular church, while he is also the head of the universal Church. The very structure of the Church demands that there should be a duty on every single person to uphold his own local or particular church.

The support to a member church must always be in harmony and good balance with the belief and support given to the universal Church. There is no precise measure to determine how much a Christian should give to his particular community and how much to the universal congregation of the Church. Such measure can only be determined by taking into account a call and a mandate: the vocation of an individual person or of a distinct community. Even in the case of the same person, of the same community, the contribution can be shifting and changing according to needs, and their existing capacity to give.

Now we have come to the point where we can speak more explicitly about the duty of religious communities to uphold the local, particular church. It is a duty from which there is no exception and no exemption. But the duty is not the same in every group.

Religious institutes that are exempt from the jurisdiction of the local ordinary and subject to the direct supervision of the Holy See, have a fundamental universality, a call and a mandate to go to local churches where the need is greater.[8]

They are freed from the power of the local bishop, not in order to be total free-lancers in the Church, but to be free to serve anywhere in any local church. Because of the universal call and mandate of such religious institutes, their world-wide organization, their capacity to move from one place to another should be respected. But once they are settled within the boundaries of the local church or in the territory of a particular church in the broader sense, they must blend into the local scene; they must even strike roots in the local soil in order to bring forth good fruit. They should not be a source of disruption, but a source of strength.[9]

Similar considerations apply to various communities of pontifical right. As a rule their vision goes beyond the limits of a particular church, their aspirations often stretch far and wide. But they too, are at some place and have the duty to serve the people of God *there*.

Then there are the institutes of diocesan right. They dedicate themselves to the service of the universal Church through serving exclusively near a local church. They are not superior or inferior to the others; they simply have their own distinctive vocation and dedication.

The duty to respect and to serve a particular church springs not only from a law imposed by God through the structures of the Church, but also from the respect due to differences manifest in our human nature and in our historical traditions. The upholding of the local church originates in a deep belief in the Incarnation; in the blending of divine and human elements in the Christian community. The gift of God may be similar all around but it takes different shapes and forms in various places.

Second Question: How Do We Perceive Existentially, Understand Rationally, and Be at Home Practically With Religious Communities?

The question sounds broad but the focus of our inquiry is strictly circumscribed again. We do not wish to reflect over all the aspects of the existence and life of religious communities. We want to know, to understand and help them in their relationship to the local and particular church. This is the proper scope of our inquiry.

A short survey of the development of religious communities in their relationship to the local or particular church will be good grounding again for further reflection.

Our survey will be limited to a few facts arising in the history of the Western Church.

The birth and expansion of the monastic movement from the sixth into the ninth century can be described in a somewhat unusual way: the autonomous monasteries that sprang up first in Italy, and then on the continent of Europe, also in the British Isles, had much of the characteristics of a local church. The monasteries were cities of God, distinguished from the cities of man. The brethren gathered around the Abbot to offer their praise and thanksgiving to God.[10]

In some places, the bishop exercised a certain amount of power over them. In other places, due often to distance, the monks lived and died within their own monastery, with no interference from any ecclesial authority. By the eighth century however, the weakness of being alone and not being in communication with a broader segment of the Church became manifest. Signs of decline and decay were setting in.

The eighth century that witnessed the movement of Cluny also saw an increasing awareness of the need for greater unity among religious communities. Monasteries of different places, provinces, regions and countries placed themselves under the power of the Abbot of Cluny. Such close unity clearly constituted a new relationship to both the particular and universal Church. In fact, without the help of the church of Rome, that is the pope, they could not have achieved what they did. With Cluny, an organizational breakthrough had been made.

In the eleventh century, the movement of Citeaux brought about again a new type of union of monasteries built more on a bond of love than on any legal structure.

In the thirteenth century, Francis and Dominic were certainly dedicated servants of local churches, but soon they moved beyond this: they embraced the whole of Christendom. They brought their own new approach toward serving both the local and the universal Church. They had a strongly developed sense of universality, without, however, turning their backs on local needs.[11]

The sixteenth century is the time when new continents opened up. Discoverers and colonizers set out to conquer new lands. That is the time of the foundation of the Society of Jesus. The Jesuits seemingly had no allegiance to any local church. They were devoted to the pope. But further examination shows that while they set out on their apostolic journeys, often sent by the pope himself, for the sake of the universal Church, once they arrived, they went to extraordinary lengths to build and to uphold local churches in India, in Japan, in South America. Paradoxically, they left their native churches to become all to the natives in faraway places.[12]

The nineteenth and the twentieth centuries bring a new development. There are many apostolic foundations; some more for the sake of the universal Church, some definitely for the sake of particular churches. Both trends are represented: to serve the universal Church, and to work for the welfare of local churches.

Here our historical survey ends and our reflections begin.

The ecclesial character of religious communities; or, how are they related to the Church?

Our aim here is to articulate with some clarity an understanding of the obvious fact of history that religious communities exist in the Church and they are in the service of our Christian people.

1. The birth, the development, the existence and the work of religious communities is nothing else than a particular manifestation of the life of the Church.[13] A religious community, independently from the Church, has no life. When a community prospers, it is growing in the life that was given to the Church. This statement should be stressed today since some religious communities have become so involved in reflecting on their own life that they have lost sight of the source of their life. They work within a narrow horizon, and never find what they are seeking so anxiously.

Also, once we understand the fact that there is no life in religious communities except what comes from the Church, it is easier to understand the history of those communities which once prospered spiritually but later grew old and died. There is not necessarily any shame in that. Human persons too, are born, develop, prosper, grow old and die. God may well call a community into existence to provide for the needs of the times; he may well call another one for new needs. We are not privy to his designs. We should give praise for the vocation we have and should not covet what we do not have. Those who are anxiously asking whether or not religious life will survive lock themselves into the limits of a wrong question. The right question is: is there an abundance of life in the Church? If so, that life will manifest itself in new ways that we cannot foresee. There will be always foolish persons around, such as were Francis of Assisi, Ignatius of Loyola, Teresa of Avila, to surprise us, to shock us, and to entice us to follow them. If we put our hope where it naturally belongs, that is, in the Church, our anxieties may well disappear.[14]

2. A religious community may have many goals, all of them good and right. But there is a built-in purpose in every community that seeks and obtains approval from the Church. They publicly proclaim that the words

of life are with the visible Church. They want to be publicly recognized by the Church, they want to have their way of life authenticated as good enough to follow Christ.

The legal formalities of obtaining approval for a new religious community have a deep theological significance. As often happens in the Church, the beauty is all within. A community asks for public incorporation into the structures of the Church. Such a quest is the fruit of an act of faith in the wisdom and the power of the Church. When such incorporation is granted, behind the test of the document there is a quiet recognition that the Church has seen grace operating in the community. It is an approval of the way of life of the group, of their service to the community. The foundation for the understanding of government and obedience in religious communities is their ecclesial character. The Church gives them a public mandate. When they accept it, they obey the call to service.[15]

3. Yet, the mandate from the Church does not make all the communities the same. Each retains its own particular character and personality. Each is called to serve both the universal and local church in different ways.

There are and there will be communities who have their origin and the scope of their life within a local or particular church. There they were born, there they live, work and die. We all know such groups. Their gift is precious beyond telling. In Lesotho, who can serve the local church better than a congregation of native sisters?

There are communities whose organization may spread throughout the universal Church. Members are easily transferred from one place to another, according to need. Their vocation is to blend the universal mission with service in one place. The Franciscan or Dominican friars or the Jesuits would be typical examples of such communities. But let us recall that when a European is sent to Japan, and takes up some apostolic work there, his mandate is to affirm and uphold through every available means the church of Japan. Missionary adaptation or "inculturation" is really an effort toward building the local church. No matter how universal the vocation of a community is, eventually service must be given at a place that *is* the local or particular church.

The duty of the Church to uphold religious communities; or, how can religious communities be affirmed by the Church?

The Church affirms a religious community through the act of public approval. But that is just the beginning. The initial act should be followed by unceasing help and encouragement to promote the integration of religious into the life of the Church, both universal and particular. Respect for the way of life of each group should be the fundamental rule that governs the attitude of the Holy See or of the diocesan bishop. There is no single rule to say how this respect should go.

In the case of a contemplative monastery, respect may mean the appreciation of the prayers offered by those monks and nuns, of the sacrifice of their lives. In the case of an apostolic community, the situation is different; they are taking part in the practical work of evangelization. The Church mandates them to preach and to perform deeds of charity. They should be given an opportunity to share their experience with others. In the diocese, they should be taken into the planning, even into the decision-making, process. Indeed, there is an ancient tradition to invite abbots of independent monasteries and, a newer practice, to invite superiors general of exempt religious orders, to an ecumenical council. To have religious present at synods, held either on regional or diocesan levels, would be not only fair and just, but it would be according to our traditions, too.

Such can be the affirmation of religious life in practice. At this point it is interesting to note that the development from synods to episcopal conferences is somewhat a departure from the old tradition of the Church. Surely, the episcopal body has a unique position in the universal Church, and the residential bishop is in charge of his diocese. But the bishop needs the religious to carry out well their own mandate received through their consecration. It is necessary for them to be in steady contact with religious who carry so much of the burden of daily work in the Church and the churches. If religious share the pastoral work of the bishops, they should also have some part in planning and evaluating the same work.[16]

Third Question: What Is the Relationship Between the Particular Church and Religious Communities, and How Should This Relationship Develop?

The relationship between a particular church and religious communities is a dynamic living relationship that must be created anew all the time.

Legal norms cannot do more than give a framework that is always inadequate to generate life, but good enough to protect life that comes from deeper sources.

Legal norms by their very nature are abstract, impersonal, and general. They are meant for typical cases irrespective of the persons involved, and of their historical circumstances. But in real life there are only concrete situations and living persons and communities. The relationship depends on the personality of the bishop on the one side, of the religious community on the other side. They must work out their relationship concerning particular issues.[17]

Perhaps this relationship is best described through analogies.

The obvious analogy of *call and response* can be used. The bishop calls on the religious community and asks for help to build the Church, to announce the good news, to do the good deeds of charity. When the religious hear this call they must respond out of their own resources. The response of an enclosed community may well be in offering prayers for the needs of the diocese; the response of a group of Dominican friars may well be in preaching in the diocese. The religious too, may call on the local church for help and encouragement; they may well need it.

They may play another role in the diocese. They may call people to a better service of the Lord. They can act as the conscience of the community. Their independence and freedom allows them to do so, provided they can do so without presumption.[18]

The *analogy of the body* can be recalled also. The religious community must find its own identity in the body of the church, before it can function properly. The community is a member of the local church, with its own structure and role. It would not be in the interest of the local church to weaken a member group. On the contrary, it must promote their welfare. It must respect their identity, must use them properly for the purpose they have been created.[19]

Such relationship cannot be regulated by the rules of justice only.

Justice gives birth to rights that must be respected, and certainly should not be bypassed and neglected. Nonetheless, a living dynamic relationship cannot be created if both sides stand on their rights. Such an attitude would lead to a dead end where all the participants become captive to their own rigidity and dedication to strict justice.[20]

Good relationships between the local church and religious living and working in it must be created continuously by both sides. There is no other way of creating it than by charity that means to give. Neither side should ask first what is due to them, but rather what is it that they can give to the other. Only then will there be a new spirit that builds the church instead of destroying it; a new spirit that brings unity to the whole body instead of fragmenting it.

Conclusion

As we reach our conclusion we may well experience contradictory feelings.

On the one side, we experience frustration. After all we did not succeed in finding precise rules and fixed principles to determine the relationship of the local church and religious communities. We found only changing and shifting patterns and the need to create relationships where they do not exist according to our expectations.

On the other side we experience contentment because we are guided by the Spirit of God and the intelligence of believers rather than by rigid rules. After all, the Lord himself did not give many detailed instructions to his disciples. He gave them his Spirit to guide them in all. With the help of the Spirit they have built the Church.

They were guided more by a person than by words. Our hope, too, is in a person, in the same Spirit of Christ. He is with us, in the local church and in the religious communities. Yet, our hope is also in the dedication and intelligence of Christian people on both sides, in the local church and in religious communities. They, together, can create their relationship anew. By doing it, they will experience the joy of the Incarnation; they will share the agony of the Cross. Yet, throughout it all, they will be blessed and will know a contentment that is in a small way the anticipation of the gift of the Resurrection.

Notes

1. *Parvus error in principio magnus est in fine* in "De ente et essentia," beginning.

2. Such understanding is the fruit of both contemplation and rational reflection. We must first accept the mystery through faith and then seek the understanding of it.

3. We do not intend to down-play the importance of a diocese. It is a natural unit in the church, sacramentally and organizationally. Nonetheless, the life of a given diocese ordinarily does not differ significantly, if at all, from the life of neighboring dioceses. But, often enough, a group of dioceses displays significant differences from the way another group lives. The local churches of Holland form a unity that is quite distinct under many aspects from the dioceses of Germany. Organizationally, the division of the universal Church into dioceses is of permanent importance; but, historically, the larger units have played a more important role. The term "particular" is used in our text loosely; its meaning is to be determined from the context. At times, it refers to a diocese. More often it refers to a larger unit: to several dioceses grouped together, displaying a common understanding of the mysteries, using similar rites in worship, cooperating closely in apostolic work.

4. The theological principle cannot be stressed enough. We do not begin with a definition; we begin with the contemplation of an event in the history of the Church. We seek to reach some understanding through the contemplative perception of the mystery. Therefore, our vision will never be so complete as apparently a definition is. Even if we are able to reach a good understanding, it remains incomplete and leaves plenty of possibility for further progress.

5. As succeeding generations of Christians may focus on different aspects of the same mystery, and give practical emphasis to their vision, in a similar way, churches existing in the same historical period may build up differing understandings of the same mystery, and order their practices accordingly, not in the sense of contradicting each other, but rather, in the sense of completing each other's perception. The same mountain can be looked at by explorers from the North, and by explorers from the South. Their differing vision of the same mountain is complementary, not contradictory. The contemplation of God's mighty deeds in our history, deeds that are certainly permanent, gives rise to perceptions and understandings that are distinct and complementary. We see the origin of particular churches in

such different perceptions, followed by different practices.

6. At any time of Christian history, a diocese can be called a particular church organizationally. There is one community, with a bishop presiding over it. But beyond any organization, there is a sacramental unity in the diocese; if the universal Church is a sacrament, so is the diocese. "This Church of Christ is truly present in all legitimate local congregations of the faithful which, united with their pastors, are themselves called churches in the New Testament" *Lumen Gentium*, 26.

7. Vatican Council II strongly upheld the dignity of, and the right of, the local church. For instance: "That Church, Holy and Catholic, which is the Mystical Body of Christ, is made up of the faithful who are organically united in the Holy Spirit through the same faith, the same sacraments, and the same government and who, combining into various groups held together by a hierarchy, form separate churches or rites. Between these, there flourishes such an admirable brotherhood that this variety within the Church in no way harms her unity, but rather manifests it. For it is the mind of the Catholic Church that each individual church or rite retain its traditions whole and entire, while adjusting its way of life to the various needs of time and place" *Orientalium ecclesiarum*, 2.

8. A paradoxical statement; nonetheless it is true. Exempt religious orders mostly used their freedom from local episcopal jurisdiction to go from one place to another, either to help the churches most in need, or through missionary activity, to give birth to new churches. Sometimes the privilege of exemption helps specific activities in the service of the universal Church, such as, to sponsor an International School of Theology in Rome or elsewhere.

9. The strength they give to the local church eventually rebounds to the strength of the whole.

10. To describe the monastic movement in terms of *fuga mundi,* that is flight from the world, only, is to do injustice to history. Granted that to flee the world was an important motive for people who wanted to join the monastic community, still their main motive was to build the city of God among the cities of man. The monastery was as self-contained as the small cities built on the tops of the hills and mountains of Italy. Yet, there was a difference: praise and thanksgiving were offered to God, day and night. The task of the earthly city was *opus hominum,* the work of man; the task in the city of God was *opus Dei,* work that belonged to God. Admittedly, the theme of "fleeing the world" is stressed in contemporary monastic literature. But such writings must be contrasted with documents, such as the Rule of St. Benedict, where the ongoing praise of God and his service takes the central place; also, with the fact that the monks did not hesitate to go out into the world of barbarians in central and northern Europe to bring them the good news of Christ, and to teach them all that they found precious in human culture. A monastery could truly be called a "local" or "particular" church except, perhaps, for the fact that it was not presided over by

a bishop. But the monks were dedicated to the service of the universal Church probably more than they realized. Without understanding their universal orientation, we cannot understand the conversion of Europe.

For a wisely controversial book on the rise and fall of religious communities, see *Vie et mort des ordres religieux* by Raymond Hostie (Paris: Cesclee de Brouwer, 1972).

For a classical exposition of the development of religious orders, see *From Pachomius to Ignatius* by David Knowles (Oxford: Claredon Press, 1966).

11. The Middle Ages, also, saw the foundation of religious orders that were principally devoted to the works of the universal Church. There were orders to promote the Crusades, or to take part in them; to protect the possession of the Holy Land; to give themselves for the redeeming of the captives, and so forth.

12. The history of the Jesuits shows eloquently that the service of the universal Church can never be separated from the service of particular churches, and vice versa. They could not have been more dedicated to the universal Church. They accepted a mandate from the pope, and the pope only. Yet once they established themselves at a given place, they did everything to enter into the culture of the natives. They helped them, in every way that was compatible with Christian faith and the universality of the Church, to build new churches with strong particular traditions. In China, they devised and fought for specific rites in the vernacular suitable for the Chinese culture and mentality. They attempted to do the same in India. In South America, they sided with the natives against the conquistadores, and gave life to local churches within the framework of the so-called "reductions," that is, autonomous Indian settlements leading a strong community life reminiscent, somewhat, of the early church of Jerusalem. History shows that to serve the universal Church redounds to the good of particular churches.

13. We like to stress that the life of religious communities is nothing else than a particular manifestation of the life of the Church. There is no such thing as the Church on one side and religious communities on the other, either helping each other in harmony, or being in open conflict. The member is not separate from the body; all life of the member is the life of the body.

Religious life cannot be conceived of as charismatic life independent and separate from the institutional life of the Church. Charisma and structures, although distinct, can no more be separated from each other in the Church than the flesh and blood of a human person can be separated from his bones. The skeleton, ugly and unfriendly as it is, gives support and proportion to the beauty of the flesh that covers it. Charisma and institutions must work together.

14. There is no need that is as great today as the need for purification of our faith in the Church, and the right understanding of what kind of community Jesus has founded. One conception should be discarded right

from the start (in the terms of Karl Rahner, it could be called a "silent heresy"): the Church is a community of holy persons throughout. While it is true that there will always be persons of extraordinary holiness raised by God among his people, there will always be many in the Church who are sinners, and glorify God by proclaiming his mercy. The Church is a human community, a community of sinners. Yet, because the Spirit of God is faithful to her, she will never lose or corrupt the word of God, provided the proclamation of the word takes place with full apostolic authority. Human limitations and fragility, however, will always be present and manifest in the Church till the end of time, be it in the hierarchy, be it in the people. To love the Church means to love the community as it is, and above all, to have the internal disposition to give what we can to this community. There is little love in those who continually expect to receive. There is love in those who know how to be compassionate. A religious community is one with the Church if the members are steadily asking themselves what they can give to her so that she can grow in goodness, into a greater likeness to Christ.

For a more detailed explanation of these principles, see "How to Be One With the Church Today" in *Blessed Are Those Who Have Questions,* by Ladislas Orsy (Denville, N. J.: Dimension Books, 1976).

Perhaps the best and most rewarding way of acquiring the right theological understanding of the Church is to read and study its history. The real Church, supported by the Spirit, is there in its beauty and fragility. A merely conceptual and systematic approach may lead the unwary to a dream—beautiful and unreal. Once a person surrenders to the dream, he will be frustrated by the harsh and true reality, that is, by the Church as it exists.

15. Indeed, the roots of a theology of obedience in religious life are there in the mandate that the community receives from the Church. There is a sacramental character to such a mandate, since the Church itself is a sacrament. (The seven signs are particular manifestations of the life of the Church.) Obedience to such a great mandate should not be confused with obeying ordinary human rules and regulations that are part and parcel of the life of every community, religious or not. Through the vow of obedience, a person gives himself or herself explicitly, visibly, to the Church. It is the sacrifice of legitimate freedom to accept a mission from the Church in which, behind human structures, the Spirit of God lives.

16. There are few countries where the health and progress of the Church depend so much on education as in the United States. Much of this work is sponsored, directed, or done by religious men and women. Yet, when the most important policy-making body for the pastoral life of the Church meets, that is, when the episcopal conference deliberates, or decides, religious are absent and are given only a very limited opportunity to contribute before, during, or after the meeting—a lack of balance, and the

Church is poorer for it.

17. It is interesting to note that, with all the ingenuity of canon lawyers at her disposal, the Church never succeeded in working out clear and entirely satisfactory norms to regulate the relationship between the local ordinary and religious communities of pontifical right, or those enjoying the privilege of exemption. Why? Because it is easy to state some theological principles such as: the bishop is the supervisor of all apostolic works in the diocese; or, religious must be free to regulate their internal affairs, and to carry out their apostolate according to their constitutions. But, it is difficult to make detailed norms applicable everywhere. Nor will the new proposed legislation overcome this problem. If anything, history proves the insufficiency of strict legal solutions.

18. A religious community of international dimensions can do much to bring a local church out of its own isolation, and to make it aware of the universal Church. The very presence of the members of a community that works world-wide for the Church is a reminder to the faithful that they too belong to a community over which the sun never sets.

19. This implies respect for the particular charism of an institute. The local church should not try to use the religious for work contrary, or alien, to their own calling.

20. While it is right to work for justice, we should never lose sight of the fact that justice is the minimum of charity. Justice can proclaim what is due to each person and group and does establish a balance in the life of a human community. Yet the stability of an organization built on justice only remains precarious. To achieve contentment and happiness, it is necessary to have charity all around. By charity, we do not mean charitable handouts, but strong love that consists in giving, not only advice or things, but ourselves. A society in which each vindicates his or her own rights is built on a shaky foundation. A society in which each one is intent on giving what he has to others, is like a house built on a rock. This is obviously true of the Church, but it is equally applicable to any secular society. The great national heroes of the past were those who were able to give to others, not counting much what they were giving. From what we just said, no one should conclude that the cause of justice is not urgent, and that we should not work for it. Quite simply, as Christians, we must say that justice, in itself, is not enough. The strength and perfection of love is a vital need for every human being and every human society. The great idea of balance and welfare through the virtue of justice ought to be completed by the foolishness of love that God revealed through his Son. See the *Conclusion* in *Morale Internationale,* by Rene Coste (Paris: Desclee, 1964).

For general orientation about the great problems of the world, and for spiritual recreation, all at once, see *Return to the Center,* by Bede Griffiths (Springfield, IL: Templegate, 1977). From the Center will those actions flow that bring love, peace, and justice to all men.

Towards a Sacramental and Social Vision of Religious Life

Philip J. Rosato, S.J.

Volume 36, 1977, pp. 501-513.

Today there are signs that the crisis which has marked religious life since Vatican II is waning. Religious watched the pendulum swing from an overly institutional conception of vowed life during the pre-conciliar period, to an overly individual conception of the vows during the period directly after the Council. If the one conception was so communal that the individual religious suffocated due to a lack of personal freedom and self-worth, the other was so intensely individualistic that the religious froze due to isolation and loneliness as each one sought separately to gain freedom and identity. The one extreme was God-centered almost to the detriment of the human; the other was man-centered almost to the point of excluding the divine. Now a new synthesis of these opposing conceptions is emerging. There is a felt need to correlate the spiritual and the human, the ecclesial and the personal, the eschatological and the psychological.[1] Thus a more sacramental understanding of religious life is in the air. Today's religious are struggling to keep God-centeredness and man-centeredness together in fruitful tension, just as the two foci of an ellipse, though distinct, form one ovular figure. This paper will aim at developing some of the dimensions of this new turn in the theology of the religious life.

Religious Life and Contemporary Theology: Living the Third Section of the Creed

One way of schematizing the different theologies behind each of the extremes noted above would be to look to the Apostles' Creed, a key statement of Christian belief and a touchstone of all theology. Previously religious life was too Father-centered, too centered on the first section of the creed. The vows took on such an ethereal and transcendent dimension that many religious stifled their humanity in order to live out their promise to the Father. The other extreme, centered solely on the second (Son) section of the creed, resulted in an incarnational or Christ-centered theology of religious life. In this model the humanity of the individual religious could find breathing room again; Jesus of Nazareth was seen as a paradigm of human freedom and self-possession. This Son-centered spirituality, though a corrective to the first model, proved in the end to lead many religious to such an affirmation of the human person that the need to lose one's self and to qualify self-centeredness through radical openness to the divine dimension was overlooked. Many religious ceased to pray, viewed community life as a denial of their freedom and the institution of the Church and of their own congregation itself as a hindrance to social relevance and engagement as well as to self-fulfillment. As religious search for a new balance today, it might be possible that a theology of the Spirit, that is, of the third section of the creed, could offer them a new model by which to combine Father-centeredness and Son-centeredness.[2] If the Spirit is the bond of love between the Father and the Son, it may be that Spirit-theology could lead to a synthetic theology of religious life which, grounded in love for God and man, avoids stressing either God's transcendence over his immanence, or God's immanence over his transcendence. A Spirit-centered theology of the religious life could well bring religious back to the kind of balance which is currently being sought in the mainstream of theological speculation today.[3]

Why is this so? The third section of the creed links the Spirit with the pneumatic life of the community, with sacrament, service and mission. "I believe in the Holy Spirit, in the one, holy catholic and apostolic Church. I believe in the communion of saints." According to the Spirit-model, religious life would be viewed as a specific way of living within the communion of the saints. The third section also affirms the reality of forgiveness and of grace: "I believe in one baptism for the forgiveness of sins." If this were underlined, religious life could be seen as a special way of living out the Christian life of forgiveness and of being totally dependent on baptismal grace.[4] Finally, the third section stresses the eschatological hope of all Christians for themselves and for the whole cosmos: "I believe in the resurrection of the body and life everlasting." According to this phrase, religious must be marked as men and women of daring, of vision, of hope. In short, a theology of religious life based on the third section of the creed would be pneumatic, ecclesial, apostolic, dependent on grace and eschatological. In a word, it would be sacramental; it would take both the divine and the human most seriously and keep them in continual tension.

But sacramental means more than bringing the divine and the human into a synthetic vision. Sacrament in this context also has to do with the sign-function which makes religious life distinctive. Religious live from grace more visibly and more unmistakably, that is, more sacramentally, than other Christians. Their life is not better than that of the baptized layman or laywoman, but it is less ambiguous a sign, a pointer, a witness to the reality of grace.[5] Religious live at the center of the Church and yet point to its eschatological edge. They live in the world as much as lay people do, but they are fascinated by the frontier, by the "not yet" of the promised kingdom of God. Religious life thus has a prophetic and end-time character. This particular form of ecclesial life gives unmistakable and visible expression to the pneumatic, enthusiastic and eschatological elements of faith which are essential to the whole Church. Religious manifest God's victorious grace in the world by pointing beyond the world. The community of religious humbly gives witness to the reality of paschal grace for all men and women by living totally from forgiveness and from hope. Sacramental thus means that religious unmistakably witness to the divine and to the human in Christ and in his Church, and that Christ's restless dynamism and his restful faithfulness to God and man are most clearly symbolized in the world through the lives of religious in the Church.[6] The religious as such are at rest and yet restless, very human and very close to God as Christ was. This is the sacramental, Spirit-centered quality of religious life.

It would be wrong, therefore, to separate the sacramental character of religious life from its social character. For the social and the sacramental go hand in hand. The vows are not private promises; they are public signs in the midst of the world which offer promise to all men and women of the ultimate alleviation of want and pain at the eschatological fulfillment of the human and of the natural world. Too often in the past the theology of the vows had too little to do with the poverty of the world, with its loneliness and search for love and intimacy, with its desire for independence and freedom. Poverty, chastity and obedience were, as it were, divorced from the real needs of others. Today it is important to view the vows in light of the social and human problems of the whole community of men and women.[7] Only in this light will religious life maintain its true sign-function. In the midst of human poverty, voluntary poverty says no to man's injustice and lack of concern for the brokenhearted and the hungry. In the face of the sexual loneliness and frustration of contemporary society voluntary chastity says no to man's search for warmth merely through uncommitted pleasure. In the midst of a world crying out for freedom, voluntary obedience says no to man's use of brute power and violence to bring about a more independent future. Today the sign-function of religious life, its sacramental witness to the power of the Spirit of God, must be seen as most relevant to the social problems of the day. The more identical religious are to their vows, the more relevant they will be to society in its deepest yearning for liberation.[8]

The future of religious life, therefore, must be more sacramental and more social. The rest of this paper will try to spell out these two themes by examining each of the three vows. One preliminary question, however, still remains. Which of the vows, by its very nature, is most clearly primary, in that it best demonstrates the sacramental and social dependence of religious on grace? It would seem that obedience is primary, since, though many Christians may live a poor and a chaste life, only religious live out poverty and chastity in the context of obedience to other members of the communion of saints in their particular religious institute.[9] Religious find God's will for them by discerning the needs of the world with the help of the religious superiors in the community. Furthermore, obedience is the hallmark of Christ's own relationship to the Father; he humbled himself to the conditions of his human existence and became obedient unto death. In what follows, therefore, the main stress will be put on obedience as *the* distinctively evangelical way of living in the communion of saints. Then poverty and chastity will be seen in light of obedience. Finally community life itself will be viewed as resulting from the three vows and as essential to the prophetic and critical apostolate of the religious in the world. In this way it is hoped that a view of the religious life of the future will be presented which is both more balanced and more relevant, more sacramental and more social.

Obedience and the Human Cry for Freedom: Becoming Independently Loyal Religious

When the early Christian communities came together, they were known for their desire to discover God's will for them through corporate discernment which had as its aim a concerted effort to preach the gospel and minister to the needy. Each member of the community was aware of his or her own gifts and was allowed to exercise them in the common task of witnessing to the grace of Christ in the world. Yet each individual was also loyal to the whole community. This type of fruitful balance between individuals and the institution led the early Christians to see the relevance of their life-style for those outside the community who were searching for freedom as well as for unity.[10] For too long religious superiors in the Church did not allow individual religious to be independent, to exercise personal responsibility or to find ways of making religious life relevant to the hunger for freedom in the world which marks the history of modern man. As religious look into the future, it seems that obedience is a possible way of expressing both the sacramental and the social dimension of being a Christian. Obedience is not the loss or relinquishment of personal freedom, but the means by which religious are more open to grace and more sensitive to the cry for liberation which is being heard throughout the globe.[11]

Through obedience religious give witness both to the interrelation of the divine and the human in the world, and to the freedom of the gospel which has profound significance for the liberation which is so desired by all today.

The religious obedience of tomorrow must therefore become more sacramental, that is, more unmistakably a sign of the divine and the human dimensions of freedom. The religious must become an independently loyal person. This means that more personal freedom on the part of the individual should lead to greater corporate fidelity and commitment rather than to less. If before, obedience either constricted religious or left them so free that they were not working together in a concerted way, obedience in the future must combine a healthy sense of individual independence with a pronounced sense of corporate responsibility for the preaching of the gospel and for the service of the whole human community. The more self-determined and independent a religious is, the more ready he or she should be to accept the discernment of the community as it decides how the apostolate can be carried out effectively. Thus obedience in the future should not be understood as submission to traffic laws which govern the well-being of the community, but as a quality of ecclesial existence which is not an end in itself but which exists for the concerted apostolate of witness and service.[12] The individual charisms of religious should be fostered so that the ecclesial service of the whole congregation is intensified. In this way obedience will have a pneumatic and eschatological character and be an unmistakable sign that the Church depends totally on grace by discovering God's will through a genuine listening to the fellowship of the saints.

Once religious obedience regains its original sign-value by producing men and women for the Church who are independently loyal, this vow will no longer be seen as simply a private matter between the individual religious and God through his or her superiors. Obedience will be a sign to the whole society in which the religious lives and works. It will broadcast the fact that a life of faith has tremendous import for the liberation movement.[13] What all men and women seek is a way of being free individually and corporately; in their scepticism over whether such a realization of corporate freedom is possible, they turn away from Christian revelation and ground their freedom on some other basis. Religious who can live in obedience and who are still free to contribute their talents and energies to the human task of building up the world in expectation of the coming kingdom of God offer the broader society around them a paradigm of human freedom in brotherhood. This societal dimension of religious obedience is not as emphasized as it should be. Religious tend to view themselves in abstraction from the world which is searching for a genuine form of freedom. The eschatological sign-function of obedience, however, is that it speaks not only to those in the Church and in the congregation, but also to those outside it who yearn for liberation. In the future religious obedience must be so conceived and so lived that it becomes a beacon of hope for those who hunger for independence in the context of interdependence.[14] In this way religious obedience is itself an invitation to faith in Jesus Christ and to hope in him and his Spirit as the guarantors of man's search for liberation within a community.

Poverty and the Human Cry for Justice: Becoming Self-possessed, Sharing Religious

As was the case with obedience, religious poverty was often presented as an ascetical norm by which an individual religious could attain detachment from the world and lean towards God alone. This concept of poverty, however, had two debilitating effects: it made religious doubt their own self-worth by creating in them guilt feelings concerning their use of material things, and it isolated religious poverty from real poverty and thus deprived the former of its relevance for the latter. Many religious lost all sense of their own personal dignity by never becoming responsible in their use of possessions. Often they were not taught how to treasure and protect the goods at their disposal. Poverty was more a matter of not using something than it was of sharing goods with the needy and the hungry. As religious look to the future, it seems that religious poverty will be a way of becoming self-possessed and yet sharing persons.[15] This vow should not make religious childishly dependent on superiors, but responsible Christians who share all they have and are with others. Religious poverty should open the hearts of religious to the cry of the poor for bread, for protection and for justice. The vow of poverty can only do this if it becomes more sacramental and more social.

The religious poverty of tomorrow must take on its original sign-function. It must be an eschatological sign of hope in the midst of human want. It can only do so if religious freely choose to identify with the poor in order to bring them to faith in Christ's promise to be with them in their hunger and to alleviate their misery. Religious are not destitute, but they freely elect to be like the very poor, so as to share whatever excess goods they have with their brothers and sisters in poverty.[16] In effect religious pattern forth a model of a sharing Christian community to the whole Church. In this way religious poverty regains its prophetic and end-time character. It urges the whole Church to be equally concerned with the hungry and encourages those who live in unjust circumstances to hope in the Christ who became poor for their sake and who is present to them through the love of religious. The poverty of religious is therefore not an end in itself, but a form of ecclesial life for the destitute, so that they can hear the gospel and taste its power. Religious who are self-possessed, sharing people give witness to their dependence on grace in the use and possession of material goods. They are an unmistakable sign to the world that the Christian community does not exist for itself and is not insensitive to human misery.[17] Religious poverty is a catalyst which makes the whole Church bring the grace of Christ into the homes and the hearts of the poor.

Religious poverty, as a sacramental sign, must rediscover its sociological roots as well as its theological significance. Just as the Eucharist is a meal which has social as well as religious dimensions, since Christ cannot be recognized in the eucharistic bread if he is not first recognized in the poor and the hungry, so religious poverty presupposes that the religious choose poverty because they recognize Christ's presence among those who are in ghettoes, in prisons, in nursing homes and in soup kitchens.[18] By being poor, religious also identify with Christ in the helpless, the confused, the power-less, the uneducated and the injured even in the midst of affluence. This identification is not, as the Marxists claim, the way in which Christians sanction injustice. Rather the religious chooses to be identified with the poor so that Christ's promise of ultimate liberation from want becomes a present reality for the destitute. The charity which being voluntarily poor makes possible is nothing else than the religious' desire to feed the poor in the name of Christ and thus to bring them more than bread, shelter, technical assistance and organizational techniques. The religious witnesses to God's grace in the face of the evil that does more than deprive the poor of food and power, but also deprives them of dreams and hope.[19]

Chastity and the Human Cry for Warmth and Fidelity: Becoming Sexual and Celibate Religious

At a time when the sexual revolution is sending shock waves through the institution of marriage, religious celibacy certainly takes on a different character than it did only a decade ago. In the past most people viewed the religious as asexual people who lacked human affection and warmth. This critique was partially justified. Many religious were taught to suppress their sexual feelings and even more their sexual identity. The beauty of human sexuality was often underplayed in formation, and religious were encouraged to live as though they did not have bodies, feelings, sexual roles or psychological needs for intimacy and friendship. Recently religious have rediscovered how to be at peace with the fact that they are sexual beings, and are now learning to live with their sexuality by making it a vital source of energy and enthusiasm in their apostolates.[20] Yet there is a deeper mean-ing to religious chastity which is opening up to religious in the face of modern man's frustration and loneliness in an age of sexual liberty. Many people feel isolated even in the most intimate of relationships and are exasperated when the experience of marital love disintegrates into infidelity, separation or divorce. As religious become more aware of the need for bal-ance in their daily lives as celibates, they must also become more aware of the social significance of their total dependence on grace in the matter of sexuality as this speaks to those who are unable to make any kind of lasting commitment.[21]

There is no doubt that the religious chastity of tomorrow must be more sacramental than it ever was before. Religious must be human and warm as well as genitally pure. The more their bodies and hearts belong to God, the more they must be at the service of the love and the friendship of Christ. Celibacy can no longer be an escape from affectionate relationships which can lead others to faith.[22] A sacramental conception of chastity means that religious must be more free to give witness to the depth of divine love by practicing human love faithfully. Religious can only do this not by suppressing, but by channeling their sexual feelings and needs. Religious celibacy must not be seen as a relinquishment of sexual identity, but as a free renunciation of valid, though ambiguous, human intimacy and exclusiveness. Human sexuality is therefore an important force in the Church since it gives men and women the power to introduce others into the loving relationship with God which is the end of all love.[23] A sacramental religious chastity would aim to combine a true love of God with a true love of other men and women. Often the sign-function of religious chastity is lost when religious fail to love deeply on a human level precisely because they do not love deeply on the supernatural level. A proper balance of both affectionate love for God and affectionate love for others is the challenge of being both sexual and celibate. Only if the religious loves genuinely, does he or she witness to the eschatological goal of all human love when Christ will return in glory to lead to completion the men and women of all ages who have sought to reach out to others and commit themselves to him through them.

The sacramental, then, cannot be seen in isolation from the social. If religious free themselves from exaggerated egoism in the form of self-serving gratification which results in insensitivity to the needs of others, it is only for the sake of the kingdom of Christ and for the sake of others who are lonely, frustrated, unfree sexually or subjected to sexual abuse and lack of fidelity.[24] There is thus a very legitimate social aspect to religious chastity. This vow is not simply a matter of private devotion; it has by its very nature a sociological function. This function is not simply critical in that it protests against the excesses which result from sexual force. The sociological function of religious chastity is also positive. The religious models forth a pattern of human love which is not merely a blind effort to distract man from death through embracing sexual pleasure. Christian love, as the religious lives it, symbolizes God's unswerving love for all and thus lends to human love the character of a relationship with the source of all affection and warmth—God's own trinitarian community of love. Just as obedience offers the human search for independence an ultimate vindication, and just as religious poverty offers human want ultimate hope, so religious chastity has a social significance. It offers the lonely and the frustrated, who see human love as the only escape from absurdity, a vision of love which ultimately vindicates their own disillusionment over human infidelity and hard-heartedness.[25] In the person of the religious a type of faithful human love is experienced which points to divine love and which thus attests that there is a deep meaning to human tears and hurt. In this sense religious chastity is sacramental as well as social.

Religious Community and Christian Mission: the Locus of Healing Criticism

The basic thesis of this paper is that, just as religious faith in general has a sociological dimension in that it is concerned with justice, so also does religious life. The more identical religious are with their own tradition, the more able they are to criticize the society around them when it fails to live up to its responsibility to heal broken men and women.[26] Just as the whole Church serves faith by promoting justice, so the religious community lives out its prophetic and end-time sign-function by bringing the healing presence of Christ to the unfree, the poor and the lonely. The other theme, which has been woven into the first, is that religious can only be signs of a critical and healing love if they themselves are balanced. Only if religious channel human talent and divine grace into an on-going sacramental synthesis, can they carry out their call to be Christ's healing presence where men and women harm each other by not living according to human and religious values. The quest for personal identity which many religious are going through today is not irrelevant to the quest for the social relevance of the whole Church which is more pressing.[27] This paper would like to assert that a more sacramental type of religious life would lead to a more socially relevant, precisely because socially critical, understanding of vowed life.

In effect this paper is advocating that a Spirit-centered Christology be the model for an understanding of the sacramental, that is, the spiritual and the social, significance of religious life today. For the Spirit-filled Jesus did not allow himself to be categorized or to be understood solely in terms of any of the typical expectations which were prevalent in his time. Instead he insisted on his identity as the one who proclaimed that the kingdom of God is near. The close identification between Spirit-theology and eschatology in the Scriptures leads us to see that Jesus' eschatological message was the fruit of his Spirit-filled being.[28] In him God's future broke into the world of time. God's kingdom dawned upon man and offered the whole cosmos the ability to head towards a new future that was guaranteed to it by the fully Spirit-filled and glorified Jesus. A Spirit-filled person and a Spirit-filled community, therefore, is essentially a critical one; it is restless until the cosmos is complete, until the kingdom of God breaks definitely into its midst. Yet it is also at rest because that kingdom is already a present phenomenon through the Spirit's activity in the ecclesial community specifically and in the whole cosmos as well.[29] Religious who live together at the heart of the Church are particularly the locus where the Spirit's activity everywhere is made most visible and most incandescent. A religious community is a critical community because it is not totally at peace until the kingdom is manifestly present.

This critical function of religious communities in the Church adds a special character to all of the vows, to their life together and to their apostolate. As indicated in this paper, all of the vows are eschatological, and therefore critical, by nature. They do not criticize society for the sake of criticism, but in order to awaken all men and women to the presence of God's kingdom which is already hidden among them. Religious are also critical of each other since they are compelled to urge their brothers and sisters to live in the presence of the coming God and to view all things, and especially the community itself, as elements of an as yet incomplete cosmos which needs the healing and purifying presence of the Spirit.[30] If religious are critical of many aspects of their community life, it is not because they are discontent by nature, but because they long for the ever-fuller manifestation of the kingdom in their community, and thus call their fellow religious to be what they are meant to be: a sign of the eschatological promise of God in the every-day life of the world. Religious witness to God's coming in the midst of man's coming and going. The same is true of the apostolate. Religious seek to make their work a sign of the eschatological promise of God. If any work loses this end-time character and does not sign forth to others a longing for God's ultimate fulfillment of all creatures, it has lost its salt. Religious community, therefore, is not a haven of peace, but a place where members of the communion of saints strive to be ever more Church, ever more a community of pilgrims who await the coming of the Lord and work to prepare his way.[31]

In the end religious communities, like the Lord whom they follow, cannot be categorized since they have a unique mission. That mission is service of men and women in the world with the specific intention of opening them to the Spirit who is the bringer of the kingdom. Religious are not private individuals with an interior depth and an exterior way of life which facilitates and disciplines their co-existence for its own sake. Religious are social beings whose religious commitment is a public sign of God's promise. Their life is sacramental because it is a confluence of the material and the spiritual, the social and the religious, just as the being of Jesus was and remains sacramental.[32] Life in the third section of the creed is essentially sacramental life. A visible community of men and women exist in unity, in holiness, in universal openness and in apostolic service. They proclaim forgiveness and look to hope; they allow the Holy Spirit to work among men, so that he can create a human body of men and women who are joined in word and sacrament to Jesus Christ. They are living signs in each generation of the Church that the Spirit-filled Jesus will return and that he is indeed already among men and women who wait in hope for him.

The special form of life in the communion of saints and of life in the context of the third section of the creed make religious a healing and yet critical presence in society. As independently loyal, as self-possessed and sharing, as sexual and celibate persons who live in community and witness

to the social dimension of the gospel, religious are a model Church in miniature, a local congregation of believers who have a sacramental as well as a
social function.[3] Their very existence is a visible sign that Spirit-filled individuals in community can heal the brokenhearted and at the same time
criticize the social institutions which are indifferent to the unfree, the poor
and the lonely. In light of the thesis which forms the underpinnings of this
paper, namely that religious life is both sacramental and social, it can be
said that to deny either element would be to lessen both the identity of
religious life and its sociological relevance. The vows of religious make them
into a community which can heal as well as criticize. Religious stand up
in the center of the Church and, like Jesus at Nazareth's synagogue,
identify themselves with the words from Isaiah which he chose to define
his own mission:

> The Spirit of the Lord is upon me,
> because he has anointed me
> to preach good news to the poor.
> He has sent me to proclaim release
> to the captives
> and recovering of sight to the blind,
> to set at liberty those who are oppressed,
> to proclaim the acceptable year of
> the Lord (Lk 4:18-19).

This is the sacramental and social function of religious life. The vows
speak to the world in a way which reminds all men and women of the
healing work of Jesus of Nazareth and which causes them to gaze into the
future and to be critical of the present, since they wait for the promise that
"the kingdom of the world has become the kingdom of our Lord and of his
Christ" (Rv 11:15).

NOTES

[1] This search after a synthesis is evident in the *Documents of the XXXII General
Congregation of the Society of Jesus* (Washington: The Jesuit Conference, 1975), the
central theme of which is stated as "Our Mission Today: The Service of Faith and
the Promotion of Justice," pp. 17-43.

[2] Karl Barth and Hans Urs von Balthasar, *Einheit und Erneuerung der Kirche* (Frei-
burg: Paulusverlag, 1968), p. 12.

[3] Avery Dulles, *Models of the Church* (New York: Doubleday & Co., 1974), pp.
58-70, where Dulles discusses the Church as a sacrament, a model which balances
visible and invisible aspects of the Church most directly.

⁴Joseph Ratzinger, *Introduction to Christianity*, trans. by J. R. Foster (New York: The Seabury Press, 1969), pp. 257-259.

⁵Karl Rahner, "The Life of the Counsels," *Theology Digest* XIV (1966) 224-227.

⁶Karl Barth, *Dogmatics in Outline*, trans. by G. T. Thomson (New York: Harper & Row, 1959), p. 148.

⁷*Documents of the XXXII General Congregation of the Society of Jesus*, p. 13.

⁸Jürgen Moltmann, *The Crucified God: The Cross of Christ as the Foundation and Criticism of Christian Theology*, trans. by R. A. Wilson and J. Bowden (New York: Harper & Row, 1974), pp. 7-18.

⁹Karl Rahner, "A Basic Ignatian Concept: Some Reflections on Obedience," trans. by Joseph P. Vetz *Woodstock Letters* 86 (1957), pp. 302-305. As opposed to others, such as Ladislas Örsy whose work is cited below, Rahner chooses obedience and not chastity as the central vow, and sees poverty and chastity as two ways of living out the total commitment to grace which obedience signifies.

¹⁰See Martin Hengel, *Poverty and Riches in the Early Church* (Philadelphia: Fortress Press, 1974).

¹¹Karl Rahner, "A Basic Ignatian Concept: Some Reflections on Obedience," pp. 299 and 308.

¹²Ladislas M. Örsy, *Open to the Spirit: Religious Life after Vatican II* (Washington: Corpus Books, 1968), pp. 159-160.

¹³Gustavo Gutierrez, *A Theology of Liberation: History, Politics and Salvation*, trans. by Sr. Caridad Inda and John Eagleson (Maryknoll: Orbis Books, 1973), pp. 104-105.

¹⁴Avery Dulles, *The Survival of Dogma: Faith, Authority and Dogma in a Changing World* (New York: Doubleday & Co., 1971), pp. 52-57.

¹⁵Horacio de la Costa, "A More Authentic Poverty," *Studies in the Spirituality of Jesuits* VIII (1976), pp. 56-57.

¹⁶David B. Knight, "St. Ignatius' Ideal of Poverty," *Studies in the Spirituality of Jesuits* IV (1972), pp. 25-30.

¹⁷Philip Land, "Justice, Development, Liberation and the Exercises," *Studies in the International Apostolate of Jesuits* V (1976), pp. 19-21.

¹⁸Philip J. Rosato, "World Hunger and Eucharistic Theology," *America* 135 (1976), pp. 47-49.

¹⁹Jürgen Moltmann, *Man: Christian Anthropology in the Conflicts of the Present*, trans. by John Sturdy (Philadelphia: Fortress Press, 1974), pp. 116-117.

²⁰Donald Goergen, *The Sexual Celibate* (New York: Seabury Press, 1974), pp. 115-116.

²¹John C. Haughey, *Should Anyone Say Forever?: On Making, Keeping and Breaking Commitments* (New York: Doubleday & Co., 1975), pp. 101-105.

²²Ladislas M. Örsy, *op. cit.*, pp. 94-97, where Örsy develops his thesis that virginity is the source of all other aspects of religious consecration. See also: Vincent O'Flaherty, "Some Reflections on Jesuit Commitment," *Studies in the Spirituality of Jesuits* III (1971), pp. 42-46.

²³Donald Goergen, *op. cit.*, pp. 220-223. See also: Pierre Teilhard de Chardin, *The Divine Milieu* (New York: Harper & Row, 1960), pp. 81-86.

²⁴John O. Meany, "The Psychology of Celibacy: An In-depth View," *Catholic Mind* LXIX (1971), pp. 18-20.

²⁵Peter L. Berger, *A Rumor of Angels: Modern Society and the Rediscovery of the Supernatural* (New York: Doubleday & Co., 1969), pp. 53-75.

²⁶Pedro Arrupe, "The Hunger for Bread and Evangelization: Focus on the 'Body of Christ, the Church' in the Service of Faith and the Promotion of Justice," *Interna-*

tional Symposium on Hunger: The 41st International Eucharistic Congress (Philadelphia: St. Joseph's College Press, 1976), pp. 21-24.

[27]John Courtney Murray, *The Problem of God Yesterday and Today* (New Haven: Yale University Press, 1964), pp. 119-121.

[28]C. K. Barrett, *The Holy Spirit in the Gospel Tradition*, 5th ed. (London: SPCK Press, 1970), pp. 153-156.

[29]Wolfhart Pannenberg, *The Apostles' Creed in the Light of Today's Questions*, trans. by Margaret Kohl (Philadelphia: The Westminster Press, 1972), pp. 139-143.

[30]Pierre Teilhard de Chardin, *The Divine Milieu*, p. 112. See also: Avery Dulles, "The Church, the Churches and the Catholic Church," *Theological Studies* XXXIII (1972), pp. 222-224.

[31]Avery Dulles, *Models of the Church*, pp. 149-150.

[32]Edward Schillebeeckx, *Christ, the Sacrament of the Encounter with God* (New York: Sheed and Ward, 1963), pp. 13-20.

[33]Karl Rahner, "The Life of the Counsels," *Theology Digest* XIV (1966), pp. 226-227.

Ministry Rooted in the Vows

Mary T. Rattigan, C.S.J.

Volume 37, 1978, pp. 321-332.

Simply stated, ministry refers to the service rendered in the name of Jesus Christ. Such service is a faith-response to our being sent to continue the mission of Jesus in the world. At the moment, religious are experiencing new vistas of ministry being opened up to them. They also perceive their call to service as stemming directly from the acknowledgment and development of their gifts and talents. Current involvement in ministry, then, calls for an increased ability to discern individual gifts for service and an appreciation of emerging diversity in form and style. We are asked to keep in mind St. Paul's injunction: "There are all sorts of service to be done, but always to the same Lord, working in all sorts of different ways in different people. . . . The particular way in which the Spirit is given to each person is for a good purpose" (1 Co 12:5-7). Regardless of its form, ministry can be broadly defined as those efforts directed to bringing the love and power of God to fruition in the world. Such efforts to build up the kingdom of God ultimately spring from a consciousness of the meaning of Christian mission. Hence, an understanding of ministry, which is normally the way mission is expressed, must be sought in the theology of mission. In the first place, mission theology pinpoints the Church's need to become a perfect sign of Christ in the world. It reminds us, moreover, that the whole Church, everywhere and in all its members, is missionary. To be Christian and to be Church means to be "chosen" for service, to carry on the work of Christ in the world. It also places a heavy emphasis on the fact that although a

295

plurality of ministries exists, there is only one mission—the mission of the risen Jesus. This single mission, which has been entrusted to the members of his Church, is said to incorporate three elements. First, we share in this mission when we announce the new life received in Christ which makes the love and power of God available here and now. Second, acceptance of this mission demands that our lifestyle give credibility to this announcement. This requires a witness to the process of being personally transformed by the love and power of God. Third, we are invited to extend God's love and power by our actions so that the kingdom may be realized to a greater extent in history. From the theology of mission, then, it is possible to delineate the essential features of a life of service. And, to the extent a sense of mission becomes a personal reality for us, we can experience a reason for being "sent" and an urgency to respond to the kingdom-vision.

Both a growing consciousness of the meaning of mission and the development of multiple forms of ministry are demanding that a second look be given to the evangelical vows. These factors, among others, are forcing religious to face the question of how the vows commit them to ministry. The need to understand the vowed life in relation to ministry is especially felt by those actively engaged in combating social injustice. The call to work for justice, equality and peace is demanding an articulation of the vows which is consonant with the social mission of the Church. By the same token, religious are wondering whether new aspects of the vows might not be emerging as they seek to confront the issues of justice, peace and equality. In either case, an understanding of the vowed life in the context of mission and ministry is deemed extremely important at this point of time. In fact, a more adequate theology of religious life cannot be expected until an examination of the vows in relation to ministry is undertaken. Apostolic religious have a need to deepen their insights into the vows as a renewal of their baptismal commitment to service, to conceive of themselves as a community with a "commission" that shares the Church's mission responsibility, and to think of religious profession as the public acceptance of this mandate to mission. The reflections which follow are intended to increase our understanding of the role of the vows in ministry, whether that ministry occurs within the Christian community itself or in society at large.

Another Look at the Vows

Religious have traditionally expressed their response to the call of discipleship through the vows of poverty, chastity and obedience. Until Vatican II, a certain clarity of understanding and expectation accompanied the evangelical life. But all too often in the past, the expression of the vows was equated with certain kinds of behavior, such as using material goods, abstaining from genital sexuality, and listening to the superior. With the renewal of religious life, however, the interpretation of the vows began to shift. Developments in theology, psychology and the social sciences forced traditional notions of the vows to be placed under severe scrutiny. For more than a decade now, serious questioning and confusion have surfaced over the relevance of the vowed life to contemporary society. The ambiguity which surrounds the present living of the vowed life is multifaceted. Uncertainty has emerged as to whether the vows themselves constitute one's religious consecration. Objection has been voiced over the traditional vocabulary still employed for the vows. Doubt has also arisen regarding their very number, with the attendant suggestion that a single, more comprehensive term be used to designate the commitment to religious life. The complexity of the situation is brought to even sharper focus when divergent interpretations are included in the picture. Some perspective can be gained, however, when we recall that the internal thrust of the early years of renewal, with its intensely personalistic and communal concerns, permeated most attempts to rethink the vows. In retrospect we can appreciate the emphasis which had to be placed on calling forth individual religious to fuller personhood and responsibility. We also realize that community life demanded that interpersonal relationships be fostered and that new structures of authority and government be adopted. But religious have now reached the point of desiring that their vows be perceived as integrally related to mission, as giving expression to their call to minister in Jesus' name. While much study remains to be done on the relation of vows to the personal and communal aspects of our life, consideration must presently be given to the strongly sensed need to relate the vows more concretely to the apostolic or service dimension of religious life. The desire to seek ways of living the vows which will best express the call to mission can be recognized from the type of question being asked: What contribution can the vows make toward a more effective realization of the mission of Jesus in the world today? In what way do the vows enable religious to be effective ministers of the gospel, particularly in the area of social justice?

It may be asked, why the current trend to relate the vows to ministry? Why do religious feel challenged to examine the vows as a source from which true ministry can flow? It is significant, I believe, that the renewed interest in the vows occurs at a time when religious have already given considerable attention to the spiritual resources needed for ministry. They have opted, for the most part, for a more intense personal spirituality. In an effort to reaffirm the importance of a deep prayer life, they are actively pursuing the charismatic movement, directed retreats, continued spiritual direction, and so forth. In line with this interest in spirituality, attention now focuses on the vows as spiritual resources which can be brought to bear on a life of service. As the thirst for spirituality extends itself to the vows, it represents a search for both a depth-dimension to life and a greater sense of integration. This depth-dimension can be characterized as a rootedness or centeredness which will serve to ground our apostolic service. The vows hold out the promise of effecting a sense of rootedness since they encapsule basic orientations and values which, if explicated and claimed as one's own, can provide roots or centering. Besides seeking deeper roots for service, religious are taking a fresh look at the vows out of a need to experience a greater degree of integration. They are led to wonder in what sense the vows can be considered an integrative force. Faced with a frequent sense of disharmony and discrepancy in ministry, they are led to inquire about the ability of the vows to "make whole." In other words, can the vows act as a unifier between the vision proposed by ministry and the reality actually achieved? In a world where it is exceedingly difficult to experience any synthesis or integration, religious feel that the vowed life deserves to be reappraised for its integrating impact on their lives. Assumed in the quest for integration, however, is the underlying assumption that the vows cannot be viewed as external to service. Any authentic living of the vows will consist of ministering to the needs of others, especially those who are victims of injustice and oppression. We turn now to consider the spiritual resources offered by the vows when ministry is conceived as the presence of God's love and power in the world.

Ministry as Presence

One way to look at ministry is to regard it as presence. As the word is used here, presence is synonymous with the term *sacrament* taken in its broadest meaning. As an expression of mission, the object of ministry is to be a sign of God's transforming love and power. One who ministers is seen to be a symbol through which the God-life received in Jesus is embodied. The form which this kind of ministry takes is that of leading others to experience the divine element in their own lives and of bringing this to fuller expression. Ministry as sacramental, then, is concerned with fostering a response to the transforming love and power of God at work in the world. As a participation in the mission of Jesus, ministry partakes of the very mystery which marked the mission and ministry of Jesus himself. In this regard, St. John's gospel offers a clarification of the nature of this mission, and consequently, contributes towards an understanding of ministry as presence. The chief work of Jesus, as presented by the fourth evangelist, lies essentially in revealing the Father's love and power: "To have seen me is to have seen the Father" (Jn 14:9). The concept of ministry espoused here centers on Jesus being the presence of God in the world. Important for us, however, is the promise which accompanies this revelation for those who believe: ". . . to perform the same work as I do myself" (Jn 14:12). As the perfect image of the Father, Jesus gives his Spirit so that we may enjoy a similar relationship to God, and thus share his likeness of being a revelation of God in the world. Despite our limitations, we have been commissioned to be sacraments of the transforming love and power of God. This is the great mystery of ministry—a mystery which the vows help to disclose. Still further reinforcement for viewing ministry as presence is found in the fourth gospel with the recorded statement of Jesus: ". . . I consecrate myself for their sakes now, that they may be consecrated in truth" (Jn 17:19). Central to this Johannine emphasis is his notion of truth, which means to "make holy." Jesus himself is the truth, the holiness of God visibly manifested. His mission is to effect a greater possession of the truth which he is. Judged in this light, discipleship becomes a mandate to bear the message of the Father's love in our life. To be consecrated in truth, therefore, implies a process whereby the love and power of God can become enfleshed in us—a process which designates our apostolic mission: to make visible the presence of God in the world. From this perspective, ministry rests on the conviction that our life itself, which is a primary form of presence, is meant to be shared with those around us. It summons us to be vehicles of God's transforming love and power.

Above all else, then, a ministry of presence asks that we witness to life in its transcendent dimension. The religious consecration of perpetual chastity, in particular, conveys a presence which elicits belief in the mystery of God's transforming love and power. This becomes possible when being unmarried for the sake of the kingdom is understood for what it actually encompasses. As St. Paul indicates, an unmarried woman "can devote herself to the Lord's affairs." His reason for extolling virginity, however, stems from the fact that she can give her "undivided attention to the Lord" (1 Co 7:32-35). All too often this passage has been interpreted solely in terms of the availability which religious possess for apostolic activity. But suggested by this Pauline directive is a relation of intimacy—a relation characteristic of those who have allowed the love and power of God to come to fruition in their lives. Seen in this light, chastity commits religious to deepen their own relationship to the Lord, and to undertake the task of concretizing this love in their relations with others. The goal of vowed chastity is judged to be concomitant with the witness called for in ministry—a witness to the mystery of God's transforming love and power. To remain celibate for the sake of the kingdom is itself a sign, and one which inserts religious into the very heart of mystery. It signifies a mystery not only to those we serve but it also continues to be an enigma even for those who have embraced it. The vow of chastity provides a way of saying concretely with our life something of the mystery which must be accepted by all persons, namely, we are made to live in and for mystery, particularly its eschatological aspect—the final destiny which brings this mystery to fulfillment. Its witness might well be to offer others the opportunity to question their lives, what is the meaning of their lives, their goal. Quite simply, this becomes possible when religious cause others to wonder why. To be a catalyst for eliciting these questions requires that our life-style palpably express a personal consecration to the mystery of God's transforming love and power. Consequently, a ministry of presence is concerned with the values and attitudes which we embody in our relationships with others. Granted this, the challenge facing religious is whether people around us can even glimpse the mystery of God's transforming power from the way we live both as individuals and as communities. It must be asked, too, whether we facilitate the possibility of others arriving at a fuller sense of themselves as vessels of God's presence in the world. Since a ministry of presence centers on personal relationships, it places a high priority on the kind of person we are rather than on any works we may perform. To what extent, then, does the vowed life enable this focus of our personhood to be reflected in our service? One instance worth noting is the way the vows help religious to go beyond the "performance principle." In a culture which tends to judge persons according to the efficiency with which they execute tasks, it is extremely difficult to maintain the primacy of personhood. Vowed chastity can foster the possibility of our being person-oriented. By refusing to be defined by our work or achievements, we can offer a challenge to the pragmatic strain underlying our culture. When we identify ourselves in terms of our relationships, we should be in a better position to view others in terms of who they are rather than what they accomplish. To strike a happy balance between a life of presence and a task-oriented one is no easy achievement. In the interests of reality, the vows should at least prevent our service from being dominated by the standard of efficiency— despite the fact that our service must indeed be efficient and competent.

In connection with a work-ethic, a certain "market-orientation" can easily creep into the ministry of religious. Such marketable elements as success, relevance, prestige, and income should not form the criteria for apostolic service. Neither a choice of ministry nor a judgment regarding its effectiveness should be made on the basis of popularity, remuneration, low-risk factors, or other marketable values. In this regard, both the vows of poverty and obedience, as steps taken in faith, have a great deal to do with ministry. They offer a direction and a challenge to the choices we make and to the attitudes we espouse. The recent association of vowed poverty with work, the fact that religious are "subject to the common law of labor," serves to illustrate how a market-orientation might become operative for us. Since Vatican II, as we know, poverty has shifted from limiting the use of possessions to the consent of the superior to earning one's own living and aiding the poor with one's resources. Because of this expectation that they be self-supporting, religious might find themselves choosing an area of service based on remuneration. Also, in view of the growing elderly population in religious communities, they might feel pressured into accepting a form of ministry which would contribute to the financial support of the community. Whatever the reasons, religious must at least recognize the subtle temptation posed by the exhortation to earn one's own living. Vowed obedience, which is concerned with the choices we make, demands a prayerful discernment regarding our motives for service. It asks that our choices proceed from values clearly based in the gospel. When we seek the

Spirit's direction for engagement in ministry, obedience makes it incumbent upon us to see that apostolic choices are not subjected to market values.

The vowed life, then, is meant to root ministry in its transcendent and relational dimensions. And the concept of personal presence allows us to perceive the dynamic relationship which exists between ministry and the vows. While ministry refers primarily to the presence or sacramental embodiment of God's love and power in the world, it must also bear the marks of suffering love. To witness to God's transforming presence requires that we undergo the sufferings inherent to bringing the kingdom of God to a fuller realization.

Ministry as Suffering Love

Suffering love is the hallmark of Christian ministry. This kind of love demands some explanation due to the recent emphasis on personalism and fulfillment in religious life. Clarification is also needed because the word *suffering* is ordinarily thought in terms of pain of mind or body, or as bearing the consequences of some illness or wrongdoing. At times it even conjures up a kind of self-sacrifice typical of the past which is now seen as destructive to personal growth and holiness. As the term is used here, *suffering* refers to the capacity to be acted upon, to be changed or moved by another. Suffering love means that we allow persons and events to enter our life so as to shape the response we make. It implies a vulnerability which results from permitting our actions to be defined by what the other requires. When our ministry takes its shape from the needs around us, it opens the door to true empathy and compassion in serving others. Personal conflict, adjustment, and denial will necessarily flow from this kind of loving, thereby contradicting a common misunderstanding that love always results in personal satisfaction. Suffering love is none other than the reverse side of self-giving love. Both aspects of love constitute the true nature of personalism. Otherwise, we have a pseudo-personalism which calls for the giving of our personal being but does not allow us to be transformed by our relations with others. For ministry, suffering love means that interdependence and reciprocity will mark the experience of truly serving others. Those who minister must have the capacity both to receive and to give, the willingness to be shaped as well as to create.

Suffering love can best be understood in the context of the mission of Jesus. Although we tend to equate Jesus' sufferings solely with the events surrounding the crucifixion, the gospels reveal that his sufferings resulted from the demands which love made upon him. His identification with the poor and outcasts, his contention with evil in its many forms, and his assistance to the sick and infirm are but a few examples of how Jesus allowed persons and events to elicit the kind of response needed. In a very real sense, then, his response was shaped by his ministry in that he allowed himself to be moved by the other, to take in the truth of each situation. As a consequence, his suffering love became the sign of his vocation to establish the kingdom, of his love for the Father and for all persons. The suffering involved in taking in the needs of others and responding accordingly had indeed the power to communicate love and to effect a new bond or communion with those to whom he ministered. Ultimately, it can be said that Jesus' sufferings resulted from fidelity to the mission he had received. The vulnerability entailed in his being faithful exemplifies an active suffering rather than a patient submission to fate. In other words, Jesus suffered because of what he stood for, because of his message and deeds. For us, too, the witness entailed in ministry will be the personal vulnerability of suffering love. In this sense, the vows, particularly obedience, have implications for ministry. Of the three vows, obedience seems to exert little influence on our day-to-day service. Often it is relegated to community life or to situations which involve a change of ministry. It is possible, however, to view the vow of obedience from a much broader perspective, namely, as a participation in Jesus' vocation to suffering love. This notion finds support in *The Epistle to the Hebrews* where we find obedience and suffering linked together. Speaking of Jesus, the author notes: "Although he was Son, he learned to obey through suffering . . ." (5:8). As the word "learned" indicates, Jesus' obedience was characterized by personal growth, and this process of growth extended over his lifetime. Also connoted by growth in obedience through suffering is an active reception of all that his ministry entailed as well as an intensely personal struggle. As the temptations suggest, Jesus was no stranger to the human longing for control and power over his own destiny in that he wrestled with the possibility of adopting a messianic role which would effect a more "successful" ministry.

The obedience of religious, like that of Jesus, consists in being faithful to our mission of service. It rests on a vision of faith which sees persons and events as indicators of the kind of response we ought to make in a given situation. To labor with Christ today requires that we undergo a similar experience of suffering love, with its active reception of struggle and misunderstanding. Listening to the direction of the Spirit and enduring the tensions which are part and parcel of ministry are avenues which will open us up to growth in faithful obedience. Because of the long-suffering involved in learning obedience, sporadic attempts will be less than adequate. Only a constant adherence to one's mission of service will suffice as a witness to this dimension of suffering love. As we engage in ministry, moreover, we can expect to deal with the temptation to dull the kingdom-vision. Perhaps one of the surest signs of participating in the mission of Jesus is that we experience a sense of being "stretched" beyond ourselves. If we are truly ministering we can expect the frustration and tension which accompanies all service, namely, the tension between the vision and the actuality, between the yet-to-be-fulfilled aspect of the kingdom and its

present degree of actualization. Because of our basic yearning for completion and satisfaction, we find it difficult to live with brokenness, unfinished business, to be forever simply ''on the way.''

At times we are tempted to adopt a "messianic complex," thereby relating
to the world around us in god-like fashion. In so doing, we would seek to take
things into our own hands, to manage and control their outcome, and to set
up our own standards for judging the effectiveness of our actions. The vows
help to remind us that we have been called to work for the extension of God's
reign of love, and that it is God who gives the increase. Quite pointedly, suffering
love brings us face-to-face with the deepest mystery of ministry, that of being
servants of the kingdom.

Because the ministry of suffering love requires a critical evaluation of our
vulnerability and creative receptivity, the vow of poverty has an important role
to play. Specifically, vowed poverty asks that we be open with respect to the
form or expression which our ministry takes. It calls us out of any sense of
self-sufficiency which might accompany a competency achieved. A sense of self-
sufficiency in ministry can only prove to be distracting. Far too much energy
can be expended in efforts to protect positions of real or imagined importance.
This proclivity for being self-sufficient is most clearly evidenced in the resentment
of newcomers for the threat they pose to our replacement. When driven by a
fear of loss, whether in status or in replacement, we begin to operate at a low-risk
level. When grasped by a sense of possessiveness, we undertake only those
activities which are considered safe, those which ensure prestige or eliminate
competition. Vowed poverty, therefore, enjoins us to assess those sources of
security which we may have erected for ourselves. It asks that subtle forms of
self-worship such as success and prestige be unmasked for what they truly are.
Because possessiveness impedes the kind of vulnerability demanded by suffering
love, religious poverty asks that we assume a posture of tentativeness with respect
to the form which our ministry takes. Such tentativeness presupposes a willingness to let go of the security of the past in order to move into the future. In
some cases, the risk involved in remaining flexible will result in a call to a new
form of ministry or to a modified response in our present ministry. In any case,
a radical trust and dependence upon the loving power of God is being called
forth in us as we search for the particular expression our ministry should assume.

The vulnerability required by suffering love also finds nourishment in vowed
chastity. The ''mystical'' dimension of chastity, with its faith-decision to embrace
the non-rational or mysterious aspect of life, exacts an acceptance of the fact
that life can be neither totally controlled nor ultimately possessed. Of its very
nature, vowed chastity leads to risk, to the unpredictable, and to the unknown.
It beckons us to love with an openness which prevents intrusions and other forms
of inconveniences from being regarded as impingements upon our "projected
plans" for service. In its "social" dimension, vowed chastity is also an important
asset for ministry. To the extent we have personally embraced a non-possessive
stance towards life, we can expect to be non-threatening persons. Those in our

presence should not find it necessary to draw upon their defenses, to play games or to put on false facades. By a simple and vulnerable lifestyle, religious can become disarming persons, those who grant others the freedom to be who they truly are. Consequently an atmosphere can be created which maximizes the acceptance and contribution of personal gifts and talents, thus paving the road to ministry becoming a mutual venture between those who serve and those who are served.

Ministry Rooted in Freedom

Both views of ministry being addressed here—ministry as presence and ministry as suffering love—will necessarily engage us in the struggle to attain a greater degree of Christian freedom. And Jesus, as the paradigm of this freedom, offers us the model. When we meditate on the gospels we find that he ministered in a way that freed others, that empowered and enabled them. For example, Mary Magdalene and the Samaritan woman were enabled to accept the seeds of new life which had come within their reach. In such cases, Jesus used his power to empower others. If we are to engage in a life-giving ministry, we must be freed from those obstacles which hinder this kind of service from occurring. The vowed life, understood in the sense of personal liberation, can be said to foster the freedom needed for ministry. First of all, how does the vow of poverty free us to serve in a life-giving manner? As we know, evangelical poverty does not center on either economic status or material deprivation. For apostolic religious, the vitality of one's service, with its attendant signs of peace and joy, has always been intrinsically linked to evangelical poverty. Poverty implies a freedom from ourselves (detachment) and a single-heartedness (attachment) for the service of God's kingdom. Stated in other words, poverty aims at a self-emptying so that we can devote everything that we are and have to others. By a voluntary limitation of possessions and other forms of self-sufficiency, a self-emptying ensues which places us in a situation of being poor, namely, of being ultimately dependent upon God's love and power. Inner freedom, which is a goal of vowed poverty, comes from placing our trust in God rather than in our own resources. Its specific apostolic witness consists in having chosen to have less than we could have attained. In so doing, we can demonstrate our belief that the kingdom of God is not dependent upon success in the areas of prestige, possessions or power. Vowed poverty, it is hoped, should also free religious to give a fuller response to Jesus' injunction: "You have received without paying; you must give without charge" (Mt 10:8). As we come to a greater awareness of our God-given gifts, we should be enabled to give of ourselves, in particular, to share our talents, education, time and psychic energy.

The freedom for ministry which vowed chastity promotes is that of non-possessiveness. In vowing chastity, we promise to eradicate the strong natural desire to restrict our love and concern to those claiming a priority through family or friendship. At times, we are even called to love without reciprocity. In such cases, we are asked to love those persons not in a position to respond to the love we offer, the fearful, the lonely, and the voiceless minority in society. In a positive sense, then, vowed chastity facilitates the freedom needed to develop multirelationships, to move beyond our personal propensity for exclusive and reciprocal relationships. Because all relationships are fragile, but specifically those demanded by vowed chastity, a freedom is needed to sustain them and keep them from deteriorating into avenues of self-aggrandizement. If our ministry is not to turn into a forum where unfulfilled personal needs are ventilated, we must be in touch with our own drives and needs. In fact, only when such personal needs as the desire to be the center of attention or the need to exercise control over the lives of others have been acknowledged, can we bracket them in order to address the needs of others.

The basis for freedom in ministry also lies in vowed obedience. Often ministry is not experienced as life-giving because of our insensitivity to the gifts which others possess. All too easily we become oblivious to the potential of others and succumb to our own myopic view. Religious obedience, on the other hand, implies a freedom to experience the world around us so that persons and events can mediate the kind of response called for in ministry. In this way, our ministry will be able to align itself more closely in both form and content to the spiritual, social and political needs of the people we serve. Vowed obedience, a pledge to carry out the mission of Jesus in a public manner, requires that our decisions be augmented by a faith-vision. As the gospels indicate, Jesus never did his "own thing," but sought to do his Father's will. In a special way, obedience can prevent us from acting out of impulse, mood or selfishness if we bring our choices to the authority which resides in the community for ratification. In so doing, obedience will direct the choices we make and free us to undertake with hope and courage the service which faith identifies with the will of God.

Reciprocal Relation of Ministry and Vows

Ministry and religious vows can be said to exert a reciprocal influence on each other. Engagement in ministry offers a challenge to the vowed life, and likewise, the vows provide for a deeper immersion into ministry. One way this reciprocal relation of vow and ministry is being experienced today is through the call to stewardship. As a matter of justice, Christians are being asked to exercise responsible stewardship regarding the resources of the world. The concept of stewardship, which is based on the idea that the world's resources do not belong absolutely to any individual, group, nation, or generation holds that resources should be viewed as gifts received and entrusted to our use and care. As such, it calls for a sharing which stems from a consciousness of the common good and a concern that the poor can participate in these available resources. Although the notion of stewardship is directed mainly to the resources of food and energy, it can be extended to include a much broader sphere. Stewardship and its consequent sharing can be applied to all the gifts of life which have been entrusted to us, whether they be talents, time, or physic energy. Certainly, a lifestyle which incorporates the right use of material resources as well as a voluntary limitation of material goods is a need in today's world. The concept of stewardship, then, can find a valuable source of support in vowed poverty. The question is: will religious place the "sharing and sparing" aspects of their life in relation to the wider social issue of justice? Put in other words, how can our sharing and sparing be increased to bring about a more significant social witness?

Just as the social demands of ministry can contribute to a greater understanding of the vowed life, so too, a lived experience of the vows can enhance our vision of ministry. Involvement in ministry, as we have noted, immerses us in the paradox of discipleship. And like any paradox, the tension involved is difficult to maintain. Although not a condition for discipleship, nevertheless, the vows are gifts given to realize this end. In fact, the values symbolized in the commitment of the vows are those which are basic to ministry itself. They designate a life committed to the kingdom, and hence, call for a transformation from our old self, with its attitudes, ways of thinking and acting. When the vows are perceived in terms of the transformation required by discipleship, they can then be translated into a lifestyle consonant with the call of ministry. A truly powerful means of witnessing to God's transforming power in the world is offered to those called to love as celibates for the sake of the kingdom, to live in a simple and sharing fashion, and to be obedient to finding ways of serving others.

Religious Life as Acted Prophecy

James Fitz, S.M.

Volume 41, 1982, pp. 923-927.

Religious life is a mystery, a call to a particular form of Christian discipleship. The call is part of that great mystery of God's love for a person and that person's faithful response to God's love. For this reason, words cannot adequately capture the total reality of the call. Yet we seek understanding and intelligibility for our faith. For this reason, Christians have always struggled, as we do today, to articulate that faith. Religious, too, strive to articulate the values and reasons for living their religious life.

During the past three years as a director of novices, I have had the privilege of sharing my understanding of religious life with the new members of our religious order. In this presentation, to the novices the image of religious life as acted prophecy has been the most helpful theological model. In this article, I would like to explore briefly the role of the prophet in the Old Testament, Jesus as prophet, and then explain how religious life fulfills a similar role in the Church.

Acted Prophecy

In his book, *The Prophetic Imagination,* Walter Brueggeman describes the prophetic ministry in the Judeo-Christian tradition in the following way:

> The task of prophetic ministry is to nurture, nourish, and evoke a consciousness and perception alternative to the consciousness and perception of the dominant culture around us.[1]

This alternative consciousness and perception criticizes the existing social order, and it energizes the community by presenting a vision of an alternative way of living. Jeremiah is a prophet whose prime ministry was to criticize the existing social order (although he does proclaim a new vision, e.g. Jr 31:31-34). Deutero-Isaiah's prophetic message was primarily to energize a community broken by exile.

307

Jesus has been traditionally referred to as a prophet and, as Brueggeman points out, Jesus fulfills both prophetic functions.[2] He challenges the dominant consciousness by his readiness to forgive sin, to heal on the Sabbath, and to eat with outcasts. He proclaims an alternative consciousness which is most clearly described in the Beatitudes (Mt 5:1-13; Lk 6:20-23).

In studying the prophetic tradition, it is interesting to note that the prophets proclaimed their message not only by word but also by the way they lived. There are a number of examples of acted prophecy in the Old Testament. Jeremiah breaks the earthenware jar (19:1 - 20:6); wears a yoke (27:1-22); purchases a field (32:1-44); does not take a wife or have a son or daughter (16:1-4); and does not enter into feasting (16:8-9). Ezekiel cuts his beard and hair (5:1-15); imitates the flight of an exile (12:1-20); and does not mourn properly the death of his wife (24:15-24). Finally we have a striking model of acted prophecy in Hosea who takes a harlot for a wife and is faithful to her despite her unfaithfulness. These prophets proclaimed a message, a word of the Lord by the way they lived. The actions of Jesus, mentioned above, can also be seen as acted prophecy.

It is important to note that some of the acted prophecies were not clear actions; they were explained by the words of the prophet. The actions were intended to raise questions in the observers. An explanation by the prophet could then be given concerning the meaning of these actions, although the explanations were not always satisfactory or acceptable to the audience. Being rejected or misunderstood is often part of the prophetic mission.

This image of acted prophecy, I believe, explains well the call to religious life. We, as religious, are called to live in such a way that others are forced to ask questions about the meaning of our actions. When asked, we have the opportunity to proclaim the values of God's kingdom. Hopefully our actions and words will both criticize the existing sinful and unjust social consciousness and energize the Church and world by presenting an alternative way which brings hope.

The implications of religious life as acted prophecy are manifold. I would like to share just a few of the ways that the traditional elements of religious life can be understood as acted prophecy that both criticize and energize. I will focus on the traditional vows: chastity, poverty and obedience, as well as on prayer and community. Hopefully these beginning explorations of religious life as acted prophecy will spur further reflections on this theological image.[3] In this article I will focus on religious life as acted prophecy in our American culture since I am most familiar with that culture. But I believe this way of viewing religious life is transcultural.

Chastity

In our culture, sex is presented as the ultimate in life in much of our film and literature. Sex has become an end in itself rather than a means to intimacy and the generation of new life. Or, on another level, sex is seen as a means to overcome loneliness. Like drugs, alcohol, or other experiences, sex is seen as a means to escape loneliness and obtain instant intimacy. Celibate chastity challenges the view that sex is all, and rejects the concomitant depersonalization that comes with that view. It also challenges the use of sex to escape loneliness.

At the same time, celibate chastity energizes by presenting an alternative vision. It proclaims that the end of life is intimacy with God and with others. Celibate chastity, joyfully lived, points to what must ultimately be the end of any lifestyle.

As the opening words of the Lord's prayer indicate, Christian love is to be characterized by intimacy and universality. God is our *Father* (Abba), that is, we are called to a love which is best symbolized by the intimate love of a family. God is *our* Father, that is, we are called to relate to all our brothers and sisters. Just as married couples energize the Church by their witness to the intimate aspect of Christian love, so religious energize the Church by their witness to the universality of Christian love.

The celibate religious can energize also by showing an alternative way of dealing with loneliness. Rather than escaping loneliness, one embraces it so that it can become a means of growth and development. Loneliness can nurture solitude, friendship, and our relationship with God.[4] It points to the ultimate fulfillment of our longings. As Augustine prayed to our Father: "Our hearts are restless until they rest in you."[5]

Poverty

In our culture, the underlying statement of many television commercials is that happiness depends on what you own and, of course, on owning the particular product being advertised. There is a tendency in our culture to judge one's self-worth on what one owns or achieves or earns. The vow of poverty for most religious entails a sharing of common goods (rather than having individual ownership) and a simplicity of lifestyle (as difficult as it is to come to an adequate definition of this phrase). The vow of poverty, therefore, challenges the over-riding cultural tendency to build self-worth on material goods.

The vow of poverty energizes by presenting an alternative way. A life of sharing material goods, of caring for others, and of giving rather than amassing goods, joyfully lived by religious, presents a hope-filled alternative to the consumer oriented society which is depleting the earth's resources and which still leaves many going to bed hungry each night. The spirit of poverty goes beyond the sharing of material goods. It includes the sharing of time, of affirmation and of love. In our culture the greatest "poverty" may be the lack of psychological and spiritual health. A religious community imitating the love of Christ can be a source of great healing to those who need affirmation, love, time—that is, who need the "goods" of the healthy psychic and spiritual life.

Obedience

Power is a good thing; it can be a positive and healing force in our lives. Jesus was a powerful person. "Someone touched me; I know that power has gone forth from me" (Lk 8:46). But power can also be negative and destructive. The desire to control one's life and the lives of others can become a demonic force, can become detrimental both to oneself and to others. If the desire to control becomes an ultimate value in one's life, the effects can be disastrous. We have witnessed this demonic use of power in people such as Adolf Hitler and Idi Amin. The vow of obedience challenges the use of power. Power is to be seen as a means, not an end.

Those living the vow of obedience can energize others by witnessing to an alternative form of power, the power of service. Individual religious, and religious communities truly living obedience, truly listening to the word of the Lord, can be effective models of this alternative use of power. The vow of obedience implies listening, being attentive to the will of God. The truly obedient religious (and religious community) will imitate Christ, who came to serve and not to be served. The truly obedient religious (and community) will be able to echo the prayer of Jesus, "Thy will be done," and the prayer of Mary, "Behold the handmaid of the Lord, be it done to me according to your word."

Prayer

In our culture, activity and productivity are important values. People often are led to believe they are worth only what they do, what they produce. Many going through the retirement process have to struggle with the feeling of uselessness precisely because they are no longer doing and producing. A life of prayer is a direct challenge to this tendency of our society. Prayer emphasizes the value of being, not doing. It balances the value of producing with the value of receiving. One's self-worth is not based on what one produces but on the fact that one is a creature of God, loved by God.

In our culture, one of the criticisms of our welfare system is based on the underlying assumption that we should get only what we have worked for. Prayer, especially the prayer of thanksgiving, challenges this presupposition. Much of what we have has been graciously given to us, without a bit of work on our part. Prayer challenges us to realize that everything we have is ultimately gift from God.

Besides challenging our cultural presuppositions, a praying community presents an alternative. The truly prayerful, contemplative community becomes a thankful community. Such a community, then, becomes willing and able to share its gifts with others. "The gift you have received, give as gift" (Mt 10:8). The prayerful community can witness to our society the values of leisure, contemplation and play.

Prayer is also important in developing a contemplative attitude toward life. It helps us keep a proper perspective on the meaning of life. It helps us focus on the most important values, the values of the kingdom. Sincere and regular prayer returns us to the center, love, which is the greatest gift (I Co 13:13) and the greatest commandment (Mt 22:34-40). Possibly the greatest acted prophecy of a contemplative religious community is to call all of us back to this center.

Community

Finally, our contemporary culture is characterized by segregation and alienation. Racism, sexism, and other forms of alienation are present. Competition often furthers this feeling of alienation. The religious community, by living the Gospel, can challenge the structures that depersonalize and alienate; it can proclaim an alternative way. "This is how all will know you for my disciples, your love for one another" (Jn 13:35). A religious community of very different personalities living a life of true love (that is, the members truly care about their own and others' spiritual growth[6]) can give hope that the power of faith and the gospel can unite persons amidst great diversity. Religious community can be a great sign of hope to a world threatened daily by violence and hatred.

Conclusion

Religious life, as a charism in the Church, has endured many changes during the centuries of its existence. Like the prophets of the Old Testament, like Jesus himself, religious have often been on the cutting edge of change, criticizing when others were satisfied with the status quo, and bringing hope when others were despairing. This article has explored a few of the ways religious can criticize and energize by their vows, their prayer, and community life.

If religious take seriously their prophetic role, they will always have a place in the Church, for the Church will always need the prophetic charism. When Ezekiel was called to be a prophet he was called to be a sentry or watchman for the house of Israel. He was to warn the people in God's name:

> If I say to the wicked man, you shall surely die; and you do not warn him or speak out to dissuade him from his wicked conduct so that he may live: that wicked man shall die for his sin, but I will hold you responsible for his death. If on the other hand, you have warned the wicked man, yet he has not turned away from his evil nor from his wicked conduct, then he shall die for his sin, but you shall save your life. If a virtuous man turns away from virtue and does wrong when I place a stumbling block before him, he shall die. He shall die for his sin, and his virtuous deeds shall not be remembered; but I will hold you responsible for his death if you did not warn him. When, on the other hand, you have warned a virtuous man not to sin, and he has in fact not sinned, he shall surely live because of the warning, and you shall save your own life (Ezk 3:18-21).

NOTES

[1] Walter Brueggemann, *The Prophetic Tradition* (Philadelphia: Fortress Press, 1978), p. 13.

[2] *Ibid.*, chapters 5 and 6.

[3] For another approach to the use of the biblical image of prophet in regard to religious life see Francis J. Moloney, *Disciples and Prophets* (New York: Crossroad Publishing Company, 1981).

[4] Anna Polcino, M.D., *Loneliness: The Genesis of Solitude, Friendship, and Contemplation* (Whitinsville, Massachusetts: Affirmation Books, 1979).

[5] Saint Augustine, *The Confessions*, Book I,I.

[6] M. Scott Peck, *The Road Less Traveled* (New York: Simon and Schuster, 1978), p. 81.

Marginality and Religious Life: Belonging to a Group Called to Risk

Patrick Sean Moffett, C.F.C.

Volume 43, 1984, pp. 842-848

When the lawyer pressed Jesus for an answer to the question "Who is my neighbor?" he responded with a story and another question: "Who in your opinion was neighbor to the man who fell among robbers?" The story contained the answer to both questions. Isn't this so characteristic of a teacher? Knowing there is little impression without expression, Jesus provides a concrete example and challenges the lawyer to discover the answer and make it his own, to learn what it means to be neighbor to another human being.

Apostolic Spirituality

What does it mean to be a brother or sister in a Church that has called us once again to renewal?

I suggest that we have been asked to reconsider the paradoxes of Christianity: of being in the world but not of the world; of being ourselves and being Christ; of being bonded to each other and available to those who need us; of being at the center and at the outposts of the Church.

The question has many forms, and each form can be approached from many perspectives. I offer a psychologist's perspective on an aspect of the issue that most engages my attention: what it means "to belong to" and "to identify with" not only Christ but also our fellow humans, our Church and our specific congregations in a time of change.

Vatican II called religious to appropriate renewal involving two simultaneous processes: "a continuous return to the sources of all Christian life and to the original inspiration behind a given community and an adjustment of the

312

community to the changed conditions of the times." (*Perfectae Caritatis*, 2).

The discernment to accompany these processes involved what the Sacred Congregation for Religious and for Secular Institutes has called the four great loyalties:

-fidelity to humanity and to our times
-fidelity to Christ and the Gospel
-fidelity to the Church and its mission in the world
-fidelity to religious life and to the charism of one's own institute
(*Religious and Human Promotion*, 13, March 1980).

Ego-extension

These loyalties describe our belongingness and indicate some aspects of our identity that we share with all of our fellow humans, others that we share with all Christians, still others that we share with all Roman Catholics, and finally some that we share with the brothers and sisters of religious congregations. As the size of the reference group becomes smaller the bonds become more numerous and more cohesive.

For one who identifies himself or herself as a religious, these loyalties are aspects of one's "extended sense of self." Gordon Allport, the psychologist credited for reintroducing the study of the person to the field of American psychology has provided a phenomenology of the self. He describes *ego-extension* as a significant aspect of the identity of the mature adult:

As we grow older we identify with groups, neighborhoods, and nations as well as possessions, clothes, homes. They become matters of importance to us in a sense that other people's families, nations, or possessions are not. Later in life the process of extension may go to great lengths to the development of loyalties and of interests focused on abstractions and on moral and religious values. Indeed, a mark of maturity seems to be the range and extent of one's feeling of self-involvement in abstract ideals. (Allport, 1955).

In *The Life Cycle Completed*, Erik Erikson provided a description of identification that goes far beyond what has too often been treated as the task of adolescence. In 1982 at the age of 80, Erikson reaffirmed his position that identification is a lifelong developmental movement from "I" to "we."

. . . we are again reminded of the lifelong power of the first mutual recognition of the newborn and the *primal* (maternal) *other* and its eventual transfer to the *ultimate other* who will "lift up His countenance upon you and give you peace." From here we could once more follow the stages of development and study the way in which in given languages the fatherhoods and motherhoods, the sisterhoods and brotherhoods of the "we" come to share a joined identity experienced as most real. But here also it is necessary to amend the very concept of a reality which, as I complained at the beginning, is all too often seen as an "outer world" to be adjusted to (Erikson, 1982).

Erikson's study is particularly relevant to religious sisterhood and brotherhood.

As to the *we*, Freud went so far to assert that "there is no doubt that the tie which united each individual with Christ is also the cause of the tie which unites them with one another. (1921), but . . . he did so in a discourse on what he called *artificial* groups such as churches or armies. The fact is, however, that all identifications amounting to brotherhoods and sisterhoods depend on a joint identification with charismatic figures, from parents to founders to gods (Erikson, 1982).

The concept of identifying with Christ is, for the psychologist, a depth phenomenon involving the most central structures of the self. These inner-personal regions of our life space are affected by outside definitions to the extent that each of us internalizes the definitions. I strive to put on Christ as I understand him, and to be loyal to my fellow humans, to my church, to my congregation as I understand them. What happens though, when the definitions change, when the media afford me a new look at the global village, when the Church tells me that I have a role to play in the building of the kingdom that is very different from the one I *thought* I had, when my religious congregation readjusts in ways that alter how I work, how I pray, and how I live?

Marginal Status/Marginal Persons

In recent Vatican statements religious congregations of women and of men have been assigned the role of being a vanguard in the process of pre-evangelization and evangelization. As such, we have been encouraged to live at the boundaries of the established Church, to attend to the needs of the poor and of the marginal, to manifest clearly in our work and in our lifestyle "an option for the poor." In effect, religious are being encouraged to internalize these options and identify ourselves with those to whom we minister. Living at the boundaries of society and of the Church, we may experience in ourselves in a way that is both challenging and threatening the anxiety characteristic of the marginal person.

The term "marginal person" is one that the German-American theorist and leader in the field of social psychology, Kurt Lewin, borrowed from sociological descriptions of immigrants to present a psychological theory of adolescence.

> [The marginal person is] one who stands on the boundary of two groups. He does not belong to either of them, or at least he is not certain about his belongingness. . . the characteristic symptoms of behavior of the marginal person are emotional instability and sensitivity. They tend to unbalanced behavior, to either boisterousness or shyness, exhibiting too much tension, and a frequent shift between extremes of contradictory behavior (Lewin, 1951).

In his application of this image Lewin describes phenomena quite familiar to those of us who have worked with adolescents:

> To some extent behavior symptomatic for the marginal man can be found in the adolescent. He too is oversensitive, easily shifted from one extreme to the other, and particularly sensitive to the shortcomings of his younger fellows. Indeed, his position is sociologically the same as that of the marginal man; he does not wish to belong any longer to a group which is, after all, less privileged than the group of adults: but at the same time he knows that he is not fully accepted by the adults. The similarities between

the position of the members of the underprivileged minority and the adolescent, and between their behavior seem to me so great that one might characterize the behavior of the marginal members of the minority as that of permanent adolescence (Lewin, 1953).

The concept of a "permanent adolescence" might be applied in a most extreme form to a psychopathology that has become quite popular in our day, replacing the hysterias of previous generations as the main focus of many members of the psychotherapeutic community. The *Diagnostic and Statistical Manual of Mental Disorders III* lists the following diagnostic criteria for the *borderline personality disorder:*

(1) impulsivity or unpredictability; (2) a pattern of unstable and intense interpersonal relationships; (3) inappropriate, intense anger or lack of control of anger; (4) identity disturbance manifested by uncertainty about several issues relating to identity, such as self-image, gender identity, long-term goals or career choice, friendship, values and loyalties; (5) affective instability: marked shifts from normal mood to depression, irritability, or anxiety; (6) intolerance of being alone; (7) physically self-damaging acts; (8) chronic feelings of emptiness or boredom (DSM III, 301.83).

To qualify for membership in this group, at least five of the eight criteria must be aspects of one's current and long-term functioning. In addition one must usually be over the age of eighteen. While many adolescents will demonstrate many aspects of the disorder, they are rarely consistent enough to meet the criteria.

Not all persons who are "marginal" with respect to their social status need be "marginal persons" in the psychological sense. The marginal person experiences himself or herself as ungrounded, as not really belonging. Those with marginal status—poor people, minorities, the handicapped, the sick, the illiterate, those unable to work, those in prison, those who are removed from the mainstream of the dominant social group, etc.—may experience themselves as well-grounded, as solidly belonging to reference groups that have very positive meaning in their own lives. They therefore do not qualify as "marginal persons."

Identification with Christ

The Church is encouraging religious to maintain marginal status among those with marginal status in our society and in our Church. We are asked to take a special portion of a meal that is offered to all the Church.

There are many different situations in which the human face can be seen today deeply marked by tears, sorrow, frustration and despair. The phenomenon on marital breakdown is widespread. The young people of many cities feel rejected because there is no work for them. Racial minorities struggle for recognition and respect. Industry is split by resentments and bitter conflict. Whole peoples and communities live with daily violence, terrorism and ruthless suppression.

In recognizing the presence of the suffering Christ in these situations, the Church is called upon first of all to be with these people, to share with them their pain and then to work for a resolution of conflicts, a reconciliation of peoples (Archbishop Derek Worlock of Liverpool to the World Synod of Bishops: *Origins*, Vol. 13: No. 21).

Christ assumed marginal status: "Foxes have holes and birds have nests, but the Son of Man has no place to lie down and rest" (Lk 9:58). Some of his relatives were marginal: "When you went out to John in the desert, what did you expect to see? . . . A man dressed up in fancy clothes?" (Lk 7:24). He urged his followers to assume marginal status: "I am sending you like lambs among wolves. Don't take a purse, or a beggar's bag, or shoes . . ." (Lk 10:3). He was also brutally realistic about the consequences of such identification: "No slave is greater than his master. If they persecuted me they will persecute you too . . ." (Jn 15:20).

A Jewish psychotherapist friend of mine once suggested that any Christian who would care to know the consequences of identifying with Christ ought to read the Kazantzakis novel, *The Greek Passion*. The hero-victim of the story has been commissioned by his village to portray the role of Christ in a passion play. What happens to him in the process makes excellent Lenten reading!

While Christ himself had, and offered to his followers marginal *status*, he was not a marginal *person*. He knew who he was, he spoke with authority, he chose to accept his destiny. He knew he was beloved of the Father and experienced acceptance in his special social group: I know mine; mine know me. And he knew what he was calling his followers to: "I have given you an example" (Jn 13:15). "Love one another as I have loved you" (Jn 15:12).

In identifying with Christ we also take on marginal *status*. We avoid becoming marginal *persons* by working at that level of ego-extension that moves us from "I" to "we." In working at being brother or sister to Christ and to others, in the building of community both within the congregation and at our apostolic sites, in striving with others in the Church to establish the "kingdom," we generate the belongingness that counteracts the alienation of marginality.

Propriate Striving

Belonging and identification call forth another aspect of the self that Gordon Allport labels "propriate striving." I do that which is appropriate for me, that which fits the emerging image of who I am and who I am becoming. As I identify with groups and causes, I initiate behaviors that are consistent with the goals of the group, which advance the cause. Propriate striving thus has an integrative function with respect to the unification of the personality. As one who puts on Christ, I seek to act as he directs—: "If you love me, keep my commandments." As a member of the Church, I assume some responsibility for her mission. As a member of a religious congregation, I seek to be brother or sister in the spirit and charism of our group and of our founder.

Psychologists, who themselves must bear some responsibility for the distortions of self-actualization evident in the narcissism of the so-called "me-generation," suggest that forms of commitment, self-sacrifice and lives-lived-for-others are appropriate expressions of self-actualization in the mature adult. Identification with Christ and with his people is a process that can be psychically healthy as well as salvific. Perhaps some day we will come to discover that those of marginal status—the poor, the meek, those who suffer persecution for justice, the peacemakers—truly are blessed on this earth. I suspect that this discovery will be related to an appreciation of a lifestyle which frees individuals to live in the graced moment of *now.* I anticipate that we will grow in an appreciation of the simple yet profound interaction-rituals by which people give meaning to their daily lives. Through actions of attending to our daily needs and those of others, we "make belief" (in ourselves, our groups, our causes, and our God) a reality for ourselves and for now.

Certainly the Eucharist is a most salient expression of belongingness, identification, and belief. It is both a symbol and a form of "propriate striving" by which individuals establish a connectedness which allows them to sustain marginal status without becoming marginal persons.

Stress

Studies of stress suggest that one does not survive on the edge for long. Even those who are very creative in accommodating themselves to the tension of marginality have occasional forays of seemingly counterproductive aggression, regression, and withdrawal. The more adjusted these individuals usually are, the more salient their deviant moments may appear to themselves and to others.

Knowing the pressures of life at the boundary, we may become more tolerant of those who withdraw or regress for a time. The tolerance will begin, as it usually does in a "wounded healer," with the realization of my own need for moments away from the pressures of the moment. Could this be a time of incubation—that personal space which ultimately will give rise to new insight and energy and enlightenment and grace—or is the individual simply scared, tired, frustrated, or lazy? There is a tension in not knowing for sure, a tension that may enhance the frustration of marginality, yet one that cannot be eliminated. It is for the religious the one persistent "maybe." It is uncertain ground of hope.

It is quite possible that religious who choose "marginal *status*" will at times experience themselves as marginal *persons,* and as such be subject to the pressures exigent upon the marginal person. Reflection on the behavior of adolescents in our care will provide hints on how behaviors in our own communities may be seen as adaptive or maladaptative aggression, regression, withdrawal, and thus pave the way to accommodation-with-respect to our own feelings of marginality.

I believe that for good and for ill these responses are already evident among us, and perhaps have been throughout the history of religious life. Even eras of great stability and security in religious life might be seen as the responses to the experience of marginality. Are not some of the ghettos of our cities the safest places for those with marginal status?

The Call to Risk

Today we hear a Church which calls us to risk, to move to the boundaries of the Church and of society. It is here at these boundaries that there exist the greatest opportunities for a creative response to the poor of our day. Here also is the greatest danger.

> Religious often find themselves in a position to experience at close range the events that affect the people whom they serve. The prophetic nature of religious life requires that religious embody the Church in her desire to give herself completely to the radical demands of the beatitudes. They are often to be found at the outposts of the mission, and they take the greatest of risks for their health and for their very lives (Religious and Human Promotion, 4, a.).

When the boundaries are perceived as frontiers our vision is brightened with renewed faith and trust. We are all marginal with respect to the worlds of the unknown. We all live somehow at the frontier of tomorrow. Some, however, position themselves to attend to that which has been. Their goal is restoration of a "sound moral order." Others face the uncertain future, a receptive field for their fantasies or visions, dreams or plans, desires or hopes. Their goal is a new world order.

While we may find ourselves looking in either direction at any given time our real task and our joy is to be present to the moment at hand, to open our hearts fully to an incarnate Christ present and appealing to us in all who draw near us or see us, or hear us—in all who through their poverty, love, and loyalty teach us what it means to be neighbor and, for us in a special way, what it means to be sister and to be brother in, with, and to Christ.

REFERENCES

Allport, Gordon, *Becoming*. London: Yale University Press, 1955.
American Psychological Association. *Diagnostic and Statistical Manual of Mental Disorders III*, 1980.
Erikson, Erik, *The Life Cycle Completed*. London: W. W. Norton & Co., 1982.
Hall, G. Stanley, *Jesus the Christ in the Light of Psychology*. New York: D. Appleton Co., 1917.
Kazantzakis, Nikos, *The Greek Passion*. New York: Simon and Schuster, 1953.
Lewin, Kurt, *Field Theory in Social Science*. London: Harper, 1964.

Postscript

Religious in Service of the Church
On Dreaming Dreams, or The Making of a Revolution
Theological Reflections on Apostolic Religious Life

Religious in Service of the Church

David L. Fleming, S.J.

Volume 41, 1982, pp. 699-703.

Ever since Pope John Paul II appointed his own personal delegate to take over the ordinary government of the Society of Jesus in October 1981, there has been speculation about the wider meaning of the papal action in regard to religious life. Some questioned whether the Jesuits were about to be suppressed by the Papacy for the second time in their history. Some wondered whether the Jesuit intervention was meant to be a signal to other religious groups of a Vatican crackdown and an attempt at control. Still others asked whether the issue concerned the religious vow of obedience—not the special Jesuit vow to the Pope about mission, but rather the vow of obedience as interpreted in the 1917 Code of Canon Law and also repeated with special emphasis in the newly proposed Code. This interpretation puts all religious, by their particular vow, in a special relationship to the Pope. Was the Pope making a test case of the Jesuits to put other religious groups on alert?

As a Jesuit and one who participated in the historic meeting of Jesuit provincials in Rome from February 23 to March 3, 1982, I suggest that there are some implications to be drawn from the Pope's address to the Jesuit participants which might be helpful for the wider family of religious men and women. I would emphasize that the Pope spoke directly to the Jesuits, and so there are specifics about his relationship to the Society of Jesus with which other religious need not concern themselves. But I believe that there are certain points in the papal address which hold an importance for the direction of religious life in general, and even more particularly for active apostolic congregations.

The Papal Address

Let me review the overall content of the Pope's talk given on February 27, 1982 in a special papal audience for the Jesuit leaders. The Pope's address lasted one hour, and its length would indicate that it was not just an incidental greeting and pious exhortation.

After briefly touching upon his own extraordinary intervention in the governmental structure of the Society (which he insisted was an act of his concern and love for the well-being of the Order), Pope John Paul reviews in the first major section of his address the purpose and contribution of the newly founded Jesuit Order in its works after the Council of Trent. He continues on with a certain detailing of the current apostolic works of the Society. Then he emphasizes within this apostolic context the need for a thorough and arduous preparation and continuing formation of the members. He closes the address by underscoring his desire that the Society of Jesus play a significant role in the Church of Vatican II after the manner that it did in the Church of Trent. Presuming the continuing efforts of the Society to respond to his desires, the Pope assures the delegates that there would be a general congregation called within a year to elect a new superior general in place of the ailing Father Pedro Arrupe. In brief, these are the main aspects of the Pope's address.

Specific Apostolic Contributions

The Pope clearly delineates four major contributions of the Society of Jesus within the Church efforts at renewal following upon the decrees of the Council of Trent. He calls attention first to the efforts at renewing the Christian people. A key element within these general efforts at renewal is given by means of the directions and various adaptations which Jesuits drew from the *Spiritual Exercises of St. Ignatius Loyola.*

Another area of Jesuit contribution is in education: the setting up of an international education system through its many colleges established throughout the Europe of the sixteenth and seventeenth centuries. Within this educational area, the Pope pays special tribute to the humanistic and scientific studies which the early Jesuits advanced.

Thirdly the Pope highlights the Jesuit effort in the seminary training and formation of clergy and in the renewal of other religious congregations. The fourth area he names is the Jesuit missionary endeavors which coincided with the discovery of the New World and the trade route expansion to India, Japan, and China.

In what might seem as an apparent aside, the Pope nuances the specific quality of contribution made by Jesuits through three concrete examples. He draws attention to the work of two individuals—Francis Xavier in India and Japan and Matteo Ricci in China—and the one-hundred-year work of many Jesuits involved in the Paraguay Reductions (a planned village development for certain South American Indians to further their own human progress and protect them from the exploitation and eventual extinction by the European colonizers).

The three examples chosen by the Pope qualify the way in which Jesuits have consistently made their contributions. Xavier represents the always-present quality of evangelization in whatever works Jesuits take on. Ricci represents the necessary adaptation of the Christian message to a particular culture and its peoples—what today we call *inculturation*. The Paraguay Reductions symbolize the necessity of bettering the social order of mankind here and now—what today we so often identify as the necessary interrelationship of faith and justice.

The Pope also points out that specific additions are needed in today's Church, and these new contributions lie in the long-range and careful work in ecumenism, in relations with other religions which we describe as "non-Christian," and finally in dialogue with the ever-increasing group of non-believers and atheists.

Implications for Religious Life

Through the call of the Second Vatican Council, the Church has required a specific renewal of religious, most especially in the updating of their own Rules and Constitutions. Over the past dozen years, much energy has been spent in trying to clarify and recapture, and restate the original charism of those who first laid the foundations of a particular congregation. Community formation programs have been far more highly organized, with personnel carefully selected and trained—sometimes so much so that *formatores* at times came to outnumber those in the formation process. Community life in all its forms and styles has been questioned, examined, and discussed so that it would seem impossible for any experiment at this point to be left untried. Then there has also been the questioning and evaluating of a religious community's apostolic works.

Remembering that religious took on all these struggles with their own internal renewal at the directive of the Church, we can better appreciate some of the implications of Pope John Paul's talk.

Context: In Service of the Church

Most religious groups, in their own effort at renewal, have discovered that there has been a certain in-turning or inward focusing. Much of it was essential for the process of a true conversion. But just as individuals can become too introspective for their own healthy human functioning, so too the same danger is present for the social group. At times, it seems that religious congregations can be so caught up in their own renewal that the renewal effort becomes an unending end in itself. The source and purpose of the renewal somehow get lost amid other details.

One of the strong implications of John Paul's address is that we all need to look again at the *context* of our religious life renewal. Granted the necessity of the particular charism influencing a religious group's own document formulations, we still presuppose that the directions for renewal remain focused far more surely as we return to the necessary foundation of Vatican II documents. Our experience shows us that we religious need to find ourselves imbued and inspired once again by the wider perspectives of the Church documents of Vatican II.

Because religious congregations can be pictured as "little churches" in an analogous way in which St. Paul speaks of the various churches of Corinth, Ephesus, and Colossae, there remains always the danger that a religious group can begin to think and to act independently, as though it were the Church. In actual fact, every religious congregation has been founded *in service of the Church.* The source of life and ministry particular to a religious group necessarily comes from the Church through its official structures. It has always been true that if the Church does not find the life or ministry of a particular religious group purposeful for the service of the Church, then there has been a suppression or a putting out of existence.

John Paul II in his address makes it plain that it is particularly appropriate at this time for religious to recall that their whole renewal process is not in terms of themselves, but *in service of the Church.* Instead of reading and rereading their own newly-formulated constitutions and directives and, even worse, writing more documents of their own making, they need once more to place these important documents in the more important context of Vatican II documents.

Quality of Service: Loyal

No one is unaware of the turmoil which has been present in the process of change in the Church after Vatican II. Religious congregations, too, have undergone the same stresses, perhaps even more intensely and violently than the Church membership at large because of their front-line roles as educators and ministers. In addition, our contemporary world of the late 1960's and 1970's was one of violence and opposing forces.

Since the process of change often begets factions and hardened positions, the Church and religious life had these problems to contend with. Because of the temper of the times, there was a natural influencing of the differing groups within religious congregations to react in the same way as any differing forces within world culture. And yet opposition is not the problem, since differing positions are a human phenomenon involved in most good decision-making. But there is a Christian principle which needs to be invoked as we work with the phenomenon of opposition. As Teilhard de Chardin is quoted as saying, "you cannot convert (change) what you do not love."

Even if there can arise misunderstandings and suspicions between a religious congregation and the official structures of the Church, the service required of the religious group needs always to be characterized as *loyal.* There can be a loyal opposition by religious to the Church hierarchy, but the emphasis should rather be placed on *loyalty* than on *opposition.* The Christian effort to effect change is brought about, sustained, and is given force by love expressed in loyalty rather than by hatred expressed in anger.

Because of the cooperation called for by Vatican II for religious groups to work ever more closely with bishops, with other religious, and with laity, there certainly will continue to be areas of conflict and opposition. Aware of the struggle involved, John Paul II makes his appeal for the kind of service which religious need more than ever to observe—a service of loyalty to the Church.

Focus: the Mission

There is no doubt that John Paul II is a pope who wants to get things done. To meet him is to encounter a man who has little time for small talk and pleasantries. Words as well as actions should not be wasted. The whole air surrounding him seems to shout out "there is so much to be done."

Concretely for active apostolic religious, John Paul defines renewal in terms of *mission*. His call clearly structures all other aspects of religious life in view of mission or apostolic service. For him, formation programs are characterized as well-structured, not in themselves, but only when viewed in the perspective of the apostolic mission of the group. So, too, community structures of government and lifestyle are not well-defined either by applying some abstract principles or by using some one cultural or psychological model. Our life structures will be more adequately formed only if they are basically adapted to the particular mission of the congregation.

Without denying the importance of community support structures and community prayer, the Pope cuts through all the enervating self-focusing still present in religious life renewal attempts, in order to point more clearly the true way to life. The source of all real life and work within every active religious group comes not from some dependence on psychological models of community or particular forms of structured lifestyle; rather, as in the original foundations, the source of life is found always most surely in the mission.

Mission fires the idealism of the young and the old alike. Mission calls us to pay the price, to bear the burden, to suffer pain, loneliness, and loss. Mission remains at the heart of the active apostolic vocation. If our focus on mission is correct, then our renewal will be moving forward along the right lines—in the direction of true life and life-giving. Any other focus can lead only to deviation and possibly death for the congregation.

The Papal Challenge

Some have said that Pope John Paul II knows little about religious life. I have no way of supporting or refuting this charge. I can witness only to his own attempt to familiarize himself with the Jesuit order well enough to speak specifically to areas of renewal. In doing his homework in this one instance, he laid out some basic challenges for religious in their renewal efforts today. He remains true to his consistent message: all ministry is in service of the Church, the Church in service to the world. Active apostolic religious congregations will surely draw new life for their renewal as they come more clearly to pray and to work *in service of the Church*.

On Dreaming Dreams, or
The Making of a Revolution

Daniel F.X. Meenan, S.J.

Volume 43, 1984, pp. 547-557.

The work of putting together the November/December 1983 issue of *Review for Religious* provides particular context to the thoughts I would like to share in these pages regarding the events of the Spring of 1983—the establishment of the pontifical commission for American bishops who were being invited to exercise themselves pastorally in regard to the religious of this country.

The lead article of that issue was a very carefully prepared and substantive address given by Archbishop John Quinn at last August's meeting of the Leadership Conference of Women Religious. Though the address was reported widely, the appearance of its text in the pages of the November/December issue was intended to make the address more available, and more permanently available, for the study and reflection of religious. This article set the tone for what would follow in that issue, and in my thoughts as I worked on that issue.

It was in the course of working on that issue, and becoming more enthused about it as it gradually took shape that I began to dream about religious life today. When the invitation came to address this gathering, I began to think also about inviting you to dream with me.

It seems to me that reaction to what was to become the central subject of that issue, the papal initiative in regard to American religious, can provide us religious with a kind of barometer for assessing our present situation. You would be able to look at this reaction in your own communities, reading whether the reaction is one of boredom, or of resentment, or of polite interest, or of discovery, or of passionate movement and involvement. As a barometer this reaction will offer an accurate indicator of where we religious are at, how open we are to anything beyond the narrow confines of our own self-interest and wisdom, how interested we are in the enterprise of religious life itself.

It seems to me that the papal commission, and the work it calls for, offer us religious a great opportunity for movement, for a rediscovery and a re-possession of our sense of direction.

The Vocation Crisis

One of the questions that the papal commission is to address is the question of declining numbers, the dearth of vocations to religious life. Why has there been such a drastic decline, both of those persevering in and of those choosing to enter religious life?

So often, when I see this question addressed, I become uncomfortable at the shape and direction of the responses offered. So often we religious seem to find havens of refuge for ourselves by affixing responsibility safely elsewhere: in the spirit of the age, in the quality of our culture and milieu, in the changed attitudes of our young people—even on the workings of the Spirit! For myself, I find that such explanations, no matter how objectively founded, to be primarily useful for offering us religious, by thus looking beyond ourselves, an excuse to hide, ostrich-like, and an alibi to shirk our own share of responsibility for the phenomenon.

What has to be looked at, and this very seriously, I am convinced is the simple fact that we religious are ourselves a very major part of the reason for the falloff in vocations. And this, at base, is because, as a group, we have lost credibility. We no longer really know who we are. I find so much of our public image to be self-serving pretentiousness and grandiosity that is utterly lacking in credibility—and even worse, that is utterly boring.

The occasion of the establishment of this papal commission, it seems to me, can be an invitation for us to rediscover just who we are supposed to be. In fact, it was constituted precisely to enable us to make specifically this discovery.

An Alternative Description of Religious

One of the items which providentially came across my desk in the midst of preparing these reflections was a batch of news releases from the Jesuit Thirty-third General Congregation which was then meeting in Rome primarily for the purpose of electing a new superior general. This batch of releases included one which tugged strongly at familiar chords within. By way of background I should mention that all newly elected superiors general of the Jesuits are obliged to present themselves at the earliest opportunity to the pope as an explicit expression of availability and service. Our new general, Peter-Hans Kolvenbach, was elected on September 13. On the 27th, he had a private audience with the pope. Upon his return from this audience, Father Kolvenbach posted a brief, handwritten note informing the congregants in general what took place. If you remember the circumstances surrounding that congregation, you will understand that there would be some apprehensiveness about any such meeting.

The note said simply:

> On Tuesday, September 27th, the Holy Father once again blessed the work of the general congregation, *and requested with insistence that the Society help him to be the Vicar of the Lord for the Church in the world of today* [emphasis added].

That is the complete text of the note.

It struck me that this brief sentence could be a very good capsule description that every religious could take to heart—be they contemplative or active—each according to his or her own vocation: to help the pope to be the Vicar of Christ for the Church today. This sentence could open great doors for flights of spiritual and Gospel-minded fancy, could invite us to dream great dreams, could give us a fundamental platform on which to stand in defining ourselves to ourselves, a norm towards which to look both for directing our work, and for evaluating our work.

Two Contemporary Examples

In Pedro Arrupe we Jesuits had been blessed with a very great man to be our general during a very trying period. He is a man who, though respected and even liked by the media, has suffered greatly at their hands in terms of misunderstanding and of misrepresentation. He is, and has always been, a profoundly loyal papal servant in his administering of the Society, one whose ambition was ever and only to serve the Lord and his Vicar.

Father Arrupe gave two very brief talks in the course of this congregation which were also included in the issue of November/December: one was an address within the congregation hall itself; the second was a homily, dictated by him but read by another at a concelebrated Mass shared by the congregants at a shrine sacred to Jesuit memory. Both of these appeared under the single title, *Nunc Dimittis* because, as with Simeon, they constitute Father Arrupe's statement of farewell: "Now, Lord, you may let your servant go in peace. . . ."

The thoughts expressed in these two brief addresses could echo through the halls of today's gathering-places of the young in much the same way that the cry of Francis Xavier reverberated through the universities of Europe in the 1500s. Then Xavier launched a massive movement and unleashed an enormous energy when he wrote a now-famous letter from India saying:

> Again and again I have thought of going round the universities of Europe, especially Paris, and everywhere crying out like a madman, riveting the attention of those with more learning than charity: "What a tragedy: how many souls are being shut out of heaven and falling into hell, thanks to you!"
>
> I wish they would work as hard at this as they do at their books, and so settle their account with God for their learning and the talents entrusted to them.
>
> This thought would certainly stir most of them to meditate on spiritual realities, to listen actively to what God is saying to them. They would forget their own desires, their human affairs, and give themselves over entirely to God's will and his choice. They

would cry out with all their heart: *Lord, here I am! What do you want me to do?* Send me anywhere you like—even to India.

The measure of this man Arrupe rings loud and clear in his description of his present affliction: "More than ever, I now find myself in the hands of God. This is what I have wanted all my life, from my youth. And this is still the one thing I want." This is what gives context to another statement in which Father Arrupe refers to the experience of St. Ignatius outside Rome, which occurred in a wayside chapel where the concelebration took place. Father Arrupe said that he has "always had a great devotion to the experience of Ignatius at La Storta," evoking as it does for him the words of the Jesuit *Formula of the Institute:*

> Whoever wishes to enlist under the standard of the Cross as a soldier of God in our Society, which we desire to be distinguished by the name of Jesus, and to serve the Lord alone and the Church his Bride, under the Roman Pontiff, the Vicar of Christ on earth. . . .

The passion of this man's zeal is evident in these farewell remarks. This is the quality that can inflame the generosity and the vision—the capacity for vision—of the young who are as generous today and as open to challenge today as they have ever been.

I suspect that part of the problem of vocations, why the energy and zeal of this man, and of others like him, have not caught hold on the imagination of the young is that his is a lonely voice, one that is counterbalanced and counteracted by such an enormous weight of evidence of confusion and indirection and cross-purposes that are at work among us religious as a group. In such circumstances, his words could not find the fertile soil that did the words of Xavier.

Father Arrupe, as a person, was God's gift to the Society in this troubled period, surely an earnest of God's intent to keep Jesuits around for a while. On the occasion of our last congregation (1975), the Jesuits had also had a contretemps with another pope, leading to another papal intervention—which you might remember as well. The details of that experience are not relevant to our purposes here. Suffice it to say that, occurring as it did in the midst of the labors of the Thirty-second General Congregation, this intervention occasioned a movement of vast discouragement among the congregants. An apathy, a pall descended upon them, overshadowing their work, and, I was told, Father Arrupe personally became the center and focus of a renewed sense of purpose and direction for them. I am told that he gave an address in the meeting hall in which he invited the congregants, sunk deep in their depression, to *rejoice* that they had been chosen to share in the cross of Christ, to embrace this humiliation as his gift.

Well, of course, such ways of speaking are so conventionally "pious"; they are words that are terribly easy to say—except for the fact that this man actually and palpably *lived* them. That, of course, makes it so very difficult to ignore the challenge of his words.

Another of the articles in the issue of last November/December was written by Vincent T. O'Keefe. This, again, was material that had providentially surfaced and seemed so consonant with the theme that was developing for that issue.

Father O'Keefe is the man whom Father Arrupe had personally chosen to be his vicar after he suffered his incapacitating stroke. Father O'Keefe was also the man who was summarily and definitively removed from office when the pope named his personal delegate and coadjutor to the Society of Jesus. Months later, this same Father O'Keefe gave a lecture entitled *Sentire cum Ecclesia* (On Thinking with the Church) in which he sets forth what a Jesuit is about as servant of the pope and of the Church. In this lecture, Father O'Keefe does not once advert to that previous experience. Rather, in addressing the Society's relationship to the pope, he simply takes for granted what the Society and its members are going to do and be by way of service to the Church.

Again, you see, the words are easy enough—except that this man is obviously living them.

This, too, is part of the reality of religious life in the Church at the present time. These two men, in their vivid faith, have as a matter of fact given us all a pretty clear idea of what *we* can do and be in the service of Christ—if we are *free* enough to have Christ, and *only* Christ, at the heart of our lives.

The Freedom to Be Apostles

Recently I was helping in the preparation of some young sisters, members of a traditional, so-called "conservative" community, in their preparation for final vows. Knowing these sisters pretty well, and also recognizing just how neuralgic is the subject of habit among religious of all persuasions, in the course of one of our discussions I asked them: "Could you conceive of a situation in which you would have to remove the habit?" They responded, simply, "No."

I wasn't very happy with that answer because of the distinct impression that it came from inhibition, not from freedom; because their response seemed to emanate from behind a set of blinders; because their answer seemed to set antecedent and unexamined limitations to their apostolate. This became, then, an opportunity to share some thoughts together on the subject of what an apostle has to hold on to absolutely, and what an apostle has to hold loosely. It was the habit, and the special, highly charged sensitivities that cluster around this topic, which provided us with so useful a locus for this discussion.

In the discussion that followed, we concluded that the apostle has to be free to follow Christ, *only* Christ, and free to be his servant as effectively as possible. This alone ought to be the basis for all life decisions of the religious. This alone would define what we need in order to be apostles, to be those "sent." Only in this freedom, neither cheaply nor easily purchased, could we really help the pope to be the Vicar of Christ.

But why is this formula apt for all religious? Why ought we, as religious, to help the pope to be the Vicar of Christ? Certainly it is not out of personal regard for the pope. Rather does it stem from the nature of our gift of ourselves to Christ and to his work.

Why are we people of the Church? It is not out of any kind of "school spirit," but because the Church *is* Christ, because he has given himself to the Church, because it and he are utterly intermeshed, intertwined, because, in the concrete, you cannot say one without saying the other.

How could we—who are Christ's—be other than people of the Church, if we are serious about our vocation? Indeed, how could we ever know the Christ to whom we respond, whom we follow, except because of his Church. The vying "models" of the Church do not change the reality of the Church in the fullness of its mystery—which is a given. We do not *choose* the Church we will serve, any more than we *create* the Christ whom we will follow.

The Making of a Revolution

When I was gathering thoughts for speaking with you, when I was beginning to have this dream about religious life, when I was asking myself: "What are you going to say when you come into a room filled with major superiors at this juncture of the history of religious in this country and in this Church—the Church in the United States?" Soon I realized that what I would want so much to say—to all religious now, at this moment, but especially to superiors—is: *"Let's have a revolution!"* Let us turn a corner—now—and all of a sudden *move*—not doing old things just because they were always done, nor new things just because they are new, but let us be free, now, to do whatever makes sense in the service of Christ. Let us have a revolution that is based on the freedom of people who have bought into Christ in such wise that utterly nothing else counts. In a world filled with violent and destructive revolution, ours would not be a revolution of negation but of affirmation. In a Church beset with confrontation and conflict, ours would not be a revolution of rejection but of conversion. Born in love, not in hate, ours would be yet another of those revolutions launched in times past by a Francis, by an Ignatius—one that utterly embraces the Church, that is utterly within the Church.

In our revolution, we could very well still be doing all the things we are doing now—so long as this really made sense—in our freedom to do and to be, the freedom of those who have nothing but Christ. At the same time, we could throw over all the things we are doing now if the following of Christ were to say to us at any point: "I have something more important for you to do now!"

I think that if we religious were to dream such a dream, if we were only just to begin living it, vocations would flock to us because there are so many people "out there" who are capable of dreaming, too—so many people who are capable of responding to a dream.

What I am proposing here is what John Paul once called "freedom for."

He said that he hears a great deal today about having "freedom from." He said that he doesn't hear very much today about having "freedom for." It is under this heading of "freedom for" that I would see our revolution taking shape as a new, or at least different way of being for Christ. This would mean, among other things, the abandonment of worrying about what anyone else is doing, the abandonment of being in reaction against what any one else is doing or has done—because none of this matters. So much of so-called renewal in religious life has been characterized by just this: reaction. What really matters is that we have the freedom just to respond to Christ, in his Church, in following his Spirit. This gives us two fundamental things of which we stand in need: a sense of identity and a norm for establishing priorities.

Identity and Priority

The first is a sense of *identity:* We are followers of Christ. This is who we are. This is who we want to be. Nothing else adequately describes us. This, simply, is whom we know ourselves to be, whom we want to be.

Now the documents establishing the papal commission, it seems to me, were an attempt to facilitate the effort to bring this pious and safe abstraction down to a more dangerously concrete level, an attempt to facilitate the effort to define ourselves, "who we are," in terms of our charisms and our healthy traditions. And it does make good sense to find one's identity this way.

One of the things, in God's providence, that drew me into my particular (Jesuit) way of life, as opposed to what drew each one of you into your particular ways of life, is that your minds, each of them, work differently from mine. And this is because, from the womb and even before, you were "engineered" quite differently by God. And so you responded to him according to inspirations which were geared to speak specifically to you. They "clicked" with you in such ways that you found yourselves drawn into your concrete religious families and traditions, to these specific ways of following Christ. Alternatively, if your decision was not as conscious as that, it was rather providential circumstance, your personal history which put you into this concrete way that is your community, and you came to find it congenial to your psyche, to the constellation of factors which constitute your personal reality.

In other words, we always see Christ through *some* optic. If we are solidly based in our particular religious tradition, we will see Christ and his Gospel through the optic of each one's Founder or Foundress. That optic, we have found, is congenial to us. It expresses the harmonious mode of our response. It is out of this, when it is integral, that there ought to come our sense of identity, one that is at once both firm and free.

This optic of the Founder or Foundress is what I call, at least in significant part, each religious family's charism. But, and this is important, charism does *not* make us different one from another! Charism makes us *free* to be different one from another. And there's all the difference in the world between these two formulations. If we are *free* to be different, it doesn't make very much difference whether we *actually are* different.

In other words, we do not have to worry about being different. All we have to worry about is being ourselves. All we have to worry about is following Christ as he is seen through the perspective of our own particular optic. If I follow Christ through the instinct, native and acquired, that I have as a Jesuit, I *am* going to be different from each of you in certain areas, I suppose. Certainly I am going to be like you in enormously broad areas—for rumor has it that you, too, are followers of Christ. But no matter how different we may be, and no matter how much the same we are, what is important is that I am *free* to be different—I am *licensed* to be different—in living out my charism, my way of being, my concrete way of following Christ.

Out of this revolutionary dream for religious that I am proposing, we would also acquire a sense of *priority* regarding what is and what is not important. We would regain that "simple eye" of which the Gospel speaks, and all things—*all* things—would be prioritized in accord with this single eye.

The Chief Revolutionaries

If we were actually to begin the enfleshment of this dream, who would be the chief revolutionaries? They would *have* to be the major superiors, of course! Or rather, put it this way: they *ought* to be the major superiors—because you are the ones who have the greatest opportunity. Our revolution would be seriously hampered if the chief revolutionaries were *not* the major superiors, because of the inertia that would have to be overcome for the revolution to take hold.

Once this vision arose before my mind, the dream began to grow, especially this concept that superiors ought to be chief revolutionaries. Superiors don't often appear to think of themselves that way, do they? But why shouldn't they? Superiors, after all, aren't your run-of-the-mill executives. They are religious! And every religious is supposed to be utterly revolutionary, because every religious ought to have only one criterion for judgment and action: Christ.

Well, if a superior were to be serious about starting a revolution in the following of Christ, if a superior were to be serious about realistically getting things moving in the area of his or her competence, then I suppose one of the first things with which the superior would have to come to terms would be the fact of limitation—what can and can't be done. The superior would have to become aware of the fact of limitation at least as much as of the presence of possibility. The superior would have to be aware not only of the personal limitations imposed by each one's own defectability, but the limitations that are also imposed by the reality of those whom the superior is to lead in this revolution. It is simply counterproductive to say to anyone: "Sprout wings and fly!" Nor should one even try. The chief revolutionary has to take persons as they are. And this has to be done without giving up one iota or one scintilla of the revolutionary spirit and dream. But in taking our co-revolutionaries as they are, we can also discover so very much of the "how" of making this revolution happen.

"Taking persons as they are" necessarily involves a refinement in one's definition of the office of superior. The revolutionary superior has to think of himself or herself rather much in terms of facilitator, of enabler, of instigator. Superiors, alas, do tend to think of themselves too often merely as administrators, as stabilizing influences, as peace-makers and hand-holders. If you superiors were to begin to think of yourselves more as facilitators and instigators, then you would see that one very crucial function that you have, if your revolution is to be a success, is to evoke out of your people what really is latently there—whatever be its concrete, limited dimension. You would have to enable your people to "buy into" your dream effectively. You would have to evoke out of them their own capacity for vision by acquiring for yourselves the difficult and not at all self-evident art of invitation.

And, somehow, in doing this you have to leave space for some members of your community to remain full of fear, to remain narrow and petty, resentful and resistant. You have to leave this space without destroying your own capacity to dream, or the capacity of so many others of your community who really can join you in your dream in their varying, limited ways. You can't legislate such participation. And the executive decisions that will be made in consequence of this fundamental revolutionary decision are obviously going to be limited by the success of your facilitation, by the success you have in inflaming your sisters or brothers into becoming your fellow-revolutionaries.

If you are to engage successfully upon your revolutionary project, then, you will have to bring your sisters or brothers along with you. And to bring your confreres along with you, you will have to bring many of them alive again. To bring them alive again, you will have to involve them actively in your dream so that·it becomes their dream, too. You will have to overcome their fear, the fear that leads them to a paralysis of spirit. And this is an enormously difficult task.

At this juncture of our history in the Church, though, it may be that the success of this *kairos,* this privileged, special moment of grace that is being offered to us in America today, is going to be measured by the success that we have, all of us, in transcending old hassles and divisions so as to arrive at a new coherence, one that lies beyond old divisions—and therefore one that eschews any resolution of conflict which would take an "I-was-right-you-were-wrong" approach. Certainly, too, a part of the breaking of old molds and the dreaming of new dreams of revolution will be our willingness to look beyond today, will be our willingness to dare, and, being willing to dare, our willingness to fail.

I told those young sisters preparing for their final vows of a letter that St. Ignatius once wrote to a provincial. This provincial, as so many of us are, was overawed by the enormity of the work he had to do, with all its risks. And, as so frequently happens when people begin to look at responsibilities that way, he became paralyzed. Having so much to do, with so much actually riding on what he did—with its attendant risks for the kingdom of God—he ended up doing nothing except to mark time by the wringing of his hands. Ignatius wrote a letter of encouragement in which, in substance, he reminded the provincial: "The work in front of you is God's work and not yours. If he wants it to succeed, it will. If he doesn't, it won't. What he wants of you is to try! So have courage—and move."

I am convinced that it is crucially important for all of us to remember often—because it is so hard to keep in mind—that it is *God's work* that we are about. We have to remember that he does not need us; he chooses to use us. He is not dependent on our success; nor, indeed, does the fulfillment of his plan necessarily call for success at all. Certainly no human failure can defeat God. If we really "owned" that idea, then could we accept limitation—our own and others—and still be willing to dare?

This consideration does not, of course, rule out prudence, though it certainly relativizes prudence. If you prudently wait until everything is safely in hand and under control, you will never do anything. The service of Christ requires vulnerability, it requires the genuine possibility of failure. This, after all, is what we mean by the Cross!

Revolution and Reaching Out

Were we to enter upon such a revolutionary scheme, I don't doubt that we really would be continuing to do many of the works that we presently do— because they make so much apostolic sense. I know, though, that there would be a qualitative difference in the way that *we* went about them. I know that there would be a greater freedom in us to try new things as well. I know, too, that there would be a greater willingness to do that most dreadful of tasks in a period of change—*evaluate* and take measure; admit failure and start over. These are all the lessons that successful revolutionaries everywhere have always known, but that we religious revolutionaries have somehow or other forgotten.

Our call to revolution and our hunger for its success also imply that we be open to collaboration with others. The making of a successful revolution demands that we genuinely seek appropriate cooperation of any others whom we can enlist, whoever they may be; it demands that we know how to use their energies to further our purposes. To invite "their" cooperation makes sense. To be trapped into not daring to try, into not daring to invite, out of fear of "them"—or worse, in reaction to "them"—makes us no longer revolutionaries but prisoners of our fears.

A subject that I am trying awkwardly to introduce is that perhaps the time has come to think again about *Consortium Perfectae Caritatis* and LCWR in terms of collaborative revolution. Wouldn't it be mind-boggling if, in a new age of revolution, there were to be a coming together of all camps into a new synthesis? Wouldn't it be mind-blowing if there were to be a bonding of dreams and of energies in the forging of a new revolution?

Of course, for this bonding to happen, for it to be authentic, the revolution would have to be kept integral. Whether this bonding could happen or not, each religious family has to be free to be authentically itself; you would have to be *free enough* to be able to become your authentic selves. All parties, of course, are always called to conversion so as to discover what their authentic selves really are. In that sense, you would have to be open to whatever is possible, while remaining true to your converted, authentic selves.

What should always be in evidence among the truly converted and the truly free would be that suppleness, that graceful flexibility which healthy living organisms have, the ability to adapt, to change—so long only as thereby Christ might be more effectively present among us. That, surely, was what Paul meant when he wrote about becoming all things to all "if thereby I might gain you" for Christ.

Conclusion

This kind of supple, exploring, explosive revolution, you see, is what we religious are supposed to be about. But I think we've forgotten this—on all sides. I think that, at base, this is why we have such a problem with vocations. We use appropriate words—but others do not see in us what the words are intended to express. And so they are not interested. And I'm not sure that I blame them.

But if we caught hold of our vision again, if we did become the Gospel revolutionaires we were supposed to be—which is no easy, simple process—there are people "out there" in droves who would love to join a cause that was worth their lives, their persons. This, I think, is what we are invited to rediscover, at least in very large part, by the recent initiatives that the pope has made toward American religious.

A beginning for us might well be to think of ourselves in terms of that capsule description offered by the pope to the new Jesuit general: "Help me to be Christ's Vicar to his people." This is what we are about. This, at least, is what we *ought* to be about. Our future legitimacy depends on our rediscovering this fact.

Theological Reflections on Apostolic Religious Life

Mary Paul Ewen, S.S.C.J., Silvia Vallejo, O.D.N., and Paul Molinari, S.J.

This document on the foundations and distinguishing features of apostolic religious life is the fruit of the work of a theological study group composed of Sisters Mary Abbott, S.S.N.D. (American), Jeanne-Francoise De Jaeger, c.r.(Belgian), Mary Paul Ewen, S.S.C.J. (English), Mary Margaret Johanning, S.S.N.D. (American), Silvia Vallejo, O.D.N. (Colombian), and Fathers Joseph Aubry, S.D.B. (Swiss), Peter Gumpel, S.J. (German), Paul Molinari, S.J. (Italian), and Egidio Vigano, S.D.B. (Italian).

The paper was prepared for the UISG (International Union of Superiors General) and intended as a basic document for further reflection, study and discussion by the membership of that union, and appeared in Volume 43, 1984, pp. 3-25.

The article originally appeared in the *USIG Bulletin* (no. 62, 1983) and is reprinted here with permission.

In recent years many efforts have been made to respond to the Church's recommendation that all religious families return to the authentic sources from which their life derives, the spirit which animates it and the mission which is typically theirs. Hence we have witnessed a movement of intense research, of renewal and adaptation.

Consequently, a growing need has been felt for certain basic clarifications: what are the proper characteristics and the distinctive qualities of that form of religious life which is apostolic religious life, and what is its spirituality? While this process of research and clarification continues, much has already been achieved at the practical level, often as a result of response to new demands; these are gradually perceived as being genuine expressions of the deepest nature of apostolic religious life, which has, in turn, been grasped with even greater clarity.

In this way a number of authentic developments have taken place of which we mention only a few. We think, for example, of a keener awareness of being in the Church and of the consequent new forms of relationship and cooperation with bishops, priests and lay people; of increased contact and collaboration with other Christian denominations; of openness to the values of non-Christian religions and of the deeply felt need for inculturation and pluriformity; of the acute perception that the promotion of justice is an integral part of the mission of the Church and of her authentic apostolic task.

This more vivid understanding of certain demands of the Gospel has prompted many to set out generously on new roads and to take seriously the appeals which come from a world and a society thirsting after peace, justice and goodness but beset with many moral and material miseries which are to a large extent the result of injustice and of the oppression deriving from it.

It is true that due to human frailty there has been the occasional excessive, and therefore misleading, emphasis placed on one or another aspect, largely because of a failure to integrate these with essential values, or to base them on adequate theological foundations. But by far the major thrust has been one of genuine, healthy development which has greatly enriched the mission of the Church in the world.

Bearing these developments in mind and in the hope of furthering and strengthening them, we feel the need of basing our reflections about apostolic religious life and its distinctive qualities on the deepest foundations, situating it clearly in the context of the life and mission of Christ and of his Church; of seeing it likewise as one of the many complementary vocations within the Body of Christ. We then hope to highlight its originality and specificity and to indicate how its constitutive elements affect the lives of those who are called to this form of life.

Chapter I
The Life and Mission of Christ Which Continue in the Church as One and Diversified

Apostolic religious life, as the terminology itself indicates, can be truly understood only in the context of salvation history, for it is intimately and inseparably related to Jesus Christ and to his Church, and to each of these precisely in their relation to humanity for whose salvation they are sent into the world.

We must then consider apostolic religious life:

a) in relation to, and in direct dependence upon Christ, the Apostle of the Father, sent by the Father to save and redeem mankind, leading it back to God and gathering it together as the "family of God";

b) in relation to this same family of God, the Church, which he unites to himself as his own Body
   - in which he finds completion
   - through which he intends to continue, complete and extend his mission
   - on which he bestows the gift of his revealing and animating Spirit.

Christ Sent by the Father to Save the Whole Human Person and All Mankind

Believers and non-believers alike are in agreement that everything which exists "on earth should be related to man as their center and crown" (*Gaudium et Spes* 12). "What is man that you would think of him? . . . You have crowned him with honor and glory" (Ps 8:4-5). The coming of the Incarnate Word into history is indeed the advent of a new world, of a new creation in which all may live with the freedom of the children of God. Jesus himself in speaking of his mission speaks in terms of life. He is "the Life," and comes that others "may have it in all its fullness"; indeed, to those "who did receive him . . . he gave power to become children of God . . . the offspring of God himself" (cf Jn 14:6; 10:10; 11:25; 1:12-13). Life, "eternal life," lies at the heart of Jesus' mission, and sums up the fruits of salvation. To bring this life, the Word who "lives" and is one with the Father from all eternity, is sent into the world. Become flesh, one of us, he is like us in all things but sin; truly the Emmanuel, truly Jesus-the-Savior, he associates himself with us in every way, living in ordinary circumstances, sharing the joys, sorrows and aspirations of those he meets, living with them so as to bring them life. Prompted by an efficacious love for the afflicted and sick, for the abandoned and marginated, he goes from village to village doing good and curing all kinds of diseases (cf Mt 9:35). He is merciful aid given to those oppressed by sin and its consequences.

At the heart of this being with and for others, he remains one with the Father. He lives *of* the Father and *for* the Father. Receiving all from him, doing only what he gives him to do, Jesus goes about doing good. He is truly "the light" shining in the darkness, enlightening whoever comes into the world, and his shining goodness reflects the tenderness and providence of the Father. He is the faithful witness: "He who sees me sees the Father" (Jn 14:9; cf Rv 1:5).

The many manifestations of his active compassion and his self-giving love aim at the salvation of the whole person—body and soul, present and future—in the resurrection; they have as their ultimate object that those who come to believe in Jesus may believe also in the One who sent him, and so have life (cf Jn 17:3). This is the object of his prayer as his longed-for hour approaches (cf Jn 17:1-9); he lays down his own life that others may receive and be animated by his own Spirit. Thus he will himself live in them; they will truly be members of his Body. In the laying down of his life, he brings this Church to life, the new People of God.[1]

But this is not accomplished without a struggle against evil and victory over sin—the work of redemption. Indeed, to say that Christ was sent to save and redeem presupposes that humanity was—as it still is—in a state of need where misery and anguish prevail, and its very existence is threatened by the oppressive forces of evil, of sin.

Awareness of this sinful condition, with its ensuing disorder and powerlessness, pervades the pages of the Old Testament, finding poignant expression in the cry: "O that the heavens would open and a Savior be given to us!" (Is 45:8), cry which is echoed also in the writings of Paul (cf Rm 7:24). It is this earthly world of "darkness," death and sin which is also the setting of John's Gospel (cf Jn 3:19-21, 31; 21:46), where humanity, being "from below" has no access to that heaven for which it longs, and which is spirit, light and life (cf Jn 1:51; 3:13,27,31; 6:31-56, etc.). It takes the One who is "from above" (Jn 3:31; 8:23) to free it from the all-pervading power of evil and lead it in the path of life.

But this very world, the work of God's hands (cf Jn 1:2-14; 9:5), is so loved by him that he sends his only Son to save it, to bring light to darkness even in the knowledge that the "darkness" would resist rather than receive him (Jn 3:16-21; 1:15). Jesus comes into the world as the Lamb who takes upon himself the burden of sin, the Savior who liberates from that sin which enslaves and alienates the sinner from God as well as from others, engendering hatred and oppression.

Jesus' mission then, consists in overcoming the darkness of sin and its consequent disorder. And since at its heart lies the haughty refusal of God and his sovereignty, Jesus, far from clinging to "equality with God" (cf Ph 2:6) accomplishes his mission by living in a spirit of total and loving dependence on the Father, even to its ultimate expression: the cross. Yielding up his Spirit into the Father's hands, he triumphs over "the prince of this world" (Jn 12:31). No longer does the force of evil dominate in order to oppress; but love, in free submission, gives all in the emptying of death, thus triumphing over death and over sin (cf Ph 2:6-11).

The Church, Body of Christ, Through Which He Intends to Continue His Mission by Bestowing the Gift of His Spirit

Thus Christ is the "first-born of many brothers" (Rm 8:29) whom he has ransomed by his love, the Good Shepherd who lays down his life for his sheep gathering them into the one fold and kingdom of the Father (cf Jn 10). Of this fold he is "in all things supreme" since "God chose to reconcile the whole universe to himself through him [Christ] alone" (cf Col 1:15-20).

Once returned to the Father, in keeping with his promise he sends the Spirit upon the disciples gathered together in prayer with Mary, Mother of the Word Incarnate, so identified with him in his mission that she is rightly called the Mother of the Church (cf Ac 1:14). Jesus had promised, "The Holy Spirit will teach you everything, and will call to mind all that I have told you" (Jn 14:26). Now his promise is fulfilled, and revelation continues, for the Holy Spirit will gradually shed light on what had, until then, been veiled and mysterious.

The Spirit had indeed been present and active in the Person and work of Jesus; he was close to the disciples but not yet "in them" (cf Jn 14:25,26; 17). Once Jesus is glorified a new phase begins: the sending of the Spirit, his coming into those who believe, and his permanent presence in the community.

Then the Spirit will keep alive the teaching of Jesus, reveal its true meaning, and make it penetrate the heart. He will guide the disciples into "all the truth" (Jn 16:13), give them true knowledge of their master (cf Jn 14:10), revealing him as the only begotten Son who is always in the bosom of the Father (Jn 1:18).

However the work of the Spirit is not only to enlighten the mind; he is "another Paraclete" (cf Jn 14:16) who will prolong, renew and deepen in the disciple, the presence of the Son and the Father, enabling the disciple who "loves" to be the living abode of both. Jesus will be in him, he in Jesus (cf Jn 14:20; 17:26).

Enlightened, vivified and sustained by the Spirit, believers become living members of the Body of Christ—the Church. Through his action in the hearts of the faithful, the Spirit constantly urges the Church to "go forth to all nations" (Mt 28:19-20), to announce the good news, to attend with compassion to the needs of a suffering humanity, and so to continue that good work of the Lord which reveals the love of the Father. As the Father, in sending Jesus into the world, remained ever with him, so those who set out to live Christ's mandate know that he is always with them; the presence of his Spirit enables them to bear witness to him, that the world may believe and have life (cf Jn 17).[2]

The promise "I am with you forever till the end of the world" (Mt 28:20) becomes a vivifying reality: the presence of the Son who once walked in the heat and the dust with his disciples, of the friend who ate with them, of the prophet, the life-giving Word. The disciples experienced this as they walked many months at his side; they experienced it even more deeply once they set about "proclaiming Jesus" (Ac 5:42; 8:35).

And this can be true also of all Christians in this eschatological age, stretching from the Pasch-Pentecost to the Parousia, in the measure that they give themselves to the service of the kingdom by living in docility to the Spirit and according to the Gospel. They are members of the People of God, building history; regenerated by the Spirit, molded by the Word of God who enlightens them on their pilgrimage towards complete fulfillment, they progressively become a new People.

Indeed such is the mission of the Church, the mission begun by Jesus who, as Risen Lord, continues to draw all to himself, and by the power of his Spirit, establishes his Church as the universal sacrament of salvation (cf *Lumen Gentium* 48). Her activity is no mere continuation of Christ's pre-paschal activity, but it flows from the same source and with the same dynamism, and thrusts forward to proclaim Christ to all peoples, and so to establish his kingdom, until the end of time (cf *Ad Gentes* 1).

In so doing, the Church places herself in intimate and true solidarity with the human race and its history, its struggles, its triumphs and tragedies, entering into the movement of Christ who died and rose again "to break the stranglehold of evil" that the world "might be fashioned anew" (cf *Gaudium et Spes* 2).

A keen awareness of being the bearer of salvation to the world leads the

Church to a constant renewal in order to be faithful to her mission. She needs to "study how to bring to modern man" that Christian message which alone "can find the answer to his questions and the energy for his commitment of human solidarity"; but account must also be taken of that "heritage of faith" which the Church must preserve in all its purity and present with clarity and persuasion (cf *Evangelii Nuntiandi* 3).

And so the Spirit, who urges the Church forward into the world to proclaim Christ to all, likewise leads her back to the memory of Jesus, to contemplate his attitudes, his words and deeds which alone can throw light on the contemporary situation. Until the very end of her pilgrimage the Church must keep her eyes fixed on the Person of Jesus to know the path to follow and to have the light needed for every step; for she too "must walk the same road as Christ walked: a road of poverty and obedience, of service and self-sacrifice to the death," thus filling up "what is wanting to the sufferings of Christ" by her own trials and sufferings (*Ad Gentes* 5).

Fundamental Unity of the Christian Life; Diversity of Forms of Christian Living; and Ways of Participating in the Mission of the Church According to Various Gifts and Vocations Given by God

a) Unity

The task of continuing the saving mission of Jesus Christ is entrusted to the entire Church, to all the members of God's family. If the Church "is crowned with the gift of the Holy Spirit," it is "for God's glory" (*Lumen Gentium* 39). This implies that all the followers of Jesus Christ must "hold on to and perfect in their lives the sanctity which they have received" (cf *Lumen Gentium* 40), by living in union with Christ and in docility to his Spirit. This means to put on the mind of Christ, to share his sentiments and dispositions of heart, to be guided by his Spirit and, with Christ, to do in all things what pleases the Father.

To do this entails entering into that eternal plan of God, in which each human person has both a place and a particular function, together with corresponding gifts and graces, whereby each can share in and contribute to the mission of the Church in a unique way.

b) Diversity

It follows then that the living out of one's union with Christ (i.e., Christian sanctity) takes on different forms. Christian sanctity is one; the life in which believers share is one, as is Christ's mission which continues in the world; but the manner of living this union with Christ and of sharing his mission is necessarily manifold and diverse; it depends upon the measure of giving of Christ (cf Eph 4:7), on the action of his Spirit who "distributes his gifts to individuals as it pleases him" (1 Co 2:11). That is why, as the Church has emphasized, each Christian "must walk along the path of living faith which arouses hope and works through charity . . . according to his own personal gifts and duties" (*Lumen Gentium* 41).

The teaching of Sacred Scripture is unequivocably clear concerning God's sovereign freedom and liberality in distributing his "graces," "gifts" and "charisms." This is amply borne out by the history of salvation where numerous examples are found of "vocations" or "calls" given only to some. These refer not merely to external tasks and offices among the People of God; but rather to genuine calls to a particular type of union with Christ and a specific way of sharing in Christ's mission which may be, as in the case of the Blessed Virgin Mary, absolutely unique and unrepeatable. In all these cases we are faced with a type of charity and a form of life which are accessible only to those who have received such a call.

This becomes clear if one considers the choice and call in their deepest reality, i.e. as creative actions of God arising solely from his free initiative. The creator and giver of life, in conferring life, communicates and keeps on communicating an impulse which, reaching the created being, gives it, from its very first instant, a particular orientation, together with the capacity to live in a given way.

Such an action, accomplished from all eternity by God—the eternal Present—is perceived and received only gradually and in time by the human being (cf Jr 1:5; Is 44:2; 49:1).

All Christians are called to sanctity, to the perfection of charity; all are called to live in union with Christ in the deepest possible way. This means that each one is called to that particular fullness of Christian life and that specific perfection of charity which corresponds to the measure of the gift received from God. It obviously cannot mean that all are called to live their union with Christ in exactly the same way, with the same modalities, the same intensity.[3] Perfection can and does vary according to the many factors, including the different gifts, which diversify the lives of individual Christians.

These theological tenets are further clarified if one considers yet another aspect of that union which the Holy Spirit brings about between the human person and Christ. Any union or relation between two persons has its own specific, unique and unrepeatable flavor, deriving from the various factors which make each person distinct and different from others. The relationships existing between any two persons and a third can never be identical; one must think rather in terms of similarity. Furthermore, relationship and union between persons affects the inmost core and tendency of the person, and engages all the manifestations of life. All this is preeminently true with regard to our personal relationship with Christ.

This principle, based on the metaphysical constitution of the human person, likewise applies to the supernatural order; grace presupposes nature, is grafted onto it and ennobles it. Even more: this diversity in the relationships between individual persons and Christ is accentuated and becomes more effective because the new life of grace is given not according to the rigid laws of distributive justice, but according to the sovereign liberality of the Lord (cf Ep 4:7). Hence, the person, elevated to the supernatural order, is endowed with personal characteristics which are even more marked than would be the case in the purely natural order.

This particular aspect of the doctrine concerning the union of Christians with Christ, and God's expectations of each one individually, finds its ultimate explanation in the nature of the Mystical Body. Here the Holy Spirit assigns to each that place and function which best befits the harmonious building up of the entire Body (cf 1 Co 12:4-30). Such a diversity of individual members, endowed by God as they are with a variety of qualities and gifts, contributes much to the vitality and beauty of the Church and to the efficacy of its mission in the world.

That is why the Church in Council, not satisfied even with clear and profound teachings about Christian life in general, went further to outline the different types of union with Christ, such as are typical of the laity, of the hierarchy and of religious, indicating how each contributes to the mission of Christ.

So it is that all are called to live in union with Christ, to live by his Spirit, and to participate in his mission, fulfilling those tasks and functions which, by God's eternal design, are theirs within the Body of Christ, and this for the well-being of all its members. For God has indeed "chosen us before the world was made, to be holy and spotless, and to live through love in his presence, determining that we should become his adopted sons through Jesus Christ, for his own kind purposes . . ." (Ep 1:4-6).

There remains one further point to be borne in mind: God's choice and call—unique in each case—affects all the dimensions of the personality, embracing as it does the totality of the human person. The human being created by God and the object of his sustaining activity is indissolubly *one,* as is also the process of human development and self-awareness. Even though we may grasp this unity with an intuitive awareness, when attempting to formulate it we are faced with our human limitations: we are unable to think or to express our thoughts unless in successive moments of time and according to various categories. Hence, while fully aware of the oneness of the person, we distinguish the various constitutive elements of that unified being, and remember also that it is as yet still in process of becoming. *Both* the constitutive elements *and* the process must be borne in mind with all their implications because each vocation is lived, not in the abstract, but in the vital, existential order. This necessarily applies to those called to apostolic religious life.

Sensitive to the impact of God's call on all the facets of the person, and yet wanting to retain a unified vision of this form of life, one could say of an apostolic religious that such a person expresses the reality of being human by being a Christian, of being Christian by living as a religious, and more specifically as an apostolic religious, member of a particular institute.

There is hardly need to emphasize that the more the implications of these realities are realized, and the more apostolic religious life and each institute develops according to its proper characteristics and to the authentic vocation of each of its members, then the more the Church, enriched "by the variety of her children's gifts, will be adorned like a bride going to meet the Bridegroom (cf Rv 21:2) and through her the infinite wisdom of God will be revealed (cf Ep 3:10)." (*Perfectae Caritatis* 1, See alloc. John Paul II, Loyola, Nov. 6, 1982, passim).

These preliminary remarks are designed to foster a deeper understanding of the existence and nature of apostolic religious life as one of God's gifts to his Church. It should also allow a better grasp of what is specifically proper to it—both as regards the spirit which animates it and the ways in which it should find its own most appropriate form of expression.

Chapter II
Apostolic Religious Life in the Church

Religious Life and Apostolic Religious Life in the Light of the Sanctity-Charity of the Church (Lumen Gentium 42, 44)

The Church then is the new People of God gathered from all nations (cf *Lumen Gentium* 4.9), the community of grace, whose newness transcends the human order (cf *Mutuae Relationes* 1); in the Church—"mystery and sacrament"—the interior elements of the Order of Salvation are intimately united to the diversified external and institutional elements which make visible the mystery of grace which she encloses (*Lumen Gentium* 8; *Mutuae Relationes* 3). Within this complex and wonderful reality, God's Spirit has raised up a form of life which "is not intermediate between the clerical and lay state, but embraces some faithful of both these states who are called to enjoy this special gift in the life of the Church and to foster, each in his or her own way, her salvific mission" (*Lumen Gentium* 43).

a) Martyrdom, Virginity, Religious Life

This special gift is that of which the same Dogmatic Constitution had previously spoken (n. 42). After dealing with the "outstanding gift" bestowed on only a few, leading them to "offer the greatest witness of love" and "the supreme proof of charity" in martyrdom, the Council speaks of virginity and life according to the evangelical counsels, linking it with martyrdom and establishing a certain parallelism between these two types of callings:

> In a like manner the holiness of the Church is fostered in a special way by the observance of the manifold counsels proposed in the Gospel by our Lord to his disciples. Outstanding among them is that precious gift of divine grace which the Father gives to some (cf Mt 19:11; 1 Co 7:7) so that by virginity, or celibacy, they can more easily devote their entire selves to God alone with undivided heart (cf 1 Co 7:32-34). This total continence embraced on behalf of the kingdom of heaven has always been held in particular honor by the Church as being a sign of charity and stimulus towards it, as well as a unique fountain of spiritual fertility in the world (*Lumen Gentium* 42).

God distributes his gifts with sovereign freedom, calling people to various, complementary walks of life, each with its own distinctive qualities, and this for the good of the entire Church. But amongst the various callings to the religious life there is one common element in which they are all rooted, namely, that all who are called to this way of life devote themselves in a special way to the Lord, imitating "Christ the virgin and poor man (cf Mt 8:20; Lk 9:58) who, by an obedience which carried him even to death on the cross (cf Ph 2:8), redeemed men and made them holy." They are impelled by the Spirit to "spend themselves ever increasingly for Christ and for his body the Church (cf Col 1:24). And the more ardently they unite themselves to Christ in a self-surrender involving their entire lives, the more vigorous becomes the life of the Church and the more abundantly her apostolate bears fruit" (*Perfectae Caritatis* 1).

In this form of life charity has its own specific quality: it prompts those whom God calls to give themselves entirely to him, thus renouncing the donation of self to another human being sought and possessed as a life-long companion. Everything is centered on Christ the Lord; already here below he is "the one thing necessary" (Lk 10:42); even without seeing him (cf 1 Pt 1:18) they belong to him, live entirely for him, and follow him unconditionally in love. Such lives bespeak the absolute and transcending primacy of God.

These persons live in time; but time cannot contain the workings of God's grace; his promise is constantly in process of being fulfilled. Saved by Jesus' death and resurrection, but saved "in hope" (Rm 8:24), they live already by his life, yet long for complete union with the Lord when he returns in glory. Not only do they pray "Thy kingdom come" (Mt 6:10) but enter into the dynamics of his saving will, announcing the kingdom, inviting all to conversion and to join the fight against evil. In the words of the Council, the religious is "totally given to God, supremely loved, and thus by a new and special title destined to the service of God . . . and more intimately consecrated to it" (*LG* 44).

b) Diversity of Institutes and Personal Vocations

How this is effected in the existential order depends on the Lord who, in the very act of calling, not only forms and moves the person in a special direction through his Spirit, but also bestows a particular sensitivity as to how the radical following of Christ should be lived out, highlighting one or another aspect of his life and mission. Through these persons, "the Church can ever more present Christ contemplating on the mountain, announcing God's kingdom to the multitude, healing the sick and the maimed, turning sinners to a new life, blessing children, doing good to all and always obeying the will of the Father who sent him" (*Lumen Gentium* 46).

So it is that this particular form of charity has found diverse concrete expressions in history and continues to do so. In fact:

> From the very infancy of the Church, there have existed men and women who strove to follow Christ more freely and imitate him more nearly by the practice of the evangelical counsels. Each in his own way, these souls have led a life dedicated to God. Under the influence of the Holy Spirit, many of them pursued a solitary life or founded religious families to which the Church willingly gave the welcome and approval of her authority.
>
> And so it happened by divine plan that a wonderful variety of religious communities grew up (*Perfectae Caritatis* 1).

In this emergence of different types of religious life throughout the centuries various founders, bearers of a "charism of foundation" with a particular ecclesial dimension, have played a decisive part. They are singular manifestations of the Church's vitality and fecundity.

However, among these forms of life there is one which, even though it exists by the will of God and has been lived generously by so many religious, has not yet been sufficiently understood and appreciated. We refer to apostolic religious life, that form of life which entails "ecclesial action" of an apostolic and charitable nature (cf *Perfectae Caritatis* 8). it must be made amply clear that the "apostolic and charitable action" of which the Council speaks is an integral part of the very nature of this type of religious life. This is so, not because of any intrinsically secular or profane note in this form of life (yet neither does it repudiate the secular), but because it undertakes such action as an expression of genuine apostolic love, and because it is entrusted to these religious by the Church herself. In fact, in the vast majority of cases such action (for example, health, culture, social communications) is oriented to the bettering of the human condition. Such concrete forms of action have then a real ecclesial density and constitute part of the very nature of religious life.

As we have said, apostolic religious life has not yet been sufficiently understood and deepened, and consequently has not yet been able to offer to the mystery of the Church that contribution of light and originality which in God's plan it is destined to make.

Apostolic Religious Life: A New and Original Form of Religious Life

The Church in Council has pointed to the distinguishing feature of apostolic religious life: apostolic and charitable activity belongs to its very nature. It is true that all forms of religious life imply apostolic love, and frequently also some form of apostolic activity; however, in this form of life there is an intrinsic union and a profound reciprocity between religious life and mission.

From the sixteenth century onwards the Church, by the very fact of granting its approbation, has accepted as a gift from God the charism proper to apostolic religious orders and congregations; nevertheless, in practice there has been a tendency to reduce this new form of life to those already in existence. Yet those who are called to apostolic religious life, and who must therefore develop a spirituality corresponding to their charism, are not monks who engage in apostolic activities but religious who are in mission in virtue of their very vocation and what it confers on them. It is a vocation in which the sending and the active mission are immediately present within God's free choice and calling.

The seed planted by the Council is beginning to bear fruit. The time has now come to define more clearly what typifies this form of religious life. In so doing one must avoid presenting apostolic religious life as essentially religious life, understanding this term in a generic sense, with apostolic activity considered as a later addition of secondary importance.

The opposite danger must also be avoided: namely, to conceive of the activity of the apostolic religious as something exterior to and separate from the context of the radical and total giving to God of both the person and the life of the apostle. Indeed, apostolic religious exercise their apostolic and charitable activity precisely because they are called, consecrated and sent by God; they accomplish it as "a sacred ministry and particular task of charity . . . confided to them by the Church" (*Perfectae Caritatis* 8) and as a gesture of that gift-of-self-in-love which is expressed as much by the service of their brethren as by the profession of the evangelical counsels. This is what the Council highlights in stressing that "the entire religious life is compentrated by an apostolic spirit and the entire apostolic activity is animated by a religious spirit" (*Perfectae Caritatis* 8).

These two aspects: religious and apostolic, must then be understood in their inseparable and mutual compenetration, or their symbiotic union.

The capacity to grasp this reality is inherent in that intimate and personal call which is the gift of a vocation to the apostolic religious life. This capacity must gradually become a vivid awareness through the daily living out of the total donation to God in love and service; only then can apostolic religious, and through them the Church, reach that true understanding which will foster the growth and flowering of their particular way of life.

The specificity of apostolic religious life is, therefore, to be seen in the fact that the giving of self to God and to his service is lived out in a life of union with Christ who is followed as the only-begotten Son of the Father, sent into the world to save it by taking flesh in the womb of Mary, Virgin and Mother, by becoming Servant and Redeemer, the entirety of whose life is determined solely by the mission entrusted to him, which is to establish the kingdom of God.

The life of the apostolic religious will be, like that of Christ himself, held as it were in dialectic tension between the two poles of salvation history, on the one hand, the Father who sends; on the other, those to whom they are sent to reveal the Father's love. With Jesus as model and source of life, apostolic religious can find within this very tension the dynamism with which to live their mission.

The Charismatic Nature of Apostolic Religious Life Intrinsically Related to the Mission of the Church and Its Prophetic Role

Apostolic religious life is a precious gift with which Christ's Spirit enriches the Church through the founders of different institutes by means of the specific charism bestowed on them. Both they and their followers receive the capacity to embody in new ways and forms that love which Christ himself lived as he accomplished his mission.

Our attention must first focus the basic element common to the founders of apostolic institutes: their salvific activity both expresses and bears witness to a profound interiority.

This interiority is rooted in their attachment to and union with Jesus Christ, the Savior sent by the Father to the world. It is this attachment which transforms their vision, leading apostolic religious progressively to see mankind with the eyes of the Savior, to love it with the heart of the Incarnate Word—the Redeemer. Their lives, insofar as they are truly inspired by their "option for the Lord and his kingdom," have an eschatological orientation and emphasize the transcendental dimension, revealing "in a unique way that the kingdom of God and its overmastering necessities are superior to all earthly considerations" (cf *Lumen Gentium* 44).

But their particular vocation binds apostolic religious to the Church and her mission in such a way that, in virtue of the charism they have received, they are called to be in the world and to commit themselves to that world to which they are sent. "Dear religious, according to the different ways in which the call of God makes demands upon your spiritual families, you must give your full attention to the needs of men, their problems and their searchings; you must give witness in their midst, through prayer and action, to the Good News of love, justice and peace. The aspirations of men to a more fraternal life among individuals and nations require above all a change in ways of living, in mentality and hearts. Such a mission, which is common to all the people of God, belongs to you in a special way . . ." (*Evangelica Testificatio* 52). In this way religious may give "singular witness to the prophetic dimension of the mission of the Church" (cf *Religious and Human Promotion,* Introduction).

All members of the Church are called to live this prophetic dimension primarily through the clarity with which their lives, in accordance with their various callings, bear witness to Jesus Christ. As for apostolic religious, they will bear this prophetic mark firstly and above all by the radical and whole-hearted living out of their call to be "those who are sent." Their prophecy is intimately united with and flows from the clarity with which they live with Christ-in-mission.

Throughout the history of the various forms of religious life, wherever the following of Christ through one or another ministry has been lived out in its authentic radicality, it has always fulfilled a prophetic role in the world. This is hardly surprising since religious life is always a return to the original inspiration of the Gospel, reminding the community of the Church that before being an institutional society, it is a communion of those who believe in Jesus Christ and who are called to announce his presence in the world, bringing to it his Spirit which frequently opposes the spirit of the world and of society.

Apostolic religious life is also prophetic by drawing the attention of all to those areas in which the world refuses to be present. The Church, prolongation of Christ, wants to be and must be wherever the poor, the suffering and the emarginated are to be found—wherever there are the victims of this world.

For this reason, and because the mission of the Church aims at bringing the life of Christ to all (embracing the reality of the whole human person) the prophetic role of these institutes will be particularly significant when they:

- unite themselves in that solidarity with the poor demanded by their mission in the following of Jesus, and commit themselves effectively as religious, and insofar as they are sent by the Church, to bring about the liberation of all, together with the promotion of justice in the world (cf *Religious and Human Promotion* 2-4);
- respond with generosity and creativity to the pastoral needs of today, thus contributing to the mission of the local Church (cf ibid., 27).

"To accomplish her mission, the Church must search out the signs of the times and interpret them in the light of the Gospel, thus responding to persistent human questions" (cf ibid., Introd.). Because they did this, certain founders, as well as some religious of outstanding holiness, have efficaciously contributed to this prophetic role of the Church, and continue to highlight for us what the Church expects of apostolic religious today.

The Diversity of Foundational Charisms of Institutes is at the Service of the Complex Mission of the Church

The action of the Holy Spirit who impels the Church in her missionary thrust, is manifest with particular clarity in the charisms which mark the being and the doing of each religious institute. It goes without saying that every congregation is animated first and foremost by the Spirit of Jesus Christ. But no congregation, just as no one person, is able to live in an integrated manner all the aspects of the Gospel. It is here that particular charisms find their place, for the charism is a gift of the Spirit which accentuates in the depths of the person a sensitivity to one or another aspect of the mystery of God in Christ. This sensitivity is translated into concrete forms of life and service according to the needs of the pilgrim People of God—which calls for a keen awareness of these needs, be they of individuals or of society as a whole; it also implies an inner, spiritual intuition as to how best to respond to them and a readiness to be involved efficaciously.

So it is that one or another facet of the Spirit of Jesus is embodied in the person and life of the founder. This is further crystalized in the foundation of a religious family; it may be given expression in the primitive texts, and be tangible also in the history and manner of being of the congregation. For the founder's charism is not only a personal gift but a grace bestowed likewise and in some measure on those who are called to be part of the same religious family. It is the sharing of this particular sensitivity which brings about that mysterious affinity between members of a congregation, which in turn gives rise to the spirit which constitutes the specific nature of the institute. The charism is like a vital seed enclosing within itself an abundance of genuine newness in the spiritual and missionary life of the Church, which future generations must continue (cf *Mutuae Relationes* 11).

The potential inherent in the foundational charism develops in the measure that communities remain actively and creatively faithful to its impulse under the continuing action of the Spirit; for recipients of the charism are in duty bound to embody and safeguard it, to maintain the dynamism from which it arose, and to accept the consequences of fidelity to it. This will allow its authentic flavor to emerge, and to enrich the life of the Church, and also to attract in a particular way those persons (new vocations) who are already—even if only germinally—endowed with the same gift and called to the same religious family.

However, such dynamic fidelity makes very practical demands. It calls for fidelity to the Lord and to his Spirit, and this in relation to that gift which God gave for the life and mission of the Church through the founders; it requires intelligent attention to the signs and circumstances which, in every age, evoke different responses, as well as the willingness to live in communion with the Church, and to participate in her mystery under the guidance of her pastors; it calls for bold initiatives, constancy in self-giving and humility in adversity. Finally, fidelity to the charism inevitably involves the cross, which, often enough, authenticates the charism with its new vision, and constitutes a helpful sign in discerning a genuine call from God (cf *Mutuae Relationes* 12).

The specific charism is, then, a source of unity, of vitality and fecundity for the religious community. This ongoing and ever-creative impulse of the Spirit in founders and their followers becomes fully inserted into the mainstream of the Church's life when the institute receives, through her approbation, the official recognition of its charismatic identity, and the mandate to pursue the mission entrusted to it.

The Church of Vatican II, aware that she is enriched by the charismatic dimension of religious life in its various forms, wishes to promote the genuine renewal of these institutes in fidelity both to the original charism and the circumstances of our times. Such renewal requires of their members that charismatic inventiveness which was typical of their founders, enabling them to respond with sensitivity and generosity to the needs of those who have always had the preference of the Church: the little ones and the poor (cf *Mutuae Relationes* 23 ff).

The Church has repeatedly expressed her conviction that she will find a great source of vitality and fecundity in the genuine revitalization of apostolic religious life; thus she affirms her hope in a religious life which will be faithful to those principles which make of it "an immense fund of generosity," and without which the Church would not be fully herself (cf *Religious and Human Promotion* 31).

Apostolic Religious, United in Community, Are Sent by the Lord and by His Church

The experience of being with Christ-in-mission according to a given modality, of giving authentic expression to the particular charism of an apostolic religious community brings about a special affinity between the members of that community, a bond of understanding, support and encouragement as well as the desire to search together with those who share the same experience.

The living out of these realities gives rise to that type of community typical of apostolic religious life.

Prior to the organization of structures or adoption of concrete expression of this bond, the communitarian dimension of apostolic religious life depends on a relational capacity and an effective closeness to the other members of the same religious family who share in the same mission of Christ which has brought them together.

Such being and sharing with the members of the community is not an end in itself. Those who gather together in Jesus' name, gather to seek, to build and to live the kingdom; be they the community of the Church or the apostolic religious community; they must become an evangelizing community because the "Good News of the Kingdom" is destined "for all people of all times" (cf *Evangelii Nuntiandi* 13).

Personal encounter with the Risen Lord lies at the core of an apostolic community. It is he who converts those he chooses as his witnesses, communicating his Spirit and the dynamism of his own mission, promising to be always with them—even to the end of time. The fundamental, personal experience of the Lord confers on the community, as on each of its members, the capacity to proclaim to the world that the Lord is alive. And to this both their words and their lives bear witness. Such is the teaching of the Council—that "the community is a true family gathered together in the Lord's name, rejoicing in his presence," and the unity of its members witnesses that "Christ has come" which in turn "results [in] great apostolic influence" (cf *Perfectae Caritatis* 15).

However, a community which springs from faith in the Risen Lord, which is consecrated and sent in virtue of the Word of the Lord, must be built around that Word and the celebration of the Lord's memorial if it is to exist with any degree of credibility and become an effective "message," creative of other communities of faith. The Gospel will not transform the world if it does not first transform those whom Jesus has chosen to communicate it. Hence the community needs to grow constantly in personal knowledge of the Word, in contemplative openness to its transforming power, in the capacity to hear the inner word of the Spirit so as to grasp God's designs on the world, to discern his action in themselves, in events and situations within the Church. In so doing, they strive for that creative fidelity to the charism of which we have already spoken.

The Council also points out that other source of vitality and fidelity: the sacramental life of the Church by which religious participate in a unique way in the mystery of salvation. In the Eucharist above all they experience the total self gift of Christ, and are both challenged and strengthened in their own gift of self. As they are drawn more deeply into the love of Father, Son and Spirit, and into union with them, they are impelled to greater urgency in carrying out their mission. Their sincere desire to serve the Gospel and to contribute to human promotion demands that they strive to build up communion at all levels; in this way their own community is enriched and their presence among the people becomes more stimulating and significant. They should be seen as "experts" in communion.

It is only with a deep conviction of what constitutes them as community, and with a great fidelity to the demands of their vocation, that apostolic religious will be able to be in the world a light that is not hidden and salt which keeps its flavor.

Chapter III

The Response of the Person Called to the Apostolic Religious Life[4]

Total Donation of Self to Christ and the Radical Following of Him as He Ministers to People

Apostolic religious life exists only insofar as it is lived by persons, persons who, touched by God, have received and continue to receive, a particular sensitivity which enables them to live a specific type of relationship with Jesus Christ. At the root of every vocation to apostolic religious life there is a deep and uniquely personal experience which makes a profound imprint on the person. This experience entails:

- *an encounter with God,* who has manifested himself and continues to be present in Christ Jesus, the Incarnate Word and Redeemer;
- *a call,* which flows from a gratuitous election on the part of God; for God chooses some in Christ Jesus to continue his mission of announcing and making present God's kingdom on earth. This call implies also a creative shaping of the person, making her capable of living in union with Christ-in-mission;
- *a response,* which is also a gift of grace. It takes the form of a total and unconditional donation of self to God such that one's whole being and activity are directed to the cause of the kingdom. This self-giving is lived in union with Christ and in ever-renewed docility to his Spirit;
- *a special consecration* by which God accepts the free and total gift of self. He makes the person "his own" in a particular way, communicating, by the power of his Spirit, his very own life, strength and love; sending her out to others to make present and active for them that love which she herself has experienced.

By the very fact of being thus called to the "radical following of Christ" in mission and for mission, the person is endowed with the capacity to live as Christ lived and to share his own life and destiny.

Prompted by the selfsame Spirit, the person can truly put on the mind and heart of Christ, sharing his sentiments (cf Ph 2:5-8), longing for the Father's glory and acting only in loving dependence on him. Such intensity of life in Christ calls for a sustained contemplative attitude whereby the Spirit can enlighten and guide the person in the ways of Christ.

Inherent in the call to this particular form of life with Christ is the capacity to live also, as did Jesus, in bonds of kinship with others; sharing from within their sorrows, joys and aspirations, bringing to them in genuine service and receiving from them the message of salvation, striving alongside them to spread the kingdom. Without being of the world (cf Jn 3:23; 15:19; 17:14) yet they enter into the reality of this world in all its suffering and tension with that contemplative vision which enables them to love it as God does, and to detect therein the signs indicating how to live the mission in the contemporary world and in the context of salvation history.

The distinguishing feature of this new form of religious life[5] is, then, that it is *a call to be with Christ precisely as he is intent on carrying out his mission as the One sent by the Father;* a call to union with him who lives with and in the midst of people and who spends himself for them; in a word, to live in union with him who "went about doing good" (Ac 10:38) and who "gave his life for the redemption of all" (Mt 20:28).

In the words of one great founder, Christ says to those whom he invites to follow him: "Whoever wishes to come with me, has to be content to eat with me, and similarly with regard to drinking and clothing, etc., similarly he has to toil with me by day and to wake with me at night, etc., so that he may share in my victory just as he shared in my labors" (St. Ignatius of Loyola, *Spiritual Exercises* 93).

The Giving of Self in Love to Christ and the Apostolic Charity Deriving from This Union with Him Expressed In and Through the Vows

Jesus came as the One sent by the Father to cast fire upon the earth (cf Lk 12:49), the One sent to serve (cf Mk 10:45). Whoever is called to apostolic religious life has encountered this Jesus, and, drawn into the selfsame movement of love, can respond only by a correspondingly complete gift of self; a giving of self such that one is with Jesus at the disposition of the Father to be spent in a life of active service for others.

The response made out of love for him who first loved us (cf Jn 4:10); the option for the Person of Christ who, virgin and poor, has redeemed mankind by his obedience; the union which flows from it and the consequent sharing of his form of life are totally rooted in and informed by charity, a type of charity which possesses a special quality, that which was typical of Christ the Apostle, who, sent by the Father and out of love for him, gave himself to others and sacrificed himself totally "that they may have life in abundance" (Jn 10:10).

The giving of self by which the apostolic religious expresses her exchange of love is, therefore, a vowing of her entire self to Christ, a giving of her entire person and personality in order to live and work in union with him. Her response is one single movement of charity which urges her to give herself at one and the same time to Christ, and with him to others.

When this total offering of self is received and accepted by Christ through the ministry of the Church his bride, then God himself makes the religious totally his own by consecrating her to his service by a new and special title (cf *Lumen Gentium* 44). This is a covenant of love sealed by God.

What prompts the person to engage herself in this pact of love is that disposition of heart by which "the virgins follow the Lamb wherever he goes" (Rv 14:4) and to enter into the movement of his life and mission as redeemer, the Lamb slain for the salvation of the world. Into this movement of love enter in a unique way those who give themselves to him with an undivided heart (cf 1 Co 7:32-35).

For this reason the total giving of self which has a primordial value has its privileged expression in the vow of *virginity or celibacy for the kingdom.* Not without reason the Council has always mentioned this vow in the first place, that is, before the other vows. In so doing, the Council has stressed the fact that it is *love* which brings about the giving of self to Christ. At the same time it has given us to understand that this vow, understood in its most intimate nature, implies what is more explicitly expressed through the other vows. By these a person takes on the obligation to live according to those dispositions of love through which Jesus Christ shared all that he is and has with those he was sent to redeem. He did not cling jealously to anything that was his, and in this way he has enriched us by his *poverty* (cf 2 Co 8:9). Having loved those whom the Father had given him, he further loved them to the end (cf Jn 13:1) offering himself in a sacrifice of loving *obedience* to regain what had been lost by man's disobedience (cf Rm 5:18-19).

In this unifying vision the profession of the evangelical counsels is seen in its salvific, redemptive and missionary aspect; it is seen in its apostolic dimension. The same vision enables us to appreciate with greater clarity the intrinsic unity between being religious and being apostolic.

It is obvious, then, that in apostolic religious life the union with Christ, which is sealed through profession, has a particular thrust precisely because of the specific nature of the call to this form of life. It is a union which entails a "being among" men and women—an insertion in contemporary society; an active commitment to the upbuilding of the kingdom by means of innumerable ministries, of proclamation and evangelization, of social and charitable works, of presence and collaboration with those who seek to foster a more Christian world, a society which is more just, a humanity which moves towards the fulfillment of God's plan.

The love typical of those who thus belong totally to Christ in apostolic religious life is like his. They share his incarnational closeness and self-giving to others, seeking their good without any trace of possessiveness or personal gain; on the contrary they are ready to be sacrificed for others. Retaining nothing for self, they share readily all that God has given them: talents, time and energies. Keenly aware of being poor themselves, they are open to receive from others, even to be challenged and evangelized by them.

Moreover, in this proximity and sharing, especially with the most poor and deprived, they are conscious of being bearers of a current of life flowing from the One who through obedience died to communicate his own life. They are available to every call of the Father. Intelligently faithful in the accomplishment of the mission entrusted to them, they know that by this loving submission they become channels of that grace which comes from the Redeemer.

Such an intensity of active commitment, such refinement of love expressed through service, such warmth of human and supernatural love is the fruit of an attachment to Christ who has prompted such a total self-oblation to him.

We know only too well that because of the frailty of human beings, this union is frequently obscured by miseries and weaknesses. The response to Christ and to his expectations must, moreover, be given in the context of a world and a society which often are opposed to the plans of God. Consequently, our union with Christ passes through phases of growth and regression, of struggles and difficulties as well as of successes and victories. Hence, our affective and effective relationship with Christ must constantly be nourished and intensified.

Prayer as Relationship: The Very Texture of Life for the Apostolic Religious

At the core of the vocation to apostolic religious life there is, then, the constant creative action of God infusing that particular form of theological charity of which the only adequate expression is total belonging to Jesus Christ alone.

This specific type of relationship with Jesus Christ, unique in each case, impinges upon all the dimensions of the person and all the aspects of her life as apostolic religious. Under the impulse of the Holy Spirit, it increases in depth and intimacy as the person grows in conformity with his ways and his will, and this in the very midst—and indeed by means of—the struggles, the joys and sorrows of the mission itself.

The charity which binds the person in a relationship of virginal love to Christ-in-mission, is that same charity which is, increasingly, the dynamic source of all her apostolic undertakings, making of them that "prayer" which is the very texture of life for an apostolic religious.

This in no way implies that the apostolic religious disregards the need for time given to prayer "face to face"—to the contemplation of Jesus Christ; on the contrary. However, unlike the person called to a monastic or contemplative form of life, the basic thrust of the apostolic religious is to be with Christ-in-mission, i.e., sent out to be spent for others, normally by engagement in some kind of apostolic activity. If, and in the measure that these apostolic activities are truly animated by and flow from union in love with Jesus Christ, then they are genuine prayer. In this sense one holy Founder—Don Bosco—proclaimed the validity of apostolic work, saying "work is prayer."[6] Such was the pattern of Christ's own life whose entire being and doing flowed from his union with the Father (cf Jn 5:19-20; 8:28,38; 12:49,50; 13:3; 14:24, etc.).

If then such God-willed action is prayer because charity is its source, then that same charity which binds the person to Christ demands, of its very nature, that time be given exclusively to the contemplation of Christ, in prolonged moments of prayer. It is then that the apostolic religious, open and vulnerable to God's action, grows in likeness to the heart and mind of Christ, seeing with his eyes, seeking, with him, the glory of the Father, and thus becoming more apt to do his work. Then, too, the separateness of prayer and action dissolves as both are unified in one integrated movement flowing from relationship with the Lord.

Growth in relationship with Christ, as in the integration of prayer and action, also demands familiarity with the *word of God,* with its penetrating, purifying, guiding and challenging power (cf Heb 4:12; 2 Tm 3:16, etc.). It is likewise the fruit of active and enlightened participation in the mystery of salvation through the *liturgy* "where the power of the Holy Spirit acts upon us through sacramental signs" (*Lumen Gentium* 50), through the *sacraments,* in particular the Eucharist, memorial of the Lord's Passover, of his complete giving of self for others which is the animating principle and inspiration of apostolic religious life.

All this is intimately linked with the divers historico-social and cultural aspects of the milieu where the religious lives and works, together with the tensions and difficulties inherent in extending Christ's kingdom therein. But to speak of the Spirit acting in the world means nothing if not that the Spirit is alive and active in the hearts of believers, moving and empowering them with the Spirit of the Risen Lord, to find him always and to make of all situations and events the very stuff of their prayer, of their union with him.

Furthermore, in this the apostolic religious, although responding as a unique individual to a deeply personal call, is not alone even were she physically apart from others. Given over to Christ for them, she carries these "others" for whom and to whom she is sent always in her heart, those who share the same calling and the same charism; she does it in the context of and in union with the local and the universal Church of which she is a part.

The integration of prayer and action in the life of the apostolic religious, the maturing of that type of prayer particularly appropriate to this form of life, is a gradually evolving, and often a falteringly progressive experience. But, however falteringly, if lived in sincere response to God's ongoing call and constantly molding action, it gives rise to that Christ-mindedness which should characterize the true apostle. Not only the way of life, but the very heart of the person becomes apostolic, open to the Father, ready to be sent into his life-giving mission, able to see the world with the eyes of Christ, and, guided by his Spirit, to seek sincerely the signs indicating how to continue his saving work in today's world.

This last point evokes the whole area of *discernment,* but may seem to restrict its scope. For far from being an occasional exercise, discernment is an ongoing, God-given capacity to know, to "sense" what is of God. It likewise springs from charity, from the unique bond of love with Jesus Christ to which each one is called precisely as an apostolic religious. For where this bond of love is truly alive, it is that very love which is quick to discern in a quasi-instinctive manner, and in the course of daily events, what is of God and pleasing to him.

Lest this, exacting as it is, appear too simplistic, too facile for today's complex world, it may be added that the process embraces the use of the other faculties. However, as stressed previously, since God's action extends to *all* dimensions of the human person, then when the response to God's call is authentic and generous, all the faculties (e.g. the capacity to reason, to judge, to will) are brought under the sway and into the service of theological charity. Ultimately it is still the "love" that discerns—with a discernment that may well transcend the dictates of human wisdom.

Such discernment can never be anything but personal; however, it can never be *exclusively* personal because it is made in the context of a community. At times it also engages all the members of the community as a family gathered together in the Lord's name to contribute to the life and mission of the Church. But what we have said above holds good even here. For the authenticity of this discernment is intimately related to the quality of the "discerning hearts" (1 K 3:9 ff) which constitute the community, and on the personal sincerity with which they seek God's will.

Summary

We have considered some of the personal implications of a call to apostolic religious life: the constitutive elements of such a call, how the response involves a total donation of self which has a bearing on all the aspects of the personality, how the relationship of virginal love with Christ, once established, is the source from which all else flows and which integrates the twofold elements of prayer and apostolic activity, and gives rise to Christ-like apostolic attitudes and the capacity for genuine discernment.

However, the individual thus called, although called and responding to the call necessarily as an individual, is likewise a social being, an individual within *a community:* the community of the Church, the people of God, and furthermore, in virtue of the various charisms, a member of a specific religious family within the Church. This has its effect on all the aspects of apostolic life, and the particular charisms will add further qualifications and albeit subtle refinements to the religious consecration and mission itself as well as to the manner in which the vows are lived. Over and above the experience of being called to apostolic religious life, there is the experience of carrying that particular sensitivity or charism which binds the members of a religious family to the founder as well as to each other in a particular way, and which is one of the deepest roots of a religious community.

NOTES

[1] With regard to all this see the rich text of Eucharistic Prayer IV: "Even when he disobeyed you and lost your friendship, you did not abandon him to the power of death, but helped all men to seek and find you.

"Again and again you offered a covenant to man, and through the prophets taught him to hope for salvation. Father, you so loved the world that in the fullness of time you sent your only Son to be our savior. He was conceived through the power of the Holy Spirit and born of the Virgin Mary, a man like us in all things but sin.

"To the poor he proclaimed the good news of salvation, to prisoners freedom, and to those in sorrow joy. In fulfillment of your will he gave himself up to death; but by rising from the dead he destroyed death and restored life."

See also the words of John Paul II in his encyclical letters *Redemptor Hominis,* especially nn. 8,9,10, and *Dives in Misericordia,* especially nn. 7,8.

[2]See the following sentence of the Eucharistic Prayer IV which sums up in a very dense way what we have tried to express: "That we might live no longer for ourselves but for him, he sent the Holy Spirit from you, Father, as his first gift to those who believe, to complete his work on earth and bring us the fullness of grace."

[3]It was precisely to prevent such misunderstandings that the Theological Commission of the Council discarded the draft stating that all Christians are called to the "same" (*eadem*) sanctity. And for the same reason the Council was careful to present the Christian's life of union with Christ as "one" and yet "diversified," the diversity deriving from the rich variety of gifts granted by God which in turn leads to the variety of functions, offices and states of life within the Church and the various ways of sharing her mission. See the relevant and important passages of *Lumen Gentium* 39,40,42.

[4]This section, dealing as it does wih the response of individual persons, necessitates the use of personal pronouns in the singular. In the context of material presented for the consideration of women religious, these are obviously in the feminine gender. However, the contents of the entire paper hold for all apostolic religious.

[5]One can speak of a new form of religious life because since the sixteenth century the Holy Spirit has raised up in the Church orders of clerics regular, then congregations of men and women, both clerical and lay, in which typically monastic or conventual elements were abandoned so as to allow their members to dedicate themselves *entirely* to works of evangelization or charitable activity. Thus, a quite new type of religious life came into being: the apostolic religious life.

[6]Confirmed authoritatively by Pius XI who in answer to a petition made by Don Rinaldi, third successor of Don Bosco, said "Work and prayer are one: work is prayer, and prayer is work" (*Atti del Capitolo Superiore della Pia Società Salesiana,* Anno III, June 24, 1922, n. 15).